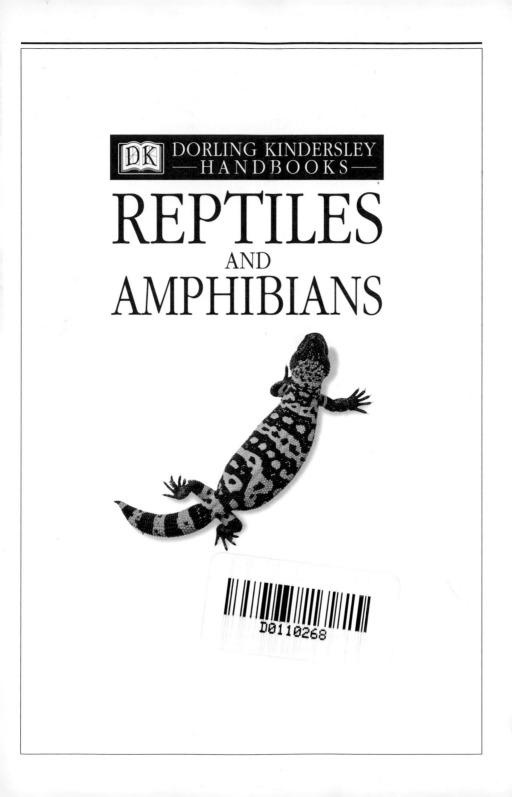

DORLING KINDERSLEY
—HANDBOOKS—

REPTILES
AND
AMPHIBIANS

DORLING KINDERSLEY
HANDBOOKS

REPTILES
AND
AMPHIBIANS

MARK O'SHEA AND TIM HALLIDAY

Editorial Consultant
DAVID A. DICKEY
(American Museum of Natural History)

A Dorling Kindersley Book

Dorling DK Kindersley

LONDON, NEW YORK, SYDNEY, DELHI, PARIS, MUNICH, AND JOHANNESBURG

Series Editor Peter Frances
US Series Editor Jill Hamilton
Series Art Editor Vanessa Hamilton
Production Controller Michelle Thomas
DTP Designers Robert Campbell, Louise Waller
Picture Research Andy Sansom
Category Publisher Jonathan Metcalf
Deputy Art Director Bryn Walls

———— 🦎 ————

Produced for Dorling Kindersley by

studio cactus ©

13 SOUTHGATE STREET WINCHESTER HAMPSHIRE SO23 9DZ

Project Editors Polly Boyd, Lesley Riley
Project Art Editors Sharon Rudd, Ann Thompson
Project Manager Kate Grant

———— 🦎 ————

First American Edition, 2001
2 4 6 8 10 9 7 5 3 1

First published in the United States in 2001 by
Dorling Kindersley Publishing, Inc.
95 Madison Avenue
New York, New York 10016

0-7894-5964-7 (flexibind)
0-7894-7632-0 (hardcover)

Reproduced by Colourscan, Singapore
Printed and bound by
Kyodo Printing Co., Singapore

see our complete
catalog at
www.dk.com

CONTENTS

AUTHORS' INTRODUCTION

The study of reptiles and amphibians, called herpetology, encompasses approximately 11,000 living species, ranging from tiny South American poison-dart frogs to huge Indo-Pacific crocodiles. Reptiles and amphibians are among the most successful and diverse animals on Earth, and many have fascinating lifestyles, intriguing adornments, striking colors and camouflage patterns, and deadly toxins. Some are ferocious predators.

AMPHIBIANS first appeared on Earth around 400 million years ago and were the dominant land animals for over 80 million years. However, the large, armored, fishlike predators of the Carboniferous period (350–270 million years ago) were quite unlike modern amphibians, which are smaller and lack the body armor and the tough skeletons of their ancestors. Modern amphibians appeared around 200 million years ago. When the supercontinent Pangaea broke up during the Jurassic period, about 150 million years ago, species were dispersed with the land masses, which is why they have proliferated worldwide despite their inability to tolerate saltwater. Today, the Class Amphibia contains approximately 4,550 species in three orders.

Although the reptiles date back to the Upper Carboniferous period, most orders (including the marine mosasaurs, the flying pterosaurs, and the terrestrial dinosaurs) died out about 65 million

EARLY ANCESTOR
Amphibians are thought to have evolved from lobe-finned fish not unlike the lungfish of today. This fossilized lungfish, which was found in Scotland, is more than 400 million years old.

years ago, most likely due to a natural cosmic or climatic disaster. The class Reptilia, as recognized today, is an artificial rather than a natural taxonomic group because it omits birds. Birds are placed in the separate class Aves but are now thought to be the closest living relatives of crocodilians (crocodiles and alligators). The ancestors of the turtles evolved about 200 million years ago, and early crocodilians diverged from lepidosaurians (ancestors of snakes, lizards, and tuataras) about 100 million years ago. The Class Reptilia contains about 6,660 species in four orders.

POISON-DART FROG
Often brilliantly coloured, poison-dart frogs are active by day; this is unusual because the majority of amphibians are active only during the hours of darkness. Some species are highly poisonous.

DISTINGUISHING FEATURES

Amphibians and reptiles, along with mammals and birds, are tetrapods – vertebrates with four limbs (although some, such as snakes and caecilians, no longer have any limbs). Amphibians are separated from other tetrapods by the need to return to water to reproduce because their eggs lack a protective shell. Most pass through a larval stage or series of stages. Reptiles, however, do not need water to breed, since their eggs are protected by a toughened shell. Some reptiles have advanced further still, and the young develop inside the body of the female. Reptiles are protected from desiccation by a waterproof skin, whereas amphibians possess a scaleless, water-permeable skin. Amphibians and reptiles are cold-blooded, relying on local conditions to raise their bodies to active temperatures.

TIGER SALAMANDER

Many salamanders superficially resemble lizards. They are, in fact, amphibians and have smooth, scaleless skin. Although the Tiger Salamander is a land-dwelling species, it returns to water to breed. It lays masses of gelatinous eggs that stick to underwater vegetation and develop into aquatic larvae.

mottled pattern continues on long tail

bright coloration alerts predators to toxic skin

legs adapted for terrestrial lifestyle

◁ ALLIGATOR
Some reptiles are adapted for aquatic lifestyles. The American Alligator preys on fish and turtles, but it also takes mammals and birds. It lays eggs on land and protects its young from predators.

▽ GIANT LIZARD
Weighing up to 310lb (140kg), the Komodo Dragon is the world's largest lizard. It is deceptively agile and will ambush wild pigs, deer, and even humans.

CLASSIFICATION

All lifeforms are classified by biologists into five kingdoms. All animals are placed in the kingdom Animalia, which is subdivided into phyla. The subphylum Vertebrata comprises those animals with a backbone within the phylum Chordata (animals with a spinal chord). Amphibia and Reptilia are two classes within the the Vertebrata. Examples of the main subdivisions are listed below.

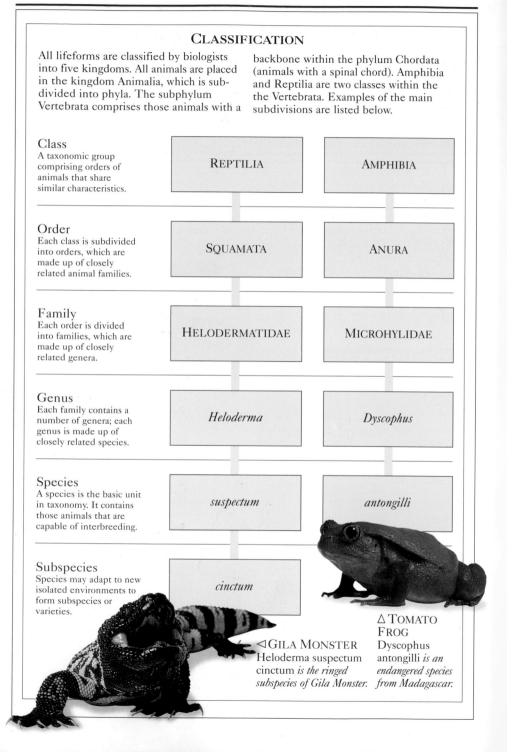

Class
A taxonomic group comprising orders of animals that share similar characteristics.

REPTILIA

AMPHIBIA

Order
Each class is subdivided into orders, which are made up of closely related animal families.

SQUAMATA

ANURA

Family
Each order is divided into families, which are made up of closely related genera.

HELODERMATIDAE

MICROHYLIDAE

Genus
Each family contains a number of genera; each genus is made up of closely related species.

Heloderma

Dyscophus

Species
A species is the basic unit in taxonomy. It contains those animals that are capable of interbreeding.

suspectum

antongilli

Subspecies
Species may adapt to new isolated environments to form subspecies or varieties.

cinctum

△ TOMATO FROG
Dyscophus antongilli *is an endangered species from Madagascar.*

◁ GILA MONSTER
Heloderma suspectum cinctum *is the ringed subspecies of Gila Monster.*

HOW THIS BOOK WORKS

THIS BOOK is first divided into two sections: reptiles and amphibians. It is then further divided into orders. Individual species entries are arranged according to family within the section for the order. The sample page below shows two typical entries: the top entry is taken from the amphibian section, and the bottom entry is taken from the reptile section.

family to which species belongs, written in roman type with initial capital letter •

two-part scientific name, written in italic type with initial capital letter •

current population status: rare, endangered, common, or locally common •

map indicates region or regions where individual • *species occurs*

common name of individual • *species*

introduction describes physical features and other characteristics •

information on distribution and habitats •

details of eggs or neonates •

indicates • *whether species is primarily terrestrial or aquatic*

KEY TO DIET SYMBOLS
For a more detailed explanation, see p.21

🦫 Mammals
🦅 Birds
🦎 Reptiles
🐸 Amphibians
● Eggs
🐟 Fish
◉ Mollusks
〰 Worms
🕷 Arthropods
🍃 Vegetation
🍄 Fungi

KEY TO ACTIVITY SYMBOLS
For a more detailed explanation, see p.25

☼ Diurnal
☾ Nocturnal
◑ Crepuscular
○ Any time

symbol indicates time of day when • *species is active*

KEY TO VENOM SYMBOLS
Venom symbol may appear next to common name of some reptiles. For a more detailed explanation, see p.15

🐍 Highly dangerous
🐍 Potentially dangerous

full-color photograph of species •

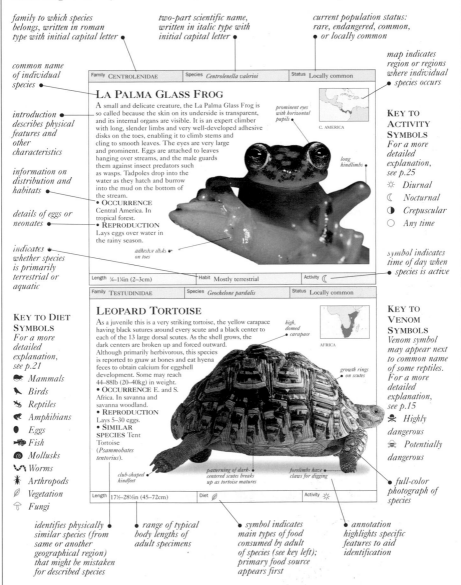

| Family CENTROLENIDAE | Species *Centrolenella valerioi* | Status Locally common |

LA PALMA GLASS FROG
A small and delicate creature, the La Palma Glass Frog is so called because the skin on its underside is transparent, and its internal organs are visible. It is an expert climber with long, slender limbs and very well-developed adhesive disks on the toes, enabling it to climb stems and cling to smooth leaves. The eyes are very large and prominent. Eggs are attached to leaves hanging over streams, and the male guards them against insect predators such as wasps. Tadpoles drop into the water as they hatch and burrow into the mud on the bottom of the stream.
• OCCURRENCE Central America. In tropical forest.
• REPRODUCTION Lays eggs over water in the rainy season.

prominent eyes with horizontal pupils

C. AMERICA

long hindlimbs

adhesive disks on toes

| Length ¾–1¼in (2–3cm) | Habit Mostly terrestrial | Activity ☾ |

| Family TESTUDINIDAE | Species *Geochelone pardalis* | Status Locally common |

LEOPARD TORTOISE
As a juvenile this is a very striking tortoise, the yellow carapace having black sutures around every scute and a black center to each of the 13 large dorsal scutes. As the shell grows, the dark centers are broken up and forced outward. Although primarily herbivorous, this species is reported to gnaw at bones and eat hyena feces to obtain calcium for eggshell development. Some may reach 44–88lb (20–40kg) in weight.
• OCCURRENCE E. and S. Africa. In savanna and savanna woodland.
• REPRODUCTION Lays 5–30 eggs.
• SIMILAR SPECIES Tent Tortoise (*Psammobates tentorius*).

high, domed carapace

AFRICA

growth rings on scutes

club-shaped hindfeet

patterning of dark-centered scutes breaks up as tortoise matures

forelimbs have claws for digging

| Length 17½–28½in (45–72cm) | Diet 🍃 | Activity ☼ |

identifies physically similar species (from same or another geographical region) that might be mistaken for described species

range of typical body lengths of adult specimens

symbol indicates main types of food consumed by adult of species (see key left); primary food source appears first

annotation highlights specific features to aid identification

WHAT IS AN AMPHIBIAN?

AMPHIBIANS ARE DIVIDED into three groups or orders: Urodeles (newts and salamanders), Gymnophionans (caecilians), and Anurans (frogs and toads). Frogs and toads have a distinctive body shape that makes them instantly recognizable, but it may be more difficult to identify newts and salamanders as their form is variable. Caecilians can be mistaken for worms or snakes.

AMPHIBIAN ANATOMY

The skin of amphibians is thin, and lacks a protective outer layer (such as the hair or feathers of mammals and birds, or the scales of reptiles). It is often moist, and the secretions produced to keep the skin moist can be toxic to deter predators. Many amphibians use their skin as a means of taking in oxygen. Most amphibians hunt by sight and have large eyes, often with a brightly colored iris. Their large eyes help them to see prey at night. Most amphibians have extremely wide mouths, which enable them to consume relatively large prey.

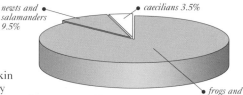

newts and salamanders 9.5%

caecilians 3.5%

frogs and toads 87%

AMPHIBIAN ORDERS

As shown in this pie chart, frogs and toads (Anura) are by far the largest order of amphibians, comprising 87 percent of all species.

ROUND   HORIZONTAL   VERTICAL

EYE VARIETY

Vertical pupils facilitate night hunting; horizontal pupils are more common for daylight vision. All newts and salamanders have round pupils.

SMOOTH   WARTY

SKIN TYPES

The skin of amphibians is often brightly colored. It may be smooth or warty, with mucus-secreting glands to keep it moist.

scaleless, water-permeable skin

large, protruding eyes for night vision

toes usually adapted for swimming

WEBBED   STICKY

AMPHIBIANS' FEET

Amphibians' toes are often webbed, to aid swimming. They may have adhesive pads to aid climbing.

FROGS AND TOADS

Frogs and toads typically have a large head with a wide mouth; a short, rigid back; small forelimbs; and very large, muscular hindlimbs. The eyes are large and protruding. The skin is smooth and often shiny in frogs, warty and dull in toads. Patterned skin provides camouflage.

TOAD
Slow-moving and unable to climb, this Common Toad walks or hops along the ground.

long toes enable treefrog to grasp stems

dull, warty skin

TREEFROG
The Red-eyed Treefrog has smooth, shiny skin. It is very agile and has adhesive toe pads to aid climbing.

body has distinctive grooves

wormlike body

CAECILIANS

Caecilians look like large earthworms; they have no legs and there are numerous grooves around the long, thin body. The pointed head is shovel-shaped and the tail is very short. They find their prey primarily by smell.

BUILT FOR BURROWING
The Mexican Caecilian is able to burrow like a worm using its shovel-shaped head.

NEWTS AND SALAMANDERS

Newts and salamanders undergo less dramatic changes than frogs and toads when they metamorphose from the larval to the adult form. They have relatively small heads; long, flexible bodies; and long tails. Those species that live in water have a deep, laterally flattened tail, which they beat from side to side when swimming. The forelimbs usually have four digits; the hindlimbs five.

brightly colored skin

△ATTRACTING FEMALES
The male Alpine Newt develops bright coloration in the breeding season to attract a mate.

deep tail aids strong swimming

◁WARNING COLORS
The Fire Salamander is brightly colored to warn predators that it is highly poisonous.

costal grooves on sides

WHAT IS A REPTILE?

REPTILES ARE DIVIDED into four orders: Testudines (turtles and tortoises); Crocodylia (crocodiles, alligators, and gharials); Rhynchocephalia (tuataras) and Squamata (scaled reptiles). The Squamata are further divided into three suborders: Sauria or Lacertilia (lizards); Amphisbaenia (worm-lizards); and Serpentes or Ophidia (snakes).

REPTILE ANATOMY

The waterproof skin of a reptile is usually covered by scales or reinforced by osteoderms (bony skin plates), but lacks the skin glands found in mammals. Coloration may be cryptic to avoid detection, or gaudy to advertise a warning. The development of senses varies between groups. Specialized organs, such as the thermosensory facial pits of certain snakes and the chemosensory tongue of snakes and some lizards, are highly advanced developments for prey location and capture.

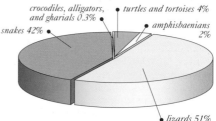

crocodiles, alligators, and gharials 0.3%
turtles and tortoises 4%
snakes 42%
amphisbaenians 2%
lizards 51%

△ REPTILE ORDERS

Snakes, lizards, and amphisbaenians (the Squamata) comprise 95% of all reptiles. At 0.03%, the tuataras are too small a group to represent on this pie chart.

GRANULAR   SMOOTH   KEELED

△ SCALES

Lizard skin varies from paperlike, granular gecko skin to the beadlike scales of heloderm lizards. Snake scales may be smooth (as in pythons) or keeled (as in desert vipers or aquatic keelbacks).

△ SHEDDING SKIN

As most reptiles grow, they shed the transparent top layer of their skins. Whereas snakes can shed their skins in one piece, the limbs of lizards prevent them from doing so, and they tend to slough their skins in pieces.

movable eyelids are found in most lizards but not in snakes

HORIZONTAL

VERTICAL   ROUND

△ EYE TYPES

Diurnal reptiles usually have round pupils but a few are horizontal; nocturnal species have vertical pupils.

tough skin is covered in scales or plates

most limbed reptiles have five toes

CROCODILES AND ALLIGATORS

Although survivors of a prehistoric lineage, modern crocodilians have a more advanced and efficient four-chambered heart than most reptiles, which typically have three-chambered hearts. Crocodilians are covered in leathery armour, often with protective osteoderms beneath the surface. With their muscular tails, webbed hind-feet, and powerful tooth-filled jaws, large crocodilians are the ultimate freshwater predators, capable of killing almost any animal that enters their domain. Not all crocodilians are dangerous to humans: the large Ganges Gharial, for example, is a fish-eating specialist. Gharials (characterized by a long, slender snout) belong to a separate family from crocodiles and alligators. Caimans are South American alligators.

powerful tail to aid swimming

armored skin

notch in jaw

△ NILE CROCODILE
Crocodiles have a notch in the upper jaw through which the fourth tooth of the lower jaw protrudes.

▽ AMERICAN ALLIGATOR
The alligator's broad snout completely covers all its teeth when the jaws are closed. The American Alligator is a heavily built swamp dweller; its blackish brown body is often covered in algae.

broad snout

massive tail aids swimming

webbed hindlimbs

▷ JACOBSON'S ORGAN
The tongue of snakes and many lizards transfers information to the chemo-sensitive Jacobson's organ in the roof of the mouth.

forked tongue

reptilian tails may be used for swimming, climbing, or defense

limbs are usually well developed but may be reduced or absent

TUATARAS

With all their close relatives extinct for over 65 million years, the two surviving species of tuatara on remote islands off New Zealand could be considered to be living dinosaurs. These curious reptiles are relatively small, slow growing, and have extremely slow reproductive and metabolic processes. Although they resemble brown iguanas, they are not closely related to snakes and lizards.

iguana-like body

TURTLES AND TORTOISES

Very different in appearance from other living reptiles, the ancestors of turtles and tortoises diverged from other reptiles over 230 million years ago. All turtles and tortoises have a shell consisting of a dorsal carapace and a ventral plastron, but in some species it is soft and leathery rather than hard and rigid. Most species live in freshwater but there are eight marine turtles and a large family of truly terrestrial tortoises. Most terrestrial species are herbivores, while most aquatic species are omnivores. The sea turtles, however, are much more specialized. They are also some of the world's greatest oceanic navigators and travelers.

△ RED-FOOT TORTOISE
A large and slow-moving rainforest herbivore, the Red-foot Tortoise relies on its strong carapace to protect it from predators.

• *carapace protects head, limbs, and body*

• *head can be completely withdrawn into shell*

◁ COMMON SLIDER
A popular pet, the American Common Slider is a typical omnivorous fresh-water turtle with a tough shell.

LIZARDS

The lizards are the most diverse suborder of reptiles, and they are also the most frequently encountered. Ranging from tiny geckos to giant monitor lizards, there is a vast diversity in shape, skeletal structure, color, reproduction, behavior, defense, and diet. Although many lizards look fearsome (and the bites of large lizards can cause serious injuries), only two species are venomous. Within lizards there is an evolutionary trend toward a reduction of the limbs to the point of complete leglessness. The loss of eyelids and ear openings may also be considered advanced traits in lizards.

lizard tails are often used to store fat and may be shed in defense •

gecko skin is fragile but many lizards have coverings of strong overlapping scales •

△ THORNY DEVIL
Some lizards are specially adapted to live in extreme conditions. The Thorny Devil inhabits arid deserts, where it lives on a diet of ants. The prickly body collects condensed desert dew and channels it to the mouth.

◁ LEOPARD GECKO
One of the most familiar of all lizards in captivity, the Leopard Gecko is a nocturnal desert dweller. Like most lizards, it is small, inoffensive, and insectivorous.

SNAKES

Snakes are characterized by their lack of limbs, eyelids, and external ear openings. Their entire body is covered in scales, which may be smooth or keeled. Unlike some lizards, which are herbivorous or at least omnivorous, all snakes are carnivorous. Snakes employ a variety of methods of locomotion and prey-handling. Some are among the most venomous animals on earth. They may lay eggs or give birth to live young. The primary sense organ of all snakes is the forked tongue, but some species are also sensitive to the body heat of their prey.

strongly keeled
body scales

PUFF ADDER
A large, stout-bodied venomous snake, the Puff Adder possesses the strongly keeled scales associated with species found in arid habitats. Its venom is potentially lethal.

typical long,
slender body

HOW DANGEROUS?

In this book, two symbols are used to denote reptiles that have potentially dangerous or highly dangerous venom.

☠ HIGHLY DANGEROUS
Species considered capable of delivering a dangerously venomous bite, including all the front-fanged venomous snakes.

☠ POTENTIALLY DANGEROUS
Venomous snakes that have large enough mouths to enable them to bite and inject large quantities of a relatively weak venom into a human.

Garter Snakes
have longitudinal
stripes

GARTER SNAKE
Fast moving, alert, and agile, the Garter Snake preys on frogs and fish. This non-venomous species is often kept as a pet.

AMPHISBAENIANS

Overshadowed by the other squamates (snakes and lizards), the usually legless amphisbaenians or worm-lizards are slender, secretive, burrowing reptiles, often mistaken for snakes or worms. Their heads are armoured for burrowing, and their tiny body scales are arranged in annular rings, further enhancing their wormlike appearance.

vestigial
eyes

annular
rings

AMPHIBIAN REPRODUCTION

MOST AMPHIBIANS gather in large numbers at a specific time of year (sometimes for only a few days) in order to breed. The breeding season is usually triggered by warm weather in temperate regions, and by the onset of the rainy season in the tropics. Within mating groups, males have to compete to attract females. Male frogs and toads, and many salamanders, clasp the female prior to mating in a tight embrace known as amplexus. In frogs and toads, fertilization is external; in most salamanders, newts, and caecilians, fertilization is internal.

LIFE CYCLE

All amphibians have a life cycle that goes through three distinct phases: egg, larva, and adult, illustrated here by the Common Toad (*Bufo bufo*). In frogs and toads, eggs are produced in clumps or strings. The eggs hatch into tiny larvae, commonly known as tadpoles, which grow rapidly and develop legs. At metamorphosis, the tadpoles leave the water, losing their tails. The tiny adults may spend several years on land, growing to adult size, before eventually returning to the water to find a mate and reproduce.

male grips female behind head

▷ MATING

Prior to mating, the toad sits on the back of the female, holding her tightly with his powerful forelimbs, while the female searches for a place to deposit her eggs. The male's hindlimbs are free to kick out at rival males. The amplexus position ensures that when the female releases her eggs they are very close to the male's vent, thus maximizing the chance that his sperm will fertilize them.

female often larger than male

egg masses laid among vegetation

▷ EGGS

Toads produce many thousands of small, black eggs, laid in long strings that are wrapped around plants. The eggs hatch into tiny tadpoles that move very little for a few days but grow by absorbing the remaining egg yolk in their bodies. Tadpoles initially have no legs, and they swim in search of food by beating their tails. An easy meal for many kinds of predator, the tadpoles of toads are nevertheless distasteful to most fish.

round black eggs laid in a string of jelly

◁ FINDING A MATE

Many frogs and toads call loudly to attract females during the breeding season, often forming a dense chorus. The call is produced by the male filling a large vocal sac with air that is shunted back and forth between the lungs and the vocal sac, passing over the vocal cords.

vocal sac

▽ ADULT TOAD

Toads grow slowly during adult life, but their final size is vital for their success in reproduction. Larger females lay more eggs, and larger males are more likely to be successful in competing for matings. Adult toads return to the water only for the few days that they need to breed.

wide mouth for eating relatively large prey

familiar adult body shape formed

warts become more prominent on skin

◁ YOUNG TOAD

At metamorphosis, the tail and gills are absorbed into the body and the tiny young toad, now breathing with lungs, emerges onto land, and soon starts to hunt for insect prey. It is very vulnerable to drying out and typically leaves the water only on rainy days.

spherical body due to tightly coiled gut

forelimbs appear

◁ OLDER TADPOLES

As tadpoles grow, their limbs develop and their body shape becomes more streamlined. The hindlimbs are the first to appear and the tail shortens. Tadpoles often swim in large schools, affording them some protection against predators and possibly also stirring up their microscopic food.

hindlimbs appear

ALTERNATIVE STRATEGIES

There are many variations on the typical
three-stage life cycle of an amphibian. Some
salamanders do not reach the typical terrestrial adult form, but become sexually mature
while still in the aquatic larval state, with
external gills. Some amphibians do not have
free-swimming larvae; instead, the larval
stage is completed inside the egg, which
hatches to produce a miniature adult.

Care and protection of the young are equally
varied. Many salamanders guard their eggs
against predators and fungal infections, and
some newts carefully wrap each egg in a
folded leaf. Many frogs protect their eggs by
laying them in a foam nest that keeps them
moist and deters predators. Parental care in
frogs also takes many forms. The developing
eggs may be retained in some part of the
body, including the mouth, skin, stomach,
or a special pouch on the back or thighs.
Poison-dart frogs carry their
tadpoles from pool to pool.

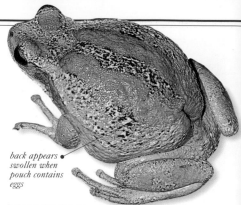

back appears
swollen when
pouch contains
eggs

△ POUCH LIFE

*The female Marsupial Frog has a pouch on its
back, which may contain over a hundred eggs. The
eggs, placed there during mating, develop into tiny
adult frogs that push their way out of the pouch
when they are fully developed.*

▷ FEMALE GREAT CRESTED NEWT

*This female Great Crested Newt is
gluing a leaf into position around
one of her eggs by pressing her
hindfeet together. This process
provides some protection for
the eggs against predation
and disease.*

feathery
external
gills

▷ EXTERNAL GILLS

*The larvae of salamanders and
newts often have large, feathery
external gills. The conspicuous
gills of this Tiger Salamander
will disappear after about 12 weeks.*

body held
upright as egg
is laid among
vegetation

△ FOAM NEST

*Male and female Foam-nest Frogs congregate to
create a vast communal foam nest to hide their
eggs. The nest is suspended over a pond.*

REPTILE REPRODUCTION

REPTILES do not possess the array of elaborate breeding strategies of amphibians, but their propagation is still highly diverse. Reproduction involves internal fertilization. Oviparity (egg-laying) and viviparity (live-bearing) are both present in reptiles, but rarely within the same species. Male reptiles find, court, and mate receptive females. Typically, female reptiles lay their eggs or give birth without any further maternal involvement.

COURTSHIP AND MATING

Courtship rituals vary considerably in reptiles, often with violent competition between males. The male Madagascan Ploughshare Tortoise, for example, has a projection on the front of its shell to roll over rival males. Male snakes court females by tracking their scent, whereas male crocodilians bellow to attract a mate. Although most reptiles abandon their eggs, crocodilians are a notable exception – females guard their nest and then remove the hatchlings to a safe "creche."

bright green body coloration

brilliant yellow and orange markings on face

◁ CLOACAL SPURS

During courtship, male boas and pythons stimulate their mates using cloacal spurs. The spur shown here belongs to a male Burmese Rock Python. Female Burmese Rock Pythons can lay over 30 eggs.

△ DISPLAY COLORS

Many reptiles have elaborate crests or striking coloration to attract a mate. This Panther Chameleon is one of the most brilliantly colored of all lizards. This species has a startling turquoise stripe and sunburst orange eye markings.

EGGS OR LIVE YOUNG

Crocodilians, turtles, tortoises, and geckos lay relatively hard-shelled eggs, but those of other lizards and snakes are soft and leathery. The embryo hatches by slitting the shell with its egg tooth. Many snake and lizard species are live-bearers, producing neonates (newborns) in embryonic membranes from which they escape within seconds of birth.

membranous birth sac

△ NEONATE BOA

Here, an Argentine Rainbow Boa emerges from its fetal sac immediately after its birth.

▷ HOGNOSE SNAKE HATCHLING

The soft, leathery egg does not crack but collapses as a hatchling emerges.

leathery shell

AMPHIBIAN FEEDING HABITS

ALL ADULT AMPHIBIANS are carnivores, feeding on a wide variety of living prey, mostly invertebrates such as insects, earthworms, millipedes, slugs, and snails. An amphibian's mouth can open very wide, enabling it to eat some surprisingly large items of food. Most amphibians are too slow-moving to be able to chase their prey, and the vast majority are "sit and wait" predators.

PART-TIME FEEDERS
The food requirements of amphibians are very much smaller than those of mammals and birds of comparable size; only in warm weather do they need to eat frequently. In winter, cold temperatures prevent them from being active and they survive on fat reserves that they have built up during the summer months. Newts, salamanders, and caecilians usually eat slow, soft-bodied prey, such as worms and slugs. Some larger amphibians, such as the notorious Marine Toad, will prey on small mammals and even birds. Some amphibians are specialist feeders. For example, the Western Narrow-mouthed Toad thrives on a diet of ants. Aquatic amphibians will eat small fish and tadpoles.

strong jaws
seize slow-
moving prey

MANDARIN SALAMANDER
This Mandarin Salamander is swallowing a worm that is nearly as long as itself. After such a large meal, it will not have to eat for several days.

SIT-AND-WAIT STRATEGY
Some frogs will leap considerable distances to catch prey, but most amphibians use their long, sticky tongue to ambush passing prey. Amphibians are generally very well camouflaged, often with elaborate patterning, and they are able to remain motionless for long periods of time. Other amphibians, such as the Green Toad, will forage for slow-moving prey.

ORNAMENTAL
HORNED
TOAD

mouse swallowed
head first

▽ CAPTURING PREY
Though extremely slow in its general movements, this Common Toad has a quick-fire, sticky tongue which it can flick out to capture its prey.

△▷ HORNED TOAD
The cryptic pattern on a horned toad provides perfect camouflage as it awaits its victim. It can capture and ingest prey, such as this mouse, nearly half its own size.

HORNED TOAD

body lunges
forward

● tongue flicks
out very
rapidly

REPTILE FEEDING HABITS

M OST REPTILES, including all crocodilians and snakes, are carnivores. Others are omnivorous; and a few are strict herbivores. Most smaller lizards and tuataras feed mainly on arthropods, but larger lizards may take much larger prey. Most amphisbaenians feed on soft invertebrates. The very wide range of reptile strategies for capturing and subduing prey is illustrated below.

HERBIVORES

In order to digest vegetation, reptiles need a specialized gut containing symbiotic microbes capable of fermenting the cellulose of ingested leaves. Most lizards that feed on leaves are iguanas or their close relatives, but a few other reptiles have also evolved specialized guts. Monkey-tail Skinks and ground-dwelling Rhinoceros Iguanas, in the Caribbean, eat plants containing compounds that are potentially deadly to other herbivores. Tortoises are typical herbivores – slow-moving, terrestrial, defenseless grazers. Hingeback Tortoises and Wood Turtles also feed on fungi. Overall, however, there are few entirely herbivorous reptiles compared to the vast number of completely carnivorous species.

MARINE HERBIVORE
The Galapagos Marine Iguana is one of the most unusual herbivores. The only truly marine lizard, it dives into the cold ocean to take mouthfuls of seaweed from the seabed.

DIET SYMBOLS

In this book, the wide variety of lifeforms consumed by reptiles are represented by eleven symbols, which are explained below. Where relevant or of particular interest, more specific information on feeding habits is given in the text for each species entry.

 MAMMALS
Preys on mammals ranging from rats and mice to antelope and wildebeest.

EGGS
Eats eggs of birds and reptiles. Some reptiles are specialist egg feeders.

ARTHROPODS
Feeds on arthropods. Arthropods such as insects and spiders provide the bulk of the diet of most small reptiles. The symbol also represents aquatic crustaceans, such as crabs and crayfish, which are preyed upon by some reptilian species.

BIRDS
Preys on birds. Some crocodilians, snakes, and large lizards eat large wading birds.

FISH
Preys on fish. Some crocodilians and turtles feed largely on fish species.

REPTILES
Preys on other reptiles. Snakes, particularly, feed on smaller reptilian species.

MOLLUSKS
Feeds on gastropods, such as slugs and snails, and on marine mollusks.

VEGETATION
Feeds on plant matter. Many tortoises and turtles are largely herbivorous.

AMPHIBIANS
Feeds on amphibians such as frogs and toads. Toxic species may be avoided.

WORMS
Feeds on worms. Also symbolizes other soft-bodied invertebrates.

FUNGI
Includes fungi in diet. Relatively few reptile species will feed on fungi.

RANGE OF CARNIVORES

Reptilian carnivores range from tiny geckos feeding on flying insects attracted to light, to Nile Crocodiles ambushing wildebeest. The majority of lizards feed on invertebrates. Some larger lizards, however, such as monitor lizards and the South American Tegus, feed on small mammals and smaller lizards as well as carrion and bird or reptile eggs. The world's largest lizard is the Komodo Dragon, which preys on deer but will take other large mammals, even humans. All snakes are carnivores, but they can be loosely subdivided into vertebrate and invertebrate feeders. Most reptiles are generalist feeders, eating a variety of prey types, but there are also many specialist feeders, one of the most curious being the American Horned Lizard, which feeds exclusively on ants. There are even snakes that specialize in eating scorpions or centipedes.

MOORISH GECKO EATING LOCUST
Insects are the primary food of most small to medium-sized lizards. Since few are dangerous to the lizard, or of large size, they require little more than powerful jaws to crush the exoskeleton prior to swallowing. Because they are extremely numerous, insects can support a large lizard population.

SPECIALIST FEEDERS

Blindsnakes feed primarily on termites; slug-eaters and thirst snakes feed on terrestrial mollusks; and mangrove watersnakes eat crabs. The King Cobra feeds primarily on other snakes, including pythons, while coralsnakes will take any cylindrical prey, including eels, other snakes, amphisbaenians, and caecilians. Anacondas, the African pythons, and the Brown Water Python have been recorded preying on crocodilians, and large anacondas and pythons are well known for their ability to swallow very large mammals, including humans. Some turtles are also specialist feeders: Leatherback Sea Turtles feed mainly on jellyfish, Hawksbill Turtles primarily feed on sponges, and the Matamata is expert at catching fish.

snake is being swallowed head first

△ SNAKE-EATING SNAKE
This mildly venomous Crowned Snake makes an easy meal for the highly venomous Sonoran Coralsnake. Snakes may be swallowed head or tail first, whereas prey with legs is ideally eaten head first.

▽ AFRICAN EGG-EATER
An egg-eating snake can engorge a whole bird's egg. After rupturing the egg within its throat, the snake will expel the shell remains from its mouth and swallow the egg's contents.

shape of egg clearly visible

head significantly smaller than egg

CATCHING PREY

Reptiles may actively stalk or lie in ambush for their prey. Once captured, the prey must be immobilized prior to ingestion. Small, harmless prey such as insects, eggs, fish, frogs, or small lizards may be swallowed alive. Larger animals must be killed before being eaten, especially those with claws and teeth. Large monitor lizards pummel their prey on the ground or crush it with their powerful jaws. Aquatic turtles use their front claws to rip prey apart. Crocodilians drown their victims and dismember them by either spinning or shaking them vigorously.

Snakes use either constriction or venom to kill. Constriction is employed by many snakes from pythons to cornsnakes – the snake coils its muscular body around its prey to prevent it from breathing. Highly venomous snakes, such as cobras and vipers, strike their prey and inject a fast-acting venom that rapidly causes death. Snakes are forced to swallow their meals whole, but they can articulate (not dislocate) their lower jaws to engorge prey that is broader than their own heads.

● hinged fangs in protective skin sheaths

◁ STRIKING PREY

Venomous snakes may be front or rear fanged (fangs under and behind the eyes). This rattlesnake is a front-fanged pitviper; it locates its prey using heat-sensitive pits, then strikes rapidly, bringing its fangs forward to enter the prey.

▷ HEAT PITS

Boas, pythons, and pit vipers have heat-sensitive pits situated on the face. The pits act together to pinpoint the precise direction and distance of prey.

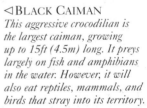

◁ BLACK CAIMAN

This aggressive crocodilian is the largest caiman, growing up to 15ft (4.5m) long. It preys largely on fish and amphibians in the water. However, it will also eat reptiles, mammals, and birds that stray into its territory.

▷ AFRICAN PYTHON

African pythons prey on large mammals such as gazelle, domestic goats, and even humans. Prey is suffocated and then swallowed head first, a process that may take several hours. Even the gazelle's bones will eventually be digested by the python's stomach juices.

MOVEMENT AND ACTIVITY

THE ACTIVITY OF REPTILES and amphibians is limited mainly by cold, since they rely on environmental heat to raise their body temperature to a level where movement is possible. Species found in cooler temperate regions may be active for only part of the year. The main threat to tropical species is the dry season, when water, food, or prey is scarce.

LOCOMOTION

Reptiles and amphibians move around in many ways: crawling, running, leaping, gliding, swimming, and burrowing. Each requires different adaptations. A pointed or shovel-shaped snout is useful for burrowing, especially if the tail bears a sharpened spike for leverage in smooth tunnels. A laterally compressed, paddle-shaped tail, flipperlike forelimbs, or webbed toes improve swimming ability. Toes may have adhesive pads, which can greatly increase climbing capabilities. Snakes use their complex systems of muscles to achieve different types of locomotion according to the terrain they have to traverse (see below).

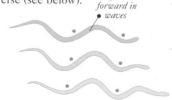

powerful hindlimbs with long, webbed toes

LEAPING
Many frogs are capable of spectacular leaps using their long, powerful hindlimbs. This Southern Leopard Frog takes a series of zigzag leaps toward water when approached by a predator.

trailing edges of ventral scales provide grip

body moves forward in waves

snake prepares to push away from its rear

RECTILINEAR
Muscle contractions along the snake's body move it directly forward in a gliding motion.

SERPENTINE
The most common type of motion, the snake pushes its body against ground irregularities.

CONCERTINA
The snake bunches its muscles at the rear and extends its front in a continuous cycle of motion.

SWIMMING
Newts, iguanas, seasnakes, and crocodiles use their long tails to drive them forward. This fire-bellied newt lashes its tail from side to side to drive itself rapidly through the water.

body flexes and tail lashes sideways to provide rapid propulsion

newt rises to surface to breathe

legs paddle rapidly to increase speed when fleeing from predators

DAY OR NIGHT

To burrowing species, day and night are no different; they surface only when rain floods their burrows. Nonburrowing reptiles and amphibians are usually active when their prey is available – many tropical snakes hunt sleeping lizards or birds at night. Frogs and toads are also active mainly at night. For species living on the tropical rainforest floor, where a tiny fraction of ambient light may be available, day and night may be little different.

BASKING

Diurnal reptiles, such as this European Eyed Lizard, bask to warm their bodies to active temperatures. If they bask too early, when ambient temperatures are still low, they risk attack by a predator.

NOCTURNAL SPECIES

The Common Leaf-tailed Gecko hides in trees during the day and emerges at night to hunt insects.

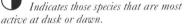

lizard stays motionless and alert to danger

ACTIVITY SYMBOLS

In this book, four symbols are used in the species profiles to indicate the time of day in which each species is active. Although most are active at night, those in temperate regions must be diurnal to remain active.

☼ DIURNAL
Indicates those reptile and amphibian species that are active during the day.

◐ CREPUSCULAR
Indicates those species that are most active at dusk or dawn.

☾ NOCTURNAL
Indicates those reptile and amphibian species that are active mainly at night.

○ ANY TIME
Indicates those species that may be active during the day or at night.

SEASONAL HABITS

Animals are active at times that are most beneficial to them, when food, prey, or mates are available and living conditions are not too extreme. In the tropics, the rainy season is often the time when most snakes are active, as are their prey. In temperate regions, reptiles and amphibians reproduce in the spring so that offspring have a chance to feed well before the oncoming winter.

RATTLESNAKES HIBERNATING

In temperate regions, reptiles and amphibians become inactive when temperatures drop below the level required for metabolic activity.

DEFENSE

AMPHIBIANS AND REPTILES use an array of strategies for defense, which may be passive or active. Passive defense involves camouflage to avoid detection or warning colors to deter predators. Active strategies range from rapid flight to the cobra's dramatic hooding. Puff Adders, Bullsnakes, and Russell's Vipers hiss very loudly; lizards may shed their tails; and frogs and toads can flatten or inflate their bodies to make them appear too large to eat, so deterring many predators.

COLOR

Many species have bright and startling colors to alert predators to toxins in the skin, as in the poison-dart frogs. Some frogs flash eyespots to confuse or frighten predators. Alternatively, coloration may be inconspicuous or cryptic to provide camouflage. Often such camouflage coloration is combined with adornments that enhance the effect, such as the curious snout protuberances of Madagascan Vinesnakes, which resemble leaf buds. Chameleons and some frogs can alter their color to match their immediate surroundings. Harmless snakes and frogs sometimes mimic dangerous species by adopting their warning patterns.

◁ CAMOUFLAGE
The brown coloration and angular shape of the Asian Leaf Frog makes it all but invisible among the decaying leaves on the forest floor.

△ WARNING
The Japanese Fire-bellied Newt has vivid red markings on its underside to warn predators that its skin contains distasteful secretions.

△ SUIT OF ARMOR
Reeve's Turtle of Southeast Asia (along with other advanced "straightneck" turtles) is able to fully retract its head into its shell for protection.

ARMOR

The most familiar armored reptiles are the turtles and tortoises, which have bony, two-piece shells. Box turtles have even evolved a means of retracting the legs and head and then closing the hinged plastron to form a box that protects them from being extracted. Many lizards that rely on retreating to a hole to avoid predators have sharply armored tails with which to block their retreats, and sand boas have strong keels on their tail scales for similar protection. Crocodilians, especially smaller species such as dwarf caimans and dwarf crocodiles, have armored osteoderms in their skin. Toxins in the skin of many amphibians may be seen as chemical armor.

PLAYING DEAD

The process of playing dead is called thanatosis. Some newts play dead to avoid the attentions of short-sighted grass snakes. Hog-nose snakes, grass snakes, and the Rinkhals will also roll over and play dead, even to the point of rolling back again, mouth agape, if turned the right way up. Thanatosis is frequently accompanied by the release of the pungent cloacal contents to repulse the predator.

▷ THANATOSIS
This grass snake is feigning death by rolling on its back with its tongue hanging limp. If the predator loses interest, the snake will make a hasty retreat.

OTHER DEFENSES

A wide range of unique defenses are employed by individual species. American Horned Toad Lizards rupture the blood vessels around the eyes and some West Indian boas bleed from the mouth in a process called autohemorrhagy. Either the blood tastes acrid to the predator or the sight is offputting. The process whereby a lizard sheds its tail to escape a predator is known as caudal autotomy.

tail severed at one of several fracture points

△ SHED TAIL
Many lizards, such as this Emerald Tree Skink, shed their tail if attacked by a predator.

new tail after eight months' growth

green color is primary passive defense

△ REGENERATED TAIL
After attack, it takes many months for a new tail, composed of cartilage, to grow to its full length. The tail can then be sacrificed again if necessary.

VENOM FOR DEFENSE

Although many snakes are venomous, the venom is used primarily for hunting. Many snakes will advertise their presence using an audible or visual signal and will bite in defense as a last resort. Spitting cobras, however, will expel a "shotgun scatter" of venom into the face of a perceived enemy. The spit causes intense pain, allowing the cobra time to escape. The only other reptiles with venom specifically for defense are the two American heloderm lizards.

hollow, interlocking segments rattle when shaken

one link added each time snake sheds skin

RATTLE
Although rattlesnakes use their venom primarily to hunt, it is a powerful deterrent to predators. The snake's rattle warns its enemies to steer clear.

DISTRIBUTION AND HABITAT

THE LIMITING FACTORS influencing the distribution of amphibians are cold, salinity, aridity, and availability of freshwater. Their permeable skins make them vulnerable to desiccation in the sun or upon immersion in seawater. Reptiles are less restricted since their scaly skin prevents desiccation. They adapt well to most conditions but are excluded from the poles and mountain peaks.

DIVERSE ENVIRONMENTS

Tropical rainforest and wetlands support the greatest range of amphibians and reptiles, but temperate forests, deserts, and grasslands are also home to a wide range of species. A few reptiles thrive in the sea or in mountainous areas. Many species have adapted to live, alongside man, in urban areas.

GRASSLANDS
Savannas, pampas, and prairies can be diverse habitats for amphibians and reptiles, accommodating burrowing snakes, lumbering tortoises, small frogs on leaf blades, and large camouflaged vipers. The main threat is drought.

DISTRIBUTION

The numbers of amphibian and reptile species and individuals are heavily dependent on temperature (although rainfall is also significant factor).

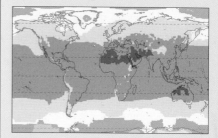

Temperature	
°C	°F
30	86
20	68
10	50
0	32
-10	14
-20	-4
-30	-22

TEMPERATURE
This map shows the Earth's average temperatures. Reptile and amphibian populations are most diverse in hot, wet areas and smaller and less varied at high altitudes and towards the poles.

DESERTS
In even the most inhospitable of deserts there are snakes feeding on lizards and lizards feeding on insects. Desert life requires adaptations for water conservation and movement on loose sand. Most activity takes place at night.

WEB-FOOTED GECKO

WETLANDS
Many amphibians, and the reptiles that feed upon them, inhabit swamps, marshes, lakes, and rivers. Some caecilians never leave the water, while frogs return to breed. Large crocodiles, snapping turtles, and rare species like the Banded Water Cobra may be found in larger watercourses.

TEMPERATE FORESTS

NATTERJACK TOAD

Less diverse than tropical forests, temperate forests are still home to a large number of newts, salamanders, leaf-litter lizards, and snakes.

TROPICAL FORESTS

Tropical forest, in its various forms, contains the most varied collection of amphibians and reptiles, including many with specialized diets or habits. Species inhabit all levels, from the soil of the forest floor to the high sunlit canopy.

ISLANDS

Species diversity is often much lower on remote islands, especially among amphibians that do not colonize well. Island populations often exhibit traits toward giantism or dwarfism. Abnormally large numbers of single species may be found.

OCEANS

The oceans are home to a few reptiles, but amphibians cannot live in saltwater.

HAWKSBILL SEA TURTLE

MOUNTAINS

Lizards are common on the lower scree slopes. A few specialized snakes, such as the Nose-horned Viper, are found at relatively high elevations but are absent from the lowlands.

NOSE-HORNED VIPER

URBAN AND SUBURBAN AREAS

Many species can adjust to man-made environments and some even thrive. Amphibians inhabit ponds on reclaimed land and in gardens, and snakes often enter to hunt them. Large, venomous snakes are sometimes found even in some of the world's major capital cities.

CONSERVATION

REPTILES AND AMPHIBIANS are under considerable threat, and every year several species become extinct. Although they often go unnoticed, many species are important to the ecology of their habitats, acting as both prey and predators, and a decline in amphibian numbers may be a sign of environmental pollution. When reptiles and amphibians become extinct, other species soon follow, so it is vital that we take as much care over them as we do over more conspicuous animals.

DECLINING POPULATIONS

Amphibians are disappearing from the world's ecosystems at an alarming rate. Apart from a number of high-profile species, such as the Costa Rican Golden Toad, population crashes have been recorded in many other species. In addition, the incidence of deformities within populations as far apart as Europe and Australia has increased noticeably in recent years. The reasons are not fully understood, but increased radiation due to ozone depletion, global warming, acid rain, and chemical pollution may all play their part. Habitat destruction is by far the greatest threat to reptile populations, although commercial exploitation (for skins and food) and introduced predators are also significant factors despite protective legislation.

• permeable skin highly sensitive to pollution such as acid rain

• bright green coloration provide camouflage in lush tropical vegetation

◁ CHUCKWALLA
Species that live on small islands, such as the Giant, or Pied, Chuckwalla, are particularly vulnerable to habitat destruction, illegal collection, and introduced predators like cats or rats. This protected species lives on two islands off Mexico.

△ LEMUR FROG
The Lemur Frog is a leaf-breeding species from Central America. In recent years it has disappeared from areas where it was once common and is now almost extinct in Costa Rica, for instance. Especially worrying is the fact that there is no obvious reason for its decline, in one of the world's most pristine environments.

crest develops to attract mate in • breeding season

▽ GREAT CRESTED NEWT
The Great Crested Newt is totally dependent on certain types of freshwater pond in order to breed. They must be deep enough to avoid drying up every year, but they should dry up occasionally so that fish and other predators cannot live in them. Ponds of this type are increasingly rare.

• bright warning coloration deters predators

COMMERCIAL EXPLOITATION

Hundreds of thousands of reptiles are sacrificed every year to feed the skin trade and the tourist industry. Despite some restrictions on the trade, tourist shops in Asia, for example, still offer ornaments made from dead reptiles, while upscale stores in prosperous countries continue to stock handbags, shoes, wallets, and other items made from reptile skins. Some of these products are from farmed crocodilians but wild populations are often exploited. Snakes and lizards are not commercially farmed, and there is only limited farming of turtles, so all products made from these species constitute a drain on wild populations, some of which have declined drastically in recent times.

▽ GREEN SEA TURTLES

Turtles are widely hunted for food and their eggs, which are often taken from slaughtered females before they are laid. Sea turtles return to the same beaches each year to nest, making them easy prey.

△ CROCODILE BAG

This handbag was made from an endangered Dwarf Crocodile, complete with head and limbs. At least 13 of the 23 surviving species of crocodilian are considered at risk. Hunting for the skin trade is the main reason for their decline.

CONSERVATION

Conservation is currently directed toward a relatively small number of high-profile species, but, as more people appreciate the need for biodiversity, the focus of attention is widening to include less conspicuous creatures. Recent conservation measures include legal protection from hunting or collection for the skin trade, and captive breeding. The Convention of International Trade in Endangered Species (CITES) has identified a large number of threatened species, and the trade in these species, or products made from them, is prohibited or strictly controlled. However, places where species diversity is greatest are often the same places where conservation measures are difficult to enforce, because of poverty, political instability, or difficulty in controlling poaching and habitat destruction.

ROUND ISLAND KEEL-SCALED BOA

This unique snake has been saved from almost certain extinction. Its small island habitat was destroyed by introduced goats, which have now been eradicated. Numbers are being built up by a captive-breeding program to prepare the species for reintroduction to its native habitat.

STUDYING AND KEEPING

ALMOST ANYONE can study reptiles and amphibians. Depending on where you live, you may have to travel some way to find them or you may be lucky enough to have a few toads or lizards in your garden. Some people are content to make casual observations while out walking; others keep reptiles and amphibians in captivity. Whatever the situation, adopt a responsible approach.

STUDYING

Compared with mammals and birds, relatively little is known about the anatomy and behavior of many reptiles and amphibians; so even amateur herpetologists using inexpensive equipment can make important observations. Records such as sightings of local species, dates of breeding activities in ponds, and numbers present will make an interesting journal, especially if pictures are included. Surveys charting population numbers over a period of time are especially valuable. Joining an amateur society or a local wildlife group puts you in touch with other enthusiasts.

△ GARDEN POND
Even a small garden pond will encourage wildlife. An amphibian pond should not contain fish, which will eat eggs and larvae.

◁ SKETCHING
Sketches of colors and markings will help you identify species later and may even enable you to keep track of individuals, because many have unique patterns.

• *sketchpad may also be useful for notes*

dial allows focus to be adjusted

△ BINOCULARS
Binoculars allow you to study the activities of reptiles and amphibians without disturbing them. Scan pond margins or openings in forests and look for tree-dwelling species where they occur.

• *distinctive shell markings aid identification*

◁ PHOTOGRAPHY
A single-lens reflex camera is best for shots of reptiles and amphibians. A close-up or macro lens and a small flashgun are also useful. You may need a telephoto lens for nervous species and a wide-angle lens for habitat shots.

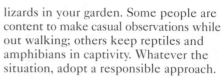

HANDLING

Only handle reptiles and amphibians when it is absolutely necessary, and only when you are sure that the species is harmless. Beware of lizards that may shed their tails, and turtles and snakes that may bite, even if they are not venomous. All species should be held firmly, and the body should be supported. A glass jar is useful for housing amphibians such as tadpoles temporarily, and a cotton bag can be used to hold snakes and lizards.

fingers out of range of jaws

△ HOLDING A TURTLE
Some turtles, even small ones, can give a nasty bite. Hold them by the back of their shell and keep your fingers well away from the head.

fingers grip snake just below head

◁ HANDLING A PET SNAKE
Hold a pet snake by gripping the front half of its body firmly – but not too tightly – and support the rest of its body in your other hand. Allow it to crawl through your hands if it wants to.

A SUITABLE HOME
Terraria (or vivaria) can be very simple or very elaborate. This one houses a colony of poison-dart frogs, whose very specific requirements include some living plants in which to hide and lay eggs.

KEEPING

Keeping reptiles and amphibians in captivity is a specialized field and you should not attempt it until you have researched the needs of the species in which you are interested. Wherever possible, buy captive-bred animals, which will adapt better to captive conditions and which will not strain natural populations. Light, temperature, and lighting are very important, and some species need a close simulation of their natural habitat if they are to remain healthy. Active species need much larger cages; some need a period of enforced hibernation in the winter. Many will thrive in captivity under the right conditions, however, and will even breed, giving further scope for the kind of observations you can make.

GUIDELINES FOR STUDY

Many reptiles and amphibians are legally protected, either locally, nationally, or internationally, because of their rarity. Others live in national parks and nature reserves, where the plants and animals are protected; the reptiles and amphibians can only be studied from a distance and so remain undisturbed. In all cases, avoid disrupting the animals and their habitats. If you are travelling in a remote place, tell someone where you are going and be particularly careful when looking for nocturnal species.

IDENTIFICATION KEY

THE KEY on pages 34 to 43 will help you identify the main families of reptiles and amphibians (most of those listed are featured in the book). First, work through the introductory key (below): this will establish whether the animal is a reptile or an amphibian, and will guide you to the relevant key. The families are identified mainly according to their physical features, but the geographical distribution of a family may be given when it will help with identification. With over 11,000 species of reptiles and amphibians in total, this key is necessarily generalized and is to be regarded as an approximate guide.

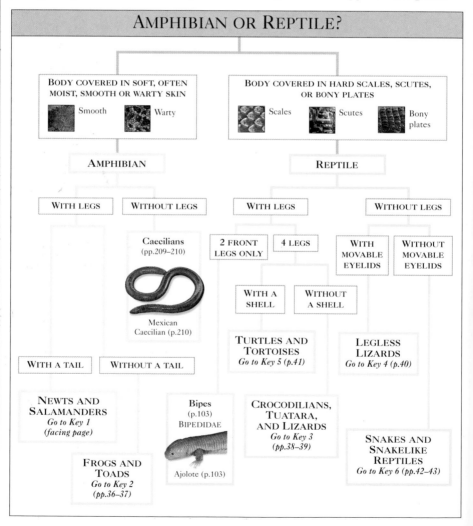

AMPHIBIAN OR REPTILE?

BODY COVERED IN SOFT, OFTEN MOIST, SMOOTH OR WARTY SKIN

Smooth   Warty

BODY COVERED IN HARD SCALES, SCUTES, OR BONY PLATES

Scales   Scutes   Bony plates

AMPHIBIAN

REPTILE

WITH LEGS   WITHOUT LEGS

WITH LEGS   WITHOUT LEGS

Caecilians
(pp.209–210)

2 FRONT LEGS ONLY   4 LEGS

WITH MOVABLE EYELIDS   WITHOUT MOVABLE EYELIDS

WITH A SHELL   WITHOUT A SHELL

Mexican Caecilian (p.210)

TURTLES AND TORTOISES
Go to Key 5 (p.41)

LEGLESS LIZARDS
Go to Key 4 (p.40)

WITH A TAIL   WITHOUT A TAIL

NEWTS AND SALAMANDERS
*Go to Key 1
(facing page)*

Bipes
(p.103)
BIPEDIDAE

CROCODILIANS, TUATARA, AND LIZARDS
*Go to Key 3
(pp.38–39)*

SNAKES AND SNAKELIKE REPTILES
Go to Key 6 (pp.42–43)

FROGS AND TOADS
*Go to Key 2
(pp.36–37)*

Ajolote (p.103)

KEY 1: NEWTS AND SALAMANDERS

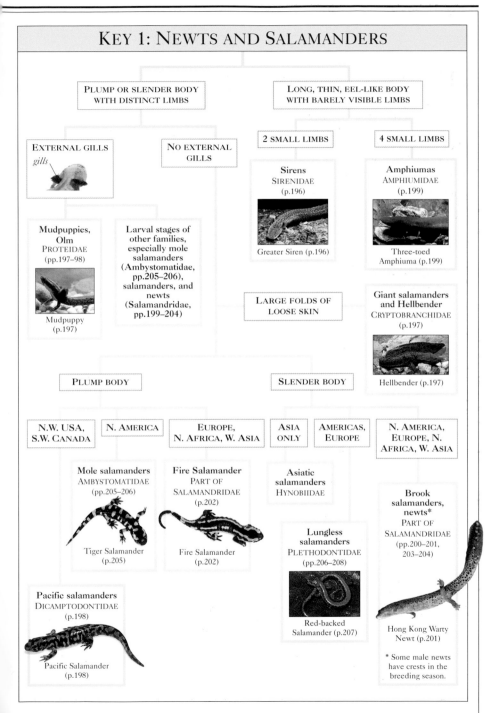

PLUMP OR SLENDER BODY WITH DISTINCT LIMBS

LONG, THIN, EEL-LIKE BODY WITH BARELY VISIBLE LIMBS

EXTERNAL GILLS

gills

NO EXTERNAL GILLS

2 SMALL LIMBS

Sirens
SIRENIDAE
(p.196)

Greater Siren (p.196)

4 SMALL LIMBS

Amphiumas
AMPHIUMIDAE
(p.199)

Three-toed Amphiuma (p.199)

Mudpuppies, Olm
PROTEIDAE
(pp.197–98)

Mudpuppy
(p.197)

Larval stages of other families, especially mole salamanders (Ambystomatidae, pp.205–206), salamanders (Salamandridae, pp.199–204)

LARGE FOLDS OF LOOSE SKIN

Giant salamanders and Hellbender
CRYPTOBRANCHIDAE
(p.197)

Hellbender (p.197)

PLUMP BODY

SLENDER BODY

| N.W. USA, S.W. CANADA | N. AMERICA | EUROPE, N. AFRICA, W. ASIA | ASIA ONLY | AMERICAS, EUROPE | N. AMERICA, EUROPE, N. AFRICA, W. ASIA |

Mole salamanders
AMBYSTOMATIDAE
(pp.205–206)

Tiger Salamander
(p.205)

Fire Salamander
PART OF
SALAMANDRIDAE
(p.202)

Fire Salamander
(p.202)

Asiatic salamanders
HYNOBIIDAE

Lungless salamanders
PLETHODONTIDAE
(pp.206–208)

Red-backed Salamander (p.207)

Brook salamanders, newts*
PART OF
SALAMANDRIDAE
(pp.200–201, 203–204)

Pacific salamanders
DICAMPTODONTIDAE
(p.198)

Pacific Salamander
(p.198)

Hong Kong Warty Newt (p.201)

* Some male newts have crests in the breeding season.

KEY 2: FROGS AND TOADS

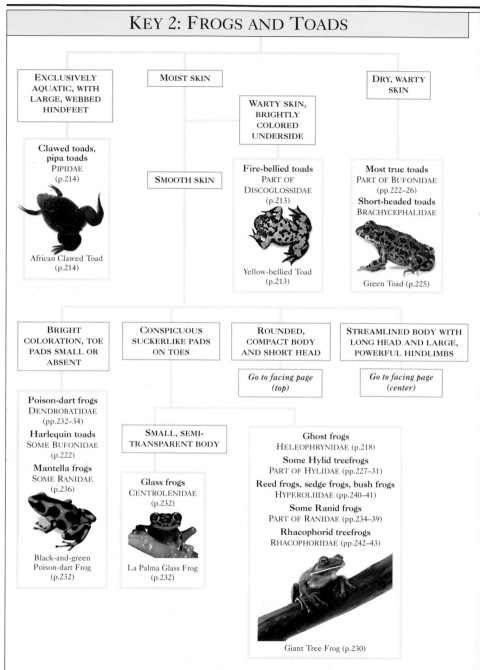

EXCLUSIVELY AQUATIC, WITH LARGE, WEBBED HINDFEET

Clawed toads, pipa toads
PIPIDAE
(p.214)

African Clawed Toad
(p.214)

MOIST SKIN

SMOOTH SKIN

WARTY SKIN, BRIGHTLY COLORED UNDERSIDE

Fire-bellied toads
PART OF DISCOGLOSSIDAE
(p.213)

Yellow-bellied Toad
(p.213)

DRY, WARTY SKIN

Most true toads
PART OF BUFONIDAE
(pp.222–26)
Short-headed toads
BRACHYCEPHALIDAE

Green Toad (p.225)

BRIGHT COLORATION, TOE PADS SMALL OR ABSENT

Poison-dart frogs
DENDROBATIDAE
(pp.232–34)

Harlequin toads
SOME BUFONIDAE
(p.222)

Mantella frogs
SOME RANIDAE
(p.236)

Black-and-green
Poison-dart Frog
(p.232)

CONSPICUOUS SUCKERLIKE PADS ON TOES

SMALL, SEMI-TRANSPARENT BODY

Glass frogs
CENTROLENIDAE
(p.232)

La Palma Glass Frog
(p.232)

ROUNDED, COMPACT BODY AND SHORT HEAD

*Go to facing page
(top)*

STREAMLINED BODY WITH LONG HEAD AND LARGE, POWERFUL HINDLIMBS

*Go to facing page
(center)*

Ghost frogs
HELEOPHRYNIDAE (p.218)
Some Hylid treefrogs
PART OF HYLIDAE (pp.227–31)
Reed frogs, sedge frogs, bush frogs
HYPEROLIIDAE (pp.240–41)
Some Ranid frogs
PART OF RANIDAE (pp.234–39)
Rhacophorid treefrogs
RHACOPHORIDAE (pp.242–43)

Giant Tree Frog (p.230)

ROUNDED, COMPACT
BODY AND SHORT HEAD
Continued from previous page

AMERICAS, ASIA, MADAGASCAR (MOSTLY SMALL WITH DULL COLORATION)	AFRICA ONLY	N. AMERICA, EUROPE, ASIA	AUSTRALASIA ONLY	N.E. MEXICO, S.E. TEXAS
Narrow-mouthed toads PART OF MICROHYLIDAE (pp.244–45)	Rain frogs PART OF MICROHYLIDAE (p.243)	Spadefoot toads PART OF PELOBATIDAE (pp.214–15)	Myobatrachid frogs MYOBATRACHIDAE (pp.216–17)	Mexican Burrowing Frog RHINOPHRYNIDAE (p.243)
Malaysian Narrow-mouthed Toad (p.245)	Bushveld Rain Frog (p.243)	Couch's Spadefoot Toad (p.215)	Sign-bearing Froglet (p.216)	Mexican Burrowing Frog (p.243)

STREAMLINED BODY WITH LONG HEAD
AND LARGE, POWERFUL HINDLIMBS
Continued from previous page

AMERICAS ONLY	Some Ranid frogs PART OF RANIDAE (pp.234–39)	Some Hylid treefrogs PART OF HYLIDAE (pp.227–31)	Paradoxical frogs PSEUDIDAE (p.226)
Leptodactylids LEPTODACTYLIDAE (pp.219–21)			
Túngara Frog (p.219)	Agile Frog (p.238)	Northern Cricket Frog (p.227)	Paradoxical Frog (p.226)

OTHER FROGS AND TOADS (DISTINGUISHING FEATURES LISTED IN THE KEY DO NOT APPLY)

Squeaker frogs and Hairy Frog (Africa only) ARTHROLEPTIDAE (p.242)	*Colostethus* species (C. and S. America) PART OF DENDROBATIDAE	New Zealand frogs (New Zealand only) LEIOPELMATIDAE	Mouth-brooding frogs (extreme South America only) RHINODERMATIDAE
Tailed Frog ASCAPHIDAE (p.211)	Midwife toads PART OF DISCOGLOSSIDAE (pp.212–13)	Parsley Frog (Europe only) PART OF PELOBATIDAE (p.216)	Seychelles frogs (Seychelles only) SOOGLOSSIDAE (p.218)

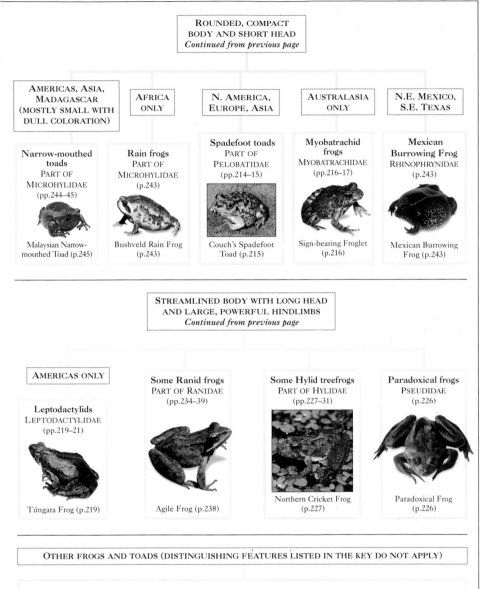

KEY 3: CROCODILIANS, TUATARA, AND LIZARDS

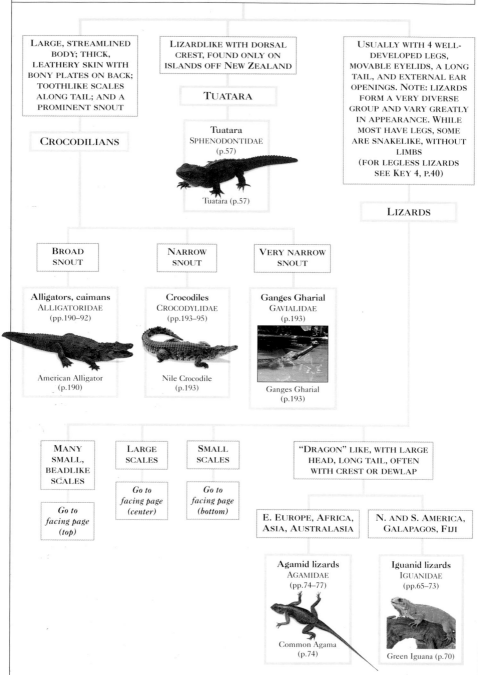

LARGE, STREAMLINED BODY; THICK, LEATHERY SKIN WITH BONY PLATES ON BACK; TOOTHLIKE SCALES ALONG TAIL; AND A PROMINENT SNOUT

CROCODILIANS

LIZARDLIKE WITH DORSAL CREST, FOUND ONLY ON ISLANDS OFF NEW ZEALAND

TUATARA

Tuatara
SPHENODONTIDAE
(p.57)

Tuatara (p.57)

USUALLY WITH 4 WELL-DEVELOPED LEGS, MOVABLE EYELIDS, A LONG TAIL, AND EXTERNAL EAR OPENINGS. NOTE: LIZARDS FORM A VERY DIVERSE GROUP AND VARY GREATLY IN APPEARANCE. WHILE MOST HAVE LEGS, SOME ARE SNAKELIKE, WITHOUT LIMBS
(FOR LEGLESS LIZARDS SEE KEY 4, P.40)

LIZARDS

BROAD SNOUT

NARROW SNOUT

VERY NARROW SNOUT

Alligators, caimans
ALLIGATORIDAE
(pp.190–92)

American Alligator
(p.190)

Crocodiles
CROCODYLIDAE
(pp.193–95)

Nile Crocodile
(p.193)

Ganges Gharial
GAVIALIDAE
(p.193)

Ganges Gharial
(p.193)

MANY SMALL, BEADLIKE SCALES

Go to facing page (top)

LARGE SCALES

Go to facing page (center)

SMALL SCALES

Go to facing page (bottom)

"DRAGON" LIKE, WITH LARGE HEAD, LONG TAIL, OFTEN WITH CREST OR DEWLAP

E. EUROPE, AFRICA, ASIA, AUSTRALASIA

N. AND S. AMERICA, GALAPAGOS, FIJI

Agamid lizards
AGAMIDAE
(pp.74–77)

Common Agama
(p.74)

Iguanid lizards
IGUANIDAE
(pp.65–73)

Green Iguana (p.70)

MANY SMALL, BEADLIKE SCALES
Continued from previous page

LONG NECK, FORKED TONGUE, POWERFUL LIMBS AND TAIL

NARROW, DEEP BODY, PREHENSILE TAIL, OFTEN HORNED OR CRESTED

BULKY ROUND BODY, SHORT LEGS, STOCKY TAIL

Monitor lizards
VARANIDAE
(pp.98–100)

Chameleons
CHAMAELEONIDAE
(pp.78–80)

Beaded Lizard, Gila Monster
HELODERMATIDAE
(pp.96–97)

Nile Monitor Lizard (p.100)

Yemeni Veiled Chameleon (p.79)

Gila Monster (p.97)

LARGE SCALES
Continued from previous page

RECTANGULAR SCALES ARRANGED IN ROWS

SMOOTH, OVERLAPPING SCALES

AFRICA ONLY

AMERICAS ONLY

AUSTRALASIA ONLY

SMALL HEAD, EYES, AND LIMBS

LARGE HEAD, EYES, AND LIMBS

Girdled lizards, plated lizards
PART OF CORDYLIDAE
(p.87)

Alligator lizards
PART OF ANGUIDAE
(p.94)
Xenosaurs
XENOSAURIDAE
(p.95)

Some skinks
PART OF SCINCIDAE
(pp.81–86)

Most skinks
PART OF SCINCIDAE
(pp.81–86)

Wonder geckos
PART OF GEKKONIDAE
(p.63)

Giant Plated Lizard (p.87)

Chinese Crocodile Lizard (p.95)

Slender Crocodile Skink (p.86)

Schneider's Gold Skink (p.83)

Wonder Gecko (p.63)

SMALL SCALES
Continued from previous page

FLATTENED BODY AND TAIL

CYLINDRICAL BODY AND TAIL

SOFT SKIN WITH RANDOM LARGE SCALES, OFTEN PADS ON TOES, USUALLY LARGE EYES

Night lizards
XANTUSIIDAE
(p.65)

N. AND S. AMERICA

EUROPE, AFRICA, ASIA

Most geckos
PART OF GEKKONIDAE
(pp.58–64)

Yellow-spotted Night Lizard (p.65)

Teiid lizards
TEIIDAE
(pp.90–93)

Sand lizards, wall lizards, and relatives
LACERTIDAE
(p.90)

Common House Gecko (p.60)

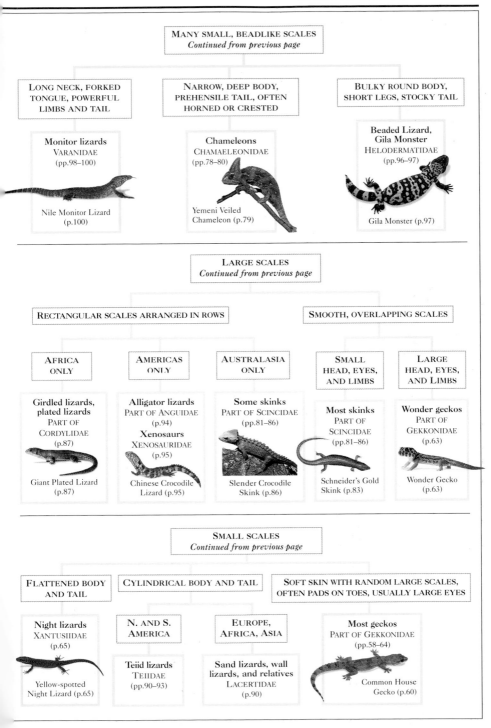

KEY 4: LEGLESS LIZARDS

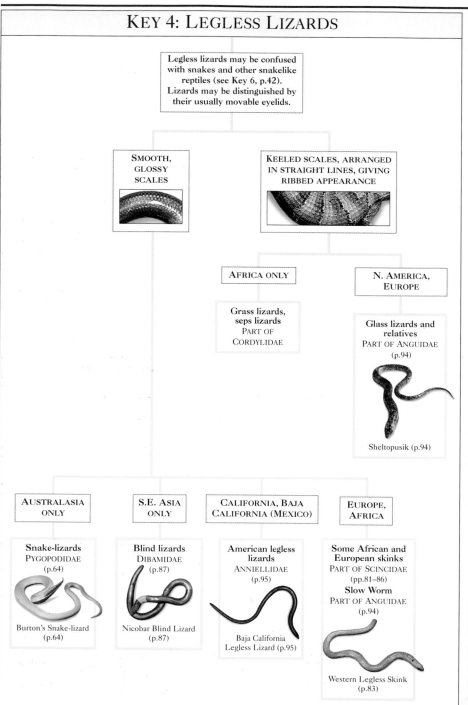

Legless lizards may be confused with snakes and other snakelike reptiles (see Key 6, p.42). Lizards may be distinguished by their usually movable eyelids.

SMOOTH, GLOSSY SCALES

KEELED SCALES, ARRANGED IN STRAIGHT LINES, GIVING RIBBED APPEARANCE

AFRICA ONLY

N. AMERICA, EUROPE

Grass lizards, seps lizards
PART OF CORDYLIDAE

Glass lizards and relatives
PART OF ANGUIDAE
(p.94)

Sheltopusik (p.94)

AUSTRALASIA ONLY

S.E. ASIA ONLY

CALIFORNIA, BAJA CALIFORNIA (MEXICO)

EUROPE, AFRICA

Snake-lizards
PYGOPODIDAE
(p.64)

Blind lizards
DIBAMIDAE
(p.87)

American legless lizards
ANNIELLIDAE
(p.95)

Some African and European skinks
PART OF SCINCIDAE
(pp.81–86)
Slow Worm
PART OF ANGUIDAE
(p.94)

Burton's Snake-lizard
(p.64)

Nicobar Blind Lizard
(p.87)

Baja California Legless Lizard (p.95)

Western Legless Skink
(p.83)

KEY 5: TURTLES AND TORTOISES

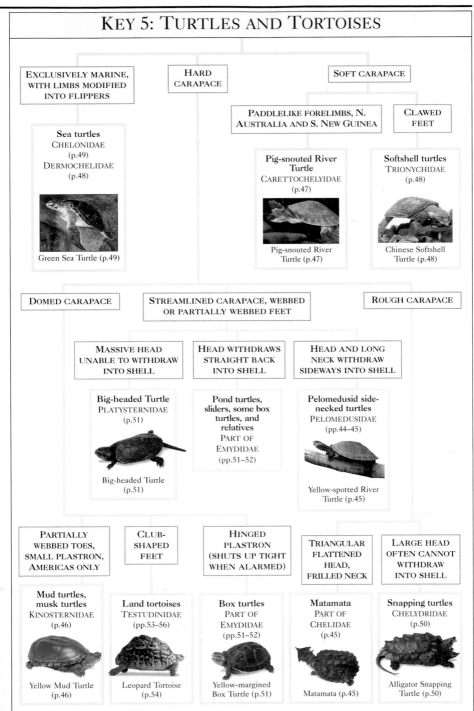

EXCLUSIVELY MARINE, WITH LIMBS MODIFIED INTO FLIPPERS

HARD CARAPACE

SOFT CARAPACE

PADDLELIKE FORELIMBS, N. AUSTRALIA AND S. NEW GUINEA

CLAWED FEET

Sea turtles
CHELONIDAE
(p.49)
DERMOCHELIDAE
(p.48)

Pig-snouted River Turtle
CARETTOCHELYIDAE
(p.47)

Softshell turtles
TRIONYCHIDAE
(p.48)

Green Sea Turtle (p.49)

Pig-snouted River Turtle (p.47)

Chinese Softshell Turtle (p.48)

DOMED CARAPACE

STREAMLINED CARAPACE, WEBBED OR PARTIALLY WEBBED FEET

ROUGH CARAPACE

MASSIVE HEAD UNABLE TO WITHDRAW INTO SHELL

HEAD WITHDRAWS STRAIGHT BACK INTO SHELL

HEAD AND LONG NECK WITHDRAW SIDEWAYS INTO SHELL

Big-headed Turtle
PLATYSTERNIDAE
(p.51)

Pond turtles, sliders, some box turtles, and relatives
PART OF
EMYDIDAE
(pp.51–52)

Pelomedusid side-necked turtles
PELOMEDUSIDAE
(pp.44–45)

Big-headed Turtle (p.51)

Yellow-spotted River Turtle (p.45)

PARTIALLY WEBBED TOES, SMALL PLASTRON, AMERICAS ONLY

CLUB-SHAPED FEET

HINGED PLASTRON (SHUTS UP TIGHT WHEN ALARMED)

TRIANGULAR FLATTENED HEAD, FRILLED NECK

LARGE HEAD OFTEN CANNOT WITHDRAW INTO SHELL

Mud turtles, musk turtles
KINOSTERNIDAE
(p.46)

Land tortoises
TESTUDINIDAE
(pp.53–56)

Box turtles
PART OF
EMYDIDAE
(pp.51–52)

Matamata
PART OF
CHELIDAE
(p.45)

Snapping turtles
CHELYDRIDAE
(p.50)

Yellow Mud Turtle (p.46)

Leopard Tortoise (p.54)

Yellow-margined Box Turtle (p.51)

Matamata (p.45)

Alligator Snapping Turtle (p.50)

KEY 6: SNAKES AND SNAKELIKE REPTILES

Snakes may be confused with legless
lizards (see Key 4, p.40). Lizards are
identified by their usually movable eyelids.

WORMLIKE, WITH SCALES
ARRANGED IN CLEAR RINGS
AROUND BODY, EYES NOT VISIBLE

LONG, SLENDER BODY
COVERED IN OVERLAPPING
OR GRANULAR SCALES

AMPHISBAENIANS

SNAKES

Amphisbaenians
AMPHISBAENIDAE
(pp.101–103)

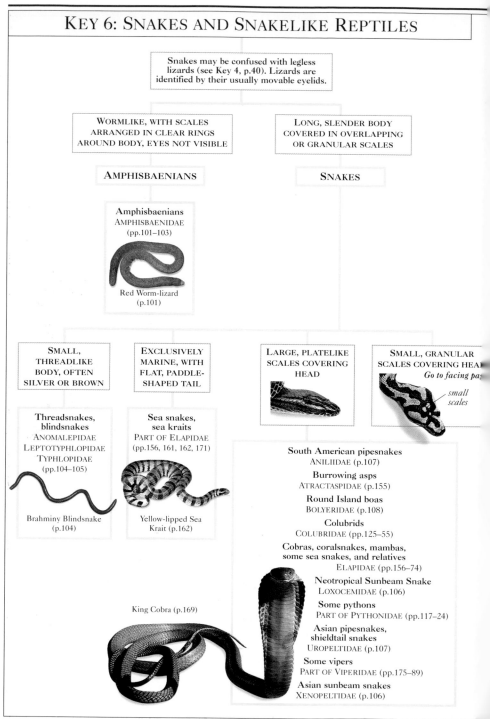

Red Worm-lizard
(p.101)

SMALL,
THREADLIKE
BODY, OFTEN
SILVER OR BROWN

EXCLUSIVELY
MARINE, WITH
FLAT, PADDLE-
SHAPED TAIL

LARGE, PLATELIKE
SCALES COVERING
HEAD

SMALL, GRANULAR
SCALES COVERING HEAD
Go to facing page

*small
scales*

Threadsnakes,
blindsnakes
ANOMALEPIDAE
LEPTOTYPHLOPIDAE
TYPHLOPIDAE
(pp.104–105)

Sea snakes,
sea kraits
PART OF ELAPIDAE
(pp.156, 161, 162, 171)

South American pipesnakes
ANILIIDAE (p.107)

Burrowing asps
ATRACTASPIDAE (p.155)

Round Island boas
BOLYERIDAE (p.108)

Colubrids
COLUBRIDAE (pp.125–55)

Cobras, coralsnakes, mambas,
some sea snakes, and relatives
ELAPIDAE (pp.156–74)

Neotropical Sunbeam Snake
LOXOCEMIDAE (p.106)

Some pythons
PART OF PYTHONIDAE (pp.117–24)

Asian pipesnakes,
shieldtail snakes
UROPELTIDAE (p.107)

Some vipers
PART OF VIPERIDAE (pp.175–89)

Asian sunbeam snakes
XENOPELTIDAE (p.106)

Brahminy Blindsnake
(p.104)

Yellow-lipped Sea
Krait (p.162)

King Cobra (p.169)

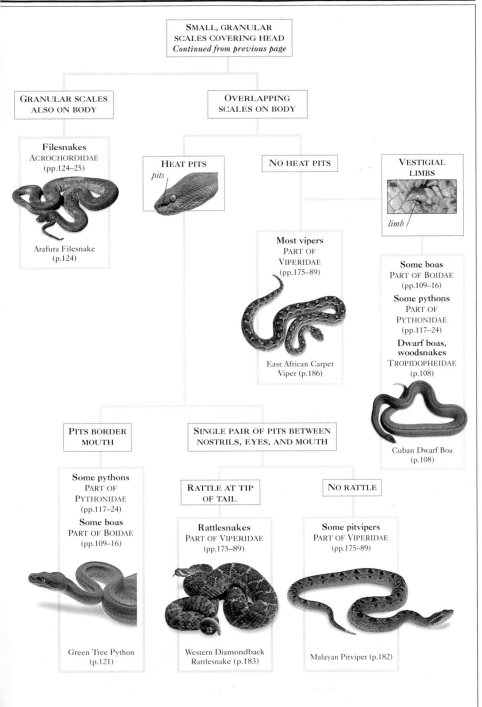

SMALL, GRANULAR SCALES COVERING HEAD
Continued from previous page

GRANULAR SCALES ALSO ON BODY

OVERLAPPING SCALES ON BODY

Filesnakes
ACROCHORDIDAE
(pp.124–25)

HEAT PITS
pits

NO HEAT PITS

VESTIGIAL LIMBS
limb

Arafura Filesnake
(p.124)

Most vipers
PART OF
VIPERIDAE
(pp.175–89)

Some boas
PART OF BOIDAE
(pp.109–16)
Some pythons
PART OF
PYTHONIDAE
(pp.117–24)
Dwarf boas, woodsnakes
TROPIDOPHEIDAE
(p.108)

East African Carpet
Viper (p.186)

Cuban Dwarf Boa
(p.108)

PITS BORDER MOUTH

SINGLE PAIR OF PITS BETWEEN NOSTRILS, EYES, AND MOUTH

Some pythons
PART OF
PYTHONIDAE
(pp.117–24)
Some boas
PART OF BOIDAE
(pp.109–16)

RATTLE AT TIP OF TAIL

NO RATTLE

Rattlesnakes
PART OF VIPERIDAE
(pp.175–89)

Some pitvipers
PART OF VIPERIDAE
(pp.175–89)

Green Tree Python
(p.121)

Western Diamondback
Rattlesnake (p.183)

Malayan Pitviper (p.182)

REPTILES

TURTLES AND TORTOISES

T HERE ARE MORE than 270 living species of turtles and tortoises, which are found in terrestrial, freshwater, and marine habitats, and in both temperate and tropical regions. The term "turtle" usually refers to a freshwater or marine species, while "tortoise" is normally reserved for a terrestrial species. "Terrapin" is a colloquial name for a freshwater turtle.

Turtles and tortoises belong to the order Testudines (or Chelonia), which is divided into two suborders. The primitive sideneck turtles (suborder Pleurodira) cannot fully retract their long necks, so when at rest they must lay their heads sideways along the inside of their shells. There are approximately 70 species of sideneck turtle, all living in freshwater. The more advanced straight-neck turtles (suborder Cryptodira) are a much larger group that live on land and in fresh- and seawater. They are able to withdraw their heads completely into their shells – the neck bending vertically in an S-shaped curve.

Tortoises and turtles range greatly in size, from the tiny Speckled Padloper (*Homopus signatus*), 2½–3¾in (6–9.5cm) long, to the massive Leatherback Sea Turtle (*Dermochelys coriacea*, p.48), which can reach up to 6ft (1.8m) in length.

Family PELOMEDUSIDAE	Species *Pelomedusa subrufa*	Status Common

AFRICAN HELMETED TURTLE

Also known as the Marsh Terrapin, this sideneck turtle is fairly uniformly patterned olive-green or brown above, sometimes with black suturing on the scutes. It also has two small tubercles under its chin and musk glands in the sides of the carapace. Unlike African black turtles (*Pelusios* species), which are its closest relatives, the African Helmeted Turtle cannot close the front of its plastron to protect its head since it lacks the necessary hinge. A voracious feeder, it will eat almost anything – from vegetation to frogs – and fine claws on its toes help it rip prey apart. It has been seen capturing and drowning doves when they come to drink, in the same way that crocodiles take wildebeest. Often living in temporary watercourses, this turtle spends the dry season burrowed in mud.
• **OCCURRENCE** Africa, Madagascar, and Yemen. In rivers, lakes, and pools.
• **REPRODUCTION** Lays 10–40 eggs.
• **SIMILAR SPECIES** African black turtles (*Pelusios* species).

AFRICA, MIDDLE EAST

low, olive-green or brown carapace

broad, powerful head and jaws

webbed feet for rapid swimming

Length 12–13in (30–32cm)	Diet	Activity

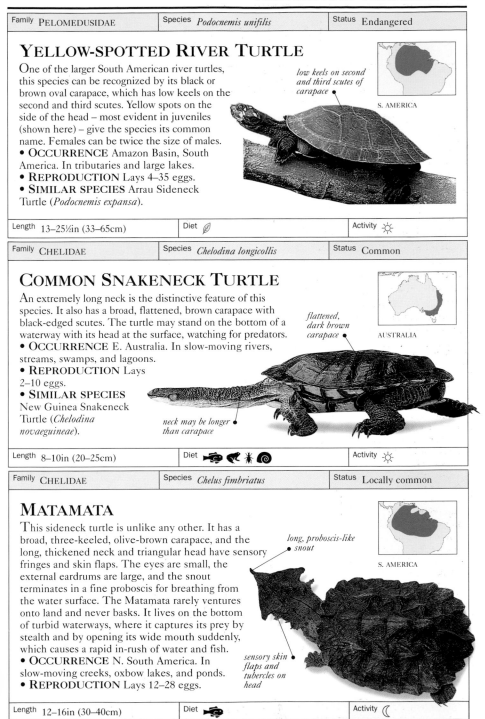

Family PELOMEDUSIDAE	Species *Podocnemis unifilis*	Status Endangered

YELLOW-SPOTTED RIVER TURTLE

One of the larger South American river turtles, this species can be recognized by its black or brown oval carapace, which has low keels on the second and third scutes. Yellow spots on the side of the head – most evident in juveniles (shown here) – give the species its common name. Females can be twice the size of males.
• **OCCURRENCE** Amazon Basin, South America. In tributaries and large lakes.
• **REPRODUCTION** Lays 4–35 eggs.
• **SIMILAR SPECIES** Arrau Sideneck Turtle (*Podocnemis expansa*).

low keels on second and third scutes of carapace •

S. AMERICA

Length 13–25½in (33–65cm)	Diet	Activity ☼

Family CHELIDAE	Species *Chelodina longicollis*	Status Common

COMMON SNAKENECK TURTLE

An extremely long neck is the distinctive feature of this species. It also has a broad, flattened, brown carapace with black-edged scutes. The turtle may stand on the bottom of a waterway with its head at the surface, watching for predators.
• **OCCURRENCE** E. Australia. In slow-moving rivers, streams, swamps, and lagoons.
• **REPRODUCTION** Lays 2–10 eggs.
• **SIMILAR SPECIES** New Guinea Snakeneck Turtle (*Chelodina novaeguineae*).

flattened, dark brown carapace •

AUSTRALIA

neck may be longer than carapace •

Length 8–10in (20–25cm)	Diet	Activity ☼

Family CHELIDAE	Species *Chelus fimbriatus*	Status Locally common

MATAMATA

This sideneck turtle is unlike any other. It has a broad, three-keeled, olive-brown carapace, and the long, thickened neck and triangular head have sensory fringes and skin flaps. The eyes are small, the external eardrums are large, and the snout terminates in a fine proboscis for breathing from the water surface. The Matamata rarely ventures onto land and never basks. It lives on the bottom of turbid waterways, where it captures its prey by stealth and by opening its wide mouth suddenly, which causes a rapid in-rush of water and fish.
• **OCCURRENCE** N. South America. In slow-moving creeks, oxbow lakes, and ponds.
• **REPRODUCTION** Lays 12–28 eggs.

long, proboscis-like snout •

S. AMERICA

sensory skin flaps and tubercles on head •

Length 12–16in (30–40cm)	Diet	Activity ☾

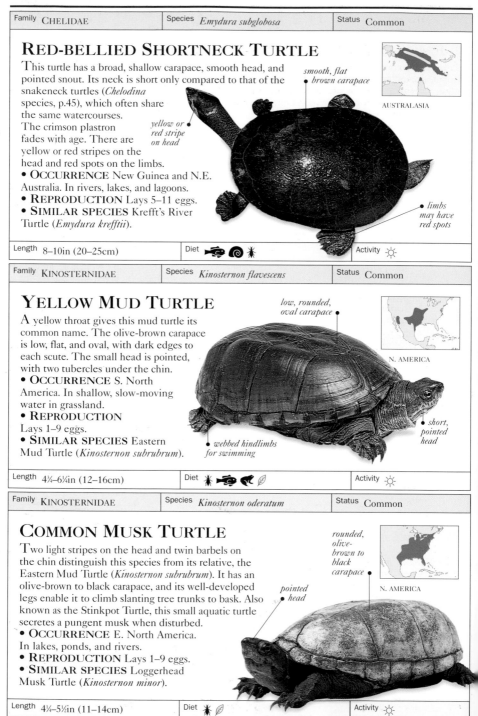

Family CHELIDAE	Species *Emydura subglobosa*	Status Common

RED-BELLIED SHORTNECK TURTLE

This turtle has a broad, shallow carapace, smooth head, and pointed snout. Its neck is short only compared to that of the snakeneck turtles (*Chelodina* species, p.45), which often share the same watercourses.
The crimson plastron fades with age. There are yellow or red stripes on the head and red spots on the limbs.
• OCCURRENCE New Guinea and N.E. Australia. In rivers, lakes, and lagoons.
• REPRODUCTION Lays 5–11 eggs.
• SIMILAR SPECIES Krefft's River Turtle (*Emydura krefftii*).

smooth, flat
• brown carapace

AUSTRALASIA

yellow or •
red stripe
on head

• limbs
may have
red spots

Length 8–10in (20–25cm)	Diet 🐟 🔵 🐜	Activity ☼

Family KINOSTERNIDAE	Species *Kinosternon flavescens*	Status Common

YELLOW MUD TURTLE

A yellow throat gives this mud turtle its common name. The olive-brown carapace is low, flat, and oval, with dark edges to each scute. The small head is pointed, with two tubercles under the chin.
• OCCURRENCE S. North America. In shallow, slow-moving water in grassland.
• REPRODUCTION Lays 1–9 eggs.
• SIMILAR SPECIES Eastern Mud Turtle (*Kinosternon subrubrum*).

low, rounded,
oval carapace •

N. AMERICA

• short,
pointed
head

• webbed hindlimbs
for swimming

Length 4¼–6¼in (12–16cm)	Diet 🐜 🐟 🐸 ✎	Activity ☼

Family KINOSTERNIDAE	Species *Kinosternon oderatum*	Status Common

COMMON MUSK TURTLE

Two light stripes on the head and twin barbels on the chin distinguish this species from its relative, the Eastern Mud Turtle (*Kinosternon subrubrum*). It has an olive-brown to black carapace, and its well-developed legs enable it to climb slanting tree trunks to bask. Also known as the Stinkpot Turtle, this small aquatic turtle secretes a pungent musk when disturbed.
• OCCURRENCE E. North America. In lakes, ponds, and rivers.
• REPRODUCTION Lays 1–9 eggs.
• SIMILAR SPECIES Loggerhead Musk Turtle (*Kinosternon minor*).

rounded,
olive-
brown to
black
carapace •

N. AMERICA

pointed
• head

Length 4¼–5½in (11–14cm)	Diet 🐜 ✎	Activity ☼

Family DERMATEMYDIDAE	Species *Dermatemys mawii*	Status Endangered

CENTRAL AMERICAN RIVER TURTLE

A large, drab brown or gray species, this river turtle has a broad, streamlined carapace, which may resemble leather in adult specimens, and a relatively small head with a short, forward-projecting, tubular snout. Although it is a freshwater turtle, it does occasionally enter brackish waters; it rarely ventures onto land.
• **OCCURRENCE** S.E. Mexico, Guatemala, and Belize. In large rivers and lakes.
• **REPRODUCTION** Lays 10–20 eggs.
• **REMARK** This is the sole living species in a family that dates back to the Cretaceous Period (which ended 65 million years ago).

C. AMERICA

dull brown or gray carapace looks like leather in adults

broad, flat carapace

slightly upturned, tubular snout tip

strongly webbed feet for swimming

Length 20–25½in (50–65cm)	Diet 🍃	Activity ☾

Family CARETTOCHELYIDAE	Species *Carettochelys insculpta*	Status Rare

PIG-SNOUTED RIVER TURTLE

This river turtle has a pitted, leathery, gray-green carapace and a reduced white plastron. Its limbs are clawed and flipperlike, resembling those of sea turtles. The carapaces of juveniles have serrated edges and a central keel. The short head ends in a broad, tubular, fleshy, piglike snout and the eyes are large. Secretive by nature, Pig-snouted River Turtles prefer shallow, slow-moving rivers with sandy or silty bottoms, into which they burrow by scooping sand over the carapace using their forelimbs. They may also enter estuarine habitats.
• **OCCURRENCE** S. New Guinea and N. Australia. In large rivers and lagoons.
• **REPRODUCTION** Lays 15–22 eggs.
• **REMARK** The Pig-snouted River Turtle has been known in New Guinea since the 1800s but the Australian populations of the species were not discovered until 1969.

AUSTRALASIA

leathery, gray-green carapace and white plastron

clawed, flipperlike limbs for swimming

Length 28–30in (70–75cm)	Diet 🍃🐟🐌	Activity ☾

Family TRIONYCHIDAE	Species *Pelodiscus sinensis*	Status Locally common

CHINESE SOFTSHELL TURTLE

As with all softshell turtles, the carapace and plastron of this species
are covered by leathery skin rather than hard scutes, although the
skeleton beneath still gives the turtle some protection. The rear of
the carapace ends in a soft, rounded skirt, and the plastron is much
reduced in size. The neck and head are long, and the long, slender
snout allows the turtle to breathe while standing on
the bottom of shallow lakes or rivers.

ASIA

• OCCURRENCE E. Asia. (Introduced
to Hawaii.) In lakes and rivers.
• REPRODUCTION Lays
12–30 eggs.
• SIMILAR SPECIES
Wattle-necked Softshell
Turtle (*Palea
steindachneri*).

*long,
proboscis-
like snout*

*grayish green
carapace with
raised ridges*

*strongly webbed
feet*

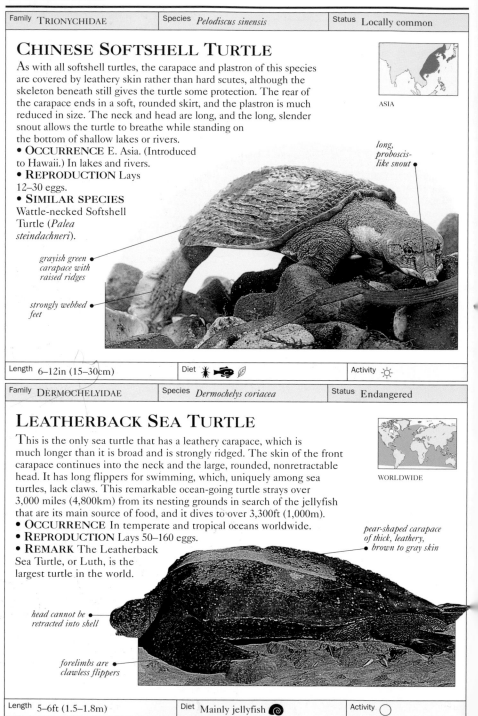

Length 6–12in (15–30cm)	Diet 🐜🐟🌿	Activity ☼

Family DERMOCHELYIDAE	Species *Dermochelys coriacea*	Status Endangered

LEATHERBACK SEA TURTLE

This is the only sea turtle that has a leathery carapace, which is
much longer than it is broad and is strongly ridged. The skin of the front
carapace continues into the neck and the large, rounded, nonretractable
head. It has long flippers for swimming, which, uniquely among sea
turtles, lack claws. This remarkable ocean-going turtle strays over
3,000 miles (4,800km) from its nesting grounds in search of the jellyfish
that are its main source of food, and it dives to over 3,300ft (1,000m).

WORLDWIDE

• OCCURRENCE In temperate and tropical oceans worldwide.
• REPRODUCTION Lays 50–160 eggs.
• REMARK The Leatherback
Sea Turtle, or Luth, is the
largest turtle in the world.

*pear-shaped carapace
of thick, leathery,
brown to gray skin*

*head cannot be
retracted into shell*

*forelimbs are
clawless flippers*

Length 5–6ft (1.5–1.8m)	Diet Mainly jellyfish 🌀	Activity ○

Family CHELONIIDAE	Species *Chelonia mydas*	Status Endangered

GREEN SEA TURTLE

This is the most familiar of the marine turtles, recognized by its mottled green or brown, shield-shaped carapace and the large, light-edged, dark scutes of the head and limbs. An ocean-going migrant, its foraging and nesting areas may be over 625 miles (1,000km) apart. It is the only marine turtle that leaves the water to bask in order to raise its body temperature. Gentle sweeps of the foreflippers make swimming effortless: this turtle can swim six times as fast as freshwater turtles. Adults are vegetarian, but juveniles also feed on marine invertebrates.
• **OCCURRENCE** In temperate and tropical oceans worldwide.
• **REPRODUCTION** Lays 100–200 eggs.
• **SIMILAR SPECIES** Loggerhead Sea Turtle (*Caretta caretta*).

smooth, shield-shaped carapace

WORLDWIDE

streamlined head

powerful flippers for high-speed swimming

Length 2½–3ft (0.8–1m)	Diet	Activity

Family CHELONIIDAE	Species *Eretmochelys imbricata*	Status Endangered

HAWKSBILL SEA TURTLE

A relatively small sea turtle, this species is easily identified by its long, narrow snout, which resembles the bill of a bird of prey. The brown, shield-shaped carapace is serrated at the back. This is the least migratory of the sea turtles, traveling only a few hundred miles in a season. On land it moves its front-left and rear-right flippers together, then its front-right and rear-left ones; other sea turtles move both front flippers together, in a more laborious dragging motion. The Hawksbill Sea Turtle is greatly affected by reef destruction and coastal pollution, both of which kill sponges, which form a major part of this turtle's diet.
• **OCCURRENCE** In tropical oceans and, occasionally, in temperate waters worldwide.
• **REPRODUCTION** Lays 32–200 eggs.
• **SIMILAR SPECIES** Loggerhead Sea Turtle (*Caretta caretta*).

flippers with tiny claws on leading edges

WORLDWIDE

snout projects into birdlike, down-turned bill

serrated edge to carapace

Length 2½–3ft (0.8–1m)	Diet Mainly sponges	Activity

| Family CHELYDRIDAE | Species *Chelydra serpentina* | Status Common |

COMMON SNAPPING TURTLE

Dull olive-green to brown in color, this stoutly built turtle has a domed, slightly serrated carapace, a powerful head and limbs, a long tail, and a reduced plastron. An adult snapping turtle is a top aquatic carnivore, preying on almost any organism small enough to swallow. The alligator is its only predator, although its nests are vulnerable to attacks from raccoons and other animals.
• **OCCURRENCE** E. and C. North America, Central America, and N.W. South America. In almost any freshwater habitat and some brackish ones.
• **REPRODUCTION** Lays 20–40 eggs.
• **SIMILAR SPECIES** Alligator Snapping Turtle (*Macroclemys temminckii*, below).
• **REMARK** Its bite can cause serious injury to fingers and toes.

N., C., & S. AMERICA

high, keeled carapace with • serrated edge

massive head with sharp jaws •

• stout, muscular tail

| Length 8–16in (20–40cm) | Diet | Activity |

| Family CHELYDRIDAE | Species *Macroclemys temminckii* | Status Endangered |

ALLIGATOR SNAPPING TURTLE

The largest freshwater turtle in the Americas, this species has a serrated and keeled carapace, and a much-reduced plastron to allow for the massive, clawed limbs. The head is large, with powerful jaws that terminate in a downturned hook. A pink, wormlike projection on its tongue is used to lure fish, which are captured as the jaws snap shut. A fully aquatic species, this turtle can remain underwater for 40–50 minutes before it has to breathe at the surface. Males grow much larger than females.
• **OCCURRENCE** S.E. US. In rivers, oxbow lakes, and bayous.
• **REPRODUCTION** Lays 10–60 eggs.
• **SIMILAR SPECIES** Common Snapping Turtle (*Chelydra serpentina*, above).
• **REMARK** The bite of even a medium-sized specimen can sever a human finger.

N. AMERICA

massive head with downturned bill •

• olive-brown carapace may be covered in algae

pink, wormlike • projection on tongue

| Length 16–31in (40–80cm) | Diet | Activity |

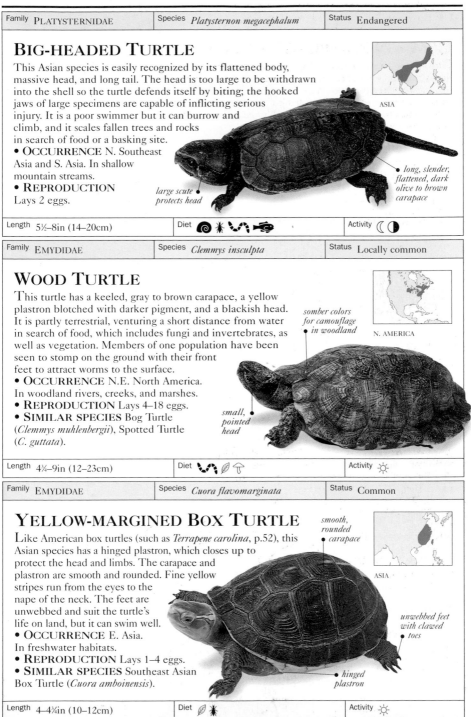

Family PLATYSTERNIDAE	Species *Platysternon megacephalum*	Status Endangered

BIG-HEADED TURTLE

This Asian species is easily recognized by its flattened body, massive head, and long tail. The head is too large to be withdrawn into the shell so the turtle defends itself by biting; the hooked jaws of large specimens are capable of inflicting serious injury. It is a poor swimmer but it can burrow and climb, and it scales fallen trees and rocks in search of food or a basking site.
• OCCURRENCE N. Southeast Asia and S. Asia. In shallow mountain streams.
• REPRODUCTION Lays 2 eggs.

ASIA

large scute
protects head

long, slender,
flattened, dark
olive to brown
carapace

Length 5½–8in (14–20cm)	Diet	Activity

Family EMYDIDAE	Species *Clemmys insculpta*	Status Locally common

WOOD TURTLE

This turtle has a keeled, gray to brown carapace, a yellow plastron blotched with darker pigment, and a blackish head. It is partly terrestrial, venturing a short distance from water in search of food, which includes fungi and invertebrates, as well as vegetation. Members of one population have been seen to stomp on the ground with their front feet to attract worms to the surface.
• OCCURRENCE N.E. North America. In woodland rivers, creeks, and marshes.
• REPRODUCTION Lays 4–18 eggs.
• SIMILAR SPECIES Bog Turtle (*Clemmys muhlenbergii*), Spotted Turtle (*C. guttata*).

somber colors
for camouflage
in woodland

N. AMERICA

small,
pointed
head

Length 4¾–9in (12–23cm)	Diet	Activity

Family EMYDIDAE	Species *Cuora flavomarginata*	Status Common

YELLOW-MARGINED BOX TURTLE

Like American box turtles (such as *Terrapene carolina*, p.52), this Asian species has a hinged plastron, which closes up to protect the head and limbs. The carapace and plastron are smooth and rounded. Fine yellow stripes run from the eyes to the nape of the neck. The feet are unwebbed and suit the turtle's life on land, but it can swim well.
• OCCURRENCE E. Asia. In freshwater habitats.
• REPRODUCTION Lays 1–4 eggs.
• SIMILAR SPECIES Southeast Asian Box Turtle (*Cuora amboinensis*).

smooth,
rounded
carapace

ASIA

unwebbed feet
with clawed
toes

hinged
plastron

Length 4–4¾in (10–12cm)	Diet	Activity

| Family EMYDIDAE | Species *Cyclemys dentata* | Status Rare |

ASIAN LEAF TURTLE

This turtle has a low, brown-and-black carapace, which is serrated at the back, and an oval brown plastron with fine black lines. Juveniles are aquatic, but adults are more terrestrial, blending into the leaf-litter on the forest floor.
• OCCURRENCE S.E. Asia. In forested freshwater habitats.
• REPRODUCTION Lays 2–4 eggs.
• SIMILAR SPECIES Stripe-necked Leaf Turtle (*Cyclemys tcheponensis*).

ASIA

black-and-white, speckled skin

small, pointed head

| Length 9½–10in (24–26cm) | Diet | Activity ☀ |

| Family EMYDIDAE | Species *Emys orbicularis* | Status Locally common |

EUROPEAN POND TURTLE

This species has a smooth, oval carapace, which is black or dark brown with yellow streaks. The head is dark with yellow spots and streaks. This turtle may be seen basking on logs or rocks but rapidly dives into the water if disturbed.
• OCCURRENCE Europe, N.W. Africa, and N.W. Asia. In still or slow-moving freshwater.
• REPRODUCTION Lays 10–16 eggs.
• SIMILAR SPECIES Mediterranean Terrapin (*Mauremys leprosa*).

smooth, domed carapace with speckled markings

EUROPE, AFRICA, ASIA

hinged plastron allows front to close slightly

| Length 8–12in (20–30cm) | Diet | Activity ☀ |

| Family EMYDIDAE | Species *Terrapene carolina* | Status Common |

COMMON BOX TURTLE

A hinged plastron allows this terrestrial turtle to make its shell into a "box," completely enclosing the soft body. The Gulf Coast Box Turtle (*Terrapene carolina major*, shown here) is one of six subspecies, and it has a uniformly brown carapace that flares outward at the back.
• OCCURRENCE E. North America and E. Mexico. In woodland, pasture, and marshland.
• REPRODUCTION Lays 1–11 eggs.
• SIMILAR SPECIES Ornate Box Turtle (*T. ornata*).

smooth carapace with central keel

N. AMERICA

head can be fully retracted inside shell

| Length 6¼–8¼in (16–21cm) | Diet | Activity ☀ |

Family EMYDIDAE	Species *Trachemys scripta*	Status Common

COMMON SLIDER

The skin of this turtle is green with yellow stripes in patterns
that vary among the 16 subspecies. The Red-eared
Slider (*Trachemys scripta elegans*, shown here)
also has a vivid red neck stripe.
• **OCCURRENCE** North,
Central, and South America.
(Introduced worldwide.)
In freshwater.
• **REPRODUCTION**
Lays 6–11 eggs.
• **SIMILAR SPECIES** River
cooters (*Pseudemys* species).

oval carapace usually green with lighter stripes

N., C., & S. AMERICA

red stripe

webbed hindfeet

Length 8–11in (20–28cm)	Diet	Activity

Family TESTUDINIDAE	Species *Geochelone carbonaria*	Status Common

RED-FOOT TORTOISE

Large red scales on the front of the forelimbs identify
this tortoise. Its long carapace is black-brown with a small
yellow center to each scute. Although still common, this
species has been over-collected for food. It is also often
caught in flash fires, lit to clear bush for cultivation.
• **OCCURRENCE** N. South America.
In savanna and savanna
woodland.
• **REPRODUCTION**
Lays 4–15 eggs.
• **SIMILAR SPECIES**
Yellow-foot Tortoise
(*Geochelone denticulata*).

black-brown carapace with yellow markings

S. AMERICA

red scales on front limbs

Length 16–20in (40–50cm)	Diet	Activity

Family TESTUDINIDAE	Species *Geochelone elegans*	Status Endangered

INDIAN STAR TORTOISE

A starlike pattern on each scute of the carapace
gives this species its common name. In adults,
each scute forms a high dome, independent of
its neighbor. The clublike feet are typical
of a tortoise that spends much of its time
walking and digging.
• **OCCURRENCE** S. Asia.
In desert and arid habitats.
• **REPRODUCTION** Lays
2–20 eggs.
• **SIMILAR SPECIES**
Burmese Star Tortoise
(*Geochelone platynota*).

scutes form high domes

ASIA

brown or black markings on yellow background

Length 12–15in (30–38cm)	Diet	Activity

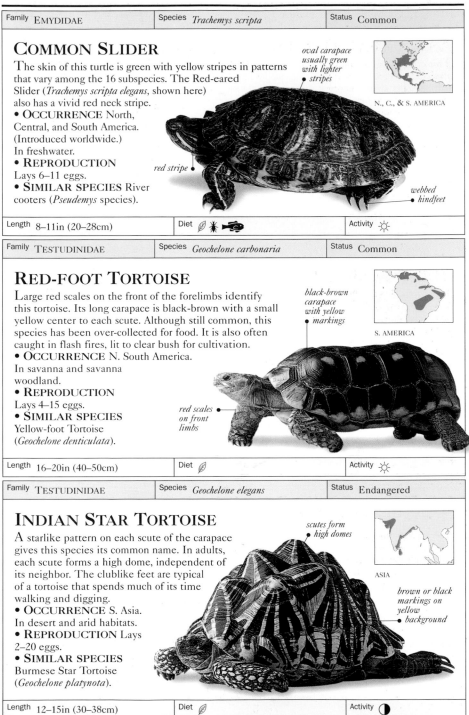

| Family TESTUDINIDAE | Species *Geochelone nigra* | Status Endangered |

GALAPAGOS TORTOISE

Formerly known as *Geochelone elephantopus*, this enormous gray tortoise has a huge carapace, massive limbs, and a small head on a very long neck. It is adapted for life on the Galapagos archipelago. Individuals on islands with ample rainfall, where the vegetation is lush, have a saddleback carapace that rises up at the front to allow the tortoise to feed on tall plants. On islands that have less rain and lower-growing plants, the carapace is classically dome-shaped.

• **OCCURRENCE** Galapagos Islands, Pacific Ocean. In rocky, volcanic terrain.
• **REPRODUCTION** Lays 10 eggs.
• **SIMILAR SPECIES** Aldabra Giant Tortoise (*G. gigantea*).
• **REMARK** The largest living "Galap" is a male in a Florida sanctuary, weighing over 880lb (400kg).

absence of small scute at center front of carapace distinguishes species from Aldabra Giant Tortoise

GALAPAGOS ISLANDS

unpatterned carapace when mature

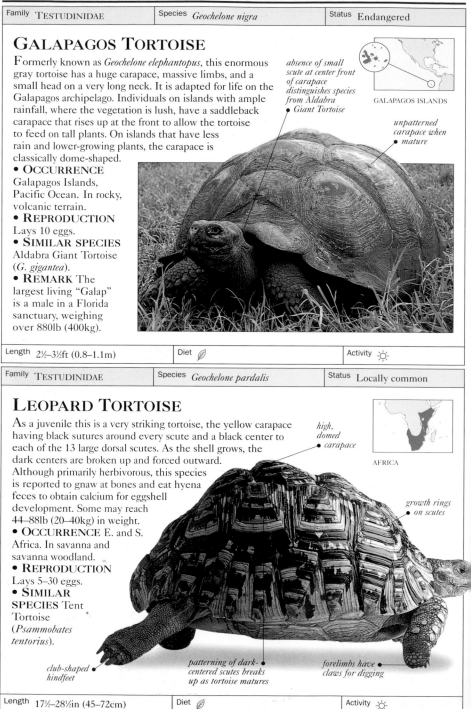

| Length 2½–3½ft (0.8–1.1m) | Diet | Activity ☼ |

| Family TESTUDINIDAE | Species *Geochelone pardalis* | Status Locally common |

LEOPARD TORTOISE

As a juvenile this is a very striking tortoise, the yellow carapace having black sutures around every scute and a black center to each of the 13 large dorsal scutes. As the shell grows, the dark centers are broken up and forced outward. Although primarily herbivorous, this species is reported to gnaw at bones and eat hyena feces to obtain calcium for eggshell development. Some may reach 44–88lb (20–40kg) in weight.

• **OCCURRENCE** E. and S. Africa. In savanna and savanna woodland.
• **REPRODUCTION** Lays 5–30 eggs.
• **SIMILAR SPECIES** Tent Tortoise (*Psammobates tentorius*).

high, domed carapace

AFRICA

growth rings on scutes

club-shaped hindfeet

patterning of dark-centered scutes breaks up as tortoise matures

forelimbs have claws for digging

| Length 17½–28½in (45–72cm) | Diet | Activity ☼ |

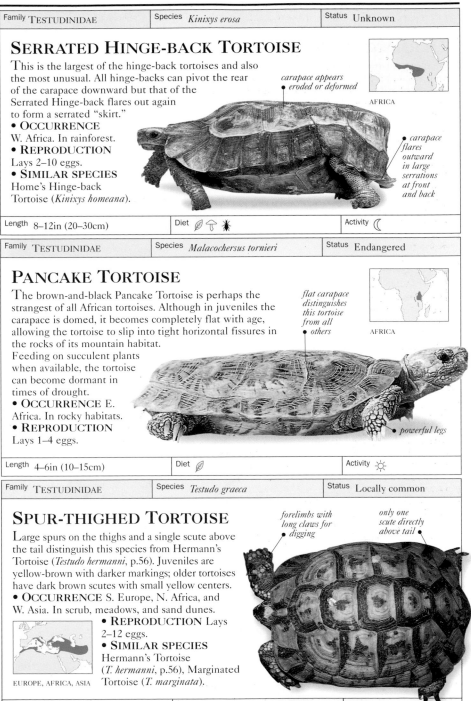

| Family TESTUDINIDAE | Species *Kinixys erosa* | Status Unknown |

SERRATED HINGE-BACK TORTOISE

This is the largest of the hinge-back tortoises and also the most unusual. All hinge-backs can pivot the rear of the carapace downward but that of the Serrated Hinge-back flares out again to form a serrated "skirt."
• OCCURRENCE
W. Africa. In rainforest.
• REPRODUCTION
Lays 2–10 eggs.
• SIMILAR SPECIES
Home's Hinge-back
Tortoise (*Kinixys homeana*).

carapace appears eroded or deformed

AFRICA

carapace flares outward in large serrations at front and back

| Length 8–12in (20–30cm) | Diet | Activity ☾ |

| Family TESTUDINIDAE | Species *Malacochersus tornieri* | Status Endangered |

PANCAKE TORTOISE

The brown-and-black Pancake Tortoise is perhaps the strangest of all African tortoises. Although in juveniles the carapace is domed, it becomes completely flat with age, allowing the tortoise to slip into tight horizontal fissures in the rocks of its mountain habitat.
Feeding on succulent plants when available, the tortoise can become dormant in times of drought.
• OCCURRENCE E. Africa. In rocky habitats.
• REPRODUCTION
Lays 1–4 eggs.

flat carapace distinguishes this tortoise from all others

AFRICA

powerful legs

| Length 4–6in (10–15cm) | Diet | Activity ☼ |

| Family TESTUDINIDAE | Species *Testudo graeca* | Status Locally common |

SPUR-THIGHED TORTOISE

Large spurs on the thighs and a single scute above the tail distinguish this species from Hermann's Tortoise (*Testudo hermanni*, p.56). Juveniles are yellow-brown with darker markings; older tortoises have dark brown scutes with small yellow centers.
• OCCURRENCE S. Europe, N. Africa, and W. Asia. In scrub, meadows, and sand dunes.
• REPRODUCTION Lays 2–12 eggs.
• SIMILAR SPECIES
Hermann's Tortoise (*T. hermanni*, p.56), Marginated Tortoise (*T. marginata*).

forelimbs with long claws for digging

only one scute directly above tail

EUROPE, AFRICA, ASIA

| Length 8–10in (20–25cm) | Diet | Activity ☼ |

Family TESTUDINIDAE	Species *Testudo hermanni*	Status Rare

HERMANN'S TORTOISE

Hermann's Tortoise has a yellowish brown to dark brown carapace, the
light markings becoming increasingly overlaid by dark pigment as the
tortoise ages. It looks similar to the Spur-thighed Tortoise (*Testudo graeca*,
p.55), the species with which it is most often confused, but it has a more
strongly domed carapace and the individual
scutes of the carapace are themselves more
domed. This species can also be distinguished
by the lack of spurs on its thighs, although there
is one on the tail tip, and the presence of two
scutes directly above the tail (the Spur-thighed
Tortoise has only one). Like all European
tortoises, this is now a protected species since
the population was severely threatened by
overcollection for food and the pet trade. Today
the main threats include bushfires, habitat
destruction, and heavy road traffic.

EUROPE

*two scutes above
tail are distinguishing
features*

- **OCCURRENCE** S. Europe. In scrub,
meadows, and sand dunes.
- **REPRODUCTION** Lays 2–10 eggs.
- **SIMILAR SPECIES** Marginated Tortoise
(*T. marginata*), Spur-thighed Tortoise
(*T. graeca*, p.55).

*spur on
tip of tail*

*strongly domed
carapace with
rounded scutes*

*yellowish brown
to dark brown
carapace*

*dark pigment
develops with age*

*club-shaped
hindlimbs with
short claws for
walking*

*forelimbs with
long claws for
digging*

Length 6–8in (15–20cm)	Diet	Activity

TUATARAS

T HE LIZARDLIKE tuataras are the last survivors of an ancient group of reptiles known as rhynchocephalians (beak-heads). All other members of the group went extinct during the Mesozoic era over 65 million years ago.

Although tuataras resemble lizards, they are classified separately because of differences in the skeleton. They also have a membranous third eyelid, not present in lizards, that passes over the open eye. Like many lizards, they have a pineal eye in the forehead. This is visible in juveniles but is shielded by skin in adults. It can register only light intensity and color but may help regulate body temperature.

Some zoologists consider tuataras to be the sole surviving members of a sister group to the lizards, snakes, and amphisbaenians. Others, however, believe they are not so closely related and that they are far older, being the most ancient group of reptiles apart from those of the turtle order Testudines. Fossils virtually identical to living tuataras exist from the late Triassic period (170 million years ago), which suggests that tuataras have one of the slowest rates of evolution of any terrestrial vertebrate. The two species of tuatara living today are therefore among the most primitive reptiles in the world.

Family SPHENODONTIDAE	Species *Sphenodon punctatus*	Status Endangered

TUATARA

In general appearance the Tuatara resembles a yellow-spotted, olive-brown iguana. It has a broad, rounded head with large eyes, powerful clawed limbs, and a raised dorsal keel of spines running down the back and stout tail, which, like that of some lizards, can be shed when attacked. Tuataras are ideally suited to life in the cool climate of their rocky islands – they have a low metabolism and feed mainly on invertebrates, and they share their burrows with seabirds. They grow extremely slowly and do not reach sexual maturity until they are at least 20 years old. Eggs gestate within the female for 12 months and, once laid, take 15 months to hatch.

- **OCCURRENCE** Islands off New Zealand. On rocky terrain.
- **REPRODUCTION** Lays 12–17 eggs.
- **SIMILAR SPECIES** Brother Island Tuatara (*Sphenodon guentheri*).
- **REMARK** Male Tuataras may live for more than 100 years.

NEW ZEALAND

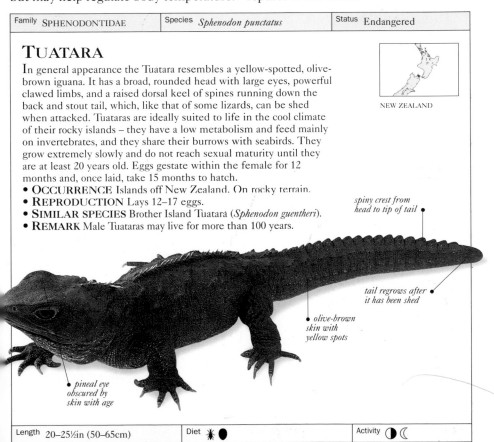

spiny crest from head to tip of tail

tail regrows after it has been shed

olive-brown skin with yellow spots

pineal eye obscured by skin with age

Length 20–25½in (50–65cm)	Diet 🐜 ●	Activity ◑ ☾

LIZARDS

T HE LIZARDS are not a natural biological group, but they are usually grouped together as Sauria, a suborder of the Squamata (which also includes snakes and amphisbaenians).

There are more than 3,400 species of lizard, and they vary considerably in appearance and behavior. Most have four well-developed legs, a relatively long tail, movable eyelids, and external ear openings. Some, however, have reduced limbs, and some are limbless – like amphisbaenians and snakes. Some lizards have fixed, transparent "spectacles" – like those of snakes – to protect their eyes, instead of movable eyelids, and some lack external ear openings. Tongues vary from the snakelike forked tongues of monitor lizards to the globular, sticky tongues of chameleons. Lizards may or may not shed their tails as a means of defense (called caudal autotomy), depending on the species.

Most lizards are nonvenomous but two species – the Beaded Lizard (*Heloderma horridum*, p.96) and the Gila Monster (*H. suspectum*, p.97) – are venomous. The saliva of the Komodo Dragon (*Varanus komodoensis*, pp.98–99) contains bacteria that can cause a fatal infection. Most other large lizards, such as iguanas and monitors, can deliver painful bites.

In this book the lizards have been divided into the traditional 17 families. However, modern taxonomists have identified a number of smaller groups within these, and now recognize up to 30 families. They have, for example, split the huge Iguanidae, with more than 800 species, into eight smaller families.

Family GEKKONIDAE	Species *Coleodactylus septentrionalis*	Status Locally common

ILHA DE MARACA LEAF-LITTER GECKO

The body of the tiny Ilha de Maraca Leaf-litter Gecko is cylindrical in shape, and it has relatively short limbs and a short tail. It is brown to gray in color with white to pale brown transverse bars, which may meet across the back, and dark and pale speckling on the upper body surfaces. On Ilha de Maraca, in Roraima, northern Brazil, this gecko is the most common terrestrial lizard and is prey to a large number of other reptiles, especially snakes. It is found in leaf-litter throughout the drier parts of the rainforest, where it feeds on soil invertebrates such as springtails.
• OCCURRENCE N. South America. On tropical rainforest floors.
• REPRODUCTION Lays 1 egg.
• SIMILAR SPECIES Meridion Leaf-litter Gecko (*Coleodactylus meridionalis*).

S. AMERICA

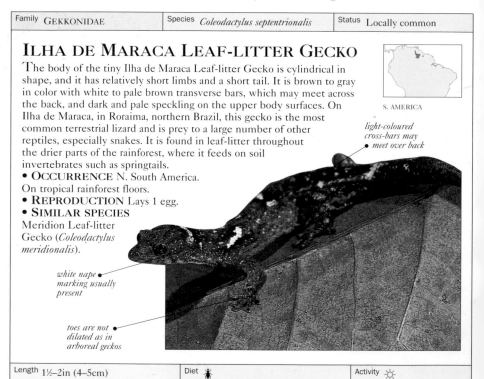

light-coloured cross-bars may • meet over back

white nape • marking usually present

toes are not • dilated as in arboreal geckos

Length 1½–2in (4–5cm)	Diet 🐜	Activity ☼

Family GEKKONIDAE	Species *Coleonyx variegatus*	Status Common

WESTERN BANDED GECKO

This gecko can be distinguished from other American desert
geckos by its soft skin and movable eyelids. It has slender limbs,
with nondilated toes. The base of the stout tail is constricted and,
in the male, has a large spur. These lizards are a
sandy color with darker cross-bands. Being
nocturnal and subterranean, they can
survive in extremely hot, arid conditions.
• OCCURRENCE S.W. US and N.W.
Mexico. In desert.
• REPRODUCTION Lays 1–3 eggs.
• SIMILAR SPECIES Barefoot Gecko (*Coleonyx
switaki*), Texas Banded Gecko (*C. brevis*).

N. AMERICA

*sandy coloration
with dark cross-
bands*

Length 3¼–4¼in (8–12cm)	Diet 🦗	Activity ☾

Family GEKKONIDAE	Species *Cyrtodactylus louisiadensis*	Status Rare

LOUISIADES BOW-FINGERED GECKO

This large, slender gecko has long legs and long,
clawed, nondilated, birdlike toes. The light brown body
and tail are patterned with broad, bold brown
bands. This arboreal species lives on tree
trunks, hunting insects, spiders, and
smaller geckos by night and sheltering
under loose bark during the day.
• OCCURRENCE N.E. Australia, New
Guinea, and Solomon Islands. In rainforest.
• REPRODUCTION Lays 1–2 eggs.
• SIMILAR SPECIES Guadalcanal Bow-
fingered Gecko (*Cyrtodactylus biordinis*).

*large head
and eyes*

OCEANIA

*long, clawed,
nondilated toes*

Length 12–13in (30–34cm)	Diet 🦗🦎	Activity ☾

Family GEKKONIDAE	Species *Eublepharis macularius*	Status Locally common

LEOPARD GECKO

Dark brown or black spots on a yellow-brown background
earn this species, also known as the Spotted Fat-tailed
Gecko, its name. The saddle-patterned juveniles, however,
look so different that they may be mistaken for another
species. It is a highly robust gecko, which seems to survive
in very harsh conditions. Like many geckos laying clutches
of two eggs, females can lay five to six clutches each year.
• OCCURRENCE S. Central Asia. In rocky desert and scrub
at altitudes of up to 8,200ft (2,500m).
• REPRODUCTION Lays 2 eggs.
• SIMILAR SPECIES Iranian
Fat-tailed Gecko (*Eublepharis
angramainyu*), Turkmensian Fat-
tailed Gecko (*E. turcmenicus*).

ASIA

*fat tail may be
food reserve*

*distinctive
"leopardskin"
markings*

Length 8–10in (20–25cm)	Diet 🦗	Activity ☾

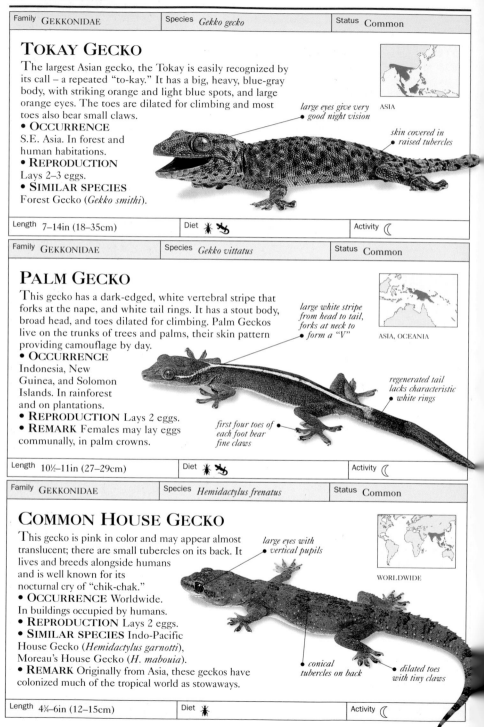

Family GEKKONIDAE	Species *Gekko gecko*	Status Common

TOKAY GECKO

The largest Asian gecko, the Tokay is easily recognized by its call – a repeated "to-kay." It has a big, heavy, blue-gray body, with striking orange and light blue spots, and large orange eyes. The toes are dilated for climbing and most toes also bear small claws.

- **OCCURRENCE**
S.E. Asia. In forest and human habitations.
- **REPRODUCTION**
Lays 2–3 eggs.
- **SIMILAR SPECIES**
Forest Gecko (*Gekko smithi*).

large eyes give very good night vision

ASIA

skin covered in raised tubercles

Length 7–14in (18–35cm)	Diet 🦎	Activity ☾

Family GEKKONIDAE	Species *Gekko vittatus*	Status Common

PALM GECKO

This gecko has a dark-edged, white vertebral stripe that forks at the nape, and white tail rings. It has a stout body, broad head, and toes dilated for climbing. Palm Geckos live on the trunks of trees and palms, their skin pattern providing camouflage by day.

- **OCCURRENCE**
Indonesia, New Guinea, and Solomon Islands. In rainforest and on plantations.
- **REPRODUCTION** Lays 2 eggs.
- **REMARK** Females may lay eggs communally, in palm crowns.

large white stripe from head to tail, forks at neck to form a "V"

ASIA, OCEANIA

regenerated tail lacks characteristic white rings

first four toes of each foot bear fine claws

Length 10½–11in (27–29cm)	Diet 🦗🦎	Activity ☾

Family GEKKONIDAE	Species *Hemidactylus frenatus*	Status Common

COMMON HOUSE GECKO

This gecko is pink in color and may appear almost translucent; there are small tubercles on its back. It lives and breeds alongside humans and is well known for its nocturnal cry of "chik-chak."

- **OCCURRENCE** Worldwide. In buildings occupied by humans.
- **REPRODUCTION** Lays 2 eggs.
- **SIMILAR SPECIES** Indo-Pacific House Gecko (*Hemidactylus garnotti*), Moreau's House Gecko (*H. mabouia*).
- **REMARK** Originally from Asia, these geckos have colonized much of the tropical world as stowaways.

large eyes with vertical pupils

WORLDWIDE

conical tubercles on back

dilated toes with tiny claws

Length 4¾–6in (12–15cm)	Diet 🦗	Activity ☾

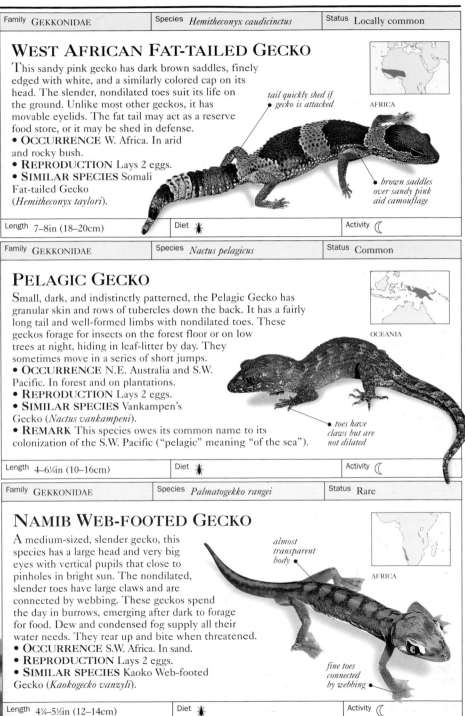

Family GEKKONIDAE	Species *Hemitheconyx caudicinctus*	Status Locally common

WEST AFRICAN FAT-TAILED GECKO

This sandy pink gecko has dark brown saddles, finely
edged with white, and a similarly colored cap on its
head. The slender, nondilated toes suit its life on
the ground. Unlike most other geckos, it has
movable eyelids. The fat tail may act as a reserve
food store, or it may be shed in defense.

*tail quickly shed if
gecko is attacked*

AFRICA

• **OCCURRENCE** W. Africa. In arid
and rocky bush.
• **REPRODUCTION** Lays 2 eggs.
• **SIMILAR SPECIES** Somali
Fat-tailed Gecko
(*Hemitheconyx taylori*).

*brown saddles
over sandy pink
aid camouflage*

Length 7–8in (18–20cm)	Diet	Activity ☾

Family GEKKONIDAE	Species *Nactus pelagicus*	Status Common

PELAGIC GECKO

Small, dark, and indistinctly patterned, the Pelagic Gecko has
granular skin and rows of tubercles down the back. It has a fairly
long tail and well-formed limbs with nondilated toes. These
geckos forage for insects on the forest floor or on low
trees at night, hiding in leaf-litter by day. They
sometimes move in a series of short jumps.

OCEANIA

• **OCCURRENCE** N.E. Australia and S.W.
Pacific. In forest and on plantations.
• **REPRODUCTION** Lays 2 eggs.
• **SIMILAR SPECIES** Vankampen's
Gecko (*Nactus vankampeni*).
• **REMARK** This species owes its common name to its
colonization of the S.W. Pacific ("pelagic" meaning "of the sea").

*toes have
claws but are
not dilated*

Length 4–6¼in (10–16cm)	Diet	Activity ☾

Family GEKKONIDAE	Species *Palmatogekko rangei*	Status Rare

NAMIB WEB-FOOTED GECKO

A medium-sized, slender gecko, this
species has a large head and very big
eyes with vertical pupils that close to
pinholes in bright sun. The nondilated,
slender toes have large claws and are
connected by webbing. These geckos spend
the day in burrows, emerging after dark to forage
for food. Dew and condensed fog supply all their
water needs. They rear up and bite when threatened.

*almost
transparent
body*

AFRICA

• **OCCURRENCE** S.W. Africa. In sand.
• **REPRODUCTION** Lays 2 eggs.
• **SIMILAR SPECIES** Kaoko Web-footed
Gecko (*Kaokogecko vanzyli*).

*fine toes
connected
by webbing*

Length 4¾–5½in (12–14cm)	Diet	Activity ☾

| Family GEKKONIDAE | Species *Phelsuma standingi* | Status Locally common |

STANDING'S DAY GECKO

yellow-green head with large eyes

This is the second largest *Phelsuma* day gecko, after the Madagascan Giant Day Gecko (*P. madagascariensis grandis*). Adults are blue-gray on the body and yellow-green on the head, with brown netlike markings and cross-bars. During basking, the blues and yellow-greens may intensify. Hatchlings are brightly banded and change coloration as they mature.
• OCCURRENCE S.W. Madagascar. In dry forest.
• REPRODUCTION Lays 2 eggs.
• REMARK The Standing's Day Gecko is protected from exploitation for trade.

MADAGASCAR

green body with brown, netlike pattern

feet with dilated toes for climbing

| Length 10–11in (25–28cm) | Diet | Activity ☼ |

| Family GEKKONIDAE | Species *Ptychozoon kuhli* | Status Common |

KUHL'S FLYING GECKO

Its irregular outline and cryptic patterning make this gecko almost invisible when resting on a lichen-covered tree trunk. The webbed toes and flaps of skin on the head, limbs, sides, and tail increase its surface area and allow it to leap from a tree and glide gracefully downward.
• OCCURRENCE S.E. Asia. In rainforest.
• REPRODUCTION Lays 2 eggs.
• SIMILAR SPECIES Burmese Flying Gecko (*Ptychozoon lionotum*).

ASIA

body with lateral flaps of skin for gliding

broad, flat tail tip distinguishes species

| Length 7–8in (18–20cm) | Diet | Activity ☾ |

| Family GEKKONIDAE | Species *Rhacodactylus leachianus* | Status Rare |

NEW CALEDONIAN GIANT FOREST GECKO

This cryptically mottled gray, green, or brown lizard lives mainly in the forest canopy or inside hollow trees, although it is occasionally encountered on tree trunks. The body is unadorned except for loose folds of skin on the sides and webbing between the toes. It primarily eats fruit – bananas and papayas – and insects, but large specimens also take small birds and mammals. In its remote island habitat it probably has few natural enemies.
• OCCURRENCE New Caledonia. In rainforest.
• REPRODUCTION Lays 2 eggs.
• SIMILAR SPECIES Bavay's New Caledonian Gecko (*Rhacodactylus chahoua*).
• REMARK The New Caledonian Giant Forest Gecko is the largest living gecko in the world.

mottled coloring provides camouflage

dilated toes aid climbing

NEW CALEDONIA

| Length 13–15in (34–38cm) | Diet | Activity ☾ |

Family GEKKONIDAE	Species *Tarentola mauritanica*	Status Common

MOORISH GECKO

Europe's largest gecko, this is a
robust, gray-brown species with a
broad, flat body and a wide head.
Several rows of tubercles running down the
body, tail, and limbs give it a spiny appearance. The toes
are dilated to form adhesive pads, with small claws at the
tips of the third and fourth toes. These geckos are often
attracted to house lights at night to feed on flying insects.
• **OCCURRENCE** S. Europe, N. Africa, and Canary Islands.
In warm, dry, coastal areas, but inland on the Iberian Peninsula.
• **REPRODUCTION** Lays 2 eggs.
• **SIMILAR SPECIES** Moorish Desert Gecko (*Tarentola deserti*).

rows of tubercles on body, limbs, and tail

EUROPE, AFRICA

eyes with vertical pupils

Length 4–6in (10–15cm)	Diet	Activity ☾

Family GEKKONIDAE	Species *Teratoscincus scincus*	Status Locally common

WONDER GECKO

Also known as the Skink Gecko, this relatively large gecko
has long legs, a cylindrical body, a large, powerful head, and
protruding eyes. Since this is a burrowing species, the toes are
not dilated for climbing. The coloration consists of a pale sandy
background with darker bands or stripes. When disturbed, the
Wonder Gecko raises its body high, emits a loud hiss, and
advances to bite, slowly waving its tail in a serpentine motion
and causing the large tail scales to rasp together audibly.
• **OCCURRENCE** Middle East
and S.W. Asia. In sandy or
clay desert and semidesert.
• **REPRODUCTION**
Lays 2 eggs.

MIDDLE EAST, ASIA

large tail scales rasp together

well-developed legs

Length 6–8in (15–20cm)	Diet	Activity ☾

Family GEKKONIDAE	Species *Thecadactylus rapicauda*	Status Locally common

TURNIP-TAILED GECKO

A bulbous tail gives this species its common name – although it is
unusual to find specimens with complete turnip-tails, since geckos
shed their tails when attacked. The broad head has large
eyes with vertical pupils. Granular scales cover
the body, and the overall patterning is of
camouflage browns and grays. The toes
end in expanded pads for climbing. Turnip-
tailed Geckos can vocalize, although they
call less frequently than smaller species.
• **OCCURRENCE** Mexico to N.
South America, and Lesser Antilles.
In rainforest and human habitations.
• **REPRODUCTION** Lays 1 egg.

N., C., & S. AMERICA

broad head with large eyes

regenerating tail

feet with dilated toes for climbing

Length 5½–7in (14–18cm)	Diet	Activity ◐

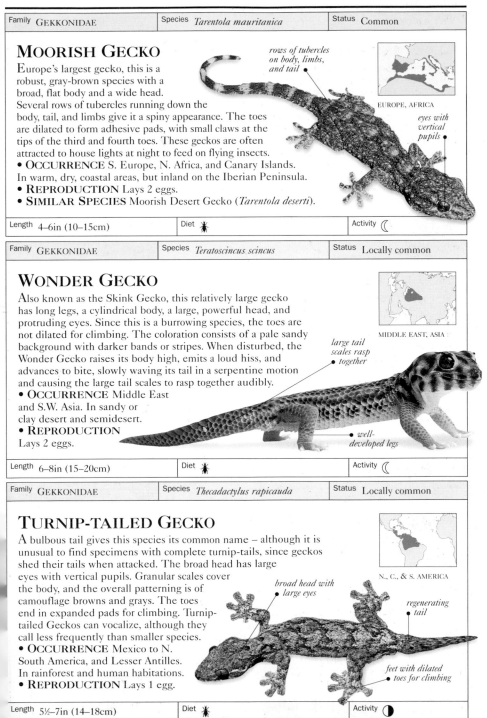

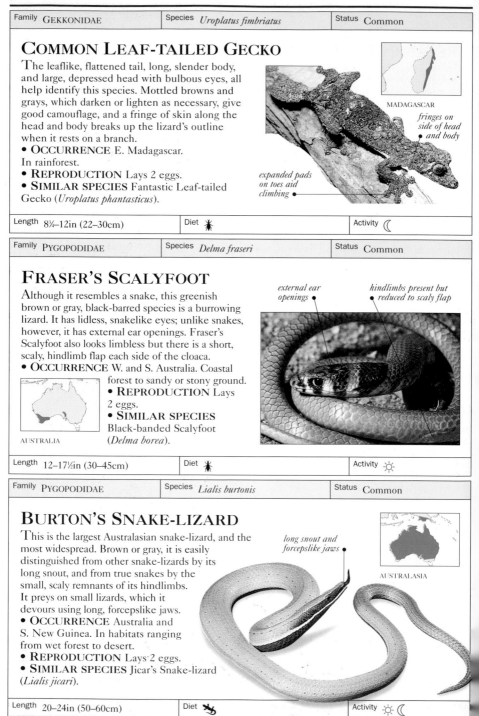

| Family GEKKONIDAE | Species *Uroplatus fimbriatus* | Status Common |

COMMON LEAF-TAILED GECKO

The leaflike, flattened tail, long, slender body, and large, depressed head with bulbous eyes, all help identify this species. Mottled browns and grays, which darken or lighten as necessary, give good camouflage, and a fringe of skin along the head and body breaks up the lizard's outline when it rests on a branch.
• OCCURRENCE E. Madagascar. In rainforest.
• REPRODUCTION Lays 2 eggs.
• SIMILAR SPECIES Fantastic Leaf-tailed Gecko (*Uroplatus phantasticus*).

MADAGASCAR

fringes on side of head and body

expanded pads on toes aid climbing

| Length 8¾–12in (22–30cm) | Diet 🐜 | Activity ☾ |

| Family PYGOPODIDAE | Species *Delma fraseri* | Status Common |

FRASER'S SCALYFOOT

Although it resembles a snake, this greenish brown or gray, black-barred species is a burrowing lizard. It has lidless, snakelike eyes; unlike snakes, however, it has external ear openings. Fraser's Scalyfoot also looks limbless but there is a short, scaly, hindlimb flap each side of the cloaca.
• OCCURRENCE W. and S. Australia. Coastal forest to sandy or stony ground.
• REPRODUCTION Lays 2 eggs.
• SIMILAR SPECIES Black-banded Scalyfoot (*Delma borea*).

external ear openings *hindlimbs present but reduced to scaly flap*

AUSTRALIA

| Length 12–17½in (30–45cm) | Diet 🐜 | Activity ☀ |

| Family PYGOPODIDAE | Species *Lialis burtonis* | Status Common |

BURTON'S SNAKE-LIZARD

This is the largest Australasian snake-lizard, and the most widespread. Brown or gray, it is easily distinguished from other snake-lizards by its long snout, and from true snakes by the small, scaly remnants of its hindlimbs. It preys on small lizards, which it devours using long, forcepslike jaws.
• OCCURRENCE Australia and S. New Guinea. In habitats ranging from wet forest to desert.
• REPRODUCTION Lays 2 eggs.
• SIMILAR SPECIES Jicar's Snake-lizard (*Lialis jicari*).

long snout and forcepslike jaws

AUSTRALASIA

| Length 20–24in (50–60cm) | Diet 🦎 | Activity ☀☾ |

Family XANTUSIIDAE	Species *Lepidophyma flavimaculatum*	Status Rare

YELLOW-SPOTTED NIGHT LIZARD

This is a medium-sized, slender lizard. Several rows of raised, tuberculate scales run down the back and the eyes are covered by snakelike "spectacles." The coloration is brown or gray, with yellow spots on the sides and dark bars on the lip scales.
brown or gray with yellow spots on sides
C. AMERICA

• OCCURRENCE Central America. In rainforest.
robust head and long neck
raised, tuberculate scales on back
• REPRODUCTION Live-bearing, 5–6 neonates.
• SIMILAR SPECIES Maya Night Lizard (*Lepidophyma mayae*).

Length 8–12in (20–30cm)	Diet	Activity

Family IGUANIDAE	Species *Amblyrhynchus cristatus*	Status Locally common

GALAPAGOS MARINE IGUANA

Gray-green in color, the Galapagos Marine Iguana becomes reddish in the breeding season. Temperature also affects color: iguanas leaving the cold ocean may be almost black; they will then bask on the rocks until warmed by the sun, when they change back to their normal gray-green. Similarities to other large iguanas include the general physique and the raised dorsal crest, but the tail is more robust and flattened like a rudder for swimming against strong currents. Because they live on kelp, eaten underwater, they have glands in the nose for excreting salt. When basking, they continually expel salt in a white spray from these glands.
GALAPAGOS ISLANDS
powerful jaws for feeding on seaweed

• OCCURRENCE Galapagos Islands. On rocky shorelines.
dark body warms quickly in sun
• REPRODUCTION Lays 2–3 eggs.
• SIMILAR SPECIES Galapagos Land Iguanas (*Conolophus* species).
• REMARK This is the only truly marine lizard in the world.

robust, rudderlike tail

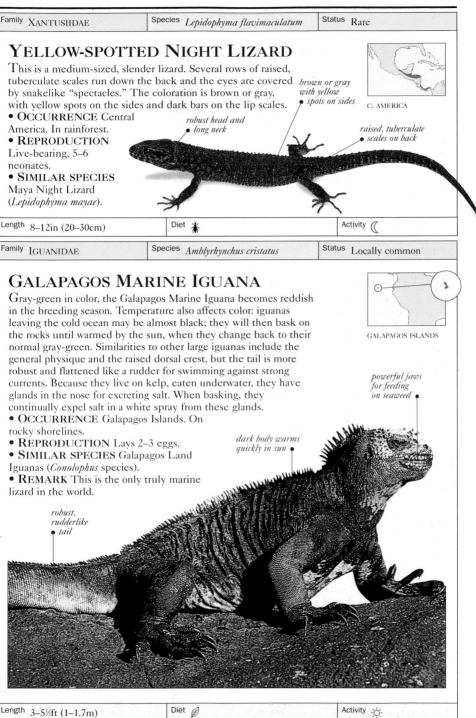

Length 3–5½ft (1–1.7m)	Diet	Activity

Family IGUANIDAE	Species *Anolis allisoni*	Status Common

ALLISON'S ANOLE

This is a relatively stout anole, which varies in color from dark brown to bright green. Males develop an electric-blue head and thorax, while females have a light stripe along the back. In both sexes, the dewlap under the chin is dark red.

long, slender, flattened head

• OCCURRENCE Cuba and the small Caribbean islands off Belize and Honduras. In dry, open sites in gardens and on plantations.
• REPRODUCTION Lays 1 egg.
• SIMILAR SPECIES Cuban Green Anole (*Anolis porcatus*).

CARIBBEAN

Length 4–6in (10–15cm)	Diet 🐛	Activity ☼

Family IGUANIDAE	Species *Anolis carolinensis*	Status Endangered

AMERICAN GREEN ANOLE

Also known as the American Chameleon, this is the only native anole in southeast US. The vivid green coloring of both sexes and the red dewlap of the males should make identification of this species easy, but some males have pink, white, or green dewlaps, and both sexes can change color. The American Green Anole was once common in gardens and other habitats, but its populations are in decline.

bright green color can change rapidly to brown

N. AMERICA

• OCCURRENCE S.E. US. In gardens and open woodland.
• REPRODUCTION Lays 1 egg.
• SIMILAR SPECIES Brown Anole (*Anolis sagrei*).

red dewlap in male

Length 4¼–8in (12–20cm)	Diet 🐛	Activity ☼

Family IGUANIDAE	Species *Anolis equestris*	Status Locally common

KNIGHT ANOLE

The largest member of its genus, the Knight Anole is bright green, occasionally brown or speckled with dark green, and it has two vivid yellow stripes under the eye and over the shoulder. The dewlap of the male is pink. The head is large and the snout is pointed. This species usually lives in palm crowns, although it is also found on other large trees. An aggressive colonizer and predator, the Knight Anole in Florida will eat the smaller Green and Brown Anoles, as well as insects and treefrogs.

CUBA, N. AMERICA

vivid yellow stripes over shoulder and through eyes

• OCCURRENCE Cuba. (Introduced to Florida.) In large trees in forests and occasionally in open areas.
• REPRODUCTION Lays 2 eggs.

Length 13–19in (33–49cm)	Diet 🐛 🐸 🦎 🍃	Activity ☼

Family IGUANIDAE	Species *Basilicus plumifrons*	Status Common

PLUMED BASILISK

The vivid green Plumed Basilisk is usually patterned
with light blue or yellow spots. It has three large crests
supported by bony spines on the head, back, and tail,
and these are especially well developed in males. At
night, basilisks sleep at the end of narrow twigs so that
they will be alerted to the approach of predatory
snakes. They escape by diving into the water below
and hiding on the stream bottom.
• OCCURRENCE S.E. Central America. By rivers
in tropical rainforest.
• REPRODUCTION Lays 15–20 eggs.
• SIMILAR SPECIES Helmeted Basilisk
(*Basilicus basiliscus*).
• REMARK Basilisks are sometimes called
Jesus Christ lizards because they run
across water on their hindfeet.

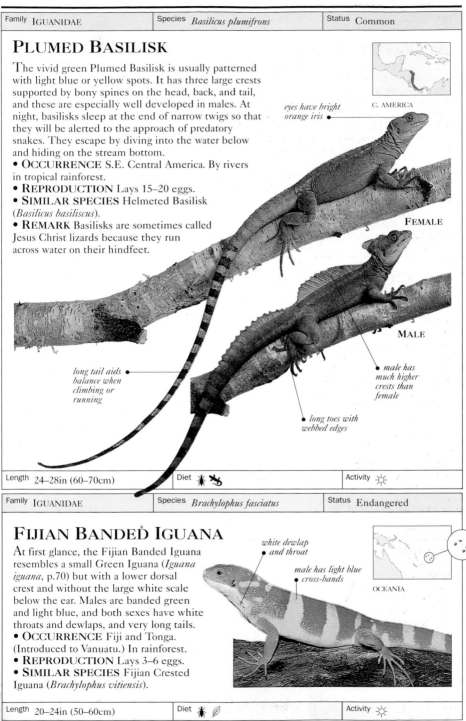

C. AMERICA

eyes have bright
orange iris •

FEMALE

MALE

long tail aids •
balance when
climbing or
running

• male has
much higher
crests than
female

• long toes with
webbed edges

Length 24–28in (60–70cm)	Diet 🐜 🦎	Activity ☼

Family IGUANIDAE	Species *Brachylophus fasciatus*	Status Endangered

FIJIAN BANDED IGUANA

At first glance, the Fijian Banded Iguana
resembles a small Green Iguana (*Iguana
iguana*, p.70) but with a lower dorsal
crest and without the large white scale
below the ear. Males are banded green
and light blue, and both sexes have white
throats and dewlaps, and very long tails.
• OCCURRENCE Fiji and Tonga.
(Introduced to Vanuatu.) In rainforest.
• REPRODUCTION Lays 3–6 eggs.
• SIMILAR SPECIES Fijian Crested
Iguana (*Brachylophus vitiensis*).

white dewlap
• and throat

male has light blue
• cross-bands

OCEANIA

Length 20–24in (50–60cm)	Diet 🐜 ◿	Activity ☼

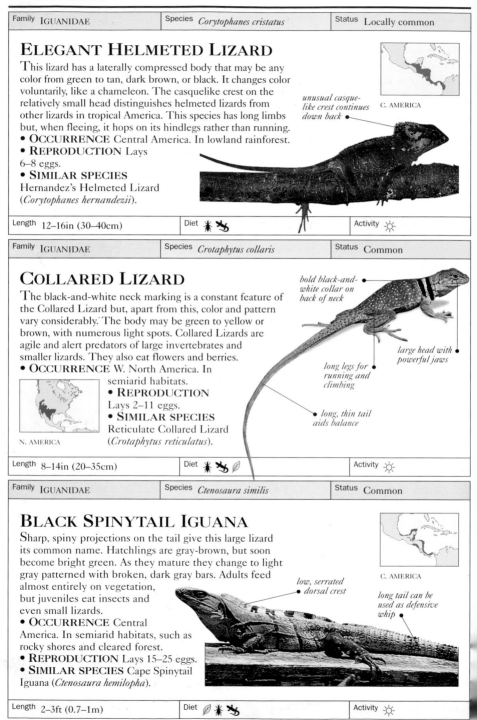

Family IGUANIDAE	Species *Corytophanes cristatus*	Status Locally common

ELEGANT HELMETED LIZARD

This lizard has a laterally compressed body that may be any color from green to tan, dark brown, or black. It changes color voluntarily, like a chameleon. The casquelike crest on the relatively small head distinguishes helmeted lizards from other lizards in tropical America. This species has long limbs but, when fleeing, it hops on its hindlegs rather than running.
• OCCURRENCE Central America. In lowland rainforest.
• REPRODUCTION Lays 6–8 eggs.
• SIMILAR SPECIES Hernandez's Helmeted Lizard (*Corytophanes hernandezii*).

unusual casque-like crest continues down back

C. AMERICA

Length 12–16in (30–40cm)	Diet 🕷 🦗	Activity ☼

Family IGUANIDAE	Species *Crotaphytus collaris*	Status Common

COLLARED LIZARD

The black-and-white neck marking is a constant feature of the Collared Lizard but, apart from this, color and pattern vary considerably. The body may be green to yellow or brown, with numerous light spots. Collared Lizards are agile and alert predators of large invertebrates and smaller lizards. They also eat flowers and berries.
• OCCURRENCE W. North America. In semiarid habitats.
• REPRODUCTION Lays 2–11 eggs.
• SIMILAR SPECIES Reticulate Collared Lizard (*Crotaphytus reticulatus*).

N. AMERICA

bold black-and-white collar on back of neck

large head with powerful jaws

long legs for running and climbing

long, thin tail aids balance

Length 8–14in (20–35cm)	Diet 🕷 🦗 🌿	Activity ☼

Family IGUANIDAE	Species *Ctenosaura similis*	Status Common

BLACK SPINYTAIL IGUANA

Sharp, spiny projections on the tail give this large lizard its common name. Hatchlings are gray-brown, but soon become bright green. As they mature they change to light gray patterned with broken, dark gray bars. Adults feed almost entirely on vegetation, but juveniles eat insects and even small lizards.
• OCCURRENCE Central America. In semiarid habitats, such as rocky shores and cleared forest.
• REPRODUCTION Lays 15–25 eggs.
• SIMILAR SPECIES Cape Spinytail Iguana (*Ctenosaura hemilopha*).

low, serrated dorsal crest

C. AMERICA

long tail can be used as defensive whip

Length 2–3ft (0.7–1m)	Diet 🌿 🕷 🦗	Activity ☼

Family IGUANIDAE	Species *Cyclura cornuta*	Status Endangered

RHINOCEROS IGUANA

The heavily built Rhinoceros Iguana is an imposing reptile, with a sturdy body and legs, a large head, and a strong, thick tail. Adults are almost uniformly gray, although juveniles may bear faint, pale cross-bars. The species takes it name from the three or five raised scales, similar to rhinoceros horns, in front of the eyes. These "horns" are most pronounced in the larger, bulkier males, which also have two enlarged areas at the back of the skull, and swollen jowls on the neck. Males are territorial, displaying by means of a series of head-bobs and rolls while turning their body sideways to intimidate their opponent with a large surface area. The diet of these iguanas includes the fruit and leaves of the manchineel (*Hippomane mancinella*) and poisonwood (*Metapium toxiferum*); both of these trees contain potentially toxic alkaloids, but the lizards have adapted to feed on them.

• OCCURRENCE Haiti and Dominican Republic, Hispaniola. In arid, rocky habitats.
• REPRODUCTION Lays 5–19 eggs.
• SIMILAR SPECIES Cuban Ground Iguana (*Cyclura nubila*).

HISPANIOLA

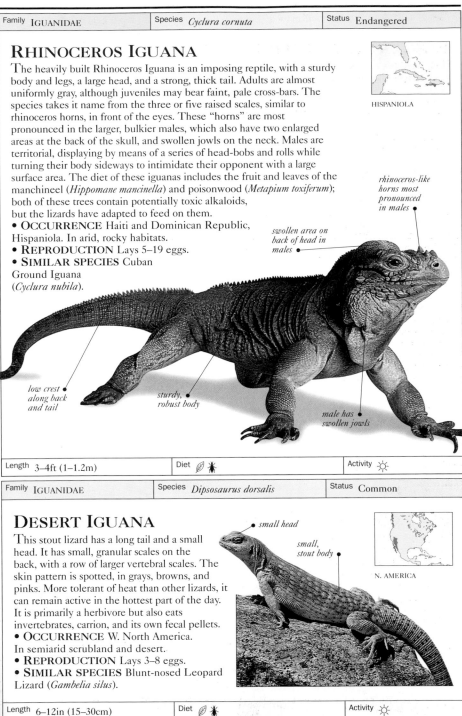

rhinoceros-like horns most pronounced in males

swollen area on back of head in males

low crest along back and tail

sturdy, robust body

male has swollen jowls

Length 3–4ft (1–1.2m)	Diet 🌿 🐜	Activity ☀

Family IGUANIDAE	Species *Dipsosaurus dorsalis*	Status Common

DESERT IGUANA

This stout lizard has a long tail and a small head. It has small, granular scales on the back, with a row of larger vertebral scales. The skin pattern is spotted, in grays, browns, and pinks. More tolerant of heat than other lizards, it can remain active in the hottest part of the day. It is primarily a herbivore but also eats invertebrates, carrion, and its own fecal pellets.

• OCCURRENCE W. North America. In semiarid scrubland and desert.
• REPRODUCTION Lays 3–8 eggs.
• SIMILAR SPECIES Blunt-nosed Leopard Lizard (*Gambelia silus*).

small head

small, stout body

N. AMERICA

Length 6–12in (15–30cm)	Diet 🌿 🐜	Activity ☀

Family IGUANIDAE	Species *Hoplocercus spinosus*	Status Rare

PRICKLE-TAIL LIZARD

With its drab coloration and patterning of reddish brown or dark brown bands alternating with light brown ones, the Prickle-tail Lizard is easily overlooked. It has an off-white nape band, but its most unusual physical attribute is its short, flat, spiny tail, which is used to block the entrance to its burrow. Unlike many other lizards, which occupy the abandoned burrows of other animals, this rare and little-known species excavates its own tubelike retreat at the base of a bush. At dusk, it emerges to hunt ants and termites, as well as larger invertebrates, such as scorpions.
• **OCCURRENCE** C. South America. In dry savanna woodland.
• **REPRODUCTION** Lays eggs (clutch size unknown).
• **SIMILAR SPECIES** Thornytail Lizard (*Uracentron azureum*).

S. AMERICA

light nape band

flat, spiny tail used to block entrance to burrow

Length 4¾–6in (12–15cm)	Diet 🐜	Activity ◑

Family IGUANIDAE	Species *Iguana iguana*	Status Common

GREEN IGUANA

Probably the best-known lizard in the world, the Green Iguana is bright green with blue markings as a juvenile and becomes more drab with maturity. Dominant males often develop bright orange forelimbs and pale heads. There are two subspecies: *Iguana iguana rhinolopha* (Central America), which has small, hornlike projections on the snout; and *I. iguana iguana* (South America), shown here, which lacks the projections. Male iguanas are highly territorial. When displaying, they stand side-on to their opponent and make themselves as large as possible by standing tall, while bobbing their heads and waving their dewlaps. The long tail is used defensively as a powerful whip; for propelling the body when swimming; and for escape (the tail is shed if it is seized). Although primarily herbivorous as adults, insects form part of the diet of juveniles and subadults.
• **OCCURRENCE** Mexico to South America. In riverine forest.
• **REPRODUCTION** Lays 20–40 eggs.
• **SIMILAR SPECIES** Lesser Antillean Green Iguana (*I. delicatissima*).

N., C., & S. AMERICA

dorsal crest runs down length of body

dewlap in male used for display

long legs and toes for climbing and running

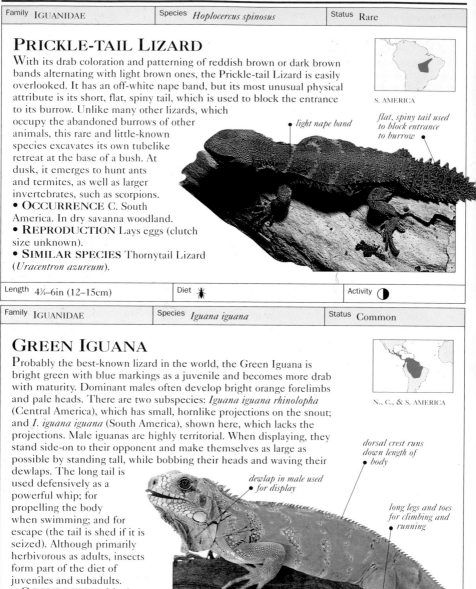

Length 5–6½ft (1.5–2m)	Diet 🍃 🐜	Activity ☀

Family IGUANIDAE	Species *Laemanctus longipes*	Status Rare

CONEHEAD LIZARD

The Conehead Lizard is a rare inhabitant of tropical forest. The body is bright green, with dark green and black markings. The head is yellow-green, with a cream-green stripe running from the lips to the shoulders, and with a highly distinctive, conelike casque at the rear.
• OCCURRENCE Mexico to Honduras. In lowland rainforest.
• REPRODUCTION Lays 3–4 eggs.
• SIMILAR SPECIES Serrated Conehead Lizard (*Laemanctus serratus*).

hard, conelike casque at rear of head

cryptic bright green coloration with darker markings

N. & C. AMERICA

long tail

slender green legs and feet

Length 16–28in (40–70cm)	Diet 🐛	Activity ☼

Family IGUANIDAE	Species *Oplurus cuvieri*	Status Common

CUVIER'S MADAGASCAN TREE SWIFT

This agile lizard is red-brown, with a series of broad, light-edged, dark bars running across the back. Unlike most other Madagascan swifts, which are rock-dwellers, this arboreal inhabitant possesses a spiny tail. The spines alternate in size, distinguishing this species from the otherwise similar Madagascan Tree Swift (*Oplurus cyclurus*).
• OCCURRENCE Madagascar. In dry woodland.
• REPRODUCTION Lays 4–6 eggs.
• SIMILAR SPECIES Madagascan Tree Swift (*O. cyclurus*).

MADAGASCAR

spines on tail

small head with pointed snout

Length 12–14½in (30–37cm)	Diet 🐛	Activity ☼

Family IGUANIDAE	Species *Phrynosoma platyrhinos*	Status Common

DESERT HORNED LIZARD

Commonly misnamed "horned toads," these lizards are squat and rounded, with a crest of horns and a single row of scales along the sides and across the throat. They are usually tan, beige, or gray, with markings that resemble pebbles in shape and color. This lizard only eats ants.
• OCCURRENCE S.W. North America. In sandy desert.
• REPRODUCTION Lays 2–16 eggs.
• SIMILAR SPECIES Coast Horned Lizard (*Phrynosoma coronatum*).

horns at back of head

N. AMERICA

cryptic tan, beige, or gray coloration

Length 3¼–4¼in (8–11cm)	Diet 🐜	Activity ☼

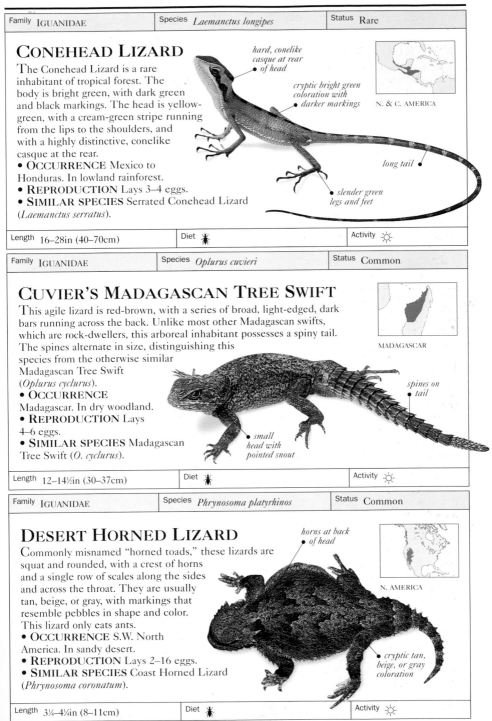

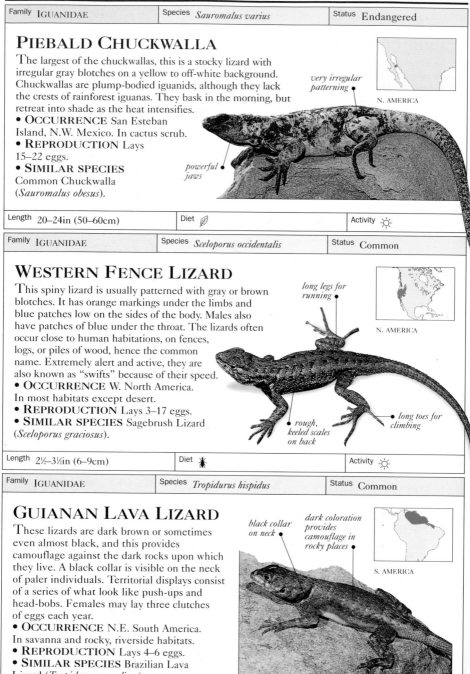

Family IGUANIDAE	Species *Sauromalus varius*	Status Endangered

PIEBALD CHUCKWALLA

The largest of the chuckwallas, this is a stocky lizard with irregular gray blotches on a yellow to off-white background. Chuckwallas are plump-bodied iguanids, although they lack the crests of rainforest iguanas. They bask in the morning, but retreat into shade as the heat intensifies.
• **OCCURRENCE** San Esteban Island, N.W. Mexico. In cactus scrub.
• **REPRODUCTION** Lays 15–22 eggs.
• **SIMILAR SPECIES** Common Chuckwalla (*Sauromalus obesus*).

very irregular patterning

N. AMERICA

powerful jaws

Length 20–24in (50–60cm)	Diet	Activity ☼

Family IGUANIDAE	Species *Sceloporus occidentalis*	Status Common

WESTERN FENCE LIZARD

This spiny lizard is usually patterned with gray or brown blotches. It has orange markings under the limbs and blue patches low on the sides of the body. Males also have patches of blue under the throat. The lizards often occur close to human habitations, on fences, logs, or piles of wood, hence the common name. Extremely alert and active, they are also known as "swifts" because of their speed.
• **OCCURRENCE** W. North America. In most habitats except desert.
• **REPRODUCTION** Lays 3–17 eggs.
• **SIMILAR SPECIES** Sagebrush Lizard (*Sceloporus graciosus*).

long legs for running

N. AMERICA

long toes for climbing

rough, keeled scales on back

Length 2½–3½in (6–9cm)	Diet	Activity ☼

Family IGUANIDAE	Species *Tropidurus hispidus*	Status Common

GUIANAN LAVA LIZARD

These lizards are dark brown or sometimes even almost black, and this provides camouflage against the dark rocks upon which they live. A black collar is visible on the neck of paler individuals. Territorial displays consist of a series of what look like push-ups and head-bobs. Females may lay three clutches of eggs each year.
• **OCCURRENCE** N.E. South America. In savanna and rocky, riverside habitats.
• **REPRODUCTION** Lays 4–6 eggs.
• **SIMILAR SPECIES** Brazilian Lava Lizard (*Tropidurus oreadicus*).

black collar on neck

dark coloration provides camouflage in rocky places

S. AMERICA

Length 5–7in (13–18cm)	Diet	Activity ☼

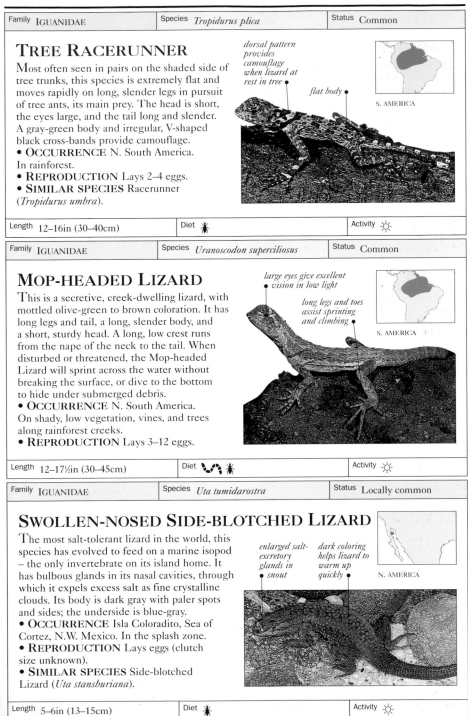

Family IGUANIDAE	Species *Tropidurus plica*	Status Common

TREE RACERUNNER

Most often seen in pairs on the shaded side of tree trunks, this species is extremely flat and moves rapidly on long, slender legs in pursuit of tree ants, its main prey. The head is short, the eyes large, and the tail long and slender. A gray-green body and irregular, V-shaped black cross-bands provide camouflage.
• OCCURRENCE N. South America. In rainforest.
• REPRODUCTION Lays 2–4 eggs.
• SIMILAR SPECIES Racerunner (*Tropidurus umbra*).

dorsal pattern provides camouflage when lizard at rest in tree

flat body

S. AMERICA

Length 12–16in (30–40cm)	Diet	Activity

Family IGUANIDAE	Species *Uranoscodon superciliosus*	Status Common

MOP-HEADED LIZARD

This is a secretive, creek-dwelling lizard, with mottled olive-green to brown coloration. It has long legs and tail, a long, slender body, and a short, sturdy head. A long, low crest runs from the nape of the neck to the tail. When disturbed or threatened, the Mop-headed Lizard will sprint across the water without breaking the surface, or dive to the bottom to hide under submerged debris.
• OCCURRENCE N. South America. On shady, low vegetation, vines, and trees along rainforest creeks.
• REPRODUCTION Lays 3–12 eggs.

large eyes give excellent vision in low light

long legs and toes assist sprinting and climbing

S. AMERICA

Length 12–17½in (30–45cm)	Diet	Activity

Family IGUANIDAE	Species *Uta tumidarostra*	Status Locally common

SWOLLEN-NOSED SIDE-BLOTCHED LIZARD

The most salt-tolerant lizard in the world, this species has evolved to feed on a marine isopod – the only invertebrate on its island home. It has bulbous glands in its nasal cavities, through which it expels excess salt as fine crystalline clouds. Its body is dark gray with paler spots and sides; the underside is blue-gray.
• OCCURRENCE Isla Coloradito, Sea of Cortez, N.W. Mexico. In the splash zone.
• REPRODUCTION Lays eggs (clutch size unknown).
• SIMILAR SPECIES Side-blotched Lizard (*Uta stansburiana*).

enlarged salt-excretory glands in snout

dark coloring helps lizard to warm up quickly

N. AMERICA

Length 5–6in (13–15cm)	Diet	Activity

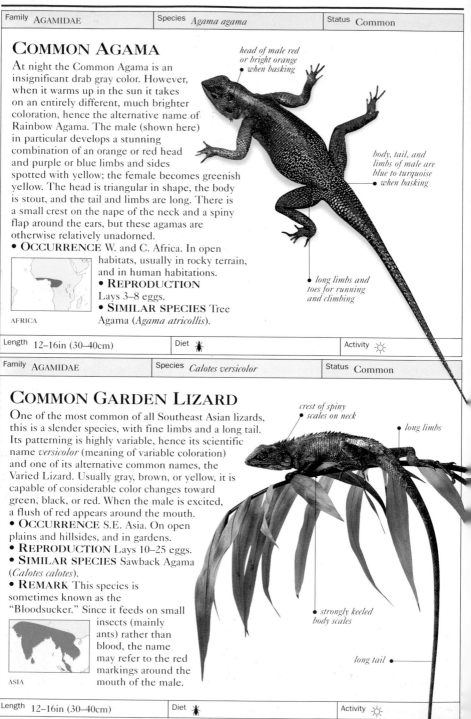

Family AGAMIDAE	Species *Agama agama*	Status Common

COMMON AGAMA

At night the Common Agama is an insignificant drab gray color. However, when it warms up in the sun it takes on an entirely different, much brighter coloration, hence the alternative name of Rainbow Agama. The male (shown here) in particular develops a stunning combination of an orange or red head and purple or blue limbs and sides spotted with yellow; the female becomes greenish yellow. The head is triangular in shape, the body is stout, and the tail and limbs are long. There is a small crest on the nape of the neck and a spiny flap around the ears, but these agamas are otherwise relatively unadorned.

head of male red or bright orange when basking

body, tail, and limbs of male are blue to turquoise when basking

long limbs and toes for running and climbing

• OCCURRENCE W. and C. Africa. In open habitats, usually in rocky terrain, and in human habitations.
• REPRODUCTION Lays 3–8 eggs.
• SIMILAR SPECIES Tree Agama (*Agama atricollis*).

AFRICA

Length 12–16in (30–40cm)	Diet 🐜	Activity ☼

Family AGAMIDAE	Species *Calotes versicolor*	Status Common

COMMON GARDEN LIZARD

One of the most common of all Southeast Asian lizards, this is a slender species, with fine limbs and a long tail. Its patterning is highly variable, hence its scientific name *versicolor* (meaning of variable coloration) and one of its alternative common names, the Varied Lizard. Usually gray, brown, or yellow, it is capable of considerable color changes toward green, black, or red. When the male is excited, a flush of red appears around the mouth.

crest of spiny scales on neck

long limbs

strongly keeled body scales

long tail

• OCCURRENCE S.E. Asia. On open plains and hillsides, and in gardens.
• REPRODUCTION Lays 10–25 eggs.
• SIMILAR SPECIES Sawback Agama (*Calotes calotes*).
• REMARK This species is sometimes known as the "Bloodsucker." Since it feeds on small insects (mainly ants) rather than blood, the name may refer to the red markings around the mouth of the male.

ASIA

Length 12–16in (30–40cm)	Diet 🐜	Activity ☼

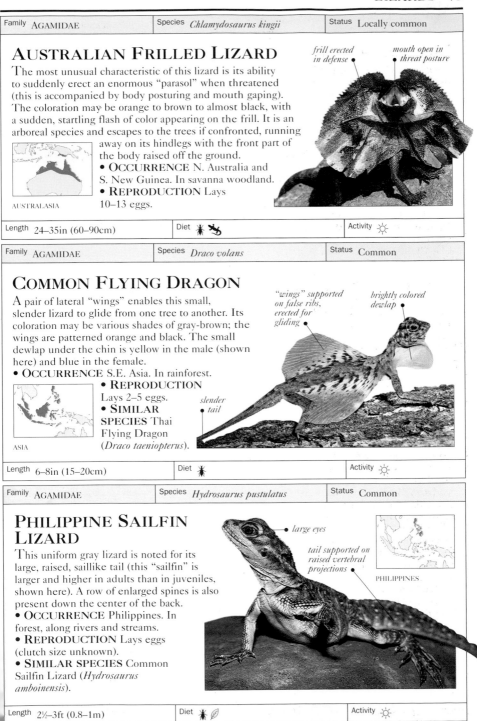

| Family AGAMIDAE | Species *Chlamydosaurus kingii* | Status Locally common |

AUSTRALIAN FRILLED LIZARD

frill erected in defense •
• *mouth open in threat posture*

The most unusual characteristic of this lizard is its ability to suddenly erect an enormous "parasol" when threatened (this is accompanied by body posturing and mouth gaping). The coloration may be orange to brown to almost black, with a sudden, startling flash of color appearing on the frill. It is an arboreal species and escapes to the trees if confronted, running away on its hindlegs with the front part of the body raised off the ground.
• OCCURRENCE N. Australia and S. New Guinea. In savanna woodland.
• REPRODUCTION Lays 10–13 eggs.

AUSTRALASIA

| Length 24–35in (60–90cm) | Diet 🐜 🦎 | Activity ☀ |

| Family AGAMIDAE | Species *Draco volans* | Status Common |

COMMON FLYING DRAGON

"wings" supported on false ribs, erected for gliding •
• *brightly colored dewlap*

A pair of lateral "wings" enables this small, slender lizard to glide from one tree to another. Its coloration may be various shades of gray-brown; the wings are patterned orange and black. The small dewlap under the chin is yellow in the male (shown here) and blue in the female.
• OCCURRENCE S.E. Asia. In rainforest.
• REPRODUCTION Lays 2–5 eggs.
• SIMILAR SPECIES Thai Flying Dragon (*Draco taeniopterus*).

slender tail •

ASIA

| Length 6–8in (15–20cm) | Diet 🐜 | Activity ☀ |

| Family AGAMIDAE | Species *Hydrosaurus pustulatus* | Status Common |

PHILIPPINE SAILFIN LIZARD

• *large eyes*

tail supported on raised vertebral projections •

PHILIPPINES

This uniform gray lizard is noted for its large, raised, saillike tail (this "sailfin" is larger and higher in adults than in juveniles, shown here). A row of enlarged spines is also present down the center of the back.
• OCCURRENCE Philippines. In forest, along rivers and streams.
• REPRODUCTION Lays eggs (clutch size unknown).
• SIMILAR SPECIES Common Sailfin Lizard (*Hydrosaurus amboinensis*).

| Length 2½–3ft (0.8–1m) | Diet 🐜 🌿 | Activity ☀ |

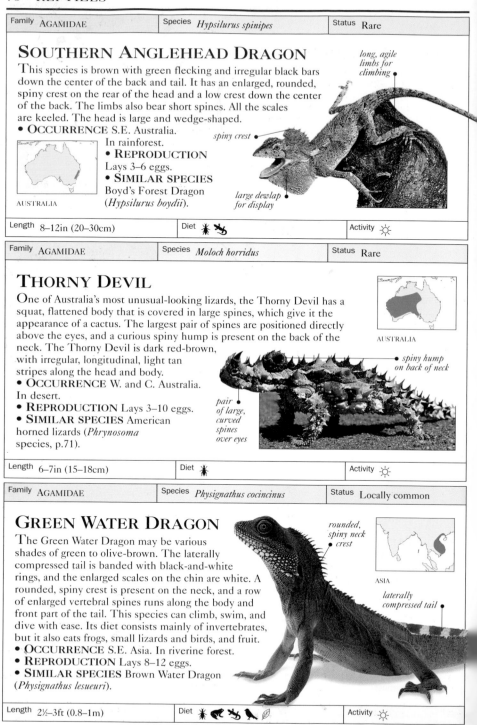

Family AGAMIDAE	Species *Hypsilurus spinipes*	Status Rare

SOUTHERN ANGLEHEAD DRAGON

This species is brown with green flecking and irregular black bars down the center of the back and tail. It has an enlarged, rounded, spiny crest on the rear of the head and a low crest down the center of the back. The limbs also bear short spines. All the scales are keeled. The head is large and wedge-shaped.

- **OCCURRENCE** S.E. Australia. In rainforest.
- **REPRODUCTION** Lays 3–6 eggs.
- **SIMILAR SPECIES** Boyd's Forest Dragon (*Hypsilurus boydii*).

AUSTRALIA

long, agile limbs for climbing

spiny crest

large dewlap for display

Length 8–12in (20–30cm)	Diet	Activity ☼

Family AGAMIDAE	Species *Moloch horridus*	Status Rare

THORNY DEVIL

One of Australia's most unusual-looking lizards, the Thorny Devil has a squat, flattened body that is covered in large spines, which give it the appearance of a cactus. The largest pair of spines are positioned directly above the eyes, and a curious spiny hump is present on the back of the neck. The Thorny Devil is dark red-brown, with irregular, longitudinal, light tan stripes along the head and body.

- **OCCURRENCE** W. and C. Australia. In desert.
- **REPRODUCTION** Lays 3–10 eggs.
- **SIMILAR SPECIES** American horned lizards (*Phrynosoma* species, p.71).

AUSTRALIA

spiny hump on back of neck

pair of large, curved spines over eyes

Length 6–7in (15–18cm)	Diet	Activity ☼

Family AGAMIDAE	Species *Physignathus cocincinus*	Status Locally common

GREEN WATER DRAGON

The Green Water Dragon may be various shades of green to olive-brown. The laterally compressed tail is banded with black-and-white rings, and the enlarged scales on the chin are white. A rounded, spiny crest is present on the neck, and a row of enlarged vertebral spines runs along the body and front part of the tail. This species can climb, swim, and dive with ease. Its diet consists mainly of invertebrates, but it also eats frogs, small lizards and birds, and fruit.

- **OCCURRENCE** S.E. Asia. In riverine forest.
- **REPRODUCTION** Lays 8–12 eggs.
- **SIMILAR SPECIES** Brown Water Dragon (*Physignathus lesueuri*).

rounded, spiny neck crest

ASIA

laterally compressed tail

Length 2½–3ft (0.8–1m)	Diet	Activity ☼

Family AGAMIDAE	Species *Pogona vitticeps*	Status Common

CENTRAL BEARDED DRAGON

The Central Bearded Dragon is a relatively flat lizard and may be any color from yellow to tan to red-brown, with faint darker markings. The back and nape of the neck are covered in spiny scales. When threatened, this lizard displays by opening its mouth and puffing out the spiny throat beard after which it is named. This bearded dragon is distinguished from other *Pogona* species by the presence of a single, regular row of enlarged conical spines along the side of the body (between the limbs) and a fringe of enlarged spiny scales across the center of the throat. Common in dry habitats, the Central Bearded Dragon is frequently observed perched on fence posts or dead tree trunks, or foraging for insects in the bark.

AUSTRALIA

• **OCCURRENCE**
E. central Australia. In dry forest and desert.
• **REPRODUCTION**
Lays 11–16 eggs.
• **SIMILAR SPECIES** Eastern Bearded Dragon (*Pogona barbata*).

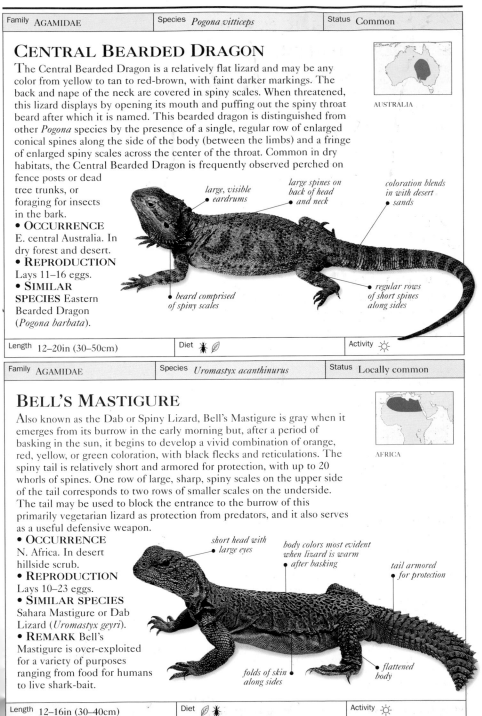

large, visible eardrums

large spines on back of head and neck

coloration blends in with desert sands

beard comprised of spiny scales

regular rows of short spines along sides

Length 12–20in (30–50cm)	Diet 🦗 🌿	Activity ☼

Family AGAMIDAE	Species *Uromastyx acanthinurus*	Status Locally common

BELL'S MASTIGURE

Also known as the Dab or Spiny Lizard, Bell's Mastigure is gray when it emerges from its burrow in the early morning but, after a period of basking in the sun, it begins to develop a vivid combination of orange, red, yellow, or green coloration, with black flecks and reticulations. The spiny tail is relatively short and armored for protection, with up to 20 whorls of spines. One row of large, sharp, spiny scales on the upper side of the tail corresponds to two rows of smaller scales on the underside. The tail may be used to block the entrance to the burrow of this primarily vegetarian lizard as protection from predators, and it also serves as a useful defensive weapon.

AFRICA

• **OCCURRENCE**
N. Africa. In desert hillside scrub.
• **REPRODUCTION**
Lays 10–23 eggs.
• **SIMILAR SPECIES**
Sahara Mastigure or Dab Lizard (*Uromastyx geyri*).
• **REMARK** Bell's Mastigure is over-exploited for a variety of purposes ranging from food for humans to live shark-bait.

short head with large eyes

body colors most evident when lizard is warm after basking

tail armored for protection

folds of skin along sides

flattened body

Length 12–16in (30–40cm)	Diet 🌿 🦗	Activity ☼

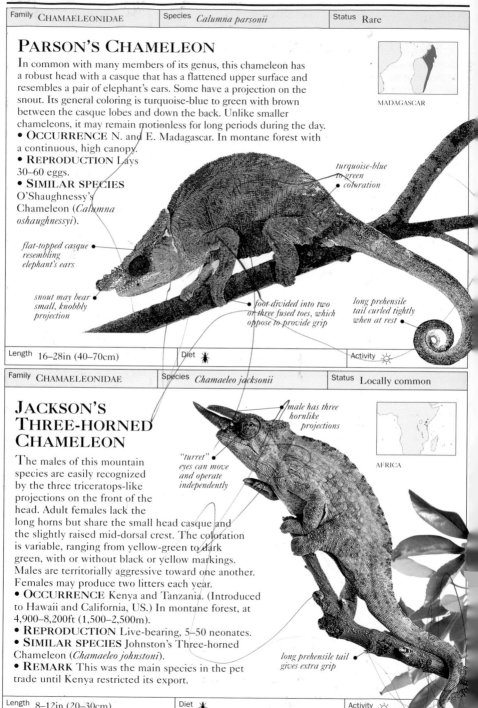

| Family CHAMAELEONIDAE | Species *Calumna parsonii* | Status Rare |

PARSON'S CHAMELEON

In common with many members of its genus, this chameleon has a robust head with a casque that has a flattened upper surface and resembles a pair of elephant's ears. Some have a projection on the snout. Its general coloring is turquoise-blue to green with brown between the casque lobes and down the back. Unlike smaller chameleons, it may remain motionless for long periods during the day.
• OCCURRENCE N. and E. Madagascar. In montane forest with a continuous, high canopy.
• REPRODUCTION Lays 30–60 eggs.
• SIMILAR SPECIES O'Shaughnessy's Chameleon (*Calumna oshaughnessyi*).

MADAGASCAR

turquoise-blue to green coloration

flat-topped casque resembling elephant's ears

snout may bear small, knobbly projection

foot divided into two or three fused toes, which oppose to provide grip

long prehensile tail curled tightly when at rest

| Length 16–28in (40–70cm) | Diet 🐜 | Activity ☀ |

| Family CHAMAELEONIDAE | Species *Chamaeleo jacksonii* | Status Locally common |

JACKSON'S THREE-HORNED CHAMELEON

The males of this mountain species are easily recognized by the three triceratops-like projections on the front of the head. Adult females lack the long horns but share the small head casque and the slightly raised mid-dorsal crest. The coloration is variable, ranging from yellow-green to dark green, with or without black or yellow markings. Males are territorially aggressive toward one another. Females may produce two litters each year.
• OCCURRENCE Kenya and Tanzania. (Introduced to Hawaii and California, US.) In montane forest, at 4,900–8,200ft (1,500–2,500m).
• REPRODUCTION Live-bearing, 5–50 neonates.
• SIMILAR SPECIES Johnston's Three-horned Chameleon (*Chamaeleo johnstoni*).
• REMARK This was the main species in the pet trade until Kenya restricted its export.

male has three hornlike projections

AFRICA

"turret" eyes can move and operate independently

long prehensile tail gives extra grip

| Length 8–12in (20–30cm) | Diet 🐜 | Activity ☀ |

Family CHAMAELEONIDAE	Species *Chamaeleo calyptratus*	Status Locally common

YEMENI VEILED CHAMELEON

Easily recognized by its high cranial casque – a peculiarity of
Arabian chameleons – the Yemeni Veiled Chameleon inhabits the
surprisingly humid coastal lowlands, mountain slopes, and high
plateaus of the southwestern corner of the Arabian
Peninsula. It has been suggested that the
helmetlike casque and accompanying forward-
folding occipital flaps may collect early
morning dew and funnel it toward the
jaws. It is possible, too, that the
casque, with its extensive
supply of blood vessels,
may act as a cooling
device – an invaluable
feature in a hot climate.
Many chameleons are
laterally compressed, but
this species is more
compressed than most, being
shaped almost like a large leaf. Its
coloration is variable, with broad
yellow and green bands above,
and blue-green and yellow
bands below. Two subspecies
are recognized. The casques
of males from the northern subspecies
(*Chamaeleo calyptratus calcarifer*) are
lower than those of the southern race
(*C. calyptratus calyptratus*), shown here.
In both cases, females have substantially
lower casques than males.
• OCCURRENCE Yemen and S.W.
Saudi Arabia. On mountain slopes and
coastal lowlands.
• REPRODUCTION Lays 27–80 eggs.

MIDDLE EAST

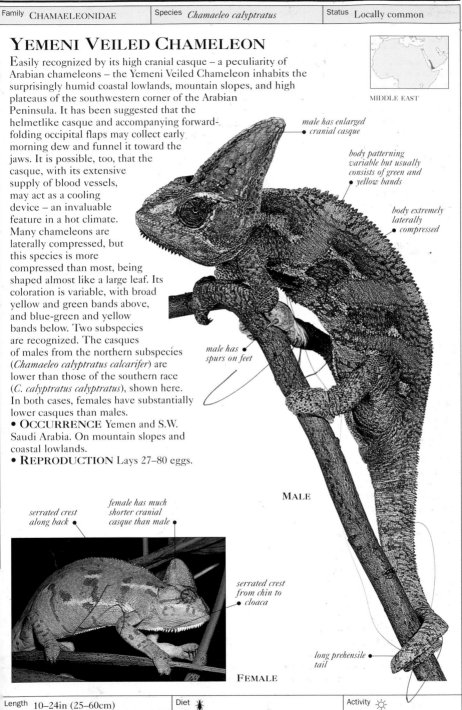

male has enlarged
cranial casque

body patterning
variable but usually
consists of green and
yellow bands

body extremely
laterally
compressed

male has
spurs on feet

MALE

serrated crest
along back

female has much
shorter cranial
casque than male

serrated crest
from chin to
cloaca

long prehensile
tail

FEMALE

Length 10–24in (25–60cm)	Diet 🐜	Activity ☼

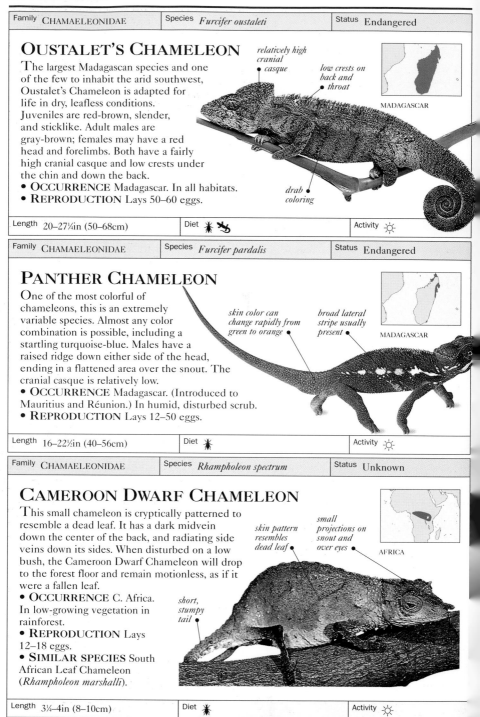

Family CHAMAELEONIDAE	Species *Furcifer oustaleti*	Status Endangered

OUSTALET'S CHAMELEON

The largest Madagascan species and one of the few to inhabit the arid southwest, Oustalet's Chameleon is adapted for life in dry, leafless conditions. Juveniles are red-brown, slender, and sticklike. Adult males are gray-brown; females may have a red head and forelimbs. Both have a fairly high cranial casque and low crests under the chin and down the back.

- OCCURRENCE Madagascar. In all habitats.
- REPRODUCTION Lays 50–60 eggs.

relatively high cranial casque

low crests on back and throat

MADAGASCAR

drab coloring

Length 20–27¼in (50–68cm)	Diet 🦗 🐛	Activity ☀

Family CHAMAELEONIDAE	Species *Furcifer pardalis*	Status Endangered

PANTHER CHAMELEON

One of the most colorful of chameleons, this is an extremely variable species. Almost any color combination is possible, including a startling turquoise-blue. Males have a raised ridge down either side of the head, ending in a flattened area over the snout. The cranial casque is relatively low.

- OCCURRENCE Madagascar. (Introduced to Mauritius and Réunion.) In humid, disturbed scrub.
- REPRODUCTION Lays 12–50 eggs.

skin color can change rapidly from green to orange

broad lateral stripe usually present

MADAGASCAR

Length 16–22½in (40–56cm)	Diet 🦗	Activity ☀

Family CHAMAELEONIDAE	Species *Rhampholeon spectrum*	Status Unknown

CAMEROON DWARF CHAMELEON

This small chameleon is cryptically patterned to resemble a dead leaf. It has a dark midvein down the center of the back, and radiating side veins down its sides. When disturbed on a low bush, the Cameroon Dwarf Chameleon will drop to the forest floor and remain motionless, as if it were a fallen leaf.

- OCCURRENCE C. Africa. In low-growing vegetation in rainforest.
- REPRODUCTION Lays 12–18 eggs.
- SIMILAR SPECIES South African Leaf Chameleon (*Rhampholeon marshalli*).

skin pattern resembles dead leaf

small projections on snout and over eyes

AFRICA

short, stumpy tail

Length 3¼–4in (8–10cm)	Diet 🦗	Activity ☀

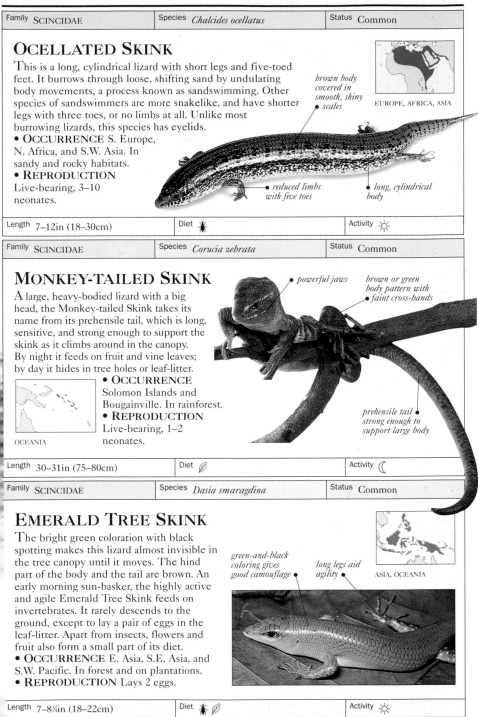

| Family SCINCIDAE | Species *Chalcides ocellatus* | Status Common |

OCELLATED SKINK

This is a long, cylindrical lizard with short legs and five-toed feet. It burrows through loose, shifting sand by undulating body movements, a process known as sandswimming. Other species of sandswimmers are more snakelike, and have shorter legs with three toes, or no limbs at all. Unlike most burrowing lizards, this species has eyelids.
• OCCURRENCE S. Europe, N. Africa, and S.W. Asia. In sandy and rocky habitats.
• REPRODUCTION Live-bearing, 3–10 neonates.

brown body covered in smooth, shiny scales

EUROPE, AFRICA, ASIA

reduced limbs with five toes

long, cylindrical body

| Length 7–12in (18–30cm) | Diet 🐜 | Activity ☼ |

| Family SCINCIDAE | Species *Corucia zebrata* | Status Common |

MONKEY-TAILED SKINK

A large, heavy-bodied lizard with a big head, the Monkey-tailed Skink takes its name from its prehensile tail, which is long, sensitive, and strong enough to support the skink as it climbs around in the canopy. By night it feeds on fruit and vine leaves; by day it hides in tree holes or leaf-litter.
• OCCURRENCE Solomon Islands and Bougainville. In rainforest.
• REPRODUCTION Live-bearing, 1–2 neonates.

OCEANIA

powerful jaws

brown or green body pattern with faint cross-bands

prehensile tail strong enough to support large body

| Length 30–31in (75–80cm) | Diet 🌿 | Activity ☾ |

| Family SCINCIDAE | Species *Dasia smaragdina* | Status Common |

EMERALD TREE SKINK

The bright green coloration with black spotting makes this lizard almost invisible in the tree canopy until it moves. The hind part of the body and the tail are brown. An early morning sun-basker, the highly active and agile Emerald Tree Skink feeds on invertebrates. It rarely descends to the ground, except to lay a pair of eggs in the leaf-litter. Apart from insects, flowers and fruit also form a small part of its diet.
• OCCURRENCE E. Asia, S.E. Asia, and S.W. Pacific. In forest and on plantations.
• REPRODUCTION Lays 2 eggs.

green-and-black coloring gives good camouflage

long legs aid agility

ASIA, OCEANIA

| Length 7–8¾in (18–22cm) | Diet 🐜 🌿 | Activity ☼ |

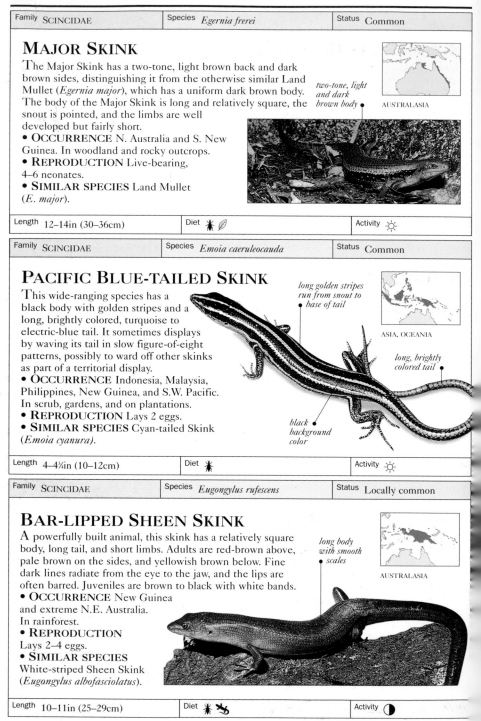

Family SCINCIDAE	Species *Egernia frerei*	Status Common

MAJOR SKINK

The Major Skink has a two-tone, light brown back and dark brown sides, distinguishing it from the otherwise similar Land Mullet (*Egernia major*), which has a uniform dark brown body. The body of the Major Skink is long and relatively square, the snout is pointed, and the limbs are well developed but fairly short.

two-tone, light and dark brown body

AUSTRALASIA

• OCCURRENCE N. Australia and S. New Guinea. In woodland and rocky outcrops.
• REPRODUCTION Live-bearing, 4–6 neonates.
• SIMILAR SPECIES Land Mullet (*E. major*).

Length 12–14in (30–36cm)	Diet 🐜 🌿	Activity ☼

Family SCINCIDAE	Species *Emoia caeruleocauda*	Status Common

PACIFIC BLUE-TAILED SKINK

This wide-ranging species has a black body with golden stripes and a long, brightly colored, turquoise to electric-blue tail. It sometimes displays by waving its tail in slow figure-of-eight patterns, possibly to ward off other skinks as part of a territorial display.

long golden stripes run from snout to base of tail

ASIA, OCEANIA

long, brightly colored tail

• OCCURRENCE Indonesia, Malaysia, Philippines, New Guinea, and S.W. Pacific. In scrub, gardens, and on plantations.
• REPRODUCTION Lays 2 eggs.
• SIMILAR SPECIES Cyan-tailed Skink (*Emoia cyanura*).

black background color

Length 4–4¾in (10–12cm)	Diet 🐜	Activity ☼

Family SCINCIDAE	Species *Eugongylus rufescens*	Status Locally common

BAR-LIPPED SHEEN SKINK

A powerfully built animal, this skink has a relatively square body, long tail, and short limbs. Adults are red-brown above, pale brown on the sides, and yellowish brown below. Fine dark lines radiate from the eye to the jaw, and the lips are often barred. Juveniles are brown to black with white bands.

long body with smooth scales

AUSTRALASIA

• OCCURRENCE New Guinea and extreme N.E. Australia. In rainforest.
• REPRODUCTION Lays 2–4 eggs.
• SIMILAR SPECIES White-striped Sheen Skink (*Eugongylus albofasciolatus*).

Length 10–11in (25–29cm)	Diet 🐜 🐛	Activity ◑

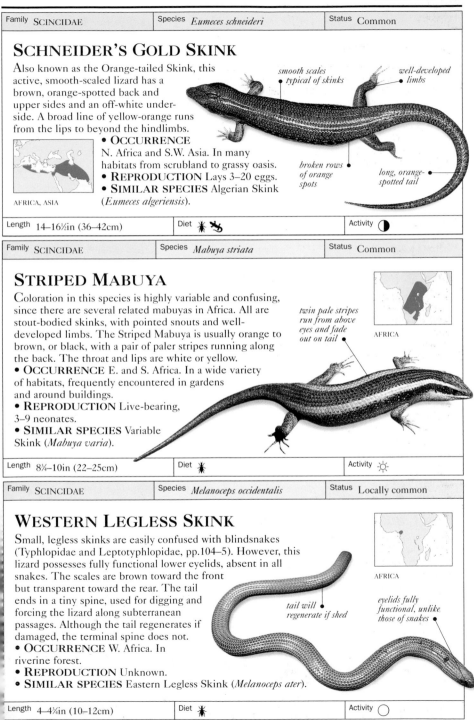

Family SCINCIDAE	Species *Eumeces schneideri*	Status Common

SCHNEIDER'S GOLD SKINK

Also known as the Orange-tailed Skink, this active, smooth-scaled lizard has a brown, orange-spotted back and upper sides and an off-white underside. A broad line of yellow-orange runs from the lips to beyond the hindlimbs.
• **OCCURRENCE** N. Africa and S.W. Asia. In many habitats from scrubland to grassy oasis.
• **REPRODUCTION** Lays 3–20 eggs.
• **SIMILAR SPECIES** Algerian Skink (*Eumeces algeriensis*).

AFRICA, ASIA

smooth scales typical of skinks
well-developed limbs
broken rows of orange spots
long, orange-spotted tail

Length 14–16½in (36–42cm)	Diet 🐜 🪱	Activity ◐

Family SCINCIDAE	Species *Mabuya striata*	Status Common

STRIPED MABUYA

Coloration in this species is highly variable and confusing, since there are several related mabuyas in Africa. All are stout-bodied skinks, with pointed snouts and well-developed limbs. The Striped Mabuya is usually orange to brown, or black, with a pair of paler stripes running along the back. The throat and lips are white or yellow.
• **OCCURRENCE** E. and S. Africa. In a wide variety of habitats, frequently encountered in gardens and around buildings.
• **REPRODUCTION** Live-bearing, 3–9 neonates.
• **SIMILAR SPECIES** Variable Skink (*Mabuya varia*).

twin pale stripes run from above eyes and fade out on tail
AFRICA

Length 8¾–10in (22–25cm)	Diet 🐜	Activity ☼

Family SCINCIDAE	Species *Melanoceps occidentalis*	Status Locally common

WESTERN LEGLESS SKINK

Small, legless skinks are easily confused with blindsnakes (Typhlopidae and Leptotyphlopidae, pp.104–5). However, this lizard possesses fully functional lower eyelids, absent in all snakes. The scales are brown toward the front but transparent toward the rear. The tail ends in a tiny spine, used for digging and forcing the lizard along subterranean passages. Although the tail regenerates if damaged, the terminal spine does not.
• **OCCURRENCE** W. Africa. In riverine forest.
• **REPRODUCTION** Unknown.
• **SIMILAR SPECIES** Eastern Legless Skink (*Melanoceps ater*).

AFRICA

tail will regenerate if shed
eyelids fully functional, unlike those of snakes

Length 4–4¾in (10–12cm)	Diet 🐜	Activity ○

Family SCINCIDAE	Species *Panaspis reichenowi*	Status Locally common

REICHENOW'S SNAKE-EYED SKINK

This slender skink is brown, patterned with darker brown and yellow, with a dark stripe runs along the sides and the underside is gray or yellow. Unlike many west African skinks, this species has transparent "spectacles" instead of movable eyelids.
• **OCCURRENCE** Cameroon, Gabon, and Fernando Po, Equatorial Guinea. In rainforest.
• **REPRODUCTION** Lays eggs (clutch size unknown).
• **SIMILAR SPECIES** Rohde's Snake-eyed Skink (*Panaspis rohdei*).

AFRICA

pointed head

dark stripe on each side

• slender, brown-and-yellow body

• long legs for running

Length 4–6in (10–15cm)	Diet 🐜	Activity ☀

Family SCINCIDAE	Species *Prasinohaema semoni*	Status Rare

GREEN-BLOODED SKINK

Cream to white below and on the sides, this arboreal skink has a cream-brown back with alternating mid- and dark brown bars across it. The body is slender, the limbs long and well developed, and the prehensile tail is used for climbing. This species and its close relatives are the only known terrestrial, green-blooded vertebrates.
• **OCCURRENCE** S. New Guinea. In forest and on coconut plantations.
• **REPRODUCTION** Lays eggs (clutch size unknown).
• **SIMILAR SPECIES** *Prasinohaema flavipes* (Green-blooded Skink).

cream body with • brown cross-bars

prehensile tail with glandular tip •   NEW GUINEA

Length 4–6in (10–15cm)	Diet 🐜	Activity ☀

Family SCINCIDAE	Species *Riopa fernandi*	Status Rare

FERNANDO PO FIRE SKINK

One of the most attractive skinks in Africa, this species is named after an island off the west coast. It is a stout, square-bodied lizard with red-and-black sides speckled with white, and a broad brown back and head. The limbs are black and reduced in size. This skink inhabits rainforest, living in burrows beneath tree buttresses. Rarely seen in the open, it will defend itself by biting if molested. In parts of Cameroon it is thought to be poisonous to the touch.
• **OCCURRENCE** W. Africa. In rainforest and on plantations.
• **REPRODUCTION** Lays eggs (clutch size unknown).

robust, squarish • body

AFRICA   vivid red markings • on sides

Length 8–14in (20–36cm)	Diet 🐜	Activity ☾ ◐

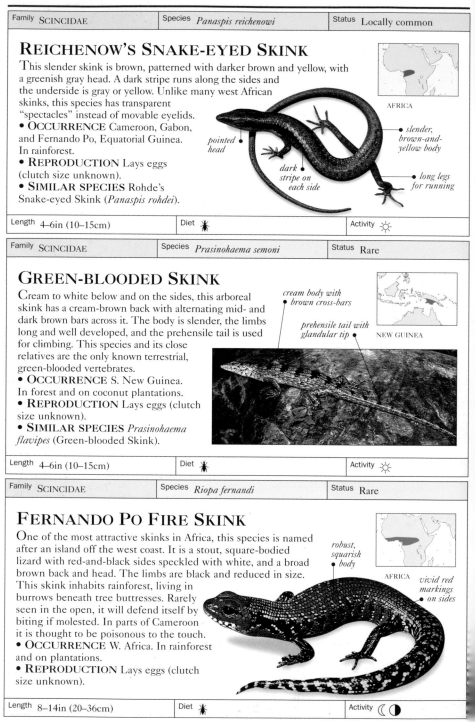

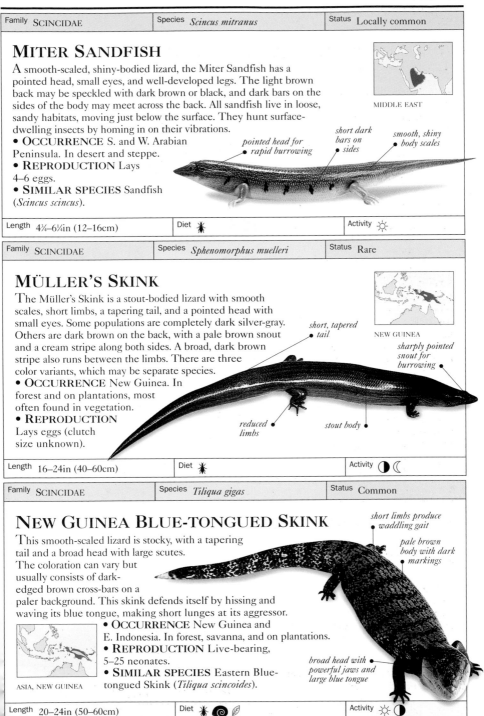

Family SCINCIDAE	Species *Scincus mitranus*	Status Locally common

MITER SANDFISH

A smooth-scaled, shiny-bodied lizard, the Miter Sandfish has a
pointed head, small eyes, and well-developed legs. The light brown
back may be speckled with dark brown or black, and dark bars on the
sides of the body may meet across the back. All sandfish live in loose,
sandy habitats, moving just below the surface. They hunt surface-
dwelling insects by homing in on their vibrations.

MIDDLE EAST

• OCCURRENCE S. and W. Arabian
Peninsula. In desert and steppe.
• REPRODUCTION Lays
4–6 eggs.
• SIMILAR SPECIES Sandfish
(*Scincus scincus*).

pointed head for rapid burrowing

short dark bars on sides

smooth, shiny body scales

Length 4¾–6¼in (12–16cm)	Diet 🐜	Activity ☼

Family SCINCIDAE	Species *Sphenomorphus muelleri*	Status Rare

MÜLLER'S SKINK

The Müller's Skink is a stout-bodied lizard with smooth
scales, short limbs, a tapering tail, and a pointed head with
small eyes. Some populations are completely dark silver-gray.
Others are dark brown on the back, with a pale brown snout
and a cream stripe along both sides. A broad, dark brown
stripe also runs between the limbs. There are three
color variants, which may be separate species.

short, tapered tail

NEW GUINEA

sharply pointed snout for burrowing

• OCCURRENCE New Guinea. In
forest and on plantations, most
often found in vegetation.
• REPRODUCTION
Lays eggs (clutch
size unknown).

reduced limbs

stout body

Length 16–24in (40–60cm)	Diet 🐜	Activity ◗ ☾

Family SCINCIDAE	Species *Tiliqua gigas*	Status Common

NEW GUINEA BLUE-TONGUED SKINK

This smooth-scaled lizard is stocky, with a tapering
tail and a broad head with large scutes.
The coloration can vary but
usually consists of dark-
edged brown cross-bars on a
paler background. This skink defends itself by hissing and
waving its blue tongue, making short lunges at its aggressor.

short limbs produce waddling gait

pale brown body with dark markings

• OCCURRENCE New Guinea and
E. Indonesia. In forest, savanna, and on plantations.
• REPRODUCTION Live-bearing,
5–25 neonates.
• SIMILAR SPECIES Eastern Blue-
tongued Skink (*Tiliqua scincoides*).

ASIA, NEW GUINEA

broad head with powerful jaws and large blue tongue

Length 20–24in (50–60cm)	Diet 🐜 ◉ 🍃	Activity ☼ ◗

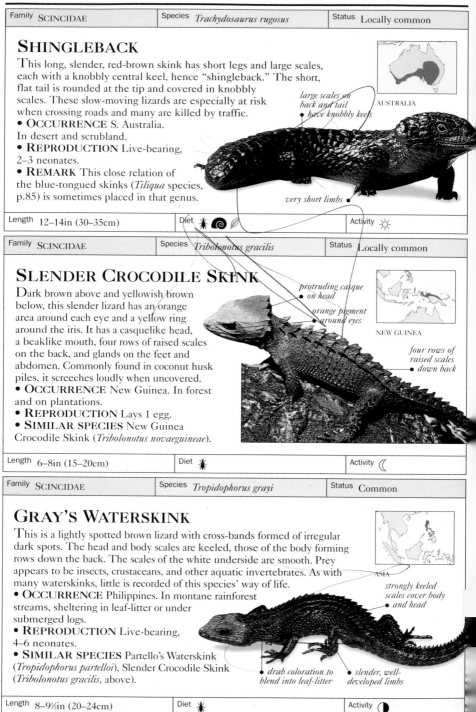

Family SCINCIDAE	Species *Trachydosaurus rugosus*	Status Locally common

SHINGLEBACK

This long, slender, red-brown skink has short legs and large scales, each with a knobbly central keel, hence "shingleback." The short, flat tail is rounded at the tip and covered in knobbly scales. These slow-moving lizards are especially at risk when crossing roads and many are killed by traffic.
• OCCURRENCE S. Australia. In desert and scrubland.
• REPRODUCTION Live-bearing, 2–3 neonates.
• REMARK This close relation of the blue-tongued skinks (*Tiliqua* species, p.85) is sometimes placed in that genus.

large scales on back and tail have knobbly keels

AUSTRALIA

very short limbs

Length 12–14in (30–35cm)	Diet	Activity ☀

Family SCINCIDAE	Species *Tribolonotus gracilis*	Status Locally common

SLENDER CROCODILE SKINK

Dark brown above and yellowish brown below, this slender lizard has an orange area around each eye and a yellow ring around the iris. It has a casquelike head, a beaklike mouth, four rows of raised scales on the back, and glands on the feet and abdomen. Commonly found in coconut husk piles, it screeches loudly when uncovered.
• OCCURRENCE New Guinea. In forest and on plantations.
• REPRODUCTION Lays 1 egg.
• SIMILAR SPECIES New Guinea Crocodile Skink (*Tribolonotus novaeguineae*).

protruding casque on head

orange pigment around eyes

NEW GUINEA

four rows of raised scales down back

Length 6–8in (15–20cm)	Diet	Activity ☾

Family SCINCIDAE	Species *Tropidophorus grayi*	Status Common

GRAY'S WATERSKINK

This is a lightly spotted brown lizard with cross-bands formed of irregular dark spots. The head and body scales are keeled, those of the body forming rows down the back. The scales of the white underside are smooth. Prey appears to be insects, crustaceans, and other aquatic invertebrates. As with many waterskinks, little is recorded of this species' way of life.
• OCCURRENCE Philippines. In montane rainforest streams, sheltering in leaf-litter or under submerged logs.
• REPRODUCTION Live-bearing, 4–6 neonates.
• SIMILAR SPECIES Partello's Waterskink (*Tropidophorus partelloi*), Slender Crocodile Skink (*Tribolonotus gracilis*, above).

ASIA

strongly keeled scales cover body and head

drab coloration to blend into leaf-litter

slender, well-developed limbs

Length 8–9½in (20–24cm)	Diet	Activity ◑

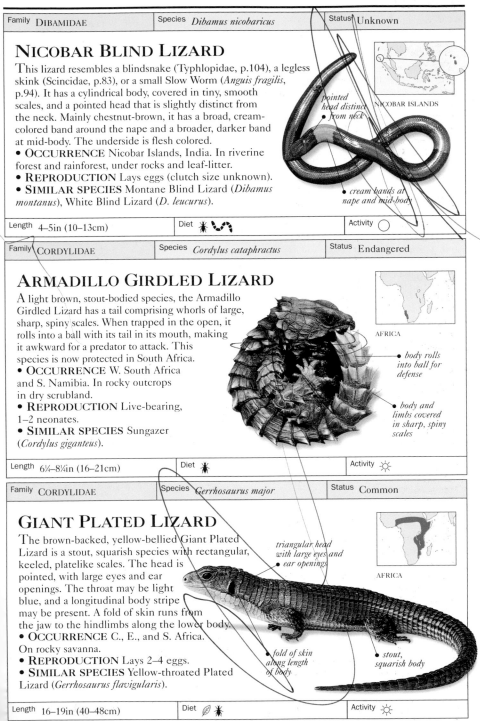

Family DIBAMIDAE	Species *Dibamus nicobaricus*	Status Unknown

NICOBAR BLIND LIZARD

This lizard resembles a blindsnake (Typhlopidae, p.104), a legless
skink (Scincidae, p.83), or a small Slow Worm (*Anguis fragilis*,
p.94). It has a cylindrical body, covered in tiny, smooth
scales, and a pointed head that is slightly distinct from
the neck. Mainly chestnut-brown, it has a broad, cream-
colored band around the nape and a broader, darker band
at mid-body. The underside is flesh colored.
• OCCURRENCE Nicobar Islands, India. In riverine
forest and rainforest, under rocks and leaf-litter.
• REPRODUCTION Lays eggs (clutch size unknown).
• SIMILAR SPECIES Montane Blind Lizard (*Dibamus
montanus*), White Blind Lizard (*D. leucurus*).

pointed
head distinct
from neck

NICOBAR ISLANDS

cream bands at
nape and mid-body

Length 4–5in (10–13cm)	Diet	Activity

Family CORDYLIDAE	Species *Cordylus cataphractus*	Status Endangered

ARMADILLO GIRDLED LIZARD

A light brown, stout-bodied species, the Armadillo
Girdled Lizard has a tail comprising whorls of large,
sharp, spiny scales. When trapped in the open, it
rolls into a ball with its tail in its mouth, making
it awkward for a predator to attack. This
species is now protected in South Africa.
• OCCURRENCE W. South Africa
and S. Namibia. In rocky outcrops
in dry scrubland.
• REPRODUCTION Live-bearing,
1–2 neonates.
• SIMILAR SPECIES Sungazer
(*Cordylus giganteus*).

AFRICA

body rolls
into ball for
defense

body and
limbs covered
in sharp, spiny
scales

Length 6¼–8¼in (16–21cm)	Diet	Activity

Family CORDYLIDAE	Species *Gerrhosaurus major*	Status Common

GIANT PLATED LIZARD

The brown-backed, yellow-bellied Giant Plated
Lizard is a stout, squarish species with rectangular,
keeled, platelike scales. The head is
pointed, with large eyes and ear
openings. The throat may be light
blue, and a longitudinal body stripe
may be present. A fold of skin runs from
the jaw to the hindlimbs along the lower body.
• OCCURRENCE C., E., and S. Africa.
On rocky savanna.
• REPRODUCTION Lays 2–4 eggs.
• SIMILAR SPECIES Yellow-throated Plated
Lizard (*Gerrhosaurus flavigularis*).

triangular head
with large eyes and
ear openings

AFRICA

fold of skin
along length
of body

stout,
squarish body

Length 16–19in (40–48cm)	Diet	Activity

Family LACERTIDAE	Species *Acanthodactylus erythrurus*	Status Common

COMMON FRINGE-TOED LIZARD

The Common Fringe-toed Lizard takes its name from a fringe of scales that runs along the edge of each toe, enabling the lizard to run freely across loose, shifting sand. Adults are brown on the back and black and yellow on the sides, and they have a white underside. A series of lengthwise white stripes or black spots may be present on the back. Juveniles are black with white stripes and a red tail. An alert lizard, this species adopts a characteristic position with the front of its body raised to watch for predators. It is found around the bases of bushes in sandy habitats.
• OCCURRENCE S. Spain, Portugal, and Morocco. In sandy scrubland.
• REPRODUCTION Lays 6–7 eggs.
• SIMILAR SPECIES Leopard Fringe-toed Lizard (*Acanthodactylus pardalis*).

EUROPE, AFRICA

extremely variable patterning on body

pointed head

small fringe of scales on toes for running across sand

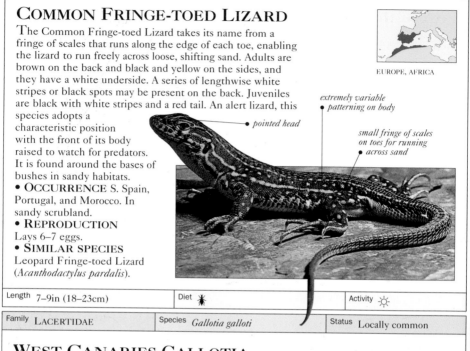

Length 7–9in (18–23cm)	Diet 🐜	Activity ☼

Family LACERTIDAE	Species *Gallotia galloti*	Status Locally common

WEST CANARIES GALLOTIA

Juvenile and female gallotias are dark brown with yellow stripes, which become obscured and replaced by large blue spots in the robustly built adult male (shown here). Gallotias live in arid conditions and feed primarily on vegetation, although they also take large insects. In the absence of snakes these lizards have few natural enemies, but they are in danger from feral cats. Some populations have become threatened.
• OCCURRENCE Canary Islands, off the coast of N.W. Africa. In rocky scrubland.
• REPRODUCTION Lays 2–7 eggs.
• SIMILAR SPECIES East Canaries Gallotia (*Gallotia atlantica*).
• REMARK Every large island in the Canaries is home to one or more species of *Gallotia*.

dark brown coloration of tail and body

long tail can be shed as means of escape

long, powerful legs for running and climbing

blue spots on throat in male

CANARY ISLANDS

Length 12–16in (30–40cm)	Diet 🌿 🐜	Activity ☼

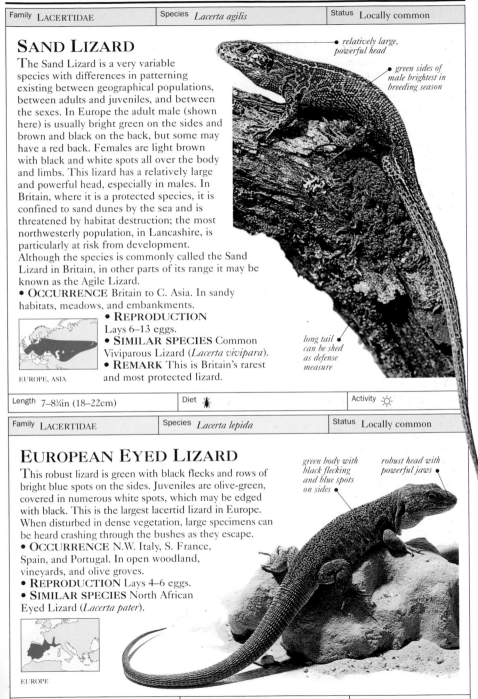

Family LACERTIDAE	Species *Lacerta agilis*	Status Locally common

SAND LIZARD

The Sand Lizard is a very variable
species with differences in patterning
existing between geographical populations,
between adults and juveniles, and between
the sexes. In Europe the adult male (shown
here) is usually bright green on the sides and
brown and black on the back, but some may
have a red back. Females are light brown
with black and white spots all over the body
and limbs. This lizard has a relatively large
and powerful head, especially in males. In
Britain, where it is a protected species, it is
confined to sand dunes by the sea and is
threatened by habitat destruction; the most
northwesterly population, in Lancashire, is
particularly at risk from development.
Although the species is commonly called the Sand
Lizard in Britain, in other parts of its range it may be
known as the Agile Lizard.
• OCCURRENCE Britain to C. Asia. In sandy
habitats, meadows, and embankments.
• REPRODUCTION
Lays 6–13 eggs.
• SIMILAR SPECIES Common
Viviparous Lizard (*Lacerta vivipara*).
• REMARK This is Britain's rarest
and most protected lizard.

EUROPE, ASIA

*relatively large,
powerful head*

*green sides of
male brightest in
breeding season*

*long tail
can be shed
as defense
measure*

Length 7–8¾in (18–22cm)	Diet 🐜	Activity ☼

Family LACERTIDAE	Species *Lacerta lepida*	Status Locally common

EUROPEAN EYED LIZARD

This robust lizard is green with black flecks and rows of
bright blue spots on the sides. Juveniles are olive-green,
covered in numerous white spots, which may be edged
with black. This is the largest lacertid lizard in Europe.
When disturbed in dense vegetation, large specimens can
be heard crashing through the bushes as they escape.
• OCCURRENCE N.W. Italy, S. France,
Spain, and Portugal. In open woodland,
vineyards, and olive groves.
• REPRODUCTION Lays 4–6 eggs.
• SIMILAR SPECIES North African
Eyed Lizard (*Lacerta pater*).

EUROPE

*green body with
black flecking
and blue spots
on sides*

*robust head with
powerful jaws*

Length 24–31in (60–80cm)	Diet 🐜 🐛 🦎 ●	Activity ☼

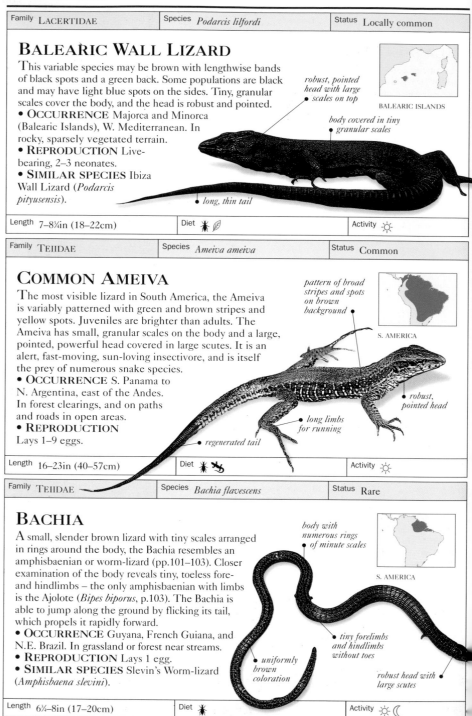

| Family LACERTIDAE | Species *Podarcis lilfordi* | Status Locally common |

BALEARIC WALL LIZARD

This variable species may be brown with lengthwise bands of black spots and a green back. Some populations are black and may have light blue spots on the sides. Tiny, granular scales cover the body, and the head is robust and pointed.
• **OCCURRENCE** Majorca and Minorca (Balearic Islands), W. Mediterranean. In rocky, sparsely vegetated terrain.
• **REPRODUCTION** Live-bearing, 2–3 neonates.
• **SIMILAR SPECIES** Ibiza Wall Lizard (*Podarcis pityusensis*).

robust, pointed head with large scales on top

BALEARIC ISLANDS

body covered in tiny granular scales

long, thin tail

| Length 7–8¾in (18–22cm) | Diet ✴ 🍃 | Activity ☀ |

| Family TEIIDAE | Species *Ameiva ameiva* | Status Common |

COMMON AMEIVA

The most visible lizard in South America, the Ameiva is variably patterned with green and brown stripes and yellow spots. Juveniles are brighter than adults. The Ameiva has small, granular scales on the body and a large, pointed, powerful head covered in large scutes. It is an alert, fast-moving, sun-loving insectivore, and is itself the prey of numerous snake species.
• **OCCURRENCE** S. Panama to N. Argentina, east of the Andes. In forest clearings, and on paths and roads in open areas.
• **REPRODUCTION** Lays 1–9 eggs.

pattern of broad stripes and spots on brown background

S. AMERICA

robust, pointed head

long limbs for running

regenerated tail

| Length 16–23in (40–57cm) | Diet ✴ 🦗 | Activity ☀ |

| Family TEIIDAE | Species *Bachia flavescens* | Status Rare |

BACHIA

A small, slender brown lizard with tiny scales arranged in rings around the body, the Bachia resembles an amphisbaenian or worm-lizard (pp.101–103). Closer examination of the body reveals tiny, toeless fore- and hindlimbs – the only amphisbaenian with limbs is the Ajolote (*Bipes biporus*, p.103). The Bachia is able to jump along the ground by flicking its tail, which propels it rapidly forward.
• **OCCURRENCE** Guyana, French Guiana, and N.E. Brazil. In grassland or forest near streams.
• **REPRODUCTION** Lays 1 egg.
• **SIMILAR SPECIES** Slevin's Worm-lizard (*Amphisbaena slevini*).

body with numerous rings of minute scales

S. AMERICA

tiny forelimbs and hindlimbs without toes

uniformly brown coloration

robust head with large scutes

| Length 6¾–8in (17–20cm) | Diet ✴ | Activity ☀ ☾ |

Family TEIIDAE	Species *Cnemidophorus gramivagus*	Status Locally common

LLANOS WHIPTAIL

As a juvenile, this species is green to brown with four fine white to yellow stripes down the back. Adults may develop a broad, dark central stripe and large white or yellow-green spots on the sides. This is a fast-moving savanna lizard, permanently alert for predators that include snakes, larger lizards, and birds.

• **OCCURRENCE** Colombia and Venezuela. On open, grassy plains (llanos).

• **REPRODUCTION** Lays 1–5 eggs.

• **SIMILAR SPECIES** Ribboned Whiptail (*Cnemidophorus lemniscatus*).

S. AMERICA

brown body with fine stripes and spots

strong limbs for running

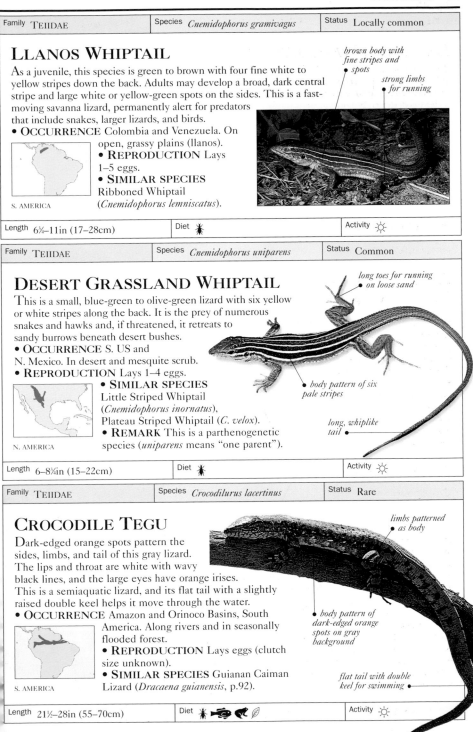

Length 6¾–11in (17–28cm)	Diet 🐜	Activity ☼

Family TEIIDAE	Species *Cnemidophorus uniparens*	Status Common

DESERT GRASSLAND WHIPTAIL

This is a small, blue-green to olive-green lizard with six yellow or white stripes along the back. It is the prey of numerous snakes and hawks and, if threatened, it retreats to sandy burrows beneath desert bushes.

• **OCCURRENCE** S. US and N. Mexico. In desert and mesquite scrub.

• **REPRODUCTION** Lays 1–4 eggs.

• **SIMILAR SPECIES** Little Striped Whiptail (*Cnemidophorus inornatus*), Plateau Striped Whiptail (*C. velox*).

• **REMARK** This is a parthenogenetic species (*uniparens* means "one parent").

N. AMERICA

long toes for running on loose sand

body pattern of six pale stripes

long, whiplike tail

Length 6–8¾in (15–22cm)	Diet 🐜	Activity ☼

Family TEIIDAE	Species *Crocodilurus lacertinus*	Status Rare

CROCODILE TEGU

Dark-edged orange spots pattern the sides, limbs, and tail of this gray lizard. The lips and throat are white with wavy black lines, and the large eyes have orange irises. This is a semiaquatic lizard, and its flat tail with a slightly raised double keel helps it move through the water.

• **OCCURRENCE** Amazon and Orinoco Basins, South America. Along rivers and in seasonally flooded forest.

• **REPRODUCTION** Lays eggs (clutch size unknown).

• **SIMILAR SPECIES** Guianan Caiman Lizard (*Dracaena guianensis*, p.92).

S. AMERICA

limbs patterned as body

body pattern of dark-edged orange spots on gray background

flat tail with double keel for swimming

Length 21½–28in (55–70cm)	Diet 🐜🐟🐌🍃	Activity ☼

Family TEIIDAE	Species *Dracaena guianensis*	Status Endangered

GUIANAN CAIMAN LIZARD

This powerful lizard has a large, robust head with strong, crushing jaws
and molarlike teeth for feeding on aquatic snails. The tongue expels the
indigestible pieces of shell. The coloration of the Guianan Caiman
Lizard is primarily bright green or brown, with an orange head. Juveniles
are a brighter green than adults. The scales of the neck are raised and
may afford some protection, while many of those on the back and tail
bear strong keels. This lizard resembles a Spectacled Caiman (*Caiman
crocodilus*, p.192), except for its broad, relatively short head, which is
similar to that of the Northern Black Tegu (*Tupinambis teguixin*,
opposite). In the dry season, the Guianan Caiman Lizard is reported
to climb trees in search of invertebrates and eggs.
• OCCURRENCE Amazon Basin, South America. In
swamps, rivers, and flooded forest.
• REPRODUCTION Lays 2 eggs.
• SIMILAR SPECIES Paraguayan
Caiman Lizard (*Dracaena
paraguayensis*).

S. AMERICA

*green or
brown body
coloration*

*broad, short orange
head contains strong,
crushing jaws*

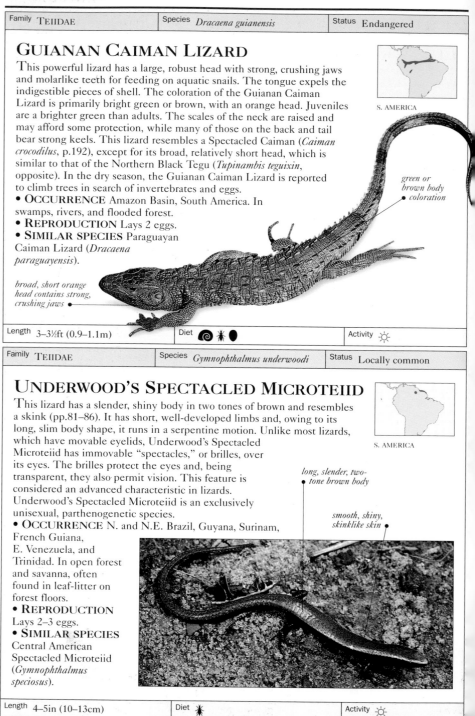

Length 3–3½ft (0.9–1.1m)	Diet 🐌 🐛 ●	Activity ☀

Family TEIIDAE	Species *Gymnophthalmus underwoodi*	Status Locally common

UNDERWOOD'S SPECTACLED MICROTEIID

This lizard has a slender, shiny body in two tones of brown and resembles
a skink (pp.81–86). It has short, well-developed limbs and, owing to its
long, slim body shape, it runs in a serpentine motion. Unlike most lizards,
which have movable eyelids, Underwood's Spectacled
Microteiid has immovable "spectacles," or brilles, over
its eyes. The brilles protect the eyes and, being
transparent, they also permit vision. This feature is
considered an advanced characteristic in lizards.
Underwood's Spectacled Microteiid is an exclusively
unisexual, parthenogenetic species.
• OCCURRENCE N. and N.E. Brazil, Guyana, Surinam,
French Guiana,
E. Venezuela, and
Trinidad. In open forest
and savanna, often
found in leaf-litter on
forest floors.
• REPRODUCTION
Lays 2–3 eggs.
• SIMILAR SPECIES
Central American
Spectacled Microteiid
(*Gymnophthalmus
speciosus*).

S. AMERICA

*long, slender, two-
tone brown body*

*smooth, shiny,
skinklike skin*

Length 4–5in (10–13cm)	Diet 🐛	Activity ☀

Family TEIIDAE	Species *Proctoporus shrevei*	Status Rare

LUMINOUS LIZARD

The Luminous Lizard is uniform olive-brown, with rough, keeled scales, short limbs, and a long, pointed head. Adult males are bright red below and possess a series of dark-edged, white-centered, portholelike spots along the sides. In the 1930s, the British naturalist Ivan Sanderson captured an adult male in a dark, remote cave in the mountains of northern Trinidad and claimed that its white markings glowed brightly for a few moments. His claims were discounted. However, research on a male captured more recently (in 1999) suggests that although it may not actually produce light, it does seem capable of absorbing and reemitting light. Its apparent luminescence may be a form of defense.

TRINIDAD

brown body with
• *rough, keeled scales*

portholelike markings
"glow" in low light
• *conditions*

• OCCURRENCE Aripo Caves, N. Trinidad. In rainforest caves.
• REPRODUCTION Lays 1 egg.
• SIMILAR SPECIES Keeled Microteiid (*Leposoma percarinatum*).

Length 4–5in (10–13cm)	Diet 🐜	Activity ☼

Family TEIIDAE	Species *Tupinambis teguixin*	Status Common

NORTHERN BLACK TEGU

The Northern Black Tegu is a large, terrestrial lizard. Coloration is generally copper-brown, with a series of broad, broken, irregular black or dark brown bars and dark speckling in between. Adult specimens become considerably darker with age. The limbs are long and powerful for running (juveniles can run on their hindlegs alone), and the long, thick tail makes a useful defensive weapon. Like monitor lizards (*Varanus* species, pp.98–100), *Tupinambis* species are large and carnivorous. They are active predators of most organisms, but they also steal the eggs of birds and caimans and feed on carrion.

S. AMERICA

powerful
head on
• *stocky neck*

transverse black
markings •

• OCCURRENCE Amazon and Orinoco Basins, South America. In forest and savanna.
• REPRODUCTION Lays 4–32 eggs.
• SIMILAR SPECIES Teiu (*Tupinambis merianae*).

long, muscular
tail used in
defense •

sturdy, long
• *limbs used for*
running

Length 2½–3ft (0.8–1m)	Diet 🐸🦎⬤🐍🐸🐜🍃	Activity ☼

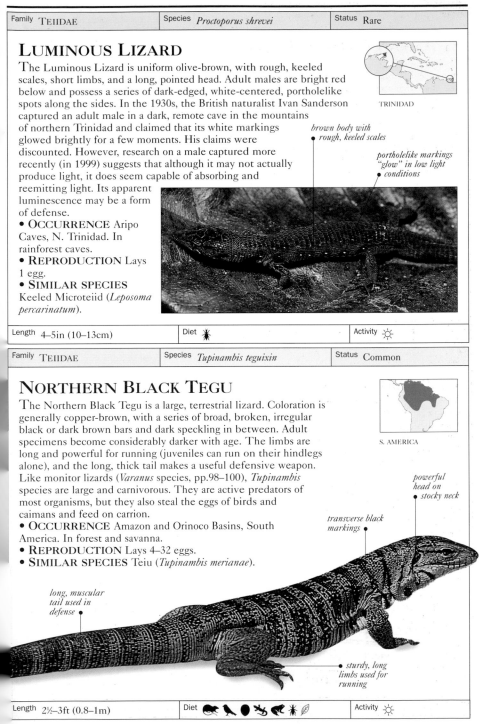

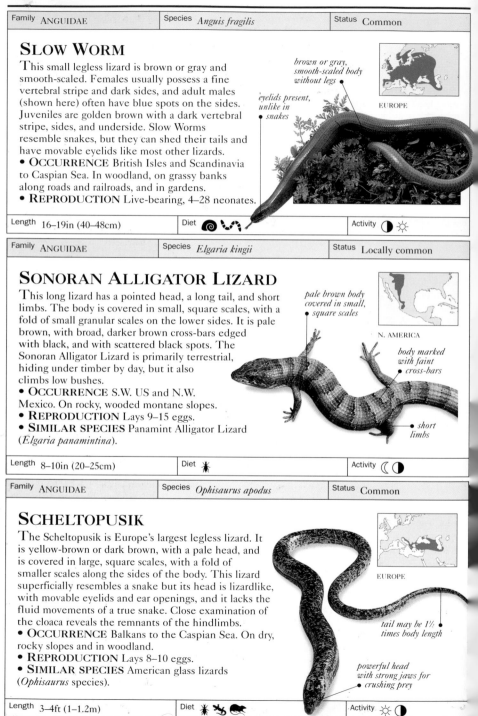

Family ANGUIDAE	Species *Anguis fragilis*	Status Common

SLOW WORM

This small legless lizard is brown or gray and smooth-scaled. Females usually possess a fine vertebral stripe and dark sides, and adult males (shown here) often have blue spots on the sides. Juveniles are golden brown with a dark vertebral stripe, sides, and underside. Slow Worms resemble snakes, but they can shed their tails and have movable eyelids like most other lizards.
• OCCURRENCE British Isles and Scandinavia to Caspian Sea. In woodland, on grassy banks along roads and railroads, and in gardens.
• REPRODUCTION Live-bearing, 4–28 neonates.

brown or gray, smooth-scaled body without legs

eyelids present, unlike in snakes

EUROPE

Length 16–19in (40–48cm)	Diet	Activity

Family ANGUIDAE	Species *Elgaria kingii*	Status Locally common

SONORAN ALLIGATOR LIZARD

This long lizard has a pointed head, a long tail, and short limbs. The body is covered in small, square scales, with a fold of small granular scales on the lower sides. It is pale brown, with broad, darker brown cross-bars edged with black, and with scattered black spots. The Sonoran Alligator Lizard is primarily terrestrial, hiding under timber by day, but it also climbs low bushes.
• OCCURRENCE S.W. US and N.W. Mexico. On rocky, wooded montane slopes.
• REPRODUCTION Lays 9–15 eggs.
• SIMILAR SPECIES Panamint Alligator Lizard (*Elgaria panamintina*).

pale brown body covered in small, square scales

N. AMERICA

body marked with faint cross-bars

short limbs

Length 8–10in (20–25cm)	Diet	Activity

Family ANGUIDAE	Species *Ophisaurus apodus*	Status Common

SCHELTOPUSIK

The Scheltopusik is Europe's largest legless lizard. It is yellow-brown or dark brown, with a pale head, and is covered in large, square scales, with a fold of smaller scales along the sides of the body. This lizard superficially resembles a snake but its head is lizardlike, with movable eyelids and ear openings, and it lacks the fluid movements of a true snake. Close examination of the cloaca reveals the remnants of the hindlimbs.
• OCCURRENCE Balkans to the Caspian Sea. On dry, rocky slopes and in woodland.
• REPRODUCTION Lays 8–10 eggs.
• SIMILAR SPECIES American glass lizards (*Ophisaurus* species).

EUROPE

tail may be 1½ times body length

powerful head with strong jaws for crushing prey

Length 3–4ft (1–1.2m)	Diet	Activity

| Family ANNIELLIDAE | Species *Anniella geroninensis* | Status Rare |

BAJA CALIFORNIA LEGLESS LIZARD

The Baja California Legless Lizard is silver to light brown, with smooth scales and a narrow vertebral stripe. The sides are white with a series of fine black longitudinal stripes. The small head is indistinct from the neck, and the eyelids are movable, as in most lizards; ear openings, usually present in lizards, are absent. These lizards hunt invertebrates just beneath the surface of the sand.
• OCCURRENCE N.W. Baja California, Mexico. In coastal sand dunes and sand flats stabilized by coarse grasses.
• REPRODUCTION Live-bearing, 1–2 neonates.
• SIMILAR SPECIES California Legless Lizard (*Anniella pulchra*), Slow Worm (*Anguis fragilis*, opposite).

N. AMERICA

silver to light brown body

small head with movable eyelids

pointed tail tip helps burrowing

| Length 4–6in (10–15cm) | Diet 🦗 | Activity ☼ ☾ |

| Family XENOSAURIDAE | Species *Shinisaurus crocodilurus* | Status Endangered |

CHINESE CROCODILE LIZARD

The Chinese Crocodile Lizard (juvenile shown here) has a wrinkled skin consisting of many strongly keeled scales. It is red to yellow-brown, with dark brown on the back and a starburst of dark lines radiating from the eye. Although primarily aquatic, this lizard also climbs into low bushes to bask.
• OCCURRENCE Guangxi, S. China. In stony montane forest streams.
• REPRODUCTION Live-bearing, 3–8 neonates.
• SIMILAR SPECIES Borneo Earless Monitor (*Lanthanotus borneensis*, below).

small camouflaged eyes

scales on back more strongly keeled than on sides

ASIA

| Length 16–18in (40–46cm) | Diet 🦗 🐟 🐸 | Activity ☼ ◑ |

| Family LANTHANOTIDAE | Species *Lanthanotus borneensis* | Status Rare |

BORNEO EARLESS MONITOR

The semiburrowing Borneo Earless Monitor is uniform dark brown in color. Several rows of raised, strongly keeled scales run down the back onto the tail, with numerous small granular scales in between. The eyes are small with functional eyelids but, as the name suggests, ear openings are absent.
• OCCURRENCE Sarawak, Borneo. In riverine forest and rainforest.
• REPRODUCTION Lays 6 eggs.

longitudinal rows of strongly keeled scales on back

dark brown, flattened body with short limbs

BORNEO

| Length 16–17½in (40–44cm) | Diet 🦎 ● 🐛 🐟 | Activity ☾ ◑ |

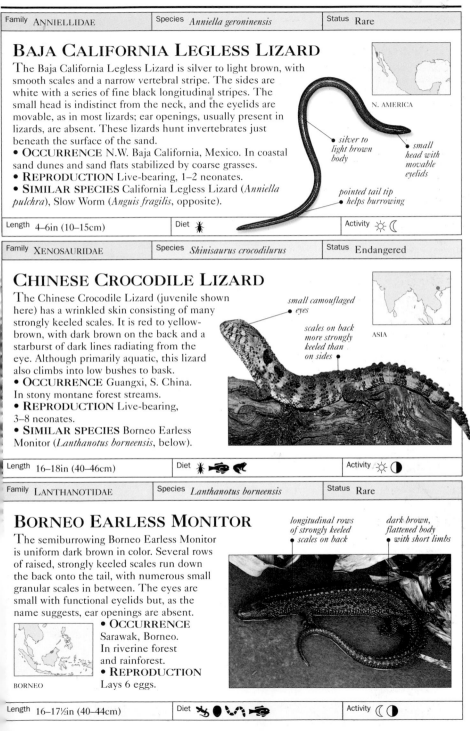

Family HELODERMATIDAE	Species *Heloderma horridum*	Status Rare

BEADED LIZARD ☠

Occurring along the Pacific coast from Guatemala to the northwestern Mexican state of Sonora, the Beaded Lizard is easily recognized, if rarely sighted. It has a stoutly built body, covered in dark brown and yellow, beadlike scales, with a relatively long neck, a rounded, slender head, powerful limbs with sharp-clawed feet, and a long, tapering tail. It is one of only two venomous lizards in the world – the other being the related, desert-living Gila Monster (*Heloderma suspectum*, opposite). The venom apparatus is situated in the lower jaw (in snakes it is in the upper jaw). Unlike snakes, the Beaded Lizard uses its venom primarily for defense. It does not need it for dealing with prey, which is comparatively small and innocuous – the largest consist of infant rodents, fledgling birds, and eggs. A forked tongue enables the lizard to locate its food. Its tenacious, chewing bite is exceedingly painful, and potentially fatal to humans. Beaded Lizards are often diurnal, but they avoid hot weather by remaining underground in their burrows during the day, and becoming nocturnal. They also frequently climb trees. Unpatterned, uniformly black-brown specimens occur in southern Mexico.

N. & C. AMERICA

longer head, neck, and tail than Gila Monster, opposite ●

• OCCURRENCE W. Mexico and Guatemala. In tropical, deciduous woodland and thornscrub.
• REPRODUCTION Lays 8–10 eggs.
• SIMILAR SPECIES Gila Monster (*H. suspectum*, opposite).
• REMARK The Beaded Lizard is known to Mexicans as "Escorpion."

● *body covered in rounded, beadlike scales*

● *powerful limbs with long claws*

● *long, tapering tail*

● *lower jaw with venom glands and venom-delivering teeth*

Length 2–3ft (0.7–1m)	Diet 🐜 🐍 🐢 🦎 ●	Activity ☼ ☾

| Family HELODERMATIDAE | Species *Heloderma suspectum* | Status Endangered |

GILA MONSTER ☠

Named after the Gila River in Arizona, this black-and-pink or
black-and-yellow, tapestry-skinned species is one of the most
distinctive lizards of North America. Distributed from Utah to
northern Sinaloa in Mexico, its range slightly overlaps that of
the more tropical Beaded Lizard (*Heloderma horridum*, opposite).
It is smaller and less robust than its relative, with a shorter
neck, shorter tail, and more rounded head. Like the Beaded
Lizard, it is venomous, with the venom mechanism in the
lower jaw, and it has a similar diet. Its sluggish appearance
is deceptive since a predatory approach may be countered
with a sudden turn and a rapid bite, resulting in a tenacious,
chewing grip and a potentially serious injection of venom.
There are two subspecies. The more northern of these,
the Banded Gila Monster (*H. suspectum cinctum*, shown
here), has a more defined pattern than the southern
Reticulated Gila Monster (*H. suspectum suspectum*).
• **OCCURRENCE** S.W. US and N.W. Mexico.
In desert and dry grassland.
• **REPRODUCTION** Lays 4–7 eggs.
• **SIMILAR SPECIES** Beaded Lizard
(*H. horridum*, opposite).
• **REMARK** The Gila
Monster is a protected
species and must not
be killed, collected,
or molested.

shorter head, neck, and tail than Beaded Lizard, opposite

rounded, beadlike scales cover body and limbs

pink or yellow coloring with black cross-bands

powerful limbs with long claws

tail can act as reserve food store

large, broad head with venom apparatus in lower jaw

snakelike forked tongue

N. AMERICA

| Length 12–20in (30–50cm) | Diet | Activity ○ |

Family VARANIDAE	Species *Varanus albigularis*	Status Common

WHITE-THROATED MONITOR LIZARD

This short-headed lizard is gray-brown with pale yellow, dark-edged markings. It climbs well and travels long distances to search for a mate or food, which consists of a wide variety of prey, including insects, birds and birds' eggs, and venomous snakes. This monitor lizard uses its long, rough tail as a defensive whip, and it can deliver a serious bite.

AFRICA

• OCCURRENCE E. and S. Africa.
In savanna woodland.
• REPRODUCTION
Lays 8–50 eggs.
• SIMILAR
SPECIES Bosc
Monitor Lizard (*Varanus exanthematicus*).

stocky tail used in defense

Length 6–7ft (1.9–2.1m)	Diet 🐜🦗🦎🐍🥚🐁	Activity ☀

Family VARANIDAE	Species *Varanus komodoensis*	Status Locally common

KOMODO DRAGON

The largest and heaviest lizard in the world, the Komodo Dragon is found on a few small, arid islands in Indonesia. It has a massive body, carried on sturdy legs, and a broad, powerful head. Adult Komodos are a fairly drab gray color but juveniles, which adopt a more arboreal existence for their own safety, are more brightly patterned. The Komodo Dragon is a formidable predator, hunting large mammals such as pigs, deer, horses, and buffalo. Before these were introduced by man, it is believed to have fed on a now-extinct pygmy elephant. Birds and reptiles, including smaller dragons, also form part of its diet, and it is known to have taken humans. It has a reputation for feeding on carrion, but since it is the only large terrestrial carnivore on the islands, most carrion is the result of dragon kills. When hunting, the Komodo Dragon ambushes large prey. If the animal escapes the initial attack but is wounded, the dragon will track it down until it dies. This may not take long, since the saliva contains virulent bacteria that rapidly cause weakness, allowing the pursuing dragon to administer a *coup-de-grace*.

long forked tongue and sense of smell enable dragon to locate carrion

drab gray body coloration

• OCCURRENCE Indonesia, on only a few islands in the Lesser Sunda archipelago (Komodo, Rintja, Gillimontang, Padar, and the western end of Flores). In savanna and woodland.
• REPRODUCTION Lays 8–27 eggs.

INDONESIA

strong tail used to knock over prey

Length 8–10ft (2.5–3.1m)	Diet 🐀 🦎	Activity ☀

Family VARANIDAE	Species *Varanus dumerilii*	Status Rare

DUMERIL'S MONITOR LIZARD

The adult of this species is light brown, with dark bars across its back. Juveniles have a more striking coloration: they are black, with bright yellow bars across the body and vivid orange on top of the head. Both adults and juveniles have a dark stripe running backward from each eye. This monitor lizard climbs well and enters water if disturbed.

ASIA

• **OCCURRENCE** S.E. Asia. In mangrove swamps and rainforest.
• **REPRODUCTION** Lays 12–23 eggs.
• **SIMILAR SPECIES** Indo-Malay Water Monitor Lizard (*Varanus salvator*).

long, keeled tail for swimming

dark stripes behind eyes

strong claws for climbing

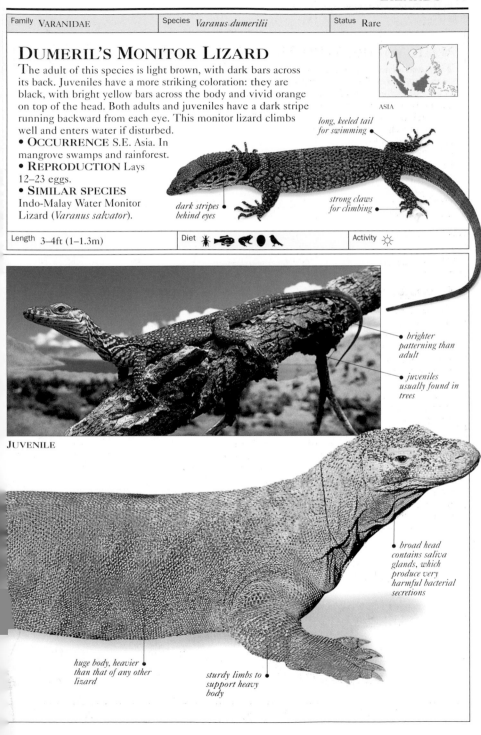

Length 3–4ft (1–1.3m)	Diet 🦗🐟🐸🥚🐦🗡	Activity ☀

brighter patterning than adult

juveniles usually found in trees

JUVENILE

broad head contains saliva glands, which produce very harmful bacterial secretions

huge body, heavier than that of any other lizard

sturdy limbs to support heavy body

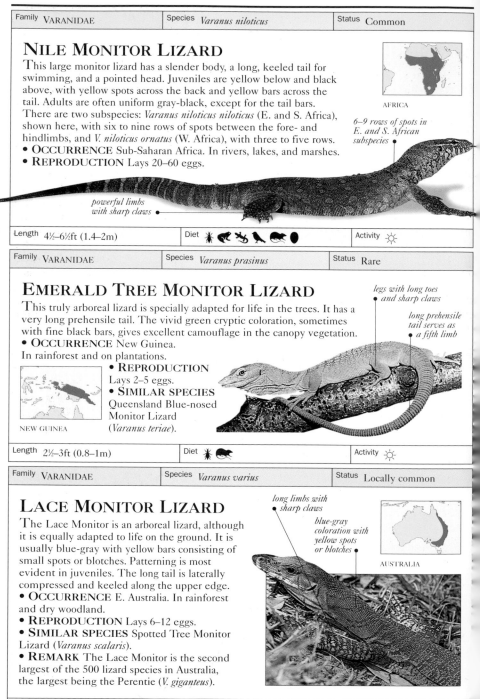

Family VARANIDAE	Species *Varanus niloticus*	Status Common

NILE MONITOR LIZARD

This large monitor lizard has a slender body, a long, keeled tail for swimming, and a pointed head. Juveniles are yellow below and black above, with yellow spots across the back and yellow bars across the tail. Adults are often uniform gray-black, except for the tail bars. There are two subspecies: *Varanus niloticus niloticus* (E. and S. Africa), shown here, with six to nine rows of spots between the fore- and hindlimbs, and *V. niloticus ornatus* (W. Africa), with three to five rows.
• OCCURRENCE Sub-Saharan Africa. In rivers, lakes, and marshes.
• REPRODUCTION Lays 20–60 eggs.

AFRICA

6–9 rows of spots in E. and S. African subspecies

powerful limbs with sharp claws

Length 4½–6½ft (1.4–2m)	Diet	Activity ☼

Family VARANIDAE	Species *Varanus prasinus*	Status Rare

EMERALD TREE MONITOR LIZARD

legs with long toes and sharp claws

This truly arboreal lizard is specially adapted for life in the trees. It has a very long prehensile tail. The vivid green cryptic coloration, sometimes with fine black bars, gives excellent camouflage in the canopy vegetation.
• OCCURRENCE New Guinea. In rainforest and on plantations.
• REPRODUCTION Lays 2–5 eggs.
• SIMILAR SPECIES Queensland Blue-nosed Monitor Lizard (*Varanus teriae*).

long prehensile tail serves as a fifth limb

NEW GUINEA

Length 2½–3ft (0.8–1m)	Diet	Activity ☼

Family VARANIDAE	Species *Varanus varius*	Status Locally common

LACE MONITOR LIZARD

long limbs with sharp claws

The Lace Monitor is an arboreal lizard, although it is equally adapted to life on the ground. It is usually blue-gray with yellow bars consisting of small spots or blotches. Patterning is most evident in juveniles. The long tail is laterally compressed and keeled along the upper edge.
• OCCURRENCE E. Australia. In rainforest and dry woodland.
• REPRODUCTION Lays 6–12 eggs.
• SIMILAR SPECIES Spotted Tree Monitor Lizard (*Varanus scalaris*).
• REMARK The Lace Monitor is the second largest of the 500 lizard species in Australia, the largest being the Perentie (*V. giganteus*).

blue-gray coloration with yellow spots or blotches

AUSTRALIA

Length 5–6½ft (1.5–2m)	Diet	Activity ☼

AMPHISBAENIANS

T HE AMPHISBAENIANS, or worm-lizards, were once considered a family within the lizards. However, they are now considered different enough to form an entirely separate group (suborder Amphisbaenia), distinct from both lizards and snakes. Authorities place the 140 known species variously in two, three, or four families (in this book, they are treated as four). Amphisbaenians occur in South America, Florida, southern Europe, north Africa, tropical Africa, and the Middle East. They live almost entirely underground, so they are seldom seen on the surface, except after rain.

Most amphisbaenians have long, slender, cylindrical bodies and possess extremely short, often truncated, tails. Indeed, the tail is so short and bluntly rounded that in Brazil these creatures are known as the "cobras de duas cabeças," meaning "snakes with two heads." They lack limbs, except for species in the unusual genus *Bipes* (p.103), which have forelimbs.

The scales covering the entire body and tail of amphisbaenians are tiny and are arranged in a series of rings, known as annuli; these make amphisbaenians superficially resemble earthworms, but they are not related. The annuli are sometimes interrupted by a long, indented fold that runs along the sides of the body. The armored head is ideal for burrowing, and the mouth and jaw are small. Both the ears and the eyes, which are vestigial areas of dark pigmentation, are hidden beneath large transparent scales.

Family AMPHISBAENIDAE	Species *Amphisbaena alba*	Status Unknown

RED WORM-LIZARD

The largest of the amphisbaenians, the Red Worm-lizard is rarely encountered above ground, except after heavy rain. The sturdy, armored white head has tiny eyes and ears, which are adapted for the detection of vibrations. A small mouth is located under the head. The head runs directly into the body without any hint of a neck. The body consists of numerous rings of tiny scales that resemble the annuli of an earthworm. The coloration is red-brown above, paler below, but without specific patterning. The Red Worm-lizard is most often found near the nests of large leaf-cutter ants because it feeds on the beetles that live in the ant-nest refuse areas.
• OCCURRENCE N. South America. In rainforest.
• REPRODUCTION Lays eggs (clutch size unknown).
• SIMILAR SPECIES Slevin's Worm-lizard (*Amphisbaena slevini*).

S. AMERICA

minute body scales arranged in numerous rings

head scales conceal eyes and ears

cylindrical body with very short, blunt tail

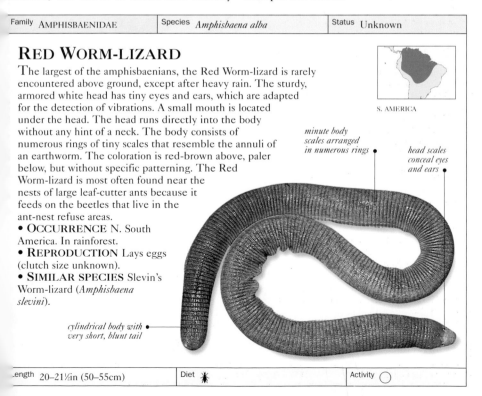

Length 20–21½in (50–55cm)	Diet	Activity

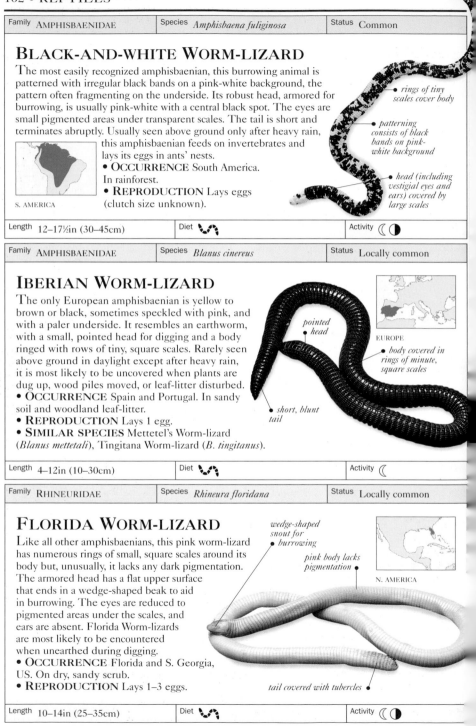

Family AMPHISBAENIDAE	Species *Amphisbaena fuliginosa*	Status Common

BLACK-AND-WHITE WORM-LIZARD

The most easily recognized amphisbaenian, this burrowing animal is patterned with irregular black bands on a pink-white background, the pattern often fragmenting on the underside. Its robust head, armored for burrowing, is usually pink-white with a central black spot. The eyes are small pigmented areas under transparent scales. The tail is short and terminates abruptly. Usually seen above ground only after heavy rain, this amphisbaenian feeds on invertebrates and lays its eggs in ants' nests.

S. AMERICA

• **OCCURRENCE** South America. In rainforest.
• **REPRODUCTION** Lays eggs (clutch size unknown).

rings of tiny scales cover body

patterning consists of black bands on pink-white background

head (including vestigial eyes and ears) covered by large scales

Length 12–17½in (30–45cm)	Diet	Activity

Family AMPHISBAENIDAE	Species *Blanus cinereus*	Status Locally common

IBERIAN WORM-LIZARD

The only European amphisbaenian is yellow to brown or black, sometimes speckled with pink, and with a paler underside. It resembles an earthworm, with a small, pointed head for digging and a body ringed with rows of tiny, square scales. Rarely seen above ground in daylight except after heavy rain, it is most likely to be uncovered when plants are dug up, wood piles moved, or leaf-litter disturbed.
• **OCCURRENCE** Spain and Portugal. In sandy soil and woodland leaf-litter.
• **REPRODUCTION** Lays 1 egg.
• **SIMILAR SPECIES** Mettetel's Worm-lizard (*Blanus mettetali*), Tingitana Worm-lizard (*B. tingitanus*).

pointed head

EUROPE

body covered in rings of minute, square scales

short, blunt tail

Length 4–12in (10–30cm)	Diet	Activity

Family RHINEURIDAE	Species *Rhineura floridana*	Status Locally common

FLORIDA WORM-LIZARD

Like all other amphisbaenians, this pink worm-lizard has numerous rings of small, square scales around its body but, unusually, it lacks any dark pigmentation. The armored head has a flat upper surface that ends in a wedge-shaped beak to aid in burrowing. The eyes are reduced to pigmented areas under the scales, and ears are absent. Florida Worm-lizards are most likely to be encountered when unearthed during digging.
• **OCCURRENCE** Florida and S. Georgia, US. On dry, sandy scrub.
• **REPRODUCTION** Lays 1–3 eggs.

wedge-shaped snout for burrowing

pink body lacks pigmentation

N. AMERICA

tail covered with tubercles

Length 10–14in (25–35cm)	Diet	Activity

Family BIPEDIDAE	Species *Bipes biporus*	Status Rare

AJOLOTE

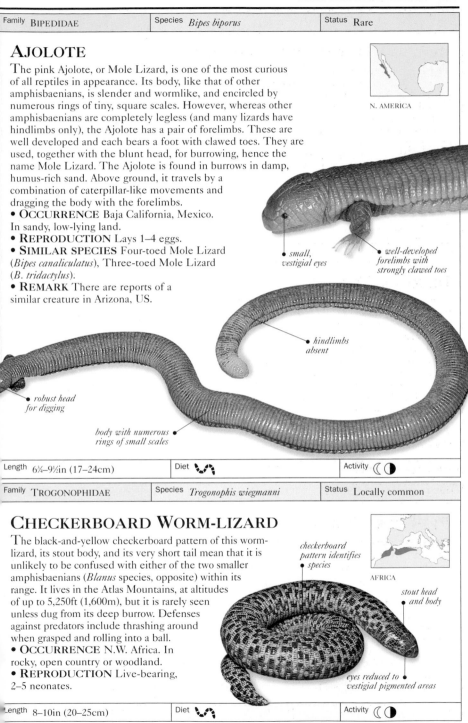

The pink Ajolote, or Mole Lizard, is one of the most curious of all reptiles in appearance. Its body, like that of other amphisbaenians, is slender and wormlike, and encircled by numerous rings of tiny, square scales. However, whereas other amphisbaenians are completely legless (and many lizards have hindlimbs only), the Ajolote has a pair of forelimbs. These are well developed and each bears a foot with clawed toes. They are used, together with the blunt head, for burrowing, hence the name Mole Lizard. The Ajolote is found in burrows in damp, humus-rich sand. Above ground, it travels by a combination of caterpillar-like movements and dragging the body with the forelimbs.
• **OCCURRENCE** Baja California, Mexico. In sandy, low-lying land.
• **REPRODUCTION** Lays 1–4 eggs.
• **SIMILAR SPECIES** Four-toed Mole Lizard (*Bipes canaliculatus*), Three-toed Mole Lizard (*B. tridactylus*).
• **REMARK** There are reports of a similar creature in Arizona, US.

N. AMERICA

small, vestigial eyes

well-developed forelimbs with strongly clawed toes

hindlimbs absent

robust head for digging

body with numerous rings of small scales

Length 6¾–9½in (17–24cm)	Diet	Activity

Family TROGONOPHIDAE	Species *Trogonophis wiegmanni*	Status Locally common

CHECKERBOARD WORM-LIZARD

The black-and-yellow checkerboard pattern of this worm-lizard, its stout body, and its very short tail mean that it is unlikely to be confused with either of the two smaller amphisbaenians (*Blanus* species, opposite) within its range. It lives in the Atlas Mountains, at altitudes of up to 5,250ft (1,600m), but it is rarely seen unless dug from its deep burrow. Defenses against predators include thrashing around when grasped and rolling into a ball.
• **OCCURRENCE** N.W. Africa. In rocky, open country or woodland.
• **REPRODUCTION** Live-bearing, 2–5 neonates.

checkerboard pattern identifies species

AFRICA

stout head and body

eyes reduced to vestigial pigmented areas

Length 8–10in (20–25cm)	Diet	Activity

SNAKES

S NAKES ARE characterized by a long, slender body covered in overlapping scales. They have no limbs (although some have vestigial claws and pelvic bones). The eyelids do not move but are fused to form transparent "spectacles," and there is no external ear. The bones of the jaws are not fused, enabling the snake to open its mouth wide, and the forked tongue is completely retractable. Only one lung is functional, the left lung usually being reduced or absent. Some primitive snakes have teeth only in one jaw; egg-eaters have no teeth at all.

There are about 2,800 species of snakes. Most are nonvenomous and do no harm to humans. Venomous snakes have specially adapted fangs through which venom is forcibly injected. In many, the fangs are at the rear of the upper jaw; of these, fewer than a dozen are dangerous. There are some 500 front-fanged venomous snakes, but many of these are also incapable of causing serious injury to humans.

Snakes are dealt with here in 16 families. However, taxonomists may recognize other combinations. Some, for example, place boas and pythons in the same family (Boidae), but they have been treated separately here to emphasize the differences between them.

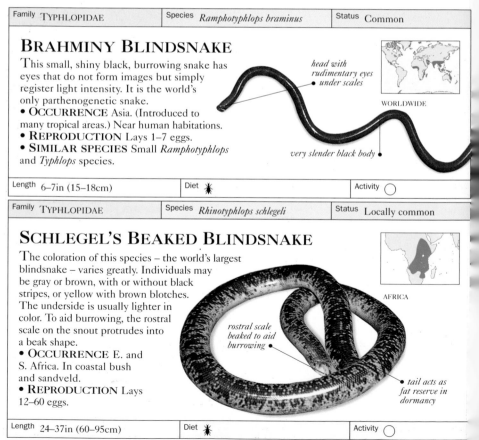

Family TYPHLOPIDAE	Species *Ramphotyphlops braminus*	Status Common

BRAHMINY BLINDSNAKE
This small, shiny black, burrowing snake has eyes that do not form images but simply register light intensity. It is the world's only parthenogenetic snake.
• **OCCURRENCE** Asia. (Introduced to many tropical areas.) Near human habitations.
• **REPRODUCTION** Lays 1–7 eggs.
• **SIMILAR SPECIES** Small *Ramphotyphlops* and *Typhlops* species.

head with
rudimentary eyes
under scales

WORLDWIDE

very slender black body

Length 6–7in (15–18cm)	Diet 🐜	Activity ◯

Family TYPHLOPIDAE	Species *Rhinotyphlops schlegeli*	Status Locally common

SCHLEGEL'S BEAKED BLINDSNAKE
The coloration of this species – the world's largest blindsnake – varies greatly. Individuals may be gray or brown, with or without black stripes, or yellow with brown blotches. The underside is usually lighter in color. To aid burrowing, the rostral scale on the snout protrudes into a beak shape.
• **OCCURRENCE** E. and S. Africa. In coastal bush and sandveld.
• **REPRODUCTION** Lays 12–60 eggs.

AFRICA

rostral scale
beaked to aid
burrowing

tail acts as
fat reserve in
dormancy

Length 24–37in (60–95cm)	Diet 🐜	Activity ◯

Family LEPTOTYPHLOPIDAE	Species *Leptotyphlops dulcis*	Status Common

TEXAS BLINDSNAKE

This blindsnake may be brown, red, or pink above, with a silvery sheen, and lighter below. A spine in the tip of the tail helps the blindsnake to force itself down narrow burrows in search of termites and ant larvae. When in a nest of ferocious ants, this species coats itself in a pheremonal body secretion that deceives the ants into thinking that the snake is part of the nest, allowing the snake to enter the larval chambers to feed in safety.

N. AMERICA

smooth, shiny scales cover body •

• **OCCURRENCE** S.W. US and N.E. Mexico. In prairies, canyons, and deserts. In crevices, under stones, and in bushes.
• **REPRODUCTION** Lays 2–7 eggs.
• **SIMILAR SPECIES** Western Blindsnake (*Typhlops humilis*).

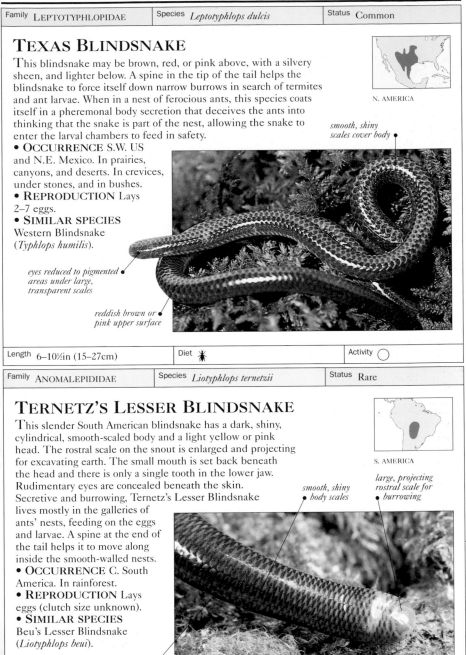

eyes reduced to pigmented areas under large, transparent scales •

reddish brown or pink upper surface •

Length 6–10½in (15–27cm)	Diet ☀	Activity ◯

Family ANOMALEPIDIDAE	Species *Liotyphlops ternetzii*	Status Rare

TERNETZ'S LESSER BLINDSNAKE

This slender South American blindsnake has a dark, shiny, cylindrical, smooth-scaled body and a light yellow or pink head. The rostral scale on the snout is enlarged and projecting for excavating earth. The small mouth is set back beneath the head and there is only a single tooth in the lower jaw. Rudimentary eyes are concealed beneath the skin. Secretive and burrowing, Ternetz's Lesser Blindsnake lives mostly in the galleries of ants' nests, feeding on the eggs and larvae. A spine at the end of the tail helps it to move along inside the smooth-walled nests.
• **OCCURRENCE** C. South America. In rainforest.
• **REPRODUCTION** Lays eggs (clutch size unknown).
• **SIMILAR SPECIES** Beu's Lesser Blindsnake (*Liotyphlops beui*).

S. AMERICA

smooth, shiny body scales •

large, projecting rostral scale for burrowing •

dark body color contrasts with lighter head •

Length 6–8¼in (15–21cm)	Diet ☀	Activity ◯

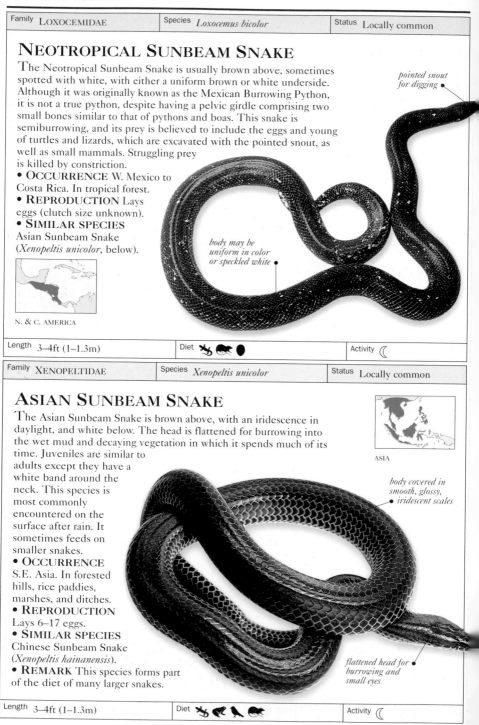

| Family LOXOCEMIDAE | Species *Loxocemus bicolor* | Status Locally common |

NEOTROPICAL SUNBEAM SNAKE

The Neotropical Sunbeam Snake is usually brown above, sometimes spotted with white, with either a uniform brown or white underside. Although it was originally known as the Mexican Burrowing Python, it is not a true python, despite having a pelvic girdle comprising two small bones similar to that of pythons and boas. This snake is semiburrowing, and its prey is believed to include the eggs and young of turtles and lizards, which are excavated with the pointed snout, as well as small mammals. Struggling prey is killed by constriction.

pointed snout for digging

• **OCCURRENCE** W. Mexico to Costa Rica. In tropical forest.
• **REPRODUCTION** Lays eggs (clutch size unknown).
• **SIMILAR SPECIES** Asian Sunbeam Snake (*Xenopeltis unicolor*, below).

body may be uniform in color or speckled white

N. & C. AMERICA

| Length 3–4ft (1–1.3m) | Diet | Activity ☾ |

| Family XENOPELTIDAE | Species *Xenopeltis unicolor* | Status Locally common |

ASIAN SUNBEAM SNAKE

The Asian Sunbeam Snake is brown above, with an iridescence in daylight, and white below. The head is flattened for burrowing into the wet mud and decaying vegetation in which it spends much of its time. Juveniles are similar to adults except they have a white band around the neck. This species is most commonly encountered on the surface after rain. It sometimes feeds on smaller snakes.

ASIA

body covered in smooth, glossy, iridescent scales

• **OCCURRENCE** S.E. Asia. In forested hills, rice paddies, marshes, and ditches.
• **REPRODUCTION** Lays 6–17 eggs.
• **SIMILAR SPECIES** Chinese Sunbeam Snake (*Xenopeltis hainanensis*).
• **REMARK** This species forms part of the diet of many larger snakes.

flattened head for burrowing and small eyes

| Length 3–4ft (1–1.3m) | Diet | Activity ☾ |

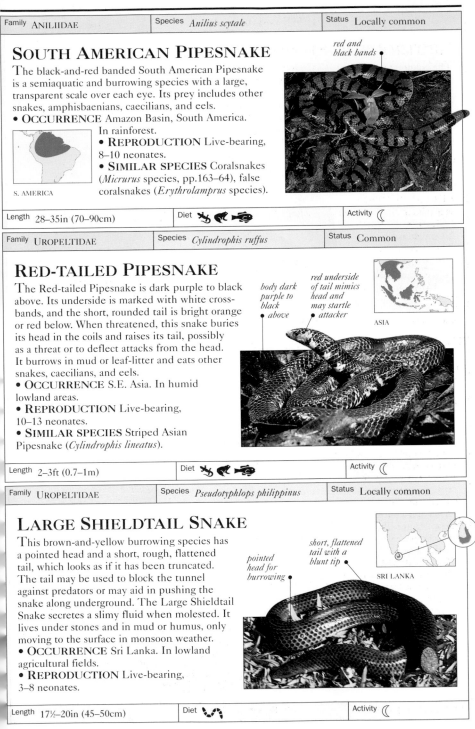

Family ANILIIDAE	Species *Anilius scytale*	Status Locally common

SOUTH AMERICAN PIPESNAKE

red and
black bands

The black-and-red banded South American Pipesnake
is a semiaquatic and burrowing species with a large,
transparent scale over each eye. Its prey includes other
snakes, amphisbaenians, caecilians, and eels.
• OCCURRENCE Amazon Basin, South America.
In rainforest.

• REPRODUCTION Live-bearing,
8–10 neonates.
• SIMILAR SPECIES Coralsnakes
(*Micrurus* species, pp.163–64), false
coralsnakes (*Erythrolamprus* species).

S. AMERICA

Length 28–35in (70–90cm)	Diet	Activity ☾

Family UROPELTIDAE	Species *Cylindrophis ruffus*	Status Common

RED-TAILED PIPESNAKE

The Red-tailed Pipesnake is dark purple to black
above. Its underside is marked with white cross-
bands, and the short, rounded tail is bright orange
or red below. When threatened, this snake buries
its head in the coils and raises its tail, possibly
as a threat or to deflect attacks from the head.
It burrows in mud or leaf-litter and eats other
snakes, caecilians, and eels.
• OCCURRENCE S.E. Asia. In humid
lowland areas.
• REPRODUCTION Live-bearing,
10–13 neonates.
• SIMILAR SPECIES Striped Asian
Pipesnake (*Cylindrophis lineatus*).

body dark
purple to
black
• above

red underside
of tail mimics
head and
may startle
• attacker

ASIA

Length 2–3ft (0.7–1m)	Diet	Activity ☾

Family UROPELTIDAE	Species *Pseudotyphlops philippinus*	Status Locally common

LARGE SHIELDTAIL SNAKE

This brown-and-yellow burrowing species has
a pointed head and a short, rough, flattened
tail, which looks as if it has been truncated.
The tail may be used to block the tunnel
against predators or may aid in pushing the
snake along underground. The Large Shieldtail
Snake secretes a slimy fluid when molested. It
lives under stones and in mud or humus, only
moving to the surface in monsoon weather.
• OCCURRENCE Sri Lanka. In lowland
agricultural fields.
• REPRODUCTION Live-bearing,
3–8 neonates.

pointed
head for
burrowing •

short, flattened
tail with a
blunt tip •

SRI LANKA

Length 17½–20in (45–50cm)	Diet	Activity ☾

Family TROPIDOPHEIDAE	Species *Tropidophis melanurus*	Status Common

CUBAN DWARF BOA

The coloration of this species is gray, tan, or red, overlaid by darker
stripes, zigzags, or blotches. This is the largest dwarf boa or woodsnake
and, like its smaller relatives, it is an agile climber, equally at home in
the treetops as under palm debris on the forest floor. Defensive
behavior includes rolling into a ball; secreting a pungent
white liquid from the cloaca; and changing
color – from dark during the day,
when inactive, to light at night,
when active.
• **OCCURRENCE** Cuba.
In rainforest, disturbed
gardens, and rocky
outcrops.
• **REPRODUCTION**
Live-bearing,
4–9 neonates.
• **SIMILAR
SPECIES** Haitian
Dwarf Boa
(*Tropidophis
haetianus*).

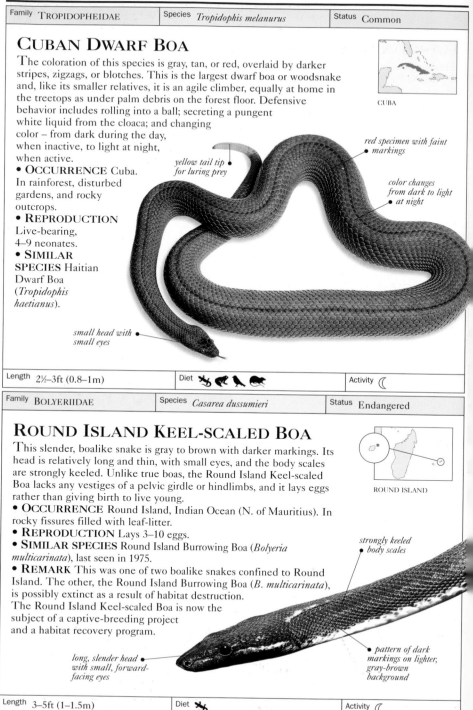

CUBA

*red specimen with faint
markings*

*color changes
from dark to light
at night*

*yellow tail tip
for luring prey*

*small head with
small eyes*

Length 2½–3ft (0.8–1m)	Diet 🦎🐀🦅🐁	Activity ☾

Family BOLYERIIDAE	Species *Casarea dussumieri*	Status Endangered

ROUND ISLAND KEEL-SCALED BOA

This slender, boalike snake is gray to brown with darker markings. Its
head is relatively long and thin, with small eyes, and the body scales
are strongly keeled. Unlike true boas, the Round Island Keel-scaled
Boa lacks any vestiges of a pelvic girdle or hindlimbs, and it lays eggs
rather than giving birth to live young.
• **OCCURRENCE** Round Island, Indian Ocean (N. of Mauritius). In
rocky fissures filled with leaf-litter.
• **REPRODUCTION** Lays 3–10 eggs.
• **SIMILAR SPECIES** Round Island Burrowing Boa (*Bolyeria
multicarinata*), last seen in 1975.
• **REMARK** This was one of two boalike snakes confined to Round
Island. The other, the Round Island Burrowing Boa (*B. multicarinata*),
is possibly extinct as a result of habitat destruction.
The Round Island Keel-scaled Boa is now the
subject of a captive-breeding project
and a habitat recovery program.

ROUND ISLAND

*strongly keeled
body scales*

*long, slender head
with small, forward-
facing eyes*

*pattern of dark
markings on lighter,
gray-brown
background*

Length 3–5ft (1–1.5m)	Diet 🦎	Activity ☾

Family BOIDAE	Species *Boa constrictor*	Status Common

COMMON BOA CONSTRICTOR

This is a widespread species with up to 10 mainland and island subspecies. These range from the dark-colored Argentinian Boa (*Boa constrictor occidentalis*) to much lighter, brown or gray specimens, often with a red tail. All, however, have saddle markings. There is also considerable variation in size: dwarf island races such as the Hog's Island Boa (*B. constrictor imperator*) reach only 3ft (1m) compared to the 13ft (4m) of mainland boas. Common Boas are powerful constrictors capable of subduing fairly large mammals, but they are not the huge giants some people believe them to be. They are not dangerous to humans although they can deliver painful bites, especially dark Central American species such as the Imperial Boa (*B. constrictor imperator*). Common Boas are mainly terrestrial but they can climb and swim well.

C. & S. AMERICA

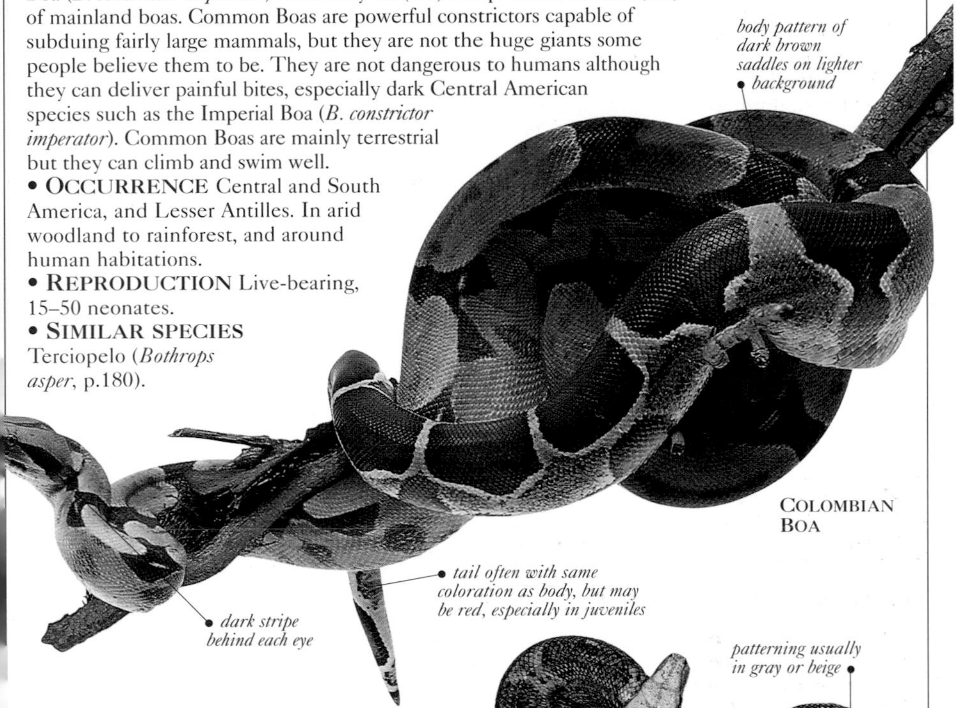

body pattern of dark brown saddles on lighter background

• **OCCURRENCE** Central and South America, and Lesser Antilles. In arid woodland to rainforest, and around human habitations.
• **REPRODUCTION** Live-bearing, 15–50 neonates.
• **SIMILAR SPECIES** Terciopelo (*Bothrops asper*, p.180).

COLOMBIAN BOA

tail often with same coloration as body, but may be red, especially in juveniles

dark stripe behind each eye

patterning usually in gray or beige

very dark body with lighter spots

HOG'S ISLAND BOA

ARGENTINIAN BOA (JUVENILE)

Length 6½–13ft (2–4m)	Diet	Activity

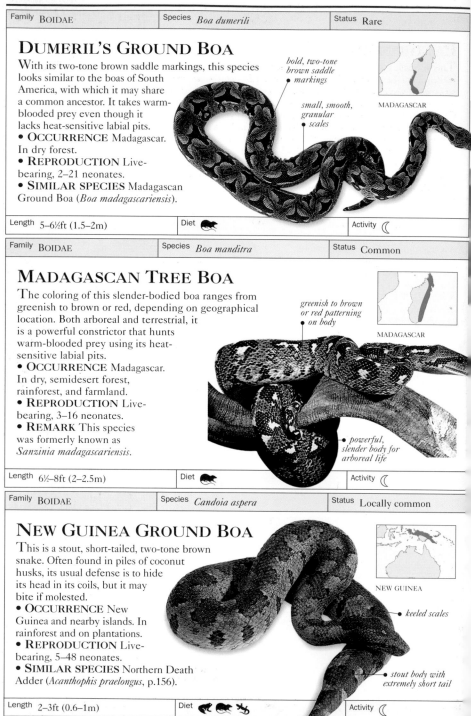

Family BOIDAE	Species *Boa dumerili*	Status Rare

DUMERIL'S GROUND BOA

With its two-tone brown saddle markings, this species looks similar to the boas of South America, with which it may share a common ancestor. It takes warm-blooded prey even though it lacks heat-sensitive labial pits.
- **OCCURRENCE** Madagascar. In dry forest.
- **REPRODUCTION** Live-bearing, 2–21 neonates.
- **SIMILAR SPECIES** Madagascan Ground Boa (*Boa madagascariensis*).

bold, two-tone brown saddle markings

small, smooth, granular scales

MADAGASCAR

Length 5–6½ft (1.5–2m)	Diet	Activity ☾

Family BOIDAE	Species *Boa manditra*	Status Common

MADAGASCAN TREE BOA

The coloring of this slender-bodied boa ranges from greenish to brown or red, depending on geographical location. Both arboreal and terrestrial, it is a powerful constrictor that hunts warm-blooded prey using its heat-sensitive labial pits.
- **OCCURRENCE** Madagascar. In dry, semidesert forest, rainforest, and farmland.
- **REPRODUCTION** Live-bearing, 3–16 neonates.
- **REMARK** This species was formerly known as *Sanzinia madagascariensis*.

greenish to brown or red patterning on body

MADAGASCAR

powerful, slender body for arboreal life

Length 6½–8ft (2–2.5m)	Diet	Activity ☾

Family BOIDAE	Species *Candoia aspera*	Status Locally common

NEW GUINEA GROUND BOA

This is a stout, short-tailed, two-tone brown snake. Often found in piles of coconut husks, its usual defense is to hide its head in its coils, but it may bite if molested.
- **OCCURRENCE** New Guinea and nearby islands. In rainforest and on plantations.
- **REPRODUCTION** Live-bearing, 5–48 neonates.
- **SIMILAR SPECIES** Northern Death Adder (*Acanthophis praelongus*, p.156).

NEW GUINEA

keeled scales

stout body with extremely short tail

Length 2–3ft (0.6–1m)	Diet	Activity ☾

Family BOIDAE	Species *Candoia carinata*	Status Locally common

PACIFIC BOA

This species is extremely variable. Some populations are terrestrial, while others are arboreal. The Pacific Ground Boa (*Candoia carinata paulsoni*) is short-tailed, stout-bodied, and may be red or grayish brown to off-white. It is terrestrial and occurs in areas where the New Guinea Ground Boa (*C. aspera*, opposite) is absent. The Pacific Tree Boa (*C. carinata carinata*) is a slender-bodied, long-tailed, arboreal snake that occurs in the same areas as the New Guinea Ground Boa. It may be brown or gray, and has an off-white patch above the cloaca.

ASIA, OCEANIA

• **OCCURRENCE** New Guinea, E. Indonesia, and the Solomon Islands. In rainforest and on cocoa and coconut plantations.
• **REPRODUCTION** Live-bearing, 4–50 neonates.
• **SIMILAR SPECIES** New Guinea Ground Boa (*C. aspera*, opposite).

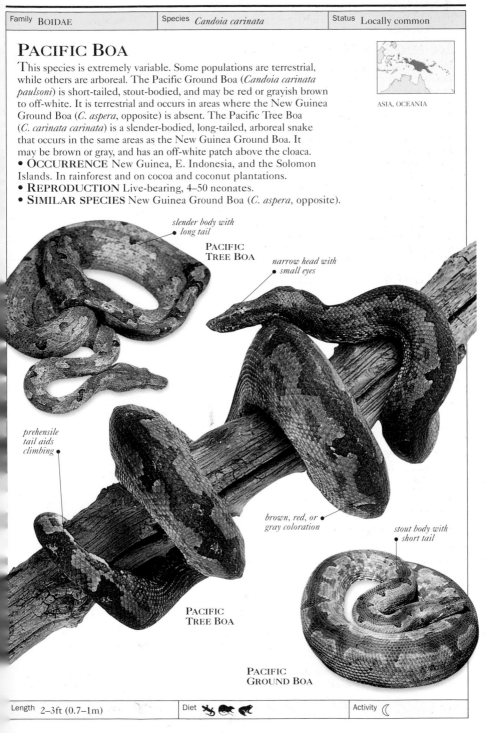

slender body with long tail

PACIFIC TREE BOA

narrow head with small eyes

prehensile tail aids climbing

brown, red, or gray coloration

stout body with short tail

PACIFIC TREE BOA

PACIFIC GROUND BOA

Length 2–3ft (0.7–1m)	Diet	Activity

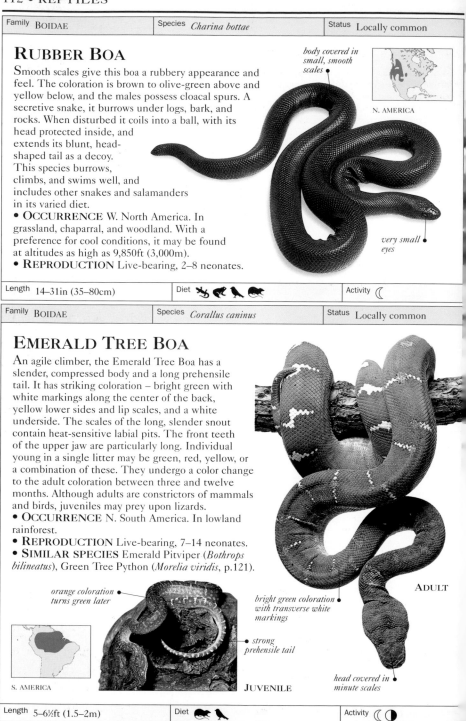

| Family BOIDAE | Species *Charina bottae* | Status Locally common |

RUBBER BOA

Smooth scales give this boa a rubbery appearance and feel. The coloration is brown to olive-green above and yellow below, and the males possess cloacal spurs. A secretive snake, it burrows under logs, bark, and rocks. When disturbed it coils into a ball, with its head protected inside, and extends its blunt, head-shaped tail as a decoy. This species burrows, climbs, and swims well, and includes other snakes and salamanders in its varied diet.
• **OCCURRENCE** W. North America. In grassland, chaparral, and woodland. With a preference for cool conditions, it may be found at altitudes as high as 9,850ft (3,000m).
• **REPRODUCTION** Live-bearing, 2–8 neonates.

body covered in small, smooth scales

N. AMERICA

very small eyes

| Length 14–31in (35–80cm) | Diet | Activity |

| Family BOIDAE | Species *Corallus caninus* | Status Locally common |

EMERALD TREE BOA

An agile climber, the Emerald Tree Boa has a slender, compressed body and a long prehensile tail. It has striking coloration – bright green with white markings along the center of the back, yellow lower sides and lip scales, and a white underside. The scales of the long, slender snout contain heat-sensitive labial pits. The front teeth of the upper jaw are particularly long. Individual young in a single litter may be green, red, yellow, or a combination of these. They undergo a color change to the adult coloration between three and twelve months. Although adults are constrictors of mammals and birds, juveniles may prey upon lizards.
• **OCCURRENCE** N. South America. In lowland rainforest.
• **REPRODUCTION** Live-bearing, 7–14 neonates.
• **SIMILAR SPECIES** Emerald Pitviper (*Bothrops bilineatus*), Green Tree Python (*Morelia viridis*, p.121).

orange coloration turns green later

S. AMERICA

JUVENILE

bright green coloration with transverse white markings

strong prehensile tail

ADULT

head covered in minute scales

| Length 5–6½ft (1.5–2m) | Diet | Activity |

Family BOIDAE	Species *Corallus hortulanus*	Status Common

AMAZONIAN TREE BOA

The Amazonian Tree Boa is a very slender, almost entirely arboreal snake with a prehensile tail. Its coloration is highly variable – it may be yellow, red, orange, gray, or reticulated black and gray. Like the Emerald Tree Boa (opposite), the Amazonian Tree Boa has heat-sensitive labial pits, vertical pupils, and long teeth in its front outer jaw. The back of the head is angular, allowing the jaws to open very wide.
• **OCCURRENCE** N. South America. In forest margins and in vegetation over water.
• **REPRODUCTION** Live-bearing, 2–12 neonates.
• **SIMILAR SPECIES** Caribbean and Venezuelan tree boas (*Corallus cooki, C. grenadensis, C. ruschenbergerii*).
• **REMARK** This is the most frequently encountered nocturnal snake in riverine forest habitats in the Amazon Basin.

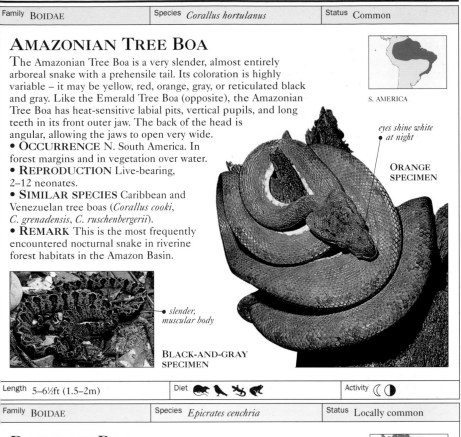

S. AMERICA

eyes shine white at night

ORANGE SPECIMEN

slender, muscular body

BLACK-AND-GRAY SPECIMEN

Length 5–6½ft (1.5–2m)	Diet	Activity ☾ ◑

Family BOIDAE	Species *Epicrates cenchria*	Status Locally common

RAINBOW BOA

The Rainbow Boa is a powerful constrictor, so named because of the iridescent sheen of its scales. Throughout its range, this boa exhibits considerable variation in body patterning. Specimens from Panama and Colombia are uniform brown, while those from Argentina are gray-brown on the sides and dark brown on the back, with lighter brown oval markings. The most striking Rainbow Boas are the orange, red, and black ones from Brazil (shown here). Most of the nine subspecies have five dark longitudinal stripes on the head, the outer stripes passing through the eye. All possess heat-sensitive labial pits.
• **OCCURRENCE** Central and South America (Panama to Argentina). In rainforest, dry woodland, and savanna grassland.
• **REPRODUCTION** Live-bearing, 10–30 neonates.

iridescent sheen resembles effect of oil on water

orange and red markings on Brazilian subspecies

C. & S. AMERICA

Length 5–6½ft (1.5–2m)	Diet	Activity ☾ ◑

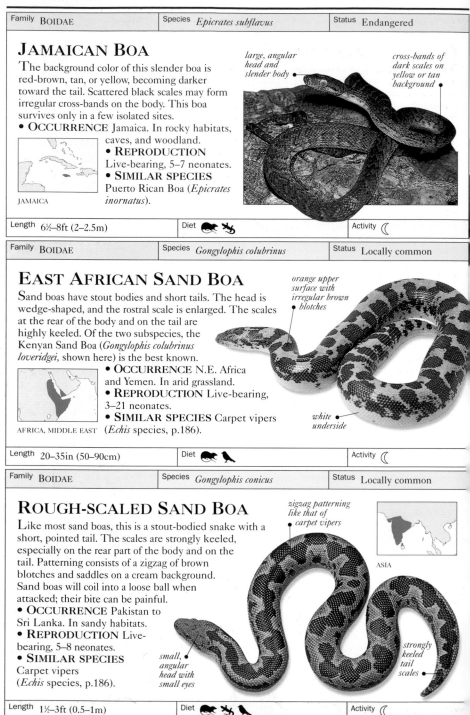

Family BOIDAE	Species *Epicrates subflavus*	Status Endangered

JAMAICAN BOA

The background color of this slender boa is red-brown, tan, or yellow, becoming darker toward the tail. Scattered black scales may form irregular cross-bands on the body. This boa survives only in a few isolated sites.

- **OCCURRENCE** Jamaica. In rocky habitats, caves, and woodland.
- **REPRODUCTION** Live-bearing, 5–7 neonates.
- **SIMILAR SPECIES** Puerto Rican Boa (*Epicrates inornatus*).

JAMAICA

large, angular head and slender body

cross-bands of dark scales on yellow or tan background

Length 6½–8ft (2–2.5m)	Diet	Activity ☾

Family BOIDAE	Species *Gongylophis colubrinus*	Status Locally common

EAST AFRICAN SAND BOA

Sand boas have stout bodies and short tails. The head is wedge-shaped, and the rostral scale is enlarged. The scales at the rear of the body and on the tail are highly keeled. Of the two subspecies, the Kenyan Sand Boa (*Gongylophis colubrinus loveridgei*, shown here) is the best known.

- **OCCURRENCE** N.E. Africa and Yemen. In arid grassland.
- **REPRODUCTION** Live-bearing, 3–21 neonates.
- **SIMILAR SPECIES** Carpet vipers

AFRICA, MIDDLE EAST (*Echis* species, p.186).

orange upper surface with irregular brown blotches

white underside

Length 20–35in (50–90cm)	Diet	Activity ☾

Family BOIDAE	Species *Gongylophis conicus*	Status Locally common

ROUGH-SCALED SAND BOA

Like most sand boas, this is a stout-bodied snake with a short, pointed tail. The scales are strongly keeled, especially on the rear part of the body and on the tail. Patterning consists of a zigzag of brown blotches and saddles on a cream background. Sand boas will coil into a loose ball when attacked; their bite can be painful.

- **OCCURRENCE** Pakistan to Sri Lanka. In sandy habitats.
- **REPRODUCTION** Live-bearing, 5–8 neonates.
- **SIMILAR SPECIES** Carpet vipers (*Echis* species, p.186).

ASIA

zigzag patterning like that of carpet vipers

small, angular head with small eyes

strongly keeled tail scales

Length 1½–3ft (0.5–1m)	Diet	Activity ☾

| Family BOIDAE | Species *Eunectes murinus* | Status Common |

GREEN ANACONDA

The green-and-black spotted coloration of the Green Anaconda makes recognition easy. The snake often grows to an immense weight and huge girth, yet moves relatively easily through the water in which it spends much of its life. Hunting by ambush from the shallows, anacondas can kill large prey, including capybara, deer, young jaguars, and even caimans. They are sufficiently powerful constrictors to kill humans, and have been known to eat them occasionally. Anacondas court and mate in the water and may form mating balls comprising several smaller males and one large female. Females also give birth in the water.

• **OCCURRENCE** N. South America. In rainforest rivers, lagoons, and seasonally flooded grassland.

• **REPRODUCTION** Live-bearing, 4–80 neonates.

• **REMARK** This is the world's largest and heaviest snake, although the Reticulated Python (*Python reticulatus*, p.123) may grow longer.

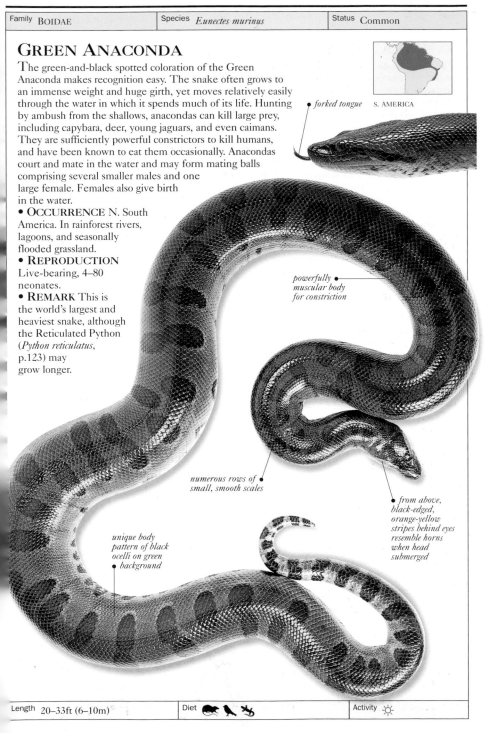

S. AMERICA

• *forked tongue*

• *powerfully muscular body for constriction*

numerous rows of small, smooth scales •

unique body pattern of black ocelli on green • background

• *from above, black-edged, orange-yellow stripes behind eyes resemble horns when head submerged*

| Length 20–33ft (6–10m) | Diet | Activity ☼ |

Family BOIDAE	Species *Eunectes notaeus*	Status Common

YELLOW ANACONDA

Also known as the Paraguayan Anaconda, this powerful constrictor is yellow with longitudinal rows of black spots on the body and a black, three-pronged arrow on top of the head. Smaller than the related Green Anaconda (*Eunectes murinus*, p.115), it also inhabits a more restricted range. The Yellow Anaconda is capable of killing capybara, large wading birds, and Yacare Caimans by constriction, but is not large enough to devour humans.
• **OCCURRENCE** S.W. Brazil, Paraguay, Bolivia, and N. Argentina. In grassland and watercourses.
• **REPRODUCTION** Live-bearing, 4–20 neonates.
• **SIMILAR SPECIES** De Schauensee's Anaconda (*E. deschauenseei*).
• **REMARK** There is a recent report of the Yellow Anaconda hybridizing with the Green Anaconda in Bolivia.

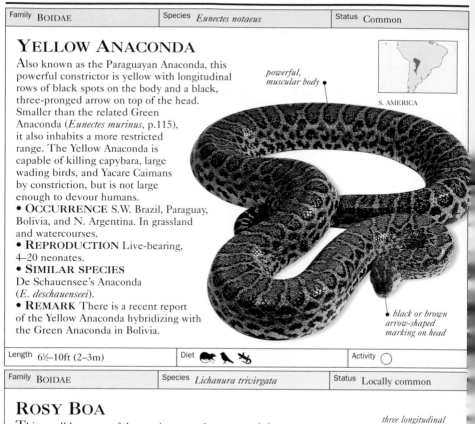

S. AMERICA

powerful, muscular body

black or brown arrow-shaped marking on head

Length 6½–10ft (2–3m)	Diet	Activity

Family BOIDAE	Species *Lichanura trivirgata*	Status Locally common

ROSY BOA

This small but powerful constrictor may be gray or pink in color, and usually has a series of three broad brown, black, or reddish longitudinal stripes down the back and sides. The underside is usually white, often spotted with darker pigment. Both males and females possess small cloacal spurs, although only the males actually use them. Rosy Boas are extremely docile snakes and rarely bite. They shelter under rocks during the day, and they may hibernate in groups in cold weather.
• **OCCURRENCE** S.W. North America. In desert and rocky scrubland (often in seasonal watercourses) at altitudes ranging from sea level to 4,000ft (1,200m).
• **REPRODUCTION** Live-bearing, 1–12 neonates.

three longitudinal stripes on body

very small eyes

body covered in smooth scales

N. AMERICA

Length 2–3½ft (0.6–1.1m)	Diet	Activity

Family PYTHONIDAE	Species *Antaresia childreni*	Status Common

CHILDREN'S PYTHON

This very small python, named after the zoologist J.G. Children, is also known as the Northern Brown Python. It is often uniform brown as an adult, although the juvenile (shown here) is more marked, with dark bars and spots crossing the head and body. These darker markings fade with age. Prey consists mainly of skinks and geckos, but this python also eats frogs, snakes, and bats.

AUSTRALIA

• OCCURRENCE
N. Australia. On rocky hillsides, in grassland and coastal forest.
• REPRODUCTION
Lays 7–20 eggs.
• SIMILAR SPECIES
Pygmy Python (*Antaresia perthensis*), Spotted Python (*A. maculosa*), Stimson's Python (*A. stimsoni*).

small, forward-pointing eyes with vertical pupils

body relatively small for a python

body patterning of juvenile often fades with age

gray, brown, or reddish brown coloration

Length 2½–3ft (0.8 1m)	Diet 🦎🐸🐦🦇🐸	Activity ☾

Family PYTHONIDAE	Species *Apodora papuana*	Status Locally common

PAPUAN OLIVE PYTHON

The Papuan Olive Python has a distinctive two-tone, green-brown body coloration. The contrasting head is light gray-brown with black interstitial skin, and heat-sensitive pits are present on the lips. A large and powerful constrictor, the Papuan Olive Python is easily capable of killing large animals (one of these pythons is on record for eating a wallaby weighing as much as 50lb/22.7kg). This species also eats other snakes, including other pythons – a 6½ft (2m) specimen was once recorded eating an Amethystine Python (*Morelia amethistina*) of the same length.
• OCCURRENCE New Guinea and E. Indonesia. In low monsoon forest, savanna woodland, and savanna.
• REPRODUCTION Lays 15–25 eggs.

head contrasts strongly with body color

heavy-set body in two shades of brown

ASIA, AUSTRALASIA

Length 12–14ft (3.6–4.3m)	Diet 🐍🦎	Activity ☾

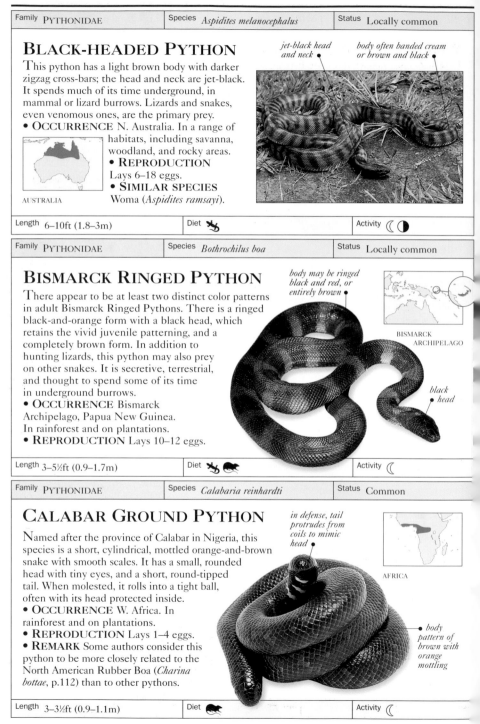

| Family PYTHONIDAE | Species *Aspidites melanocephalus* | Status Locally common |

BLACK-HEADED PYTHON

jet-black head and neck •
body often banded cream or brown and black •

This python has a light brown body with darker zigzag cross-bars; the head and neck are jet-black. It spends much of its time underground, in mammal or lizard burrows. Lizards and snakes, even venomous ones, are the primary prey.
• OCCURRENCE N. Australia. In a range of habitats, including savanna, woodland, and rocky areas.
• REPRODUCTION Lays 6–18 eggs.
• SIMILAR SPECIES Woma (*Aspidites ramsayi*).

AUSTRALIA

| Length 6–10ft (1.8–3m) | Diet | Activity |

| Family PYTHONIDAE | Species *Bothrochilus boa* | Status Locally common |

BISMARCK RINGED PYTHON

body may be ringed black and red, or entirely brown •

There appear to be at least two distinct color patterns in adult Bismarck Ringed Pythons. There is a ringed black-and-orange form with a black head, which retains the vivid juvenile patterning, and a completely brown form. In addition to hunting lizards, this python may also prey on other snakes. It is secretive, terrestrial, and thought to spend some of its time in underground burrows.
• OCCURRENCE Bismarck Archipelago, Papua New Guinea. In rainforest and on plantations.
• REPRODUCTION Lays 10–12 eggs.

BISMARCK ARCHIPELAGO

black • head

| Length 3–5½ft (0.9–1.7m) | Diet | Activity |

| Family PYTHONIDAE | Species *Calabaria reinhardti* | Status Common |

CALABAR GROUND PYTHON

in defense, tail protrudes from coils to mimic head •

Named after the province of Calabar in Nigeria, this species is a short, cylindrical, mottled orange-and-brown snake with smooth scales. It has a small, rounded head with tiny eyes, and a short, round-tipped tail. When molested, it rolls into a tight ball, often with its head protected inside.
• OCCURRENCE W. Africa. In rainforest and on plantations.
• REPRODUCTION Lays 1–4 eggs.
• REMARK Some authors consider this python to be more closely related to the North American Rubber Boa (*Charina bottae*, p.112) than to other pythons.

AFRICA

• body pattern of brown with orange mottling

| Length 3–3½ft (0.9–1.1m) | Diet | Activity |

| Family PYTHONIDAE | Species *Leiopython albertisii* | Status Common |

WHITE-LIPPED PYTHON

In New Guinea the White-lipped Python, also known as D'Albertis Python, varies considerably in color and size. Specimens from the north coast reach 6ft (1.8m) in length; they are deep brown in color, with a contrasting black head and black-and-white lip scales that look like piano keys. The southern coastal specimens are larger – about 8ft (2.4m) long – and a darker maroon-gray or green that contrasts far less with the head color. Although found in a wide variety of habitats, the White-lipped Python shows a preference for damp forests. The population in the Manus Islands, to the north of New Guinea, is separated from the mainland by several large islands on which the sole python is the Bismarck Ringed Python (*Bothrochilus boa*, opposite).
• OCCURRENCE New Guinea and nearby islands. In monsoon forest and rainforest.
• REPRODUCTION Lays 8–15 eggs.

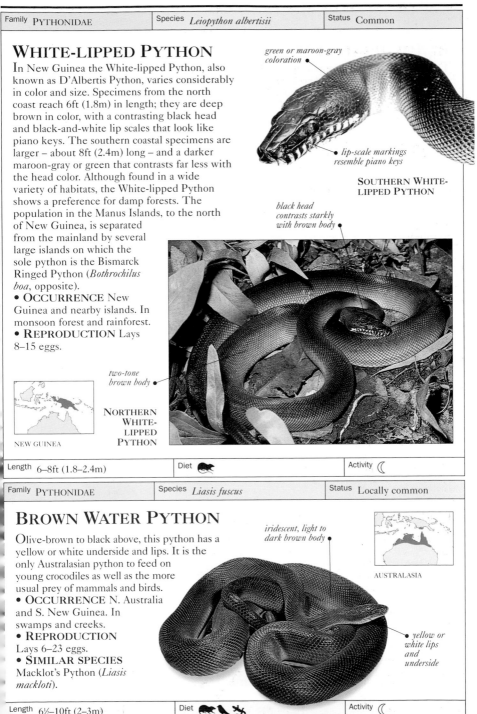

green or maroon-gray coloration

lip-scale markings resemble piano keys

SOUTHERN WHITE-LIPPED PYTHON

black head contrasts starkly with brown body

two-tone brown body

NORTHERN WHITE-LIPPED PYTHON

NEW GUINEA

| Length 6–8ft (1.8–2.4m) | Diet | Activity (|

| Family PYTHONIDAE | Species *Liasis fuscus* | Status Locally common |

BROWN WATER PYTHON

Olive-brown to black above, this python has a yellow or white underside and lips. It is the only Australasian python to feed on young crocodiles as well as the more usual prey of mammals and birds.
• OCCURRENCE N. Australia and S. New Guinea. In swamps and creeks.
• REPRODUCTION Lays 6–23 eggs.
• SIMILAR SPECIES Macklot's Python (*Liasis mackloti*).

iridescent, light to dark brown body

AUSTRALASIA

yellow or white lips and underside

| Length 6½–10ft (2–3m) | Diet | Activity (|

| Family PYTHONIDAE | Species *Morelia amethistina* | Status Common |

AMETHYSTINE PYTHON

This python's common name originates from the iridescent, amethyst-like sheen that overlays the dorsal pattern, which may be light and dark brown, or uniform yellow-brown or olive-green. The Amethystine Python has a long, slender head, covered in enlarged scales, and large, forward-facing eyes. The rows of heat-sensitive labial pits are plainly visible on the snout and the lip scales of the mouth. This agile python climbs and swims with ease.
• **OCCURRENCE** New Guinea, neighboring islands, and N. Australia (where it is recognized as a separate subspecies). In rainforest, woodland, and savanna.
• **REPRODUCTION** Lays 5–21 eggs.
• **SIMILAR SPECIES** Oenpelli Python (*Morelia oenpelliensis*).

large scales present on top of head
agile, slender body
AUSTRALASIA

| Length 8–28ft (2.4–8.5m) | Diet | Activity ☾ |

| Family PYTHONIDAE | Species *Morelia spilota* | Status Common |

CARPET PYTHON

This is the most widespread of all Australian pythons. Typically, the Carpet Python is yellow with brown cross-barring, but there are at least six subspecies in Australia and New Guinea, some of which show other coloration and patterning. The Jungle Carpet Python (*Morelia spilota cheyni*) from Queensland (shown here) is black and yellow, with stripes and large spots, while the Diamond Python (*M. spilota spilota*) of New South Wales has a black edge around every yellow scale, presenting a fine, intricate network pattern.
• **OCCURRENCE** N., E., S. Australia, and S. New Guinea. In savanna and woodland.
• **REPRODUCTION** Lays 12–54 eggs.
• **SIMILAR SPECIES** Centralian Python (*M. bredli*), Rough-scaled Python (*M. carinata*).

yellow background color
large black spots and stripes characteristic of Jungle Carpet Python
head covered in minute scales
AUSTRALASIA

| Length 6½–13ft (2–4m) | Diet | Activity ☾ |

Family PYTHONIDAE	Species *Morelia boeleni*	Status Rare

BOELEN'S PYTHON

This is a powerful python with a broad head and body. The striking pattern of iridescent blue-black, combined with the cream diagonal stripes on the throat and neck, and the black-and-white barring on the lips, are all highly distinctive. The eyes are large, with vertical pupils. Juveniles are red-brown. The natural history of Boelen's Python is poorly known owing to its fragmented range in the remote interior of New Guinea. It appears to prefer low-light, high-humidity habitats.
• **OCCURRENCE** New Guinea. In montane rainforest, above 3,280ft (1,000m).
• **REPRODUCTION** Lays 14–20 eggs.
• **REMARK** This species is the most protected reptile in Papua New Guinea.

black-and-white barring on lips

yellow-white markings extend upward from underside

NEW GUINEA

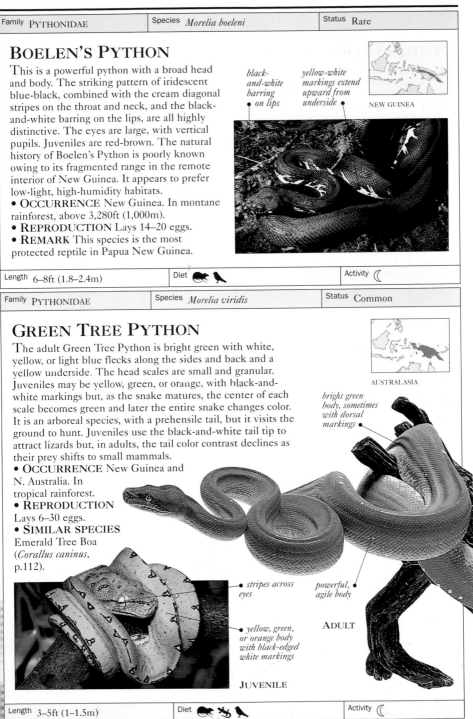

Length 6–8ft (1.8–2.4m)	Diet	Activity ☾

Family PYTHONIDAE	Species *Morelia viridis*	Status Common

GREEN TREE PYTHON

The adult Green Tree Python is bright green with white, yellow, or light blue flecks along the sides and back and a yellow underside. The head scales are small and granular. Juveniles may be yellow, green, or orange, with black-and-white markings but, as the snake matures, the center of each scale becomes green and later the entire snake changes color. It is an arboreal species, with a prehensile tail, but it visits the ground to hunt. Juveniles use the black-and-white tail tip to attract lizards but, in adults, the tail color contrast declines as their prey shifts to small mammals.
• **OCCURRENCE** New Guinea and N. Australia. In tropical rainforest.
• **REPRODUCTION** Lays 6–30 eggs.
• **SIMILAR SPECIES** Emerald Tree Boa (*Corallus caninus*, p.112).

AUSTRALASIA

bright green body, sometimes with dorsal markings

stripes across eyes

powerful, agile body

yellow, green, or orange body with black-edged white markings

ADULT

JUVENILE

Length 3–5ft (1–1.5m)	Diet	Activity ☾

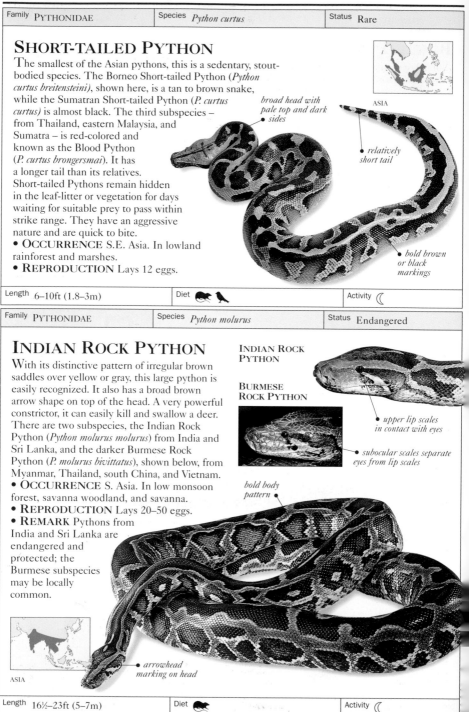

Family PYTHONIDAE	Species *Python curtus*	Status Rare

SHORT-TAILED PYTHON

The smallest of the Asian pythons, this is a sedentary, stout-bodied species. The Borneo Short-tailed Python (*Python curtus breitensteini*), shown here, is a tan to brown snake, while the Sumatran Short-tailed Python (*P. curtus curtus*) is almost black. The third subspecies – from Thailand, eastern Malaysia, and Sumatra – is red-colored and known as the Blood Python (*P. curtus brongersmai*). It has a longer tail than its relatives. Short-tailed Pythons remain hidden in the leaf-litter or vegetation for days waiting for suitable prey to pass within strike range. They have an aggressive nature and are quick to bite.
• OCCURRENCE S.E. Asia. In lowland rainforest and marshes.
• REPRODUCTION Lays 12 eggs.

broad head with pale top and dark sides

ASIA

relatively short tail

bold brown or black markings

Length 6–10ft (1.8–3m)	Diet	Activity ☾

Family PYTHONIDAE	Species *Python molurus*	Status Endangered

INDIAN ROCK PYTHON

With its distinctive pattern of irregular brown saddles over yellow or gray, this large python is easily recognized. It also has a broad brown arrow shape on top of the head. A very powerful constrictor, it can easily kill and swallow a deer. There are two subspecies, the Indian Rock Python (*Python molurus molurus*) from India and Sri Lanka, and the darker Burmese Rock Python (*P. molurus bivittatus*), shown below, from Myanmar, Thailand, south China, and Vietnam.
• OCCURRENCE S. Asia. In low monsoon forest, savanna woodland, and savanna.
• REPRODUCTION Lays 20–50 eggs.
• REMARK Pythons from India and Sri Lanka are endangered and protected; the Burmese subspecies may be locally common.

INDIAN ROCK PYTHON

BURMESE ROCK PYTHON

upper lip scales in contact with eyes

subocular scales separate eyes from lip scales

bold body pattern

arrowhead marking on head

ASIA

Length 16½–23ft (5–7m)	Diet	Activity ☾

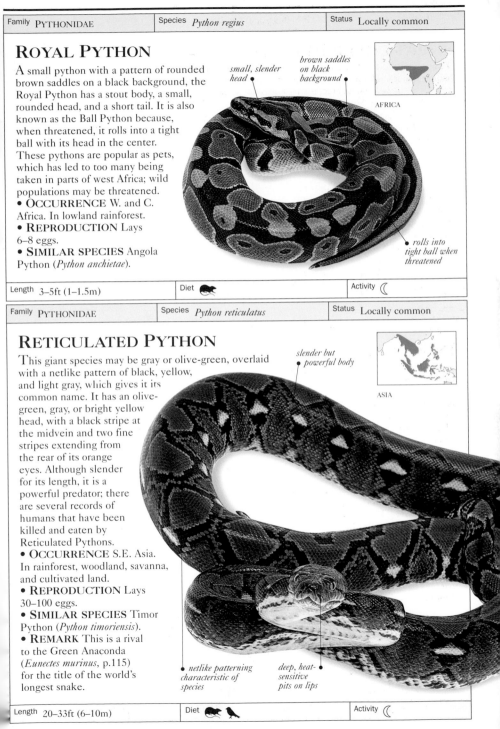

Family PYTHONIDAE	Species *Python regius*	Status Locally common

ROYAL PYTHON

A small python with a pattern of rounded brown saddles on a black background, the Royal Python has a stout body, a small, rounded head, and a short tail. It is also known as the Ball Python because, when threatened, it rolls into a tight ball with its head in the center. These pythons are popular as pets, which has led to too many being taken in parts of west Africa; wild populations may be threatened.
• OCCURRENCE W. and C. Africa. In lowland rainforest.
• REPRODUCTION Lays 6–8 eggs.
• SIMILAR SPECIES Angola Python (*Python anchietae*).

small, slender head
brown saddles on black background
AFRICA
rolls into tight ball when threatened

Length 3–5ft (1–1.5m)	Diet	Activity (

Family PYTHONIDAE	Species *Python reticulatus*	Status Locally common

RETICULATED PYTHON

This giant species may be gray or olive-green, overlaid with a netlike pattern of black, yellow, and light gray, which gives it its common name. It has an olive-green, gray, or bright yellow head, with a black stripe at the midvein and two fine stripes extending from the rear of its orange eyes. Although slender for its length, it is a powerful predator; there are several records of humans that have been killed and eaten by Reticulated Pythons.
• OCCURRENCE S.E. Asia. In rainforest, woodland, savanna, and cultivated land.
• REPRODUCTION Lays 30–100 eggs.
• SIMILAR SPECIES Timor Python (*Python timoriensis*).
• REMARK This is a rival to the Green Anaconda (*Eunectes murinus*, p.115) for the title of the world's longest snake.

slender but powerful body
ASIA
netlike patterning characteristic of species
deep, heat-sensitive pits on lips

Length 20–33ft (6–10m)	Diet	Activity (

Family PYTHONIDAE	Species *Python sebae*	Status Common

AFRICAN ROCK PYTHON

This python is the largest African snake. It is light brown, with overlaying irregular, dark brown saddles and a large, broad, dark brown, arrow-shaped marking on top of its head. African Rock Pythons are extremely powerful predators, easily capable of killing and swallowing large mammals such as antelopes and goats; there are several records of these pythons eating humans. There are two subspecies: *Python sebae sebae* and *P. sebae natalensis* (shown here); the latter has more fragmented head scales.

dark brown saddles • along body

pale brown background • color

AFRICA

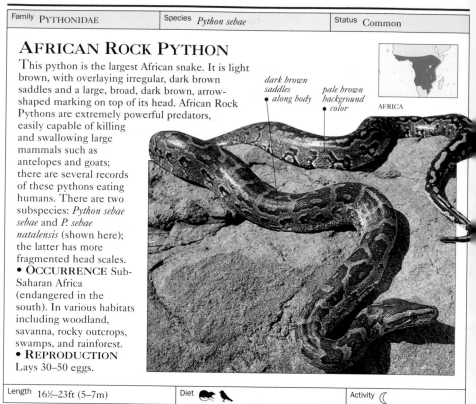

• OCCURRENCE Sub-Saharan Africa (endangered in the south). In various habitats including woodland, savanna, rocky outcrops, swamps, and rainforest.
• REPRODUCTION Lays 30–50 eggs.

Length 16½–23ft (5–7m)	Diet	Activity ☾

Family ACROCHORDIDAE	Species *Acrochordus arafurae*	Status Common

ARAFURA FILESNAKE

This gray or reddish brown filesnake is fully aquatic, so its body is unlike that of a terrestrial or arboreal snake. It has an extremely loose-fitting skin, which flattens like an oar in the water, enabling it to swim gracefully. The loose skin together with the lack of large ventral scales inhibit movement on land.

irregular, dark brown blotches on lighter • background

AUSTRALASIA

• OCCURRENCE New Guinea and N. Australia. In slow-moving freshwater rivers, lakes, and swamps.
• REPRODUCTION Live-bearing, 17 neonates.
• SIMILAR SPECIES Javan Filesnake (*Acrochordus javanicus*).
• REMARK The skins of this species are used to make the traditional "kundu" drums in New Guinea.

strongly keeled scales produce rough, filelike texture

prehensile tail for gripping submerged vegetation •

Length 5–8ft (1.5–2.5m)	Diet	Activity ☾

Family ACROCHORDIDAE	Species *Acrochordus granulatus*	Status Locally common

LITTLE FILESNAKE

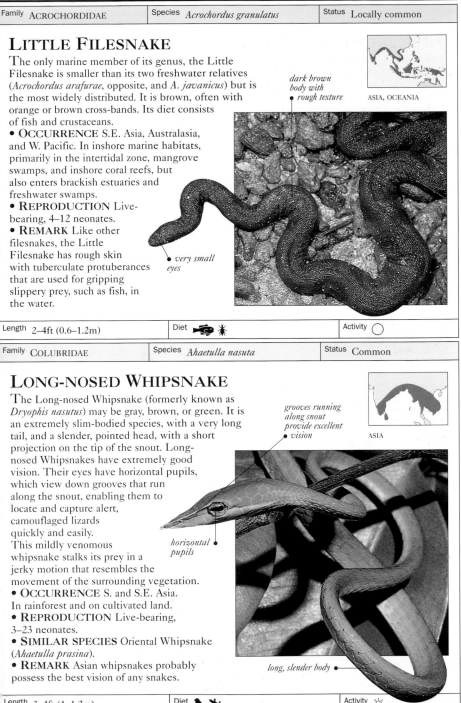

The only marine member of its genus, the Little
Filesnake is smaller than its two freshwater relatives
(*Acrochordus arafurae*, opposite, and *A. javanicus*) but is
the most widely distributed. It is brown, often with
orange or brown cross-bands. Its diet consists
of fish and crustaceans.

*dark brown
body with
rough texture*

ASIA, OCEANIA

• **OCCURRENCE** S.E. Asia, Australasia,
and W. Pacific. In inshore marine habitats,
primarily in the intertidal zone, mangrove
swamps, and inshore coral reefs, but
also enters brackish estuaries and
freshwater swamps.
• **REPRODUCTION** Live-
bearing, 4–12 neonates.
• **REMARK** Like other
filesnakes, the Little
Filesnake has rough skin
with tuberculate protuberances
that are used for gripping
slippery prey, such as fish, in
the water.

*very small
eyes*

Length 2–4ft (0.6–1.2m)	Diet	Activity

Family COLUBRIDAE	Species *Ahaetulla nasuta*	Status Common

LONG-NOSED WHIPSNAKE

The Long-nosed Whipsnake (formerly known as
Dryophis nasutus) may be gray, brown, or green. It is
an extremely slim-bodied species, with a very long
tail, and a slender, pointed head, with a short
projection on the tip of the snout. Long-
nosed Whipsnakes have extremely good
vision. Their eyes have horizontal pupils,
which view down grooves that run
along the snout, enabling them to
locate and capture alert,
camouflaged lizards
quickly and easily.
This mildly venomous
whipsnake stalks its prey in a
jerky motion that resembles the
movement of the surrounding vegetation.

*grooves running
along snout
provide excellent
vision*

ASIA

*horizontal
pupils*

• **OCCURRENCE** S. and S.E. Asia.
In rainforest and on cultivated land.
• **REPRODUCTION** Live-bearing,
3–23 neonates.
• **SIMILAR SPECIES** Oriental Whipsnake
(*Ahaetulla prasina*).
• **REMARK** Asian whipsnakes probably
possess the best vision of any snakes.

long, slender body

Length 3–4ft (1–1.2m)	Diet	Activity

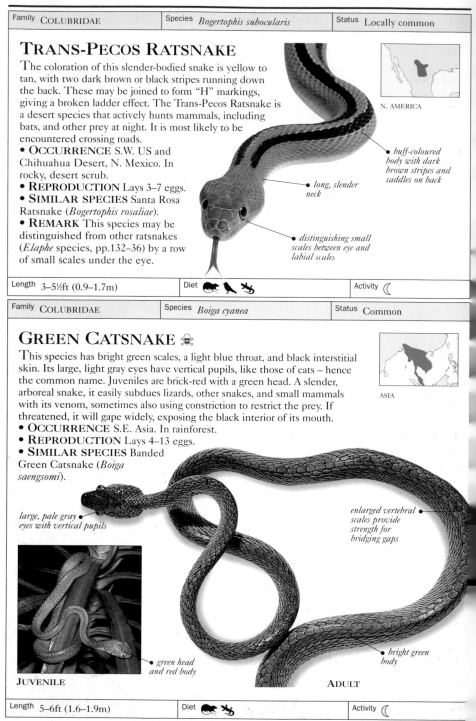

| Family COLUBRIDAE | Species *Bogertophis subocularis* | Status Locally common |

TRANS-PECOS RATSNAKE

The coloration of this slender-bodied snake is yellow to
tan, with two dark brown or black stripes running down
the back. These may be joined to form "H" markings,
giving a broken ladder effect. The Trans-Pecos Ratsnake is
a desert species that actively hunts mammals, including
bats, and other prey at night. It is most likely to be
encountered crossing roads.
• OCCURRENCE S.W. US and
Chihuahua Desert, N. Mexico. In
rocky, desert scrub.
• REPRODUCTION Lays 3–7 eggs.
• SIMILAR SPECIES Santa Rosa
Ratsnake (*Bogertophis rosaliae*).
• REMARK This species may be
distinguished from other ratsnakes
(*Elaphe* species, pp.132–36) by a row
of small scales under the eye.

N. AMERICA

*buff-coloured
body with dark
brown stripes and
saddles on back*

*long, slender
neck*

*distinguishing small
scales between eye and
labial scales*

| Length 3–5½ft (0.9–1.7m) | Diet | Activity ☾ |

| Family COLUBRIDAE | Species *Boiga cyanea* | Status Common |

GREEN CATSNAKE ☠

This species has bright green scales, a light blue throat, and black interstitial
skin. Its large, light gray eyes have vertical pupils, like those of cats – hence
the common name. Juveniles are brick-red with a green head. A slender,
arboreal snake, it easily subdues lizards, other snakes, and small mammals
with its venom, sometimes also using constriction to restrict the prey. If
threatened, it will gape widely, exposing the black interior of its mouth.
• OCCURRENCE S.E. Asia. In rainforest.
• REPRODUCTION Lays 4–13 eggs.
• SIMILAR SPECIES Banded
Green Catsnake (*Boiga
saengsomi*).

ASIA

*large, pale gray
eyes with vertical pupils*

*enlarged vertebral
scales provide
strength for
bridging gaps*

*green head
and red body*

*bright green
body*

JUVENILE

ADULT

| Length 5–6ft (1.6–1.9m) | Diet | Activity ☾ |

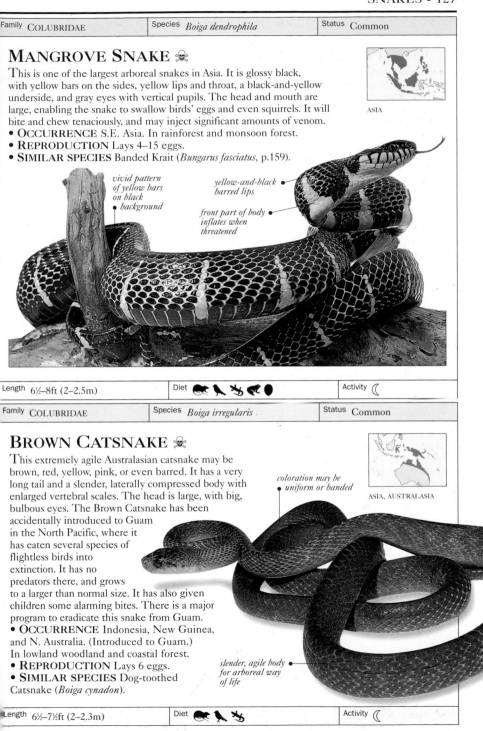

| Family COLUBRIDAE | Species *Boiga dendrophila* | Status Common |

MANGROVE SNAKE ☠

This is one of the largest arboreal snakes in Asia. It is glossy black, with yellow bars on the sides, yellow lips and throat, a black-and-yellow underside, and gray eyes with vertical pupils. The head and mouth are large, enabling the snake to swallow birds' eggs and even squirrels. It will bite and chew tenaciously, and may inject significant amounts of venom.
• **OCCURRENCE** S.E. Asia. In rainforest and monsoon forest.
• **REPRODUCTION** Lays 4–15 eggs.
• **SIMILAR SPECIES** Banded Krait (*Bungarus fasciatus*, p.159).

ASIA

vivid pattern of yellow bars on black background

yellow-and-black barred lips

front part of body inflates when threatened

| Length 6½–8ft (2–2.5m) | Diet | Activity ☾ |

| Family COLUBRIDAE | Species *Boiga irregularis* | Status Common |

BROWN CATSNAKE ☠

This extremely agile Australasian catsnake may be brown, red, yellow, pink, or even barred. It has a very long tail and a slender, laterally compressed body with enlarged vertebral scales. The head is large, with big, bulbous eyes. The Brown Catsnake has been accidentally introduced to Guam in the North Pacific, where it has eaten several species of flightless birds into extinction. It has no predators there, and grows to a larger than normal size. It has also given children some alarming bites. There is a major program to eradicate this snake from Guam.
• **OCCURRENCE** Indonesia, New Guinea, and N. Australia. (Introduced to Guam.) In lowland woodland and coastal forest.
• **REPRODUCTION** Lays 6 eggs.
• **SIMILAR SPECIES** Dog-toothed Catsnake (*Boiga cynadon*).

coloration may be uniform or banded

ASIA, AUSTRALASIA

slender, agile body for arboreal way of life

| Length 6½–7½ft (2–2.3m) | Diet | Activity ☾ |

Family COLUBRIDAE	Species *Chrysopelea paradisi*	Status Rare

PARADISE FLYING SNAKE

This is the most strikingly patterned of the flying snakes. Its body is covered in a complex speckling, which may include areas of black, green, yellow, orange, and red, forming tight chevron markings. Like all flying snakes, it is a very slender, tree-dwelling snake with a long, flat, barred head. It can make the underside of its entire body concave, enabling it to glide from the treetops when it needs to escape a predator or return to the ground quickly. It can also climb the straight trunks of coconut palms rapidly using lengthwise ridges on its scales.

• OCCURRENCE S.E. Asia. In forest and gardens.
• REPRODUCTION Lays 5–8 eggs.

entire body can be flattened for gliding

extremely bright patterning

long head has large eyes with round pupils

ASIA

Length 3–4ft (1–1.2m)	Diet	Activity ☼

Family COLUBRIDAE	Species *Clelia clelia*	Status Rare

MUSSURANA ☠

As a juvenile, the Mussurana is coral-red with a black cap and nape patch, separated by a white collar. When it reaches maturity, it undergoes a dramatic color change, becoming dark blue-black above and white below. Mussuranas are stout-bodied snakes with flat heads. They specialize in feeding on other snakes, including some venomous lanceheads (*Bothrops* species), but they will also prey on lizards and mammals. Juvenile Mussuranas are indistinguishable from juvenile false coralsnakes (*Pseudoboa* species) except for the scales under the tail – these are paired in the Mussurana, and single in false coralsnakes. Found from Guatemala to Argentina and Uruguay, the Mussurana is protected internationally.

C. & S. AMERICA

stout body with flat head

dark blue-black upper surface with white underside

large, glossy body scales, especially in adult

• OCCURRENCE Central and South America. In lowland rainforest.
• REPRODUCTION Lays 10–22 eggs.
• SIMILAR SPECIES Mexican Mussurana (*Clelia scytalina*).

Length 6½–8ft (2–2.5m)	Diet	Activity ☾

| Family COLUBRIDAE | Species *Coluber viridiflavus* | Status Common |

EUROPEAN WHIPSNAKE

This whipsnake is slender with a small head, large eyes with round pupils, and smooth scales. The front part of the body is yellow with broad, green-black cross-bars. These become increasingly dominant toward the rear of the body, and the tail is completely dark. The European Whipsnake preys primarily on lizards, which it hunts by sight and constricts within its coils. It is also extremely alert and fast moving and it will defend itself aggressively if molested. Juveniles hunt frogs, small lizards, grasshoppers, and moths.

• **OCCURRENCE** S. Europe. On dry, rocky and bushy hillsides.
• **REPRODUCTION** Lays 8–15 eggs.
• **SIMILAR SPECIES** Balkan Whipsnake (*Coluber gemonensis*), Large Whipsnake (*C. jugularis*).

slender body with smooth scales

EUROPE

body becomes darker toward rear and on tail

| Length 5–6½ft (1.5–2m) | Diet | Activity ☼ |

| Family COLUBRIDAE | Species *Coronella austriaca* | Status Locally common |

SMOOTH SNAKE

This is a gray, brown, or reddish snake with darker spots along the back, a stripe through the eyes, and darker pigment on the top of the head. The Smooth Snake preys on lizards, which it kills by constriction. It will also feed on the young of other snakes. It is the most protected reptile in Britain, where it is restricted to a small area of lowland heath in Dorset and Hampshire. Throughout the rest of its range, the Smooth Snake is not rare, although it is secretive and rarely encountered.

• **OCCURRENCE** Europe and Middle East. In heathland and dry, rocky habitats.
• **REPRODUCTION** Live-bearing, 2–15 neonates.
• **SIMILAR SPECIES** Southern Smooth Snake (*Coronella girondica*).

EUROPE, MIDDLE EAST

powerful body for constricting prey

lines of dark spots along center of back

smooth, shiny body scales

| Length 20–24in (50–60cm) | Diet | Activity ☼ |

Family COLUBRIDAE	Species *Dasypeltis scabra*	Status Common

COMMON RHOMBIC EGG-EATER

Short and slender, with a rounded head, this snake has gray or brown patterning with darker, viperlike chevrons and saddles. It climbs bushes in search of birds' nests, and it can engorge eggs three times the width of its own head. When the egg reaches the throat, projections of the snake's backbone rupture the shell. The contents are then swallowed and the shell expelled. This species is harmless but may mimic the sawlike warning sound made by the highly venomous carpet vipers (*Echis* species).
• OCCURRENCE Sub-Saharan Africa. In all habitats except rainforest and desert.
• REPRODUCTION Lays 6–18 eggs.
• SIMILAR SPECIES Carpet vipers (*Echis* species, p.186), night adders (*Causus* species).
• REMARK *Dasypeltis* species are the only snakes to lack teeth.

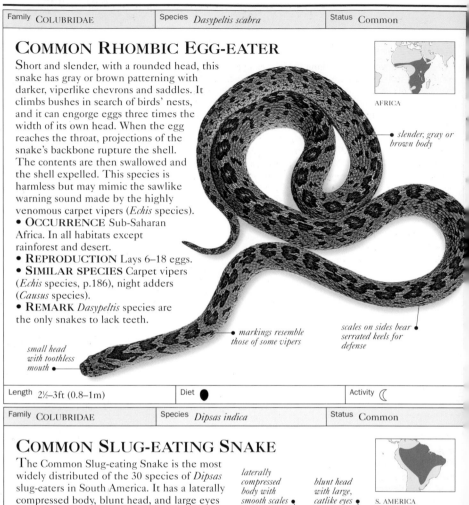

AFRICA

slender, gray or brown body

markings resemble those of some vipers

scales on sides bear serrated keels for defense

small head with toothless mouth •

Length 2½–3ft (0.8–1m)	Diet ●	Activity ☾

Family COLUBRIDAE	Species *Dipsas indica*	Status Common

COMMON SLUG-EATING SNAKE

The Common Slug-eating Snake is the most widely distributed of the 30 species of *Dipsas* slug-eaters in South America. It has a laterally compressed body, blunt head, and large eyes with vertical pupils. Coloration is light brown on the back, with faint, darker ring markings and white spots on the sides, and an unmarked underside. Most other slug-eaters are boldly marked with dark blotches. The slender shape of this snake enables it to move over very fine vegetation and span wide gaps between twigs.
• OCCURRENCE South America. In tropical rainforest.
• REPRODUCTION Lays 2–6 eggs.
• SIMILAR SPECIES Brown Blunt-headed Treesnake (*Imantodes inornatus*).
• REMARK The species name *indica* is a misnomer: the first specimen described was incorrectly labelled as coming from Sri Lanka.

laterally compressed body with smooth scales •

blunt head with large, catlike eyes •

S. AMERICA

Length 24–31in (60–80cm)	Diet ◉	Activity ☾

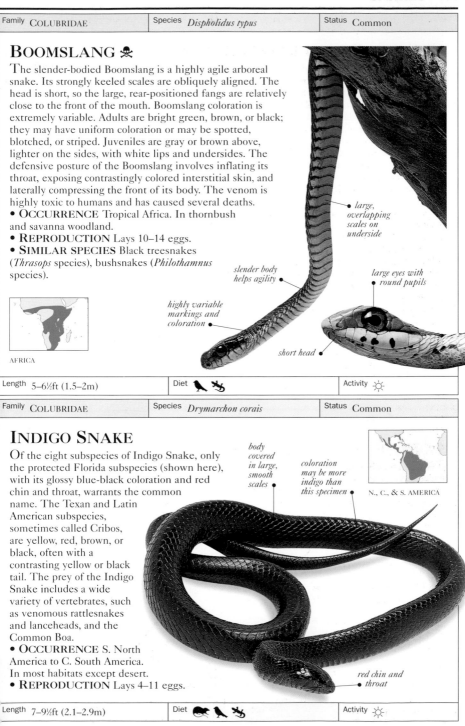

Family COLUBRIDAE	Species *Dispholidus typus*	Status Common

BOOMSLANG ☠

The slender-bodied Boomslang is a highly agile arboreal snake. Its strongly keeled scales are obliquely aligned. The head is short, so the large, rear-positioned fangs are relatively close to the front of the mouth. Boomslang coloration is extremely variable. Adults are bright green, brown, or black; they may have uniform coloration or may be spotted, blotched, or striped. Juveniles are gray or brown above, lighter on the sides, with white lips and undersides. The defensive posture of the Boomslang involves inflating its throat, exposing contrastingly colored interstitial skin, and laterally compressing the front of its body. The venom is highly toxic to humans and has caused several deaths.
- **OCCURRENCE** Tropical Africa. In thornbush and savanna woodland.
- **REPRODUCTION** Lays 10–14 eggs.
- **SIMILAR SPECIES** Black treesnakes (*Thrasops* species), bushsnakes (*Philothamnus* species).

large, overlapping scales on underside

slender body helps agility

large eyes with round pupils

highly variable markings and coloration

short head

AFRICA

Length 5–6½ft (1.5–2m)	Diet 🐦 🦎	Activity ☀

Family COLUBRIDAE	Species *Drymarchon corais*	Status Common

INDIGO SNAKE

Of the eight subspecies of Indigo Snake, only the protected Florida subspecies (shown here), with its glossy blue-black coloration and red chin and throat, warrants the common name. The Texan and Latin American subspecies, sometimes called Cribos, are yellow, red, brown, or black, often with a contrasting yellow or black tail. The prey of the Indigo Snake includes a wide variety of vertebrates, such as venomous rattlesnakes and lanceheads, and the Common Boa.
- **OCCURRENCE** S. North America to C. South America. In most habitats except desert.
- **REPRODUCTION** Lays 4–11 eggs.

body covered in large, smooth scales

coloration may be more indigo than this specimen

N., C., & S. AMERICA

red chin and throat

Length 7–9½ft (2.1–2.9m)	Diet 🐀 🐍 🦎	Activity ☀

Family COLUBRIDAE	Species *Elaphe guttata*	Status Common

CORNSNAKE

The Cornsnake is one of the best-known and most colorful of all the ratsnakes. Of the four subspecies, the most well known and typical is *Elaphe guttata guttata* from the southeastern US, which is usually orange with red saddles and sometimes has a black-and-white checkerboard underside (paler specimens from southern Florida were formerly recognized as a separate subspecies, *E. guttata rosacea*). Juvenile Cornsnakes are grey to brown and lack the colourful markings of the adult. The other three subspecies – Emory's Ratsnake or Great Plains Ratsnake (*E. guttata emoryi*), *E. guttata intermontana*, and *E. guttata meahllmorum* – occur in southern central US and northeast Mexico, and are basically gray. Cornsnakes are active predators, often encountered hunting small mammals around farm buildings or crossing roads at night. They are popular pets and several captive-bred color variants, known as "cultivars," are available. Variants include albinos, which are commonly called Snow Corns, and partial albinos that lack either black pigment (amelanistic specimens) or red or orange pigment (anerythristic specimens, commonly known as Black Corns).
• **OCCURRENCE** E. and C. North America. In a wide variety of habitats, from dry woodland and swamps to railway embankments and farmland.
• **REPRODUCTION** Lays 6–25 eggs.
• **SIMILAR SPECIES** European Leopard Snake (*E. situla*), Green Ratsnake (*E. triaspis*).

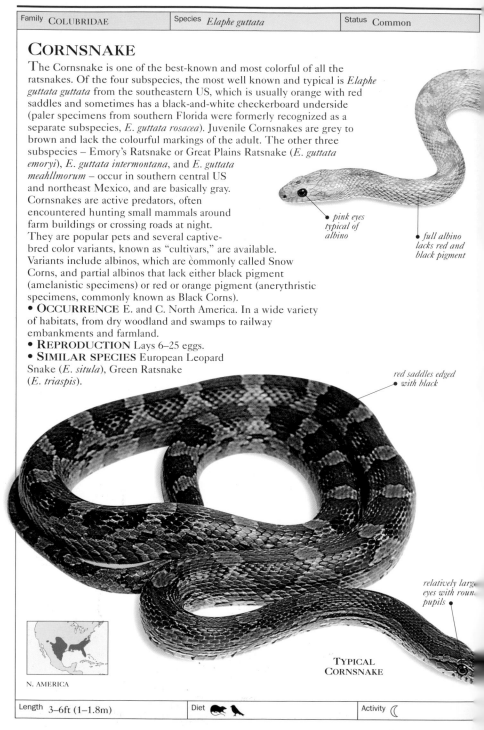

pink eyes typical of albino

full albino lacks red and black pigment

red saddles edged with black

relatively large eyes with round pupils

TYPICAL CORNSNAKE

N. AMERICA

Length 3–6ft (1–1.8m)	Diet	Activity ☾

SNOW CORN

body arched in cross
section, enabling snake to
wedge itself into bark when
scaling tree trunks ●

BLACK CORN

● skin lacks
red or orange
pigment, so
snake is gray

red saddles edged
● with white

● skin lacks
black pigment

smooth body ●
scales

AMELANISTIC
SPECIMEN

Family COLUBRIDAE	Species *Elaphe obsoleta*	Status Common

COMMON RATSNAKE

This extremely variably patterned species is divided into at least
five distinctly different subspecies, including: the Black Ratsnake
(*Elaphe obsoleta obsoleta*) in the north; the Gray Ratsnake (*E. obsoleta
spiloides*) in the south; the Yellow Ratsnake or Chicken Snake
(*E. obsoleta quadrivittata*) in the southeast; the black-and-yellow
Texas Ratsnake (*E. obsoleta lindheimeri*) in central and eastern Texas
and Louisiana; and the Orange or Everglades Ratsnake (*E. obsoleta
rossalleni*), which is confined to south Florida. These are among the
largest snakes in the US and have pugnacious dispositions. All
ratsnakes are expert climbers and they also swim well. Prey includes
large rats and squirrels, which are killed by
constriction. Juvenile ratsnakes are usually
very different in appearance from adults, the
hatchlings of Yellow Ratsnakes bearing a closer
resemblance to miniature Gray Ratsnakes.
• OCCURRENCE E. North America. Black
and Gray Ratsnakes occur mainly in deciduous
forest, but also in farmland; Yellow and Orange
Ratsnakes inhabit lowland pinelands, swamps,
and mangrove hammocks; Texas Ratsnakes
are found in drier habitats.
• REPRODUCTION Lays 5–30 eggs.
• SIMILAR SPECIES Baird's Ratsnake
(*E. bairdi*), Cornsnake (*E. guttata*, pp.132–33).

N. AMERICA

orange body coloration

ORANGE OR EVERGLADES RATSNAKE

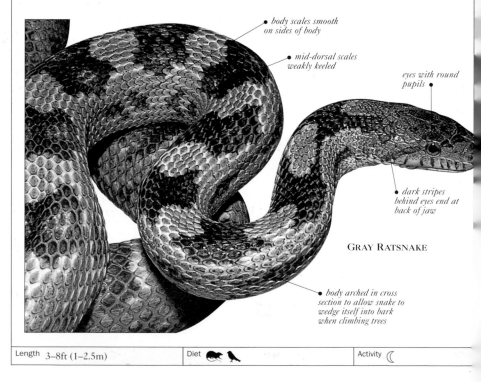

body scales smooth on sides of body

mid-dorsal scales weakly keeled

eyes with round pupils

dark stripes behind eyes end at back of jaw

GRAY RATSNAKE

body arched in cross section to allow snake to wedge itself into bark when climbing trees

Length 3–8ft (1–2.5m)	Diet	Activity ☾

Family COLUBRIDAE	Species *Elaphe longissima*	Status Common

AESCULAPIAN SNAKE

This fairly uniform olive-brown or speckled ratsnake is named after Aesculapius, the Greek god of medicine, who bore a staff entwined with a snake – the symbol of medicine today. Aesculapian Snakes are large constrictors that occur in arid, Mediterranean-type habitats, often hunting rats among the boulders of old drystone walls. Juveniles (shown here), which feed on lizards, are usually lighter with rows of dark spots. Like juvenile Grass Snakes (*Natrix natrix*, p.148), juvenile Aesculapian Snakes have a yellow collar.

EUROPE, ASIA

eyes with round pupils

checkerboard patterning on body of juvenile

• **OCCURRENCE** S. Europe and W. Asia. In dry lowland scrub and upland rocky slopes.
• **REPRODUCTION** Lays 5–12 eggs.
• **SIMILAR SPECIES** Ladder Snake (*Elaphe scalaris*).
• **REMARK** The Romans, who also worshipped Aesculapius, transported these snakes throughout the Empire in earthenware containers and introduced them into their temples, considering them to be sacred.

Length 4½–7ft (1.4–2.2m)	Diet	Activity (

Family COLUBRIDAE	Species *Elaphe mandarina*	Status Rare

MANDARIN RATSNAKE

The Mandarin Ratsnake is basically gray, with black diamond markings with yellow centers and edges on the back, and black-and-yellow chevrons over the head. Little is known about this species, but it is believed to hunt infant mice in their burrows. Although the main habitat of the Mandarin Ratsnake appears to be montane forest containing open areas and rocks, it is occasionally encountered under rocky scree and in cavities under large stones.

eyes with round pupils

black-and-yellow chevron over head

• **OCCURRENCE** E. Asia. In montane forest and rocky habitats.
• **REPRODUCTION** Lays 8 eggs.
• **SIMILAR SPECIES** Japanese Forest Ratsnake (*Elaphe conspicillata*).

ASIA

pale gray background color

black, diamond-shaped spots with large yellow centers and edges

Length 3–5ft (1–1.6m)	Diet	Activity (

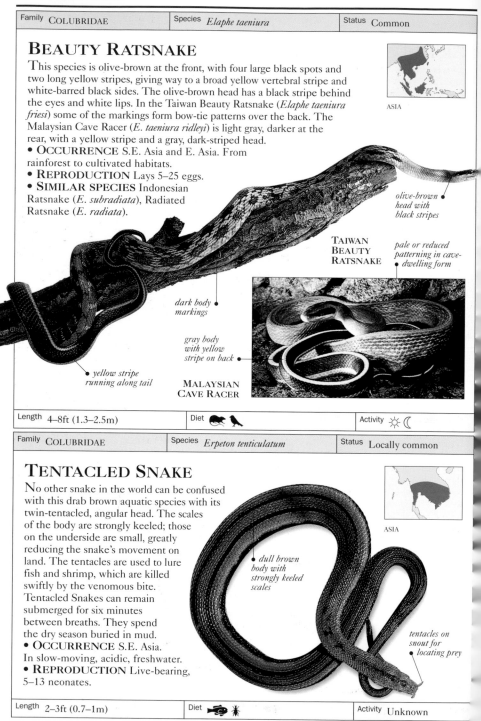

Family COLUBRIDAE	Species *Elaphe taeniura*	Status Common

BEAUTY RATSNAKE

This species is olive-brown at the front, with four large black spots and two long yellow stripes, giving way to a broad yellow vertebral stripe and white-barred black sides. The olive-brown head has a black stripe behind the eyes and white lips. In the Taiwan Beauty Ratsnake (*Elaphe taeniura friesi*) some of the markings form bow-tie patterns over the back. The Malaysian Cave Racer (*E. taeniura ridleyi*) is light gray, darker at the rear, with a yellow stripe and a gray, dark-striped head.

• OCCURRENCE S.E. Asia and E. Asia. From rainforest to cultivated habitats.
• REPRODUCTION Lays 5–25 eggs.
• SIMILAR SPECIES Indonesian Ratsnake (*E. subradiata*), Radiated Ratsnake (*E. radiata*).

ASIA

olive-brown head with black stripes

TAIWAN BEAUTY RATSNAKE

pale or reduced patterning in cave-dwelling form

dark body markings

gray body with yellow stripe on back

yellow stripe running along tail

MALAYSIAN CAVE RACER

Length 4–8ft (1.3–2.5m)	Diet	Activity ☼ ☾

Family COLUBRIDAE	Species *Erpeton tenticulatum*	Status Locally common

TENTACLED SNAKE

No other snake in the world can be confused with this drab brown aquatic species with its twin-tentacled, angular head. The scales of the body are strongly keeled; those on the underside are small, greatly reducing the snake's movement on land. The tentacles are used to lure fish and shrimp, which are killed swiftly by the venomous bite. Tentacled Snakes can remain submerged for six minutes between breaths. They spend the dry season buried in mud.

• OCCURRENCE S.E. Asia. In slow-moving, acidic, freshwater.
• REPRODUCTION Live-bearing, 5–13 neonates.

ASIA

dull brown body with strongly keeled scales

tentacles on snout for locating prey

Length 2–3ft (0.7–1m)	Diet	Activity Unknown

| Family COLUBRIDAE | Species *Fordonia leucobalia* | Status Common |

CRAB-EATING WATER SNAKE

This is a variably colored species, with yellow, orange, black, and mottled specimens. It has smooth body scales and a rounded head with small eyes and a reduced lower jaw. Also known as the White-bellied Mangrove Snake, it inhabits the zone where land and sea overlap. It shares the burrows of crabs, which are its main prey.
• **OCCURRENCE** S.E. Asia and Australasia. In mangrove swamps and estuarine mudflats.
• **REPRODUCTION** Live-bearing, 10–15 neonates.
• **SIMILAR SPECIES** Water snakes (*Enhydris* and *Myron* species).

ASIA, AUSTRALASIA

highly variable coloration including black or dark gray

yellow body coloring in some specimens

short, rounded head and small eyes

| Length 24–35in (60–90cm) | Diet 🐜🦀 | Activity ☾ |

| Family COLUBRIDAE | Species *Gonyosoma oxycephala* | Status Common |

RED-TAILED RACER

A fast-moving, alert, arboreal species, the Red-tailed Racer is usually vivid, shiny green, with a long, slender, red, brown, or gray tail; some specimens may be yellow or brown. A dark line passes through the large eyes, separating the green crown of the head from the yellow-green lips. When alarmed, this snake will inflate a secondary air sac in its throat, causing the front of the body to become enlarged and stiff, and exposing dark skin between the scales. It will gape, showing the black inside of the mouth, and strike toward its aggressor. Prey, which includes bats captured on the wing, will be constricted in the snake's muscular coils.
• **OCCURRENCE** S.E. Asia. In rainforest.
• **REPRODUCTION** Lays 5–12 eggs.
• **SIMILAR SPECIES** Green Tree Racer (*Elaphe prasina*).

ASIA

green head with dark eye-markings and yellow-green lips

long, brown or red tail

vivid green body

| Length 5–8ft (1.6–2.4m) | Diet 🐀🐦 | Activity ☀ |

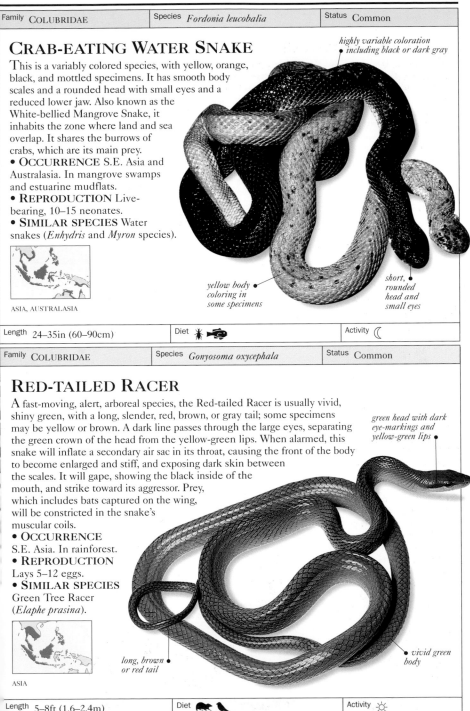

| Family COLUBRIDAE | Species *Heterodon nasicus* | Status Common |

WESTERN HOGNOSE SNAKE

The upturned snout of the Western Hognose Snake separates this species from most other North American snakes. The body is stout and pale gray, with several rows of square brown or gray blotches along the back. The large black blotches on the underside are absent on other hognose snakes.
• OCCURRENCE S. Canada, C. US, and
N.E. Mexico. In sandy areas
and prairies.
• REPRODUCTION
Lays 4–23 eggs.
• SIMILAR SPECIES
Eastern Hognose
(*Heterodon platyrhinos*),
Southern Hognose
(*H. simus*).

N. AMERICA

snout upturned for
rooting in leaf-
litter for prey

roughly keeled
body scales

gray body with brown or
gray blotches on back

| Length 16–31in (40–80cm) | Diet | Activity |

| Family COLUBRIDAE | Species *Hydrodynastes gigas* | Status Locally common |

FALSE WATER COBRA

This semiaquatic species is easily recognizable because of its large size, smooth scales, and stout body. The background color is yellow-brown, with dark brown blotches edged in black or very dark brown. There are occasional light brown patches toward the tail. The head bears a broad black streak behind the eye and a black "V" on the nape. This species spreads its neck into a cobralike hood, but it is not a true cobra.
• REPRODUCTION Lays 30–42 eggs.
• OCCURRENCE C. South
America. In flooded grassland
and forest.
• SIMILAR SPECIES
Cribo (*Drymarchon
corais*, p.131).

S. AMERICA

brown coloration
with dark-edged
blotches

broad black
streak behind
eyes

stout, smooth-
scaled body

| Length 5–6½ft (1.5–2m) | Diet | Activity |

Family COLUBRIDAE	Species *Imantodes cenchoa*	Status Locally common

BLUNT-HEADED TREESNAKE

The body of the Blunt-headed Treesnake is very light and slender,
enabling this species to venture onto the most delicate vegetation in
order to capture sleeping lizards. The blunt head is surprisingly large
in comparison to the body, and the eyes are bulbous. The scales along
the back are enlarged (they are three to four times the size of the
scales along the sides) and act as a cantilever, allowing the treesnake
to bridge wide gaps with ease. This
snake hunts its sleeping prey using its
eyes and its chemosensory tongue.
• OCCURRENCE Central and
South America. In tropical dry
and wet forests.
• REPRODUCTION
Lays 1–3 eggs.
• SIMILAR SPECIES
Central American
Treesnake
(*Imantodes
gemmistratus*).

C. & S. AMERICA

*long, very
slender, orange
• to pink body*

*flat, blunt head •
gives this snake its
common name*

Length 3–4ft (1–1.2m)	Diet 🦎🐸	Activity ☾

Family COLUBRIDAE	Species *Lamprophis fuliginosus*	Status Common

COMMON HOUSESNAKE

Probably the most ubiquitous snake in sub-Saharan Africa, the
harmless Common Housesnake is highly variable in coloration,
ranging from almost black to dark brown, sandy brown, or red. This
species may be confused with other African housesnakes. All possess
smooth scales and a long, slender head with small eyes and vertical
pupils, but the Common Housesnake usually also
has a pale streak running from the snout to
behind the eyes. Females may lay several
clutches of eggs in each breeding season.
• OCCURRENCE Sub-Saharan
Africa. In a wide variety of habitats,
including woodland, savanna,
farmland, and buildings.
• REPRODUCTION
Lays 8–16 eggs.
• SIMILAR
SPECIES Lined
Housesnake
(*Lamprophis lineatus*).

AFRICA

*pale streak runs
from snout to
• behind eyes*

*smooth brown, •
red, or black body*

Length 3–5ft (0.9–1.5m)	Diet 🐀🦎	Activity ☾

Family COLUBRIDAE	Species *Lampropeltis getula*	Status Common

COMMON KINGSNAKE

N. AMERICA

One of the best-known North American snakes, the Common Kingsnake is also one of the most variably patterned. There are between 7 and 10 subspecies. The Eastern Kingsnake (*Lampropeltis getula getula*) is also known as the Chain Kingsnake because of its body pattern of black with overlying yellow chain markings. The Desert Kingsnake (*L. getula splendida*) is similar but has more yellow speckling on the sides and a totally black mask over the head. Each black scale of the Speckled Kingsnake (*L. getula holbrooki*) has a yellow center, while the Black Kingsnake (*L. getula niger*) and the Mexican Black Kingsnake (*L. getula nigritus*) are almost entirely black. The Florida Kingsnake (*L. getula floridana*) may be brown with yellow markings, or the reverse; while the Californian Kingsnake (*L. getula californiae*) is the most variable subspecies, with both banded and striped specimens being produced from the same clutch of eggs. Primarily terrestrial, kingsnakes are powerful constrictors. They prey on small mammals, but also eat other snakes – including venomous ones such as rattlesnakes (*Crotalus* and *Sistrurus* species), to whose bites they are immune.

light vertebral stripe on brown background

• OCCURRENCE North America. In a wide variety of habitats, including woodland, farmland, and grassland.
• REPRODUCTION Lays 3–24 eggs.
• SIMILAR SPECIES Pinesnakes (*Pituophis* species, p.149).

CALIFORNIAN KINGSNAKE (STRIPED)

series of black spots down centre of back

numerous yellow speckles on black background

powerful body for constricting prey

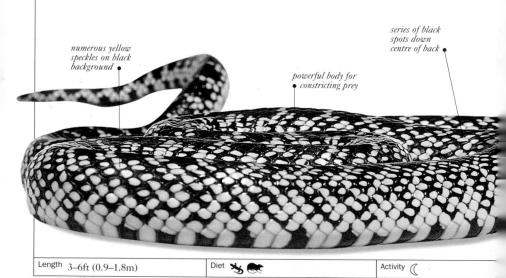

Length 3–6ft (0.9–1.8m)	Diet 🦎 🐀	Activity ☾

brown-and-yellow netlike body markings

large, smooth body scales

FLORIDA KINGSNAKE

distinctive yellow bands from head to tail

CALIFORNIAN KINGSNAKE (BANDED)

saddles may be black or brown

black mask marking over head and neck

eyes have round pupils

glossy black body with no markings

DESERT KINGSNAKE

MEXICAN BLACK KINGSNAKE

Family COLUBRIDAE	Species *Lampropeltis triangulum*	Status Common

AMERICAN MILKSNAKE

N., C., & S. AMERICA

One of the most widely distributed of all terrestrial snakes, the American Milksnake is found from southeastern Canada to Colombia and Ecuador. There are 25 subspecies, varying in size from the diminutive Scarlet Kingsnake (*Lampropeltis triangulum elapsoides*), which grows to 20in (50cm) long, to the 6½ft (2m) Ecuadorian Milksnake (*L. triangulum micropholis*). Most subspecies have characteristic red, black, and yellow (or white) banding, but in some races the red markings may be reduced to black-edged saddles on a pale background. In other races the yellow pigment may be obscured by red or black, as in the Honduran Milksnake (*L. triangulum hondurensis*). There is also an entirely black subspecies. The Central Plains Milksnake (*L. triangulum gentilis*) is paler than most other milksnakes, and the Eastern Milksnake (*L. triangulum triangulum*) is unusual in that it has red-brown saddle markings. The Mexican Milksnake (*L. triangulum annulata*) has red rings uninterrupted by black, and in the Sinaloan Milksnake (*L. triangulum sinaloae*) the first red ring is usually relatively long. Milksnakes are semiburrowing.

• **OCCURRENCE** North and Central America and N.W. South America. In a variety of habitats except true desert.
• **REPRODUCTION** Lays 5–16 eggs.
• **SIMILAR SPECIES** Arizona Kingsnake (*L. pyromelana*), coralsnakes (*Micrurus* species, pp.163–64).

body pattern of bl. and yellow bands or background

SINALOAN MILKSNAKE

first red ring usually relati• long

black pigment obscures yellow in • cross-bands

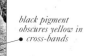

HONDURAN MILKSNAKE

Length 2–6½ft (0.5–2m)	Diet	Activity ☽

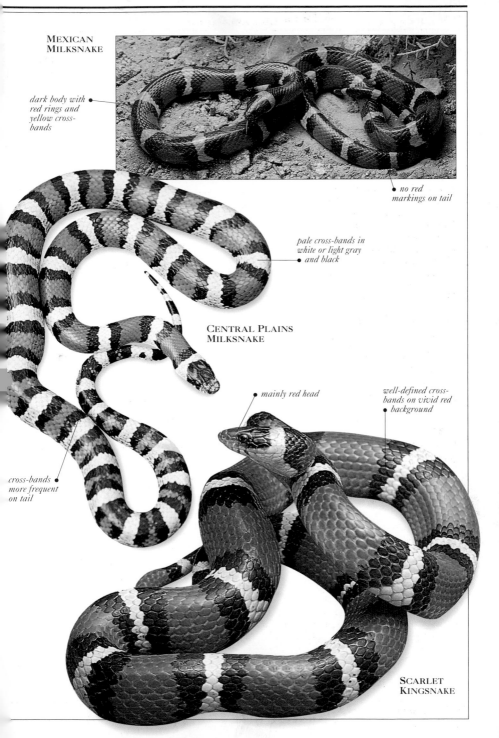

MEXICAN MILKSNAKE

dark body with red rings and yellow cross-bands

no red markings on tail

pale cross-bands in white or light gray and black

CENTRAL PLAINS MILKSNAKE

mainly red head

well-defined cross-bands on vivid red background

cross-bands more frequent on tail

SCARLET KINGSNAKE

Family COLUBRIDAE	Species *Langaha madagascariensis*	Status Locally common

MADAGASCAN LEAFNOSE VINESNAKE

The Madagascan Leafnose Vinesnake is one of the strangest-looking
snakes in the world. It is long and slender, with strongly keeled scales. Both
male and female have unusual projections on the snout. The male has a soft
spike on the snout tip; in the female, the appendage is more elaborate and
resembles a laterally compressed flower bud or fir cone. These adornments
add to the vinesnake's cryptic camouflage, so that when motionless it is
invisible to both predators and prey. Males and females also differ in their
coloration. The males are brown above and yellow below, with a distinct
line between the two colors; females are light gray with gray-brown
saddles. Although little is known about this species, it is known to
be an arboreal predator of lizards.
- **OCCURRENCE** Madagascar. In forest and woodland.
- **REPRODUCTION** Lays 3 eggs.
- **SIMILAR SPECIES** Northern Leafnose
(*Langaha pseudoalluaudi*), Southern Leafnose
(*L. alluaudi*).

MADAGASCAR

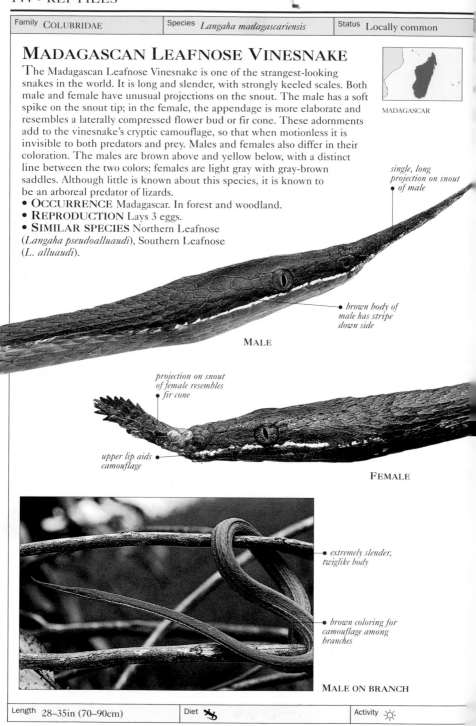

*single, long
projection on snout
of male*

*brown body of
male has stripe
down side*

MALE

*projection on snout
of female resembles
fir cone*

*upper lip aids
camouflage*

FEMALE

*extremely slender,
twiglike body*

*brown coloring for
camouflage among
branches*

MALE ON BRANCH

Length 28–35in (70–90cm)	Diet 🦎	Activity ☼

Family COLUBRIDAE	Species *Leioheterodon madagascariensis*	Status Common

GIANT MALAGASY HOGNOSE SNAKE ☠

The bold pattern of black, flecked with yellow, and dark brown saddles on a light brown background makes this an imposing species. Its large head is black above and cream below, and it has an upturned snout for excavating in leaf-litter and soft earth in search of prey. This is the largest Madagascan snake after the boas; it is also one of the island's most common snakes. Bites from the related Brown Hognose Snake (*Leioheterodon modestus*) have resulted in unpleasant symptoms, so the Giant Malagasy Hognose Snake should be treated with respect.
• **OCCURRENCE** Madagascar. (Introduced to Comoros.) In forest.
• **REPRODUCTION** Lays 5–13 eggs.

MADAGASCAR

variable body • coloration

black-and-cream head has upturned snout •

checkerboard pattern • of black and dark brown on light brown background

Length 3–5ft (1–1.5m)	Diet 🐸 🦎 🐀	Activity ☼

Family COLUBRIDAE	Species *Leptophis diplotropis*	Status Common

PACIFIC COAST PARROT SNAKE ☠

Bright green and yellow in color, with the scales of the body often edged with black, the Pacific Coast Parrot Snake blends into its woodland habitat when stationary. This species is an extremely alert predator that may be seen hunting for lizards or frogs in vegetation along riverbanks. When threatened, it rears up and inflates the curved front part of the body, then gapes widely to expose the blue-black inside of the mouth before launching aggressive strikes toward the perceived enemy. Several painful bites are on record from parrot snakes.
• **OCCURRENCE** W. Mexico. In lowland, coastal forest.
• **REPRODUCTION** Lays 1–3 eggs.
• **SIMILAR SPECIES** Common Parrot Snake (*Leptophis ahaetulla*).
• **REMARK** This is the most northern of seven species of parrot snake.

N. AMERICA

striking green-and- • yellow body color

blue-black interior to mouth •

large eyes give good • daytime vision

Length 3–5ft (1–1.5m)	Diet 🐸 🦎 🐦 🐀	Activity ☼

Family COLUBRIDAE	Species *Macroprotodon cucullatus*	Status Common

FALSE SMOOTH SNAKE

Also known as the Hooded or Cowl Snake
because of the dark head markings, this
mildly venomous lizard-eater is light gray
to brown above, with faint black markings
on the sides. A black streak runs from each
eye to the jaw. The underside is pink,
yellow, or checkerboard black and white.
• OCCURRENCE S.W. Europe and
N. Africa. In open woodland and sandy scrub.
• REPRODUCTION Lays 5–7 eggs.
• SIMILAR SPECIES Smooth Snake
(*Coronella austriaca*, p.129).

black streaks
run from
eyes to jaw

dark
markings
at rear of
head

EUROPE, AFRICA

Length 24–25½in (60–65cm)	Diet	Activity

Family COLUBRIDAE	Species *Malpolon monspessulanus*	Status Common

MONTPELLIER SNAKE

This large species is brown, sometimes striped.
It moves around rapidly in the day searching for
prey. When cornered, the snake flattens its
body, spreads its neck, hisses loudly,
and strikes quickly.
• OCCURRENCE S. Europe,
N. Africa, and S.W. Asia.
In rocky scrub and arid
semidesert.
• REPRODUCTION Lays
4–20 eggs.

long,
slender
brown body

large eyes
characteristic
of an alert,
diurnal
predator

EUROPE, AFRICA, ASIA

Length 5–6½ft (1.5–2m)	Diet	Activity

Family COLUBRIDAE	Species *Masticophis flagellum*	Status Common

COACHWHIP

The Coachwhip is extremely variably
colored. Individuals may be black,
brown, or buff, either uniform in
color or with yellow stripes or bands.
Some individuals may be entirely red or
pink. These highly active snakes hunt
using vision and run their prey down
quickly. They flee from man but bite
vigorously if handled.
• OCCURRENCE North America. In
prairies, desert, woodland, and farmland.
• REPRODUCTION Lays 4–20 eggs.
• SIMILAR SPECIES Sonoran
Whipsnake (*Masticophis bilineatus*),
Striped Whipsnake (*M. taeniatus*).

very thin,
whiplike tail

slender body
highly variable
in color

N. AMERICA

Length 3–8ft (0.9–2.5m)	Diet	Activity

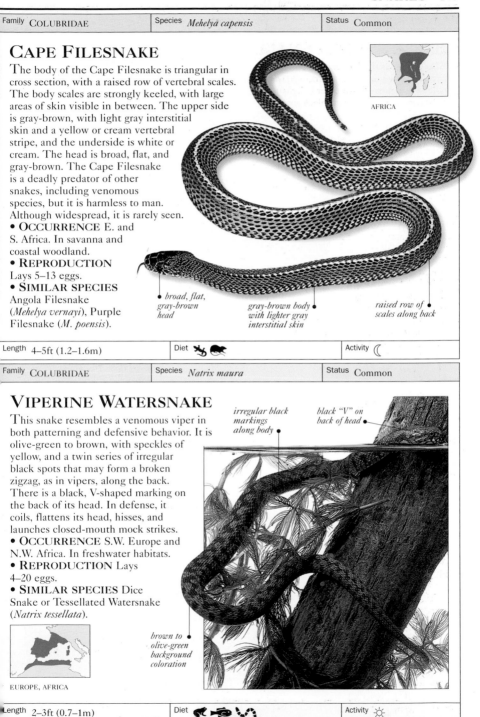

| Family COLUBRIDAE | Species *Mehelya capensis* | Status Common |

CAPE FILESNAKE

The body of the Cape Filesnake is triangular in cross section, with a raised row of vertebral scales. The body scales are strongly keeled, with large areas of skin visible in between. The upper side is gray-brown, with light gray interstitial skin and a yellow or cream vertebral stripe, and the underside is white or cream. The head is broad, flat, and gray-brown. The Cape Filesnake is a deadly predator of other snakes, including venomous species, but it is harmless to man. Although widespread, it is rarely seen.
• **OCCURRENCE** E. and S. Africa. In savanna and coastal woodland.
• **REPRODUCTION** Lays 5–13 eggs.
• **SIMILAR SPECIES** Angola Filesnake (*Mehelya vernayi*), Purple Filesnake (*M. poensis*).

AFRICA

• broad, flat, gray-brown head

gray-brown body • with lighter gray interstitial skin

raised row of • scales along back

| Length 4–5ft (1.2–1.6m) | Diet | Activity ☾ |

| Family COLUBRIDAE | Species *Natrix maura* | Status Common |

VIPERINE WATERSNAKE

This snake resembles a venomous viper in both patterning and defensive behavior. It is olive-green to brown, with speckles of yellow, and a twin series of irregular black spots that may form a broken zigzag, as in vipers, along the back. There is a black, V-shaped marking on the back of its head. In defense, it coils, flattens its head, hisses, and launches closed-mouth mock strikes.
• **OCCURRENCE** S.W. Europe and N.W. Africa. In freshwater habitats.
• **REPRODUCTION** Lays 4–20 eggs.
• **SIMILAR SPECIES** Dice Snake or Tessellated Watersnake (*Natrix tessellata*).

irregular black markings along body •

black "V" on back of head •

brown to • olive-green background coloration

EUROPE, AFRICA

| Length 2–3ft (0.7–1m) | Diet | Activity ☀ |

| Family COLUBRIDAE | Species *Natrix natrix* | Status Common |

GRASS SNAKE

Most Grass Snakes are green or olive-brown. The Barred Grass Snake (*Natrix natrix helvetica*, shown here) of western Europe is usually recognized by its double black-and-yellow collar, but this feature is less distinct in the Green-collared Grass Snake (*N. natrix astreptophora*) of Iberia and North Africa. The Balkan Grass Snake (*N. natrix persa*) has two light stripes, while the Crimean Grass Snake (*N. natrix scutata*) is spotted with black. Grass Snakes are often seen gliding across water in search of frogs. They hiss, feign death, and void their cloacal glands when threatened.
• OCCURRENCE Europe, N.W. Africa, and W. and C. Asia. In freshwater habitats.
• REPRODUCTION Lays 8–40 eggs.
• SIMILAR SPECIES Large-headed Grass Snake (*N. megalocephala*).

EUROPE, AFRICA, ASIA

green to olive-brown body with black markings

large eyes with round pupils

yellow-and-black-collar marking usually visible

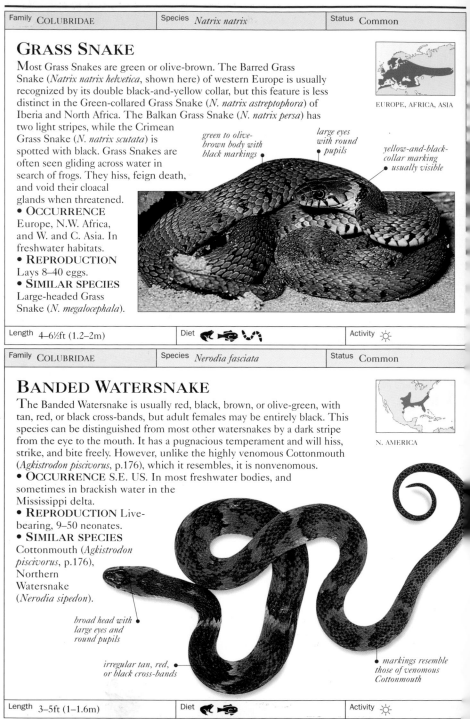

| Length 4–6½ft (1.2–2m) | Diet | Activity ☼ |

| Family COLUBRIDAE | Species *Nerodia fasciata* | Status Common |

BANDED WATERSNAKE

The Banded Watersnake is usually red, black, brown, or olive-green, with tan, red, or black cross-bands, but adult females may be entirely black. This species can be distinguished from most other watersnakes by a dark stripe from the eye to the mouth. It has a pugnacious temperament and will hiss, strike, and bite freely. However, unlike the highly venomous Cottonmouth (*Agkistrodon piscivorus*, p.176), which it resembles, it is nonvenomous.
• OCCURRENCE S.E. US. In most freshwater bodies, and sometimes in brackish water in the Mississippi delta.
• REPRODUCTION Live-bearing, 9–50 neonates.
• SIMILAR SPECIES Cottonmouth (*Agkistrodon piscivorus*, p.176), Northern Watersnake (*Nerodia sipedon*).

N. AMERICA

broad head with large eyes and round pupils

irregular tan, red, or black cross-bands

markings resemble those of venomous Cottonmouth

| Length 3–5ft (1–1.6m) | Diet | Activity ☼ |

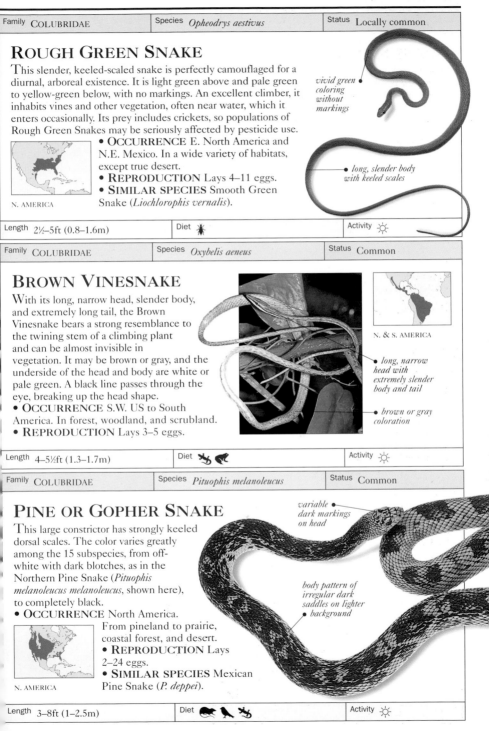

Family COLUBRIDAE	Species *Opheodrys aestivus*	Status Locally common

ROUGH GREEN SNAKE

This slender, keeled-scaled snake is perfectly camouflaged for a diurnal, arboreal existence. It is light green above and pale green to yellow-green below, with no markings. An excellent climber, it inhabits vines and other vegetation, often near water, which it enters occasionally. Its prey includes crickets, so populations of Rough Green Snakes may be seriously affected by pesticide use.

vivid green coloring without markings

- **OCCURRENCE** E. North America and N.E. Mexico. In a wide variety of habitats, except true desert.
- **REPRODUCTION** Lays 4–11 eggs.
- **SIMILAR SPECIES** Smooth Green Snake (*Liochlorophis vernalis*).

N. AMERICA

long, slender body with keeled scales

Length 2½–5ft (0.8–1.6m)	Diet 🦗	Activity ☀

Family COLUBRIDAE	Species *Oxybelis aeneus*	Status Common

BROWN VINESNAKE

With its long, narrow head, slender body, and extremely long tail, the Brown Vinesnake bears a strong resemblance to the twining stem of a climbing plant and can be almost invisible in vegetation. It may be brown or gray, and the underside of the head and body are white or pale green. A black line passes through the eye, breaking up the head shape.

- **OCCURRENCE** S.W. US to South America. In forest, woodland, and scrubland.
- **REPRODUCTION** Lays 3–5 eggs.

N. & S. AMERICA

long, narrow head with extremely slender body and tail

brown or gray coloration

Length 4–5½ft (1.3–1.7m)	Diet 🦎 🐸	Activity ☀

Family COLUBRIDAE	Species *Pituophis melanoleucus*	Status Common

PINE OR GOPHER SNAKE

variable dark markings on head

This large constrictor has strongly keeled dorsal scales. The color varies greatly among the 15 subspecies, from off-white with dark blotches, as in the Northern Pine Snake (*Pituophis melanoleucus melanoleucus*, shown here), to completely black.

- **OCCURRENCE** North America. From pineland to prairie, coastal forest, and desert.
- **REPRODUCTION** Lays 2–24 eggs.
- **SIMILAR SPECIES** Mexican Pine Snake (*P. deppei*).

N. AMERICA

body pattern of irregular dark saddles on lighter background

Length 3–8ft (1–2.5m)	Diet 🐀 🦎	Activity ☀

| Family COLUBRIDAE | Species *Psammophis subtaeniatus* | Status Common |

STRIPE-BELLIED SANDSNAKE ☠

black-edged white stripes •

slender, agile body •

This agile, fast-moving sandsnake takes its name from the twin, black-edged white stripes that occur on either side of the yellow underside. The upper side is brown with yellow stripes, and the head and neck have brown blotches and cross-bars on a lighter background.
• OCCURRENCE E. and S. Africa. In savanna and dry scrub.
• REPRODUCTION Lays 4–10 eggs.
• SIMILAR SPECIES Cape Sandsnake (*Psammophis leightoni*).

AFRICA

| Length 3–4ft (1–1.3m) | Diet | Activity ☼ |

| Family COLUBRIDAE | Species *Pseudaspis cana* | Status Common |

MOLE SNAKE

The Mole Snake is a stout-bodied, smooth-scaled snake with a pointed head and a protruding snout that is hooked downward for burrowing. Adults vary greatly in color from yellow-brown to red or black. Juveniles are patterned with a patchwork of dark brown blotches on a light brown background. The primarily subterranean adult preys mainly on moles, mole-rats, and rodents, which are captured underground. Juveniles feed on lizards. Males fight for supremacy in the breeding season and are capable of inflicting considerable damage upon one another.
• OCCURRENCE S. and S.E. Africa. In a wide variety of habitats ranging from sandy coastal scrubland to desert and hilly grassland.
• REPRODUCTION Live-bearing, 25–90 neonates.
• SIMILAR SPECIES Cape Cobra (*Naja nivea*, p.167).

AFRICA

dark spots on • light background

JUVENILE

stout body with • relatively short tail

color varies from • yellow-brown to red or black

ADULT

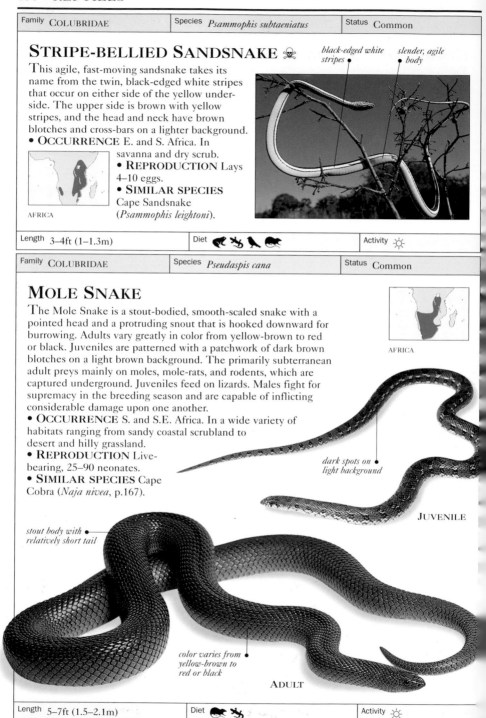

| Length 5–7ft (1.5–2.1m) | Diet | Activity ☼ |

Family COLUBRIDAE	Species *Ptyas mucosus*	Status Common

DHARMAN RATSNAKE

This very large ratsnake is brown at the front of its body and brown with darker bars toward the rear. The large head is brown, the snout tip yellow, and the labial scales yellow with black edges. The eyes are large with round pupils. This powerful snake is not a constrictor; instead, it grasps its prey and swallows it alive. Mainly terrestrial, it rarely climbs, and it seeks shelter in burrows. When alarmed, it raises its body and flattens out its neck.
• OCCURRENCE Asia. In a variety of habitats, including rainforest and open woodland.
• REPRODUCTION Lays 6–18 eggs.
• SIMILAR SPECIES King Cobra (*Ophiophagus hannah*, p.169).

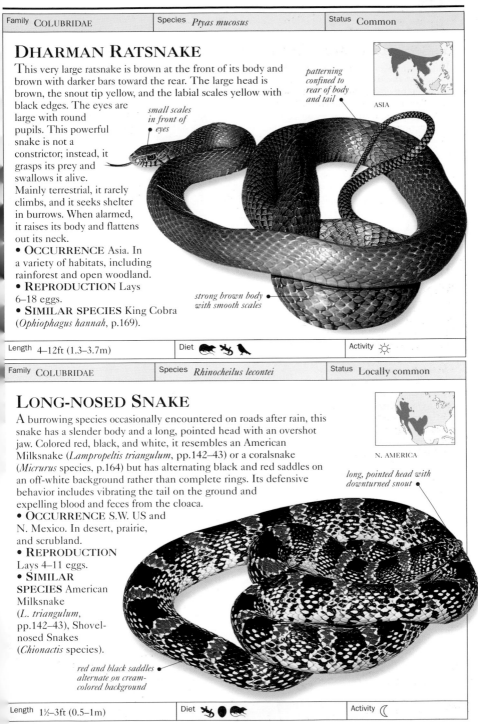

patterning confined to rear of body and tail

ASIA

small scales in front of eyes

strong brown body with smooth scales

Length 4–12ft (1.3–3.7m)	Diet	Activity ☼

Family COLUBRIDAE	Species *Rhinocheilus lecontei*	Status Locally common

LONG-NOSED SNAKE

A burrowing species occasionally encountered on roads after rain, this snake has a slender body and a long, pointed head with an overshot jaw. Colored red, black, and white, it resembles an American Milksnake (*Lampropeltis triangulum*, pp.142–43) or a coralsnake (*Micrurus* species, p.164) but has alternating black and red saddles on an off-white background rather than complete rings. Its defensive behavior includes vibrating the tail on the ground and expelling blood and feces from the cloaca.
• OCCURRENCE S.W. US and N. Mexico. In desert, prairie, and scrubland.
• REPRODUCTION Lays 4–11 eggs.
• SIMILAR SPECIES American Milksnake (*L. triangulum*, pp.142–43), Shovel-nosed Snakes (*Chionactis* species).

N. AMERICA

long, pointed head with downturned snout

red and black saddles alternate on cream-colored background

Length 1½–3ft (0.5–1m)	Diet	Activity ☾

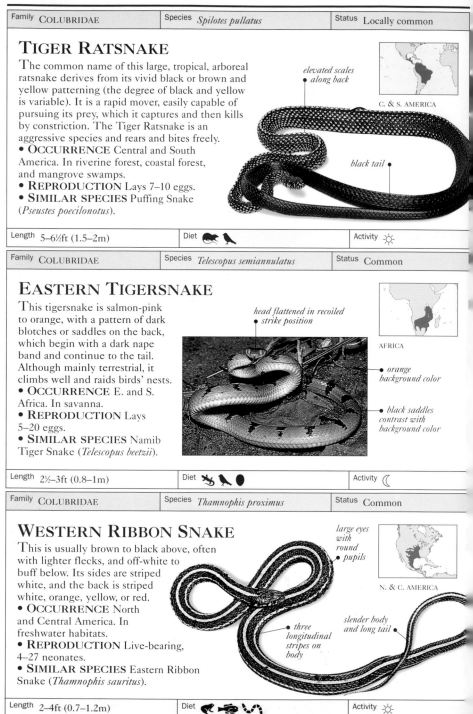

Family COLUMBRIDAE	Species *Spilotes pullatus*	Status Locally common

TIGER RATSNAKE

The common name of this large, tropical, arboreal ratsnake derives from its vivid black or brown and yellow patterning (the degree of black and yellow is variable). It is a rapid mover, easily capable of pursuing its prey, which it captures and then kills by constriction. The Tiger Ratsnake is an aggressive species and rears and bites freely.
• **OCCURRENCE** Central and South America. In riverine forest, coastal forest, and mangrove swamps.
• **REPRODUCTION** Lays 7–10 eggs.
• **SIMILAR SPECIES** Puffing Snake (*Pseustes poecilonotus*).

elevated scales along back

C. & S. AMERICA

black tail

Length 5–6½ft (1.5–2m)	Diet	Activity ☼

Family COLUMBRIDAE	Species *Telescopus semiannulatus*	Status Common

EASTERN TIGERSNAKE

This tigersnake is salmon-pink to orange, with a pattern of dark blotches or saddles on the back, which begin with a dark nape band and continue to the tail. Although mainly terrestrial, it climbs well and raids birds' nests.
• **OCCURRENCE** E. and S. Africa. In savanna.
• **REPRODUCTION** Lays 5–20 eggs.
• **SIMILAR SPECIES** Namib Tiger Snake (*Telescopus beetzii*).

head flattened in recoiled strike position

AFRICA

orange background color

black saddles contrast with background color

Length 2½–3ft (0.8–1m)	Diet	Activity ☾

Family COLUMBRIDAE	Species *Thamnophis proximus*	Status Common

WESTERN RIBBON SNAKE

This is usually brown to black above, often with lighter flecks, and off-white to buff below. Its sides are striped white, and the back is striped white, orange, yellow, or red.
• **OCCURRENCE** North and Central America. In freshwater habitats.
• **REPRODUCTION** Live-bearing, 4–27 neonates.
• **SIMILAR SPECIES** Eastern Ribbon Snake (*Thamnophis sauritus*).

large eyes with round pupils

N. & C. AMERICA

three longitudinal stripes on body

slender body and long tail

Length 2–4ft (0.7–1.2m)	Diet	Activity ☼

Family COLUBRIDAE	Species *Thamnophis sirtalis*	Status Common

COMMON GARTER SNAKE

There are 11 subspecies of Common Garter Snake, the most
widespread being the Red-sided Garter Snake (*Thamnophis
sirtalis parietalis*), which occurs just within the Arctic Circle in
southern Northwest Territories, Canada. It is black with three
vivid yellow stripes and red flashes on the lower sides. The
Eastern Garter Snake (*T. sirtalis sirtalis*) is olive-green,
with black checkerboard markings and pale
yellow stripes. The Florida Blue-striped
Garter Snake (*T. sirtalis similis*) is dark with
light blue stripes, while the San Francisco
Garter Snake (*T. sirtalis infernalis*) has black-
edged white stripes and red areas on the sides.
• **OCCURRENCE** US, Canada, and
N. Mexico. In freshwater habitats.
• **REPRODUCTION** Live-bearing, 11–23
neonates.
• **SIMILAR SPECIES** Plains Garter Snake
(*T. radix*), Western Terrestrial Garter Snake
(*T. elegans*).

N. AMERICA

twin yellow
spots often at
• rear of head

red flecks of
• interstitial skin

RED-SIDED GARTER SNAKE

checkerboard
patterning
• predominates

red head with
• large eyes

**EASTERN
GARTER
SNAKE**

• spots present on
this individual
(longitudinal stripes
are obscured)

well-defined, white •
vertebral stripe

**SAN FRANCISCO
GARTER SNAKE**

body covered in
smooth scales •

irregular, vivid •
red stripes on
sides

Length 2–4ft (0.7–1.3m)	Diet	Activity ☼

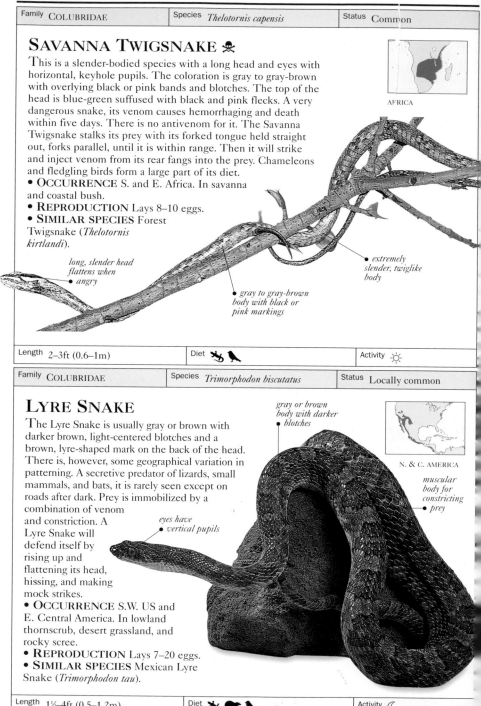

| Family COLUBRIDAE | Species *Thelotornis capensis* | Status Common |

SAVANNA TWIGSNAKE ☠

This is a slender-bodied species with a long head and eyes with horizontal, keyhole pupils. The coloration is gray to gray-brown with overlying black or pink bands and blotches. The top of the head is blue-green suffused with black and pink flecks. A very dangerous snake, its venom causes hemorrhaging and death within five days. There is no antivenom for it. The Savanna Twigsnake stalks its prey with its forked tongue held straight out, forks parallel, until it is within range. Then it will strike and inject venom from its rear fangs into the prey. Chameleons and fledgling birds form a large part of its diet.
• **OCCURRENCE** S. and E. Africa. In savanna and coastal bush.
• **REPRODUCTION** Lays 8–10 eggs.
• **SIMILAR SPECIES** Forest Twigsnake (*Thelotornis kirtlandi*).

AFRICA

long, slender head flattens when • angry

extremely slender, twiglike body

gray to gray-brown body with black or pink markings

| Length 2–3ft (0.6–1m) | Diet 🦎🐦 | Activity ☼ |

| Family COLUBRIDAE | Species *Trimorphodon biscutatus* | Status Locally common |

LYRE SNAKE

The Lyre Snake is usually gray or brown with darker brown, light-centered blotches and a brown, lyre-shaped mark on the back of the head. There is, however, some geographical variation in patterning. A secretive predator of lizards, small mammals, and bats, it is rarely seen except on roads after dark. Prey is immobilized by a combination of venom and constriction. A Lyre Snake will defend itself by rising up and flattening its head, hissing, and making mock strikes.
• **OCCURRENCE** S.W. US and E. Central America. In lowland thornscrub, desert grassland, and rocky scree.
• **REPRODUCTION** Lays 7–20 eggs.
• **SIMILAR SPECIES** Mexican Lyre Snake (*Trimorphodon tau*).

gray or brown body with darker • blotches

N. & C. AMERICA

muscular body for constricting • prey

eyes have • vertical pupils

| Length 1½–4ft (0.5–1.2m) | Diet 🦎🐦🐁 | Activity ☾ |

Family COLUBRIDAE	Species *Xenodon rabdocephalus*	Status Common

FALSE LANCEHEAD

With its lance-shaped head and broad, stocky body patterned with light and dark brown blotches, this terrestrial species can easily be mistaken for a highly venomous lancehead (*Bothrops* species, pp.180–81). However, it lacks the true lancehead's heat-sensitive pits and hinged front fangs. Its bite, although painful, is not considered dangerous. The enlarged rear teeth are designed to puncture toads, the primary prey. The round pupils of the eyes are also a distinguishing characteristic.

C. & S. AMERICA

short, stocky body with light and dark brown pattern

markings closely resemble those of venomous lanceheads

• **OCCURRENCE** Central and South America. In tropical forest, usually in damp, riverside habitats.
• **REPRODUCTION** Lays 8–12 eggs.
• **SIMILAR SPECIES** Neuwied's False Lancehead (*Xenodon neuwiedi*).

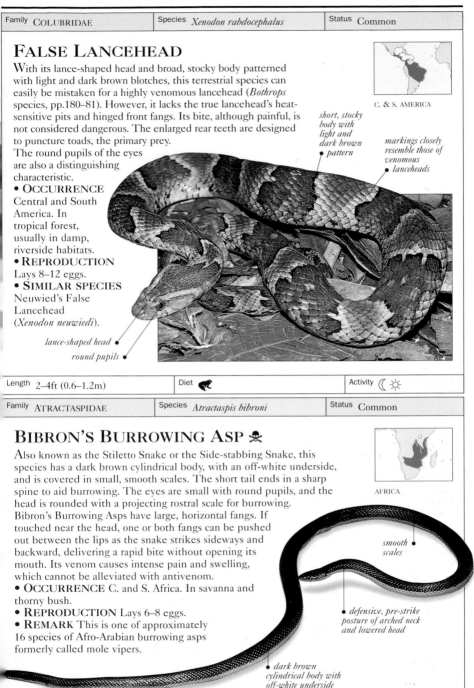

lance-shaped head

round pupils

Length 2–4ft (0.6–1.2m)	Diet	Activity

Family ATRACTASPIDAE	Species *Atractaspis bibroni*	Status Common

BIBRON'S BURROWING ASP ☠

Also known as the Stiletto Snake or the Side-stabbing Snake, this species has a dark brown cylindrical body, with an off-white underside, and is covered in small, smooth scales. The short tail ends in a sharp spine to aid burrowing. The eyes are small with round pupils, and the head is rounded with a projecting rostral scale for burrowing. Bibron's Burrowing Asps have large, horizontal fangs. If touched near the head, one or both fangs can be pushed out between the lips as the snake strikes sideways and backward, delivering a rapid bite without opening its mouth. Its venom causes intense pain and swelling, which cannot be alleviated with antivenom.

AFRICA

smooth scales

• **OCCURRENCE** C. and S. Africa. In savanna and thorny bush.
• **REPRODUCTION** Lays 6–8 eggs.
• **REMARK** This is one of approximately 16 species of Afro-Arabian burrowing asps formerly called mole vipers.

defensive, pre-strike posture of arched neck and lowered head

dark brown cylindrical body with off-white underside

Length 20–28in (50–70cm)	Diet	Activity

Family ELAPIDAE	Species *Acanthophis praelongus*	Status Common

NORTHERN DEATH ADDER ☠

In many ways, this elapid resembles a viper – it has a stout body, broad head, and secretive habits; like most vipers, it is a nocturnal, sit-and-wait ambusher. However, vipers are absent from Australasia. The Northern Death Adder has a short, slender tail, weakly keeled body scales, raised scales over the eyes, and vertical pupils. Coloration varies from gray to red, brown, or black. The slender tail tip is yellow or white to lure prey.
• OCCURRENCE N. Australia and S. New Guinea. In forest, savanna, gardens, and on plantations.
• REPRODUCTION Live-bearing, 2–8 neonates.
• SIMILAR SPECIES Southern Death Adder (*Acanthophis antarcticus*).

AUSTRALASIA

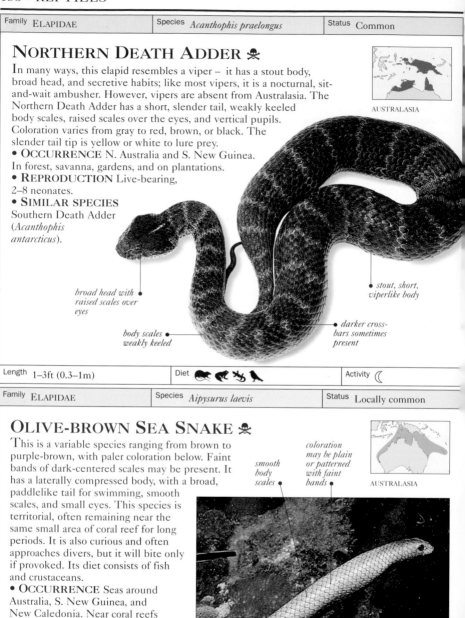

broad head with raised scales over eyes

body scales weakly keeled

stout, short, viperlike body

darker cross-bars sometimes present

Length 1–3ft (0.3–1m)	Diet	Activity ☾

Family ELAPIDAE	Species *Aipysurus laevis*	Status Locally common

OLIVE-BROWN SEA SNAKE ☠

This is a variable species ranging from brown to purple-brown, with paler coloration below. Faint bands of dark-centered scales may be present. It has a laterally compressed body, with a broad, paddlelike tail for swimming, smooth scales, and small eyes. This species is territorial, often remaining near the same small area of coral reef for long periods. It is also curious and often approaches divers, but it will bite only if provoked. Its diet consists of fish and crustaceans.
• OCCURRENCE Seas around Australia, S. New Guinea, and New Caledonia. Near coral reefs and in estuaries.
• REPRODUCTION Live-bearing, 2–5 neonates.
• SIMILAR SPECIES Brown Sea Snake (*Aipysurus fuscus*), Stokes's Sea Snake (*Astrotia stokesii*).

coloration may be plain or patterned with faint bands

smooth body scales

AUSTRALASIA

Length 4–7ft (1.2–2.2m)	Diet	Activity ○

Family ELAPIDAE	Species *Aspidelaps lubricus*	Status Locally common

SOUTH AFRICAN CORALSNAKE ☠

The South African Coralsnake has a small head with an enlarged rostral scale, and a stout body with small scales. Three subspecies are recognized: *Aspidelaps lubricus lubricus* (shown here), which lives in the southernmost part of the range and is coral-red on the back, fading to pinkish cream on the lower sides, with black bands; the Namibian *A. lubricus infuscatus*, which is off-white to gray-brown, with faint bands and a black head; and the Angolan *A. lubricus cowlesi*, which is uniform off-white to gray-brown, with a pale head.
• OCCURRENCE South Africa, Namibia, and S. Angola. In scrubland and desert fringes.
• REPRODUCTION Lays 3–11 eggs.
• SIMILAR SPECIES De Coster's Garter Snake (*Elapsoidea sundevallii decosteri*).

AFRICA

small head with enlarged rostral scale for burrowing

coral-red back, fading to coral-pink on sides, and black bands along body

stout body

smooth body scales

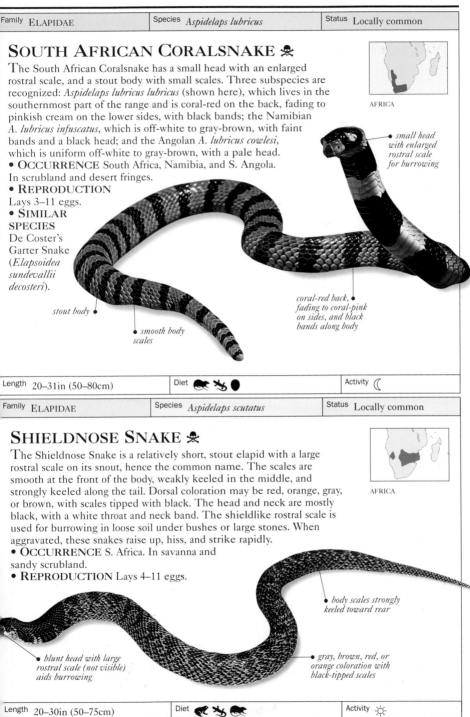

Length 20–31in (50–80cm)	Diet 🐀 🦎 ●	Activity ☾

Family ELAPIDAE	Species *Aspidelaps scutatus*	Status Locally common

SHIELDNOSE SNAKE ☠

The Shieldnose Snake is a relatively short, stout elapid with a large rostral scale on its snout, hence the common name. The scales are smooth at the front of the body, weakly keeled in the middle, and strongly keeled along the tail. Dorsal coloration may be red, orange, gray, or brown, with scales tipped with black. The head and neck are mostly black, with a white throat and neck band. The shieldlike rostral scale is used for burrowing in loose soil under bushes or large stones. When aggravated, these snakes raise up, hiss, and strike rapidly.
• OCCURRENCE S. Africa. In savanna and sandy scrubland.
• REPRODUCTION Lays 4–11 eggs.

AFRICA

body scales strongly keeled toward rear

blunt head with large rostral scale (not visible) aids burrowing

gray, brown, red, or orange coloration with black-tipped scales

Length 20–30in (50–75cm)	Diet 🐸 🦎 🐀	Activity ☀

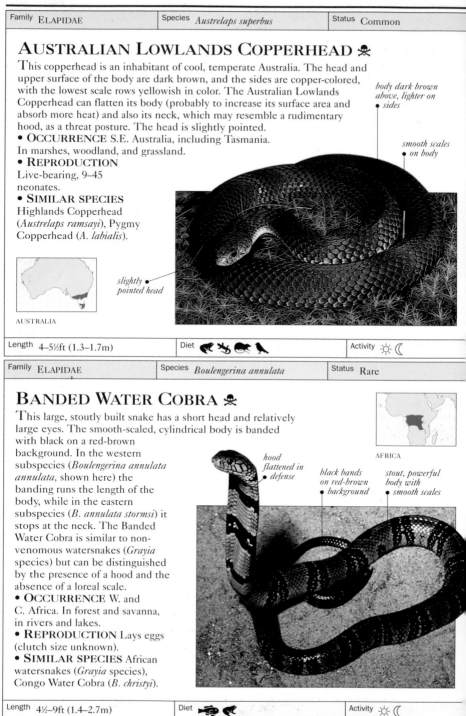

| Family ELAPIDAE | Species *Austrelaps superbus* | Status Common |

AUSTRALIAN LOWLANDS COPPERHEAD ☠

This copperhead is an inhabitant of cool, temperate Australia. The head and upper surface of the body are dark brown, and the sides are copper-colored, with the lowest scale rows yellowish in color. The Australian Lowlands Copperhead can flatten its body (probably to increase its surface area and absorb more heat) and also its neck, which may resemble a rudimentary hood, as a threat posture. The head is slightly pointed.

body dark brown above, lighter on • sides

smooth scales • on body

• **OCCURRENCE** S.E. Australia, including Tasmania. In marshes, woodland, and grassland.
• **REPRODUCTION** Live-bearing, 9–45 neonates.
• **SIMILAR SPECIES** Highlands Copperhead (*Austrelaps ramsayi*), Pygmy Copperhead (*A. labialis*).

slightly • pointed head

AUSTRALIA

| Length 4–5½ft (1.3–1.7m) | Diet | Activity ☼ ☾ |

| Family ELAPIDAE | Species *Boulengerina annulata* | Status Rare |

BANDED WATER COBRA ☠

This large, stoutly built snake has a short head and relatively large eyes. The smooth-scaled, cylindrical body is banded with black on a red-brown background. In the western subspecies (*Boulengerina annulata annulata*, shown here) the banding runs the length of the body, while in the eastern subspecies (*B. annulata stormsi*) it stops at the neck. The Banded Water Cobra is similar to non-venomous watersnakes (*Grayia* species) but can be distinguished by the presence of a hood and the absence of a loreal scale.

AFRICA

hood flattened in • defense

black bands on red-brown • background

stout, powerful body with • smooth scales

• **OCCURRENCE** W. and C. Africa. In forest and savanna, in rivers and lakes.
• **REPRODUCTION** Lays eggs (clutch size unknown).
• **SIMILAR SPECIES** African watersnakes (*Grayia* species), Congo Water Cobra (*B. christyi*).

| Length 4½–9ft (1.4–2.7m) | Diet | Activity ☼ ☾ |

Family ELAPIDAE	Species *Bungarus caeruleus*	Status Common

COMMON KRAIT ☠

The Common Krait is a large, smooth-scaled
snake with patterning consisting of white
bands on a glossy, blue-black background.
Uniform dark specimens are also common.
The head is slightly wider than the neck,
and the eyes are relatively small. The
Common Krait shelters in termite
mounds during the day, and emerges at
night to hunt other snakes, including
smaller kraits, skinks, and mammals.
• **OCCURRENCE** Pakistan and Nepal
to Sri Lanka. In savanna and woodland.
• **REPRODUCTION** Lays 8–12 eggs.
• **SIMILAR SPECIES** Jara Wolfsnake
(*Lycodon jara*), Sind Krait (*Bungarus
sindanus*).
• **REMARK** Of the 12 terrestrial krait
species in Asia, the Common Krait is
the one most often implicated in
serious snakebites.

*glossy, blue-black
body with white
• bands*

*body round
in cross
• section*

ASIA

Length 2½–5½ft (0.8–1.7m)	Diet 🐀 🦎	Activity ☾

Family ELAPIDAE	Species *Bungarus fasciatus*	Status Common

BANDED KRAIT ☠

The body of this species is ringed with yellow and black or brown
bands, and the elevated backbone presents a triangular shape in
cross section. This body shape is highly unusual, although it is also
characteristic of African filesnakes (*Mehelya* species, p.147).
During the day, the Banded Krait is extremely shy –
if uncovered, it will repeatedly hide its head
under the coils and it will not attempt to bite.
At night, however, when it is active, it can be
very dangerous. It hunts other snakes, including
Common Kraits (*Bungarus caeruleus*), and rats.
Although the Banded Krait is common, it is
rarely seen.
• **OCCURRENCE** S.E. Asia. In low-lying
grassland and woodland near water.
• **REPRODUCTION** Lays 6–12 eggs.
• **SIMILAR SPECIES** Mangrove Snake
(*Boiga dendrophila*, p.127).

ASIA

*tail ends
in stump*

*body triangular •
in cross section*

small eyes •

Length 5–7½ft (1.5–2.3m)	Diet 🐀 🦎	Activity ☾

| Family ELAPIDAE | Species *Dendroaspis angusticeps* | Status Locally common |

EAST AFRICAN GREEN MAMBA ☠

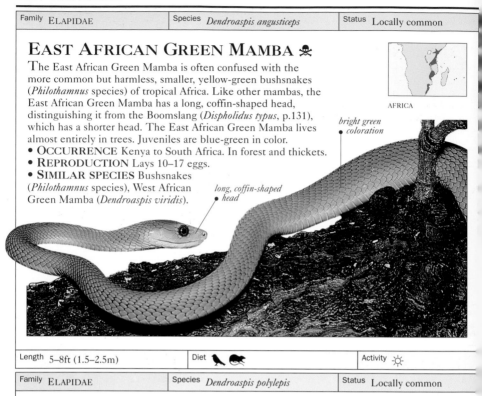

The East African Green Mamba is often confused with the more common but harmless, smaller, yellow-green bushsnakes (*Philothamnus* species) of tropical Africa. Like other mambas, the East African Green Mamba has a long, coffin-shaped head, distinguishing it from the Boomslang (*Dispholidus typus*, p.131), which has a shorter head. The East African Green Mamba lives almost entirely in trees. Juveniles are blue-green in color.
• OCCURRENCE Kenya to South Africa. In forest and thickets.
• REPRODUCTION Lays 10–17 eggs.
• SIMILAR SPECIES Bushsnakes (*Philothamnus* species), West African Green Mamba (*Dendroaspis viridis*).

AFRICA

bright green coloration

long, coffin-shaped head

| Length 5–8ft (1.5–2.5m) | Diet | Activity ☼ |

| Family ELAPIDAE | Species *Dendroaspis polylepis* | Status Locally common |

BLACK MAMBA ☠

long, coffin-shaped head

gray to brown coloration

The Black Mamba is the most venomous snake in Africa. Although it is responsible for relatively few bites, the consequences are extremely serious, with death usually occurring within an hour. Black Mambas are not usually black; they are gunmetal gray to brown, with lighter gray on the side of the head. The only black pigment is inside the mouth, which is displayed when the mamba defends itself by rearing up, flattening its neck, and gaping. Black Mambas are very alert and agile, and are at home both on the ground and in the trees.
• OCCURRENCE E. and S. Africa, with isolated records in W. Africa. In savanna woodland and thornscrub.

AFRICA

• REPRODUCTION Lays 6–17 eggs.
• SIMILAR SPECIES Black treesnakes (*Thrasops* species), Forest Cobra (*Naja melanoleuca*).

| Length 7–11½ft (2.2–3.5m) | Diet | Activity ☼ |

Family ELAPIDAE	Species *Enhydrina schistosa*	Status Rare

COMMON BEAKED SEA SNAKE ☠

This moderately slender snake is white-gray, with indistinct, pale blue-gray bands. It has a long, dagger-shaped scale on the underside of its lower jaw and a large amount of expandable skin to permit a wide mouth gape. The Common Beaked Sea Snake is very dangerous owing to its highly toxic venom and irascible temperament.

INDIAN & PACIFIC OCEANS

• **OCCURRENCE** Seas around Persian Gulf to Philippines and N. Australia. In inshore shallow bays, estuaries, and freshwater rivers.

patterning of pale blue-gray bands on lighter background

tail and rear part of body compressed

• **REPRODUCTION** Live-bearing, 3–30 neonates.
• **SIMILAR SPECIES** Zweifel's Beaked Sea Snake (*Enhydrina zweifeli*).

slender front part of body

• **REMARK** A single bite from this species may contain sufficient venom to kill from five to fifty people.

Length 3–4½ft (1–1.4m)	Diet 🐟🦗	Activity ☾

Family ELAPIDAE	Species *Hemachatus haemachatus*	Status Common

RINKHALS ☠

pointed snout

black throat

A variably patterned cobra, the Rinkhals may be uniform black or brown, speckled, or banded black and cream. It usually has a black throat. Characteristics that distinguish this southern African spitting cobra from other African cobras include its short, angular head, strongly keeled dorsal scales, and the fact that it is live-bearing (other cobras have more rounded heads, their bodies are smooth-scaled, and they lay eggs). When confronted, the Rinkhals spits venom into the face of its enemy before fleeing. If trapped, it may deter predators by shamming death in the manner of hognose snakes (*Heterodon* species, p.138) or Grass Snakes (*Natrix natrix*, p.148). All of these species "play dead" by rolling onto their backs and opening their mouths. Toads are the preferred diet of the Rinkhals.

body may be banded, spotted, or plain

• **OCCURRENCE** South Africa. In grassland.
• **REPRODUCTION** Live-bearing, 20–60 neonates.

AFRICA

• **REMARK** The Rinkhals is believed to possess the most well-developed fangs for spitting of all the cobra species.

Length 3–5ft (1–1.5m)	Diet 🐸🐸🐦	Activity ☾

Family ELAPIDAE	Species *Lapemis curtus*	Status Locally common

SHORT SEA SNAKE ☠

This species is a stout-bodied, large-headed, light brown sea snake with a lengthwise row of large brown blotches. It is also known as the Spine-bellied Sea Snake because in the male the keeled scales on the underside have short spines. An inshore species, it is probably the second most dangerous sea snake to humans after the Common Beaked Sea Snake (*Enhydrina schistosa*, p.161).

stout body with brown saddles on lighter background •

flat, paddle-shaped tail for swimming

• OCCURRENCE Persian Gulf to Australia and S. Japan. In estuaries and on coral reefs.
• REPRODUCTION Live-bearing, 1–6 neonates.
• SIMILAR SPECIES Reef Sea Snake (*Hydrophis ornatus*).

INDIAN & PACIFIC OCEANS

Length 3–3½ft (0.9–1.1m)	Diet	Activity ☼ ☾

Family ELAPIDAE	Species *Laticauda colubrina*	Status Common

YELLOW-LIPPED SEA KRAIT ☠

The black-and-blue bands are typical of sea kraits, but this species is distinguished by its yellow lips. It can move on land and in water.
• OCCURRENCE E. India to S. Japan and Fiji. On coral reefs and mangrove-fringed coastlines.
• REPRODUCTION Lays 6–18 eggs.
• SIMILAR SPECIES Large-scaled Sea Krait (*Laticauda laticaudata*).

INDIAN & PACIFIC OCEANS

black rings on body •

Length 3–6½ft (1–2m)	Diet	Activity ☾

Family ELAPIDAE	Species *Micropechis ikaheka*	Status Locally common

NEW GUINEA SMALL-EYED SNAKE ☠

dark rings become • smaller toward tail

The patterning of this smooth-scaled snake may be brown, cream, or white, with dark-edged, red or red-brown rings that increase in size and frequency toward the tail. The front part of the body may be speckled rather than ringed. The head is gray and the eyes small. By day, this snake hides in coconut husk piles and other debris.
• OCCURRENCE New Guinea. In wet forests, swamps, and on plantations.
• REPRODUCTION Lays eggs (clutch size unknown).

NEW GUINEA

small eyes •

Length 3–6½ft (1–2m)	Diet	Activity ☾

Family ELAPIDAE	Species *Micruroides euryxanthus*	Status Rare

WESTERN CORALSNAKE ☠

One of the smallest coralsnakes, this smooth-scaled species is banded with red, white or yellow, and black. It is a very secretive burrowing snake, rarely encountered on the surface. If disturbed, it will raise its tail in an elevated figure-eight, exposing the underside, in the manner of coralsnakes of the genus *Micrurus* (below and p.164). Its prey includes small snakes, such as the Texas Blindsnake (*Leptotyphlops dulcis*, p.105) and ringneck snakes (*Diadophis* species), as well as skinks.
• **OCCURRENCE** S.W. US and N.W. Mexico. In arid habitats including desert, savanna, dry woodland, and river bottoms.
• **REPRODUCTION** Lays 1–3 eggs.
• **SIMILAR SPECIES** Ground snakes (*Sonora* species), shovel-nosed snakes (*Chionactis* species).
• **REMARK** This is the only coral-snake in S.W. US and N.W. Mexico.

N. AMERICA

red, black, and white or yellow bands

small head indistinguishable from body

slender body with smooth scales

Length 16–21½in (40–55cm)	Diet	Activity ☾

Family ELAPIDAE	Species *Micrurus alleni*	Status Rare

ALLEN'S CORALSNAKE ☠

A small to medium-sized Central American species, Allen's Coralsnake is orange-red, patterned with red, yellow, and black bands. The black-and-yellow head and the eyes are small. These coralsnakes are highly venomous but very secretive. Encounters with humans are rare, and bites are unlikely due to the small size of the snakes' mouths.
• **OCCURRENCE** Nicaragua and Costa Rica. In lowland rainforest.
• **REPRODUCTION** Lays 2–3 eggs.
• **SIMILAR SPECIES** Central American Coralsnake (*Micrurus nigricinctus*), Clark's Coralsnake (*M. clarki*).
• **REMARK** It is likely that the Pacific population of Allen's Coralsnake represents a separate species.

C. AMERICA

tail raised to expose underside in defensive display

body banded in red, yellow, and black

small, slender head with small eyes

Length 2½–3½ft (0.8–1.1m)	Diet	Activity ☾

| Family ELAPIDAE | Species *Micrurus fulvius* | Status Common |

EASTERN CORALSNAKE ☠

The highly venomous Eastern Coralsnake is small and slender, with a rounded head, small eyes, and red, yellow, and black bands. It may be difficult to distinguish from tricolored colubrid snakes, which are nonvenomous; however, colubrids possess a loreal scale, which is absent in coralsnakes and other elapids. It eats mostly snakes.

rounded head with small mouth and eyes

- **REPRODUCTION** Lays 3–13 eggs.
- **OCCURRENCE** S.E. and S. US and N.E. Mexico. In dry woodland, often in leaf-litter.

smooth body scales

- **SIMILAR SPECIES** American Milksnake (*Lampropeltis triangulum*, pp.142–43), Scarlet Snake (*Cemophora coccinea*).

N. AMERICA

red, yellow, and black bands along body and head

| Length 2–3ft (0.7–1m) | Diet | Activity |

| Family ELAPIDAE | Species *Micrurus lemniscatus* | Status Common |

SOUTH AMERICAN CORALSNAKE ☠

This slender, highly venomous elapid has a rounded head with small eyes. It is similar to the Eastern Coralsnake (*Micrurus fulvius*, above), but the bands of the South American Coralsnake are in a different order and are arranged in "triads," with three black bands, separated by two white bands, on a red background.

S. AMERICA

- **OCCURRENCE** South America. In rainforest, forest along rivers, savanna, and seasonally flooded habitats.
- **REPRODUCTION** Lays 5–6 eggs.
- **SIMILAR SPECIES** Aquatic Coralsnake (*M. surinamensis*), Slender Coralsnake (*M. filiformis*).

black and white bands on red background

smooth body scales

| Length 2–4½ft (0.7–1.4m) | Diet | Activity |

Family ELAPIDAE	Species *Naja haje*	Status Common

EGYPTIAN COBRA ☠

This is a large, stout-bodied cobra, with a rounded head and smooth scales. It is highly venomous. The rostral scale is small, unlike that of the similar Snouted Cobra (*Naja annulifera*) of southern Africa, a former subspecies, which has an enlarged rostral scale. Three subspecies of *Naja haje* may be recognized: the Egyptian Cobra (*N. haje haje*, shown here), which varies from yellow-gray to brown; the Moroccan population (*N. haje legionis*), which is almost jet-black; and *N. haje arabica*, which is often yellow with a black head and neck, and occurs in the southern Arabian Peninsula (this is the only African cobra found outside the continent). When defensive, this species rears one-third of its length vertically and spreads a broad, rounded hood. If this threat is ignored, the cobra will advance toward the aggressor and, if the aggressor persists, it may eventually strike. Prey includes other snakes, toads, small mammals, and birds' eggs.

AFRICA, MIDDLE EAST

• **OCCURRENCE** N. Africa, around the Sahara Desert, and the Arabian Peninsula (*N. haje arabica* only). In savanna, dry woodland, and semidesert.
• **REPRODUCTION** Lays 10–20 eggs.
• **SIMILAR SPECIES** Snouted Cobra (*N. annulifera*).

fang sheaths (skin covering fangs) on display when cobra opens mouth

glottis (airway) visible when mouth open

broad, long hood spreads in defense

enlarged ventral scales typical of terrestrial snake

smooth, uniform brown body scales

Length 5–8ft (1.5–2.4m)	Diet	Activity

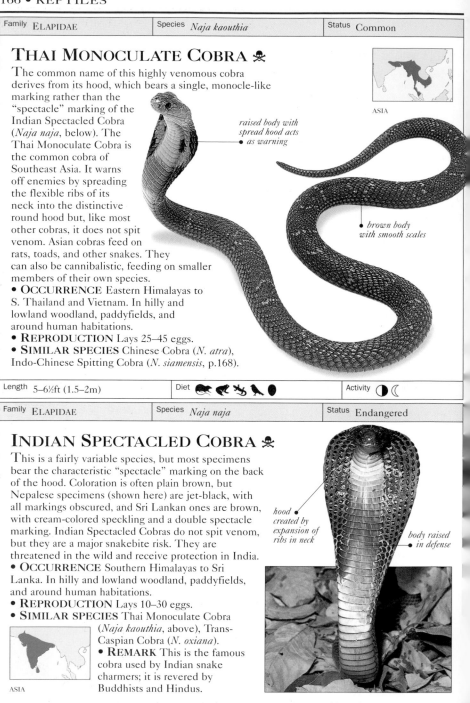

| Family ELAPIDAE | Species *Naja kaouthia* | Status Common |

THAI MONOCULATE COBRA ☠

The common name of this highly venomous cobra
derives from its hood, which bears a single, monocle-like
marking rather than the
"spectacle" marking of the
Indian Spectacled Cobra
(*Naja naja*, below). The
Thai Monoculate Cobra is
the common cobra of
Southeast Asia. It warns
off enemies by spreading
the flexible ribs of its
neck into the distinctive
round hood but, like most
other cobras, it does not spit
venom. Asian cobras feed on
rats, toads, and other snakes. They
can also be cannibalistic, feeding on smaller
members of their own species.
• **OCCURRENCE** Eastern Himalayas to
S. Thailand and Vietnam. In hilly and
lowland woodland, paddyfields, and
around human habitations.
• **REPRODUCTION** Lays 25–45 eggs.
• **SIMILAR SPECIES** Chinese Cobra (*N. atra*),
Indo-Chinese Spitting Cobra (*N. siamensis*, p.168).

raised body with spread hood acts as warning

brown body with smooth scales

ASIA

| Length 5–6½ft (1.5–2m) | Diet | Activity ◐ ☾ |

| Family ELAPIDAE | Species *Naja naja* | Status Endangered |

INDIAN SPECTACLED COBRA ☠

This is a fairly variable species, but most specimens
bear the characteristic "spectacle" marking on the back
of the hood. Coloration is often plain brown, but
Nepalese specimens (shown here) are jet-black, with
all markings obscured, and Sri Lankan ones are brown,
with cream-colored speckling and a double spectacle
marking. Indian Spectacled Cobras do not spit venom,
but they are a major snakebite risk. They are
threatened in the wild and receive protection in India.
• **OCCURRENCE** Southern Himalayas to Sri
Lanka. In hilly and lowland woodland, paddyfields,
and around human habitations.
• **REPRODUCTION** Lays 10–30 eggs.
• **SIMILAR SPECIES** Thai Monoculate Cobra
(*Naja kaouthia*, above), Trans-
Caspian Cobra (*N. oxiana*).
• **REMARK** This is the famous
cobra used by Indian snake
charmers; it is revered by
Buddhists and Hindus.

hood created by expansion of ribs in neck

body raised in defense

ASIA

| Length 4–5½ft (1.2–1.7m) | Diet | Activity ☼ ☾ |

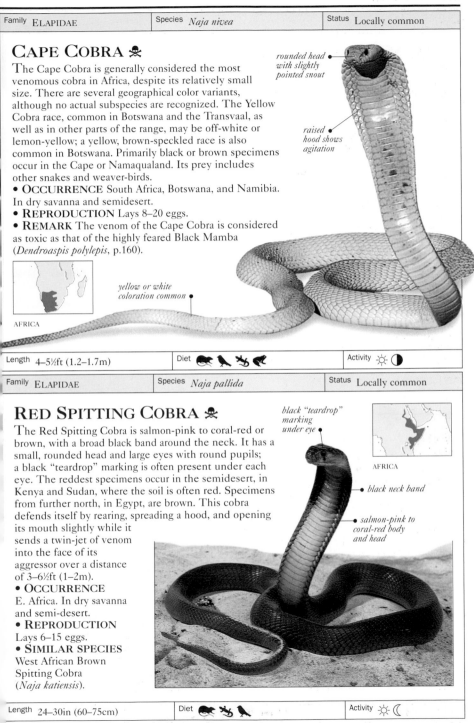

| Family ELAPIDAE | Species *Naja nivea* | Status Locally common |

CAPE COBRA ☠

The Cape Cobra is generally considered the most venomous cobra in Africa, despite its relatively small size. There are several geographical color variants, although no actual subspecies are recognized. The Yellow Cobra race, common in Botswana and the Transvaal, as well as in other parts of the range, may be off-white or lemon-yellow; a yellow, brown-speckled race is also common in Botswana. Primarily black or brown specimens occur in the Cape or Namaqualand. Its prey includes other snakes and weaver-birds.
• **OCCURRENCE** South Africa, Botswana, and Namibia. In dry savanna and semidesert.
• **REPRODUCTION** Lays 8–20 eggs.
• **REMARK** The venom of the Cape Cobra is considered as toxic as that of the highly feared Black Mamba (*Dendroaspis polylepis*, p.160).

rounded head with slightly pointed snout

raised hood shows agitation

yellow or white coloration common

AFRICA

| Length 4–5½ft (1.2–1.7m) | Diet | Activity ☼ ◑ |

| Family ELAPIDAE | Species *Naja pallida* | Status Locally common |

RED SPITTING COBRA ☠

The Red Spitting Cobra is salmon-pink to coral-red or brown, with a broad black band around the neck. It has a small, rounded head and large eyes with round pupils; a black "teardrop" marking is often present under each eye. The reddest specimens occur in the semidesert, in Kenya and Sudan, where the soil is often red. Specimens from further north, in Egypt, are brown. This cobra defends itself by rearing, spreading a hood, and opening its mouth slightly while it sends a twin-jet of venom into the face of its aggressor over a distance of 3–6½ft (1–2m).
• **OCCURRENCE** E. Africa. In dry savanna and semi-desert.
• **REPRODUCTION** Lays 6–15 eggs.
• **SIMILAR SPECIES** West African Brown Spitting Cobra (*Naja katiensis*).

black "teardrop" marking under eye

AFRICA

black neck band

salmon-pink to coral-red body and head

| Length 24–30in (60–75cm) | Diet | Activity ☼ ☾ |

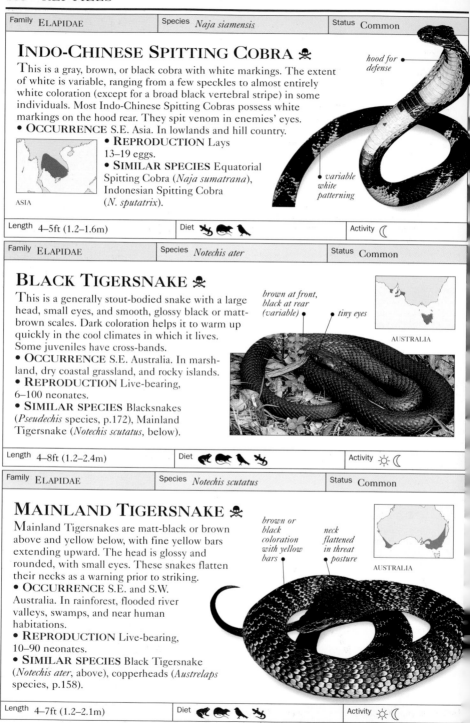

| Family ELAPIDAE | Species *Naja siamensis* | Status Common |

INDO-CHINESE SPITTING COBRA ☠

This is a gray, brown, or black cobra with white markings. The extent of white is variable, ranging from a few speckles to almost entirely white coloration (except for a broad black vertebral stripe) in some individuals. Most Indo-Chinese Spitting Cobras possess white markings on the hood rear. They spit venom in enemies' eyes.
- **OCCURRENCE** S.E. Asia. In lowlands and hill country.
- **REPRODUCTION** Lays 13–19 eggs.
- **SIMILAR SPECIES** Equatorial Spitting Cobra (*Naja sumatrana*), Indonesian Spitting Cobra (*N. sputatrix*).

ASIA

hood for defense

variable white patterning

| Length 4–5ft (1.2–1.6m) | Diet | Activity ☾ |

| Family ELAPIDAE | Species *Notechis ater* | Status Common |

BLACK TIGERSNAKE ☠

This is a generally stout-bodied snake with a large head, small eyes, and smooth, glossy black or matt-brown scales. Dark coloration helps it to warm up quickly in the cool climates in which it lives. Some juveniles have cross-bands.
- **OCCURRENCE** S.E. Australia. In marshland, dry coastal grassland, and rocky islands.
- **REPRODUCTION** Live-bearing, 6–100 neonates.
- **SIMILAR SPECIES** Blacksnakes (*Pseudechis* species, p.172), Mainland Tigersnake (*Notechis scutatus*, below).

brown at front, black at rear (variable)

tiny eyes

AUSTRALIA

| Length 4–8ft (1.2–2.4m) | Diet | Activity ☀ ☾ |

| Family ELAPIDAE | Species *Notechis scutatus* | Status Common |

MAINLAND TIGERSNAKE ☠

Mainland Tigersnakes are matt-black or brown above and yellow below, with fine yellow bars extending upward. The head is glossy and rounded, with small eyes. These snakes flatten their necks as a warning prior to striking.
- **OCCURRENCE** S.E. and S.W. Australia. In rainforest, flooded river valleys, swamps, and near human habitations.
- **REPRODUCTION** Live-bearing, 10–90 neonates.
- **SIMILAR SPECIES** Black Tigersnake (*Notechis ater*, above), copperheads (*Austrelaps* species, p.158).

brown or black coloration with yellow bars

neck flattened in threat posture

AUSTRALIA

| Length 4–7ft (1.2–2.1m) | Diet | Activity ☀ ☾ |

Family ELAPIDAE	Species *Ophiophagus hannah*	Status Locally common

KING COBRA ☠

The widely distributed King Cobra is a variable species, with adults
ranging from yellow-brown to gray-green. Juveniles are dark with yellow
bands and a series of inverted yellow chevrons on the long, narrow
hood. Some populations retain the juvenile patterning into adulthood.
King Cobras can be distinguished from other cobras by the presence of
a pair of post-occipital scales on the rear of the head. King Cobras
are unique because they "pair up" when they mate: the female
builds a plant-debris nest for their eggs and then both sexes guard
the clutch together. When threatened, the King Cobra growls,
shows a single fang, flattens its hood, and raises up to one-third
of its body off the ground. King Cobras prey mostly on
other snakes, but they occasionally eat rats or lizards.
Although they are highly venomous, few human bites
occur because the King Cobra is primarily an
inhabitant of deep forest.

ASIA

dark
coloration
with yellow
bands

• **OCCURRENCE** S. and S.E. Asia. In forest
and on plantations.
• **REPRODUCTION** Lays 20–50 eggs.
• **SIMILAR SPECIES** Dharman Ratsnake
(*Ptyas mucosus*, p.151).
• **REMARK** The King Cobra is the longest
venomous snake in the world.

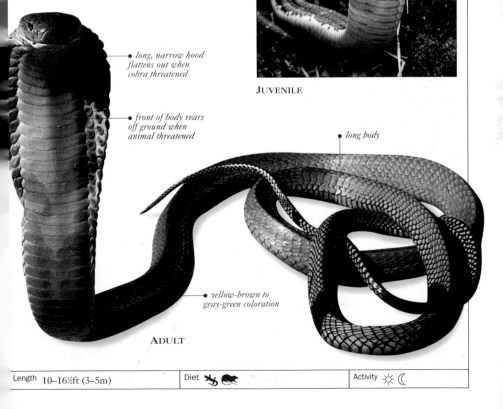

JUVENILE

long, narrow hood
flattens out when
cobra threatened

front of body rears
off ground when
animal threatened

long body

yellow-brown to
gray-green coloration

ADULT

Length 10–16½ft (3–5m)	Diet	Activity ☼ ☾

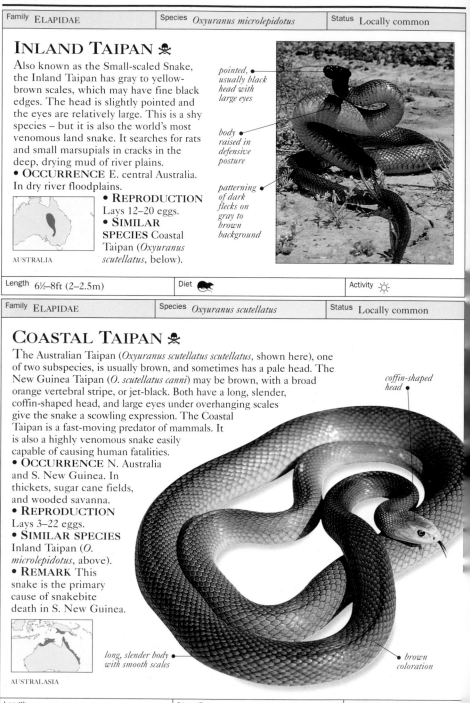

Family ELAPIDAE	Species *Oxyuranus microlepidotus*	Status Locally common

INLAND TAIPAN ☠

Also known as the Small-scaled Snake, the Inland Taipan has gray to yellow-brown scales, which may have fine black edges. The head is slightly pointed and the eyes are relatively large. This is a shy species – but it is also the world's most venomous land snake. It searches for rats and small marsupials in cracks in the deep, drying mud of river plains.
• **OCCURRENCE** E. central Australia. In dry river floodplains.
• **REPRODUCTION** Lays 12–20 eggs.
• **SIMILAR SPECIES** Coastal Taipan (*Oxyuranus scutellatus*, below).

AUSTRALIA

pointed, usually black head with large eyes

body raised in defensive posture

patterning of dark flecks on gray to brown background

Length 6½–8ft (2–2.5m)	Diet 🐀	Activity ☼

Family ELAPIDAE	Species *Oxyuranus scutellatus*	Status Locally common

COASTAL TAIPAN ☠

The Australian Taipan (*Oxyuranus scutellatus scutellatus*, shown here), one of two subspecies, is usually brown, and sometimes has a pale head. The New Guinea Taipan (*O. scutellatus canni*) may be brown, with a broad orange vertebral stripe, or jet-black. Both have a long, slender, coffin-shaped head, and large eyes under overhanging scales give the snake a scowling expression. The Coastal Taipan is a fast-moving predator of mammals. It is also a highly venomous snake easily capable of causing human fatalities.
• **OCCURRENCE** N. Australia and S. New Guinea. In thickets, sugar cane fields, and wooded savanna.
• **REPRODUCTION** Lays 3–22 eggs.
• **SIMILAR SPECIES** Inland Taipan (*O. microlepidotus*, above).
• **REMARK** This snake is the primary cause of snakebite death in S. New Guinea.

AUSTRALASIA

coffin-shaped head

long, slender body with smooth scales

brown coloration

Length 6½–12ft (2–3.6m)	Diet 🐀	Activity ☼ ☾

Family ELAPIDAE	Species *Paranaja multifasciata*	Status Rare

BURROWING COBRA ☠

Each smooth scale of the Burrowing Cobra's short, stout green body is cream with a green or black spot or edge, resulting in a reticulated or spotted pattern. In some adults, the patterning may resemble that of the Forest Cobra (*Naja melanoleuca*). The underside is immaculate cream. The short head is dark with a pale cross-band on the nape and pale

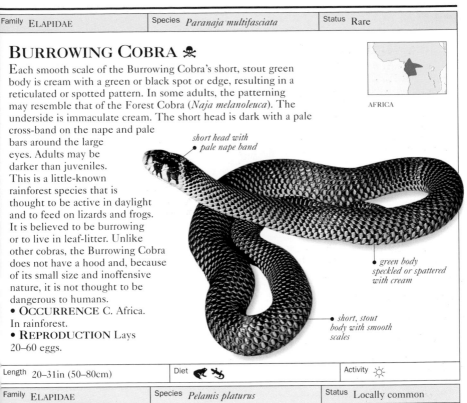

AFRICA

bars around the large eyes. Adults may be darker than juveniles. This is a little-known rainforest species that is thought to be active in daylight and to feed on lizards and frogs. It is believed to be burrowing or to live in leaf-litter. Unlike other cobras, the Burrowing Cobra does not have a hood and, because of its small size and inoffensive nature, it is not thought to be dangerous to humans.
• **OCCURRENCE** C. Africa. In rainforest.
• **REPRODUCTION** Lays 20–60 eggs.

short head with pale nape band

green body speckled or spattered with cream

short, stout body with smooth scales

Length 20–31in (50–80cm)	Diet	Activity ☼

Family ELAPIDAE	Species *Pelamis platurus*	Status Locally common

PELAGIC SEA SNAKE ☠

With its yellow-and-black body and black-spotted yellow, paddlelike tail, this is the most recognizable marine snake. It is also known as the Yellow-and-Black Sea Snake. The colors warn sharks that the snake is venomous, deterring attack. This is the world's most widely distributed snake; it may also be the most numerous, with thousands drifting together in midocean. Perfectly adapted for sea life, it has glands to excrete salt under its tongue. To rid itself of external

INDIAN & PACIFIC OCEANS

black-and-yellow coloration

parasites it twists and coils in the sea, and sloughs its skin more frequently than terrestrial snakes. Its scales butt up against each other, limiting the number of anchorage sites for parasites.
• **OCCURRENCE** Indian and Pacific Oceans. In open ocean at the surface.
• **REPRODUCTION** Live-bearing, 2–6 neonates.

paddle-shaped tail aids swimming

Length 3–5ft (1–1.5m)	Diet	Activity ☼ ☾

| Family ELAPIDAE | Species *Pseudechis australis* | Status Locally common |

KING BROWNSNAKE ☠

Australia's most widespread venomous snake, the King Brownsnake
has a brown or red body, with smooth scales, and a broad head
with large eyes. It has also been reported in southern New Guinea,
but recent research suggests that the New Guinea snake may in fact
be a new species. When threatened,
the King Brownsnake may flatten
its neck into a narrow hood
and raise its body in
preparation to strike.
• **OCCURRENCE**
Australia (excluding
the south) and S. New
Guinea. In a wide range
of habitats, from tropical
forest to desert.
• **REPRODUCTION** Lays
11–16 eggs or may be live-
bearing, 18–22 neonates.
• **SIMILAR SPECIES** Coastal
Taipan (*Oxyuranus scutellatus*,
p.170), Eastern Brownsnake
(*Pseudonaja textilis*, opposite).

AUSTRALASIA

brown or red body with smooth scales

broad head with large eyes

tail has been injured and truncated

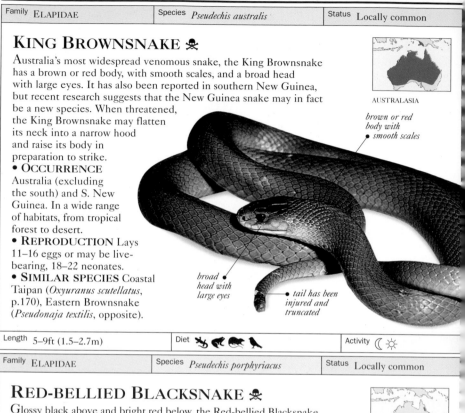

| Length 5–9ft (1.5–2.7m) | Diet | Activity |

| Family ELAPIDAE | Species *Pseudechis porphyriacus* | Status Locally common |

RED-BELLIED BLACKSNAKE ☠

Glossy black above and bright red below, the Red-bellied Blacksnake
has a rounded head with relatively large eyes. Preferring aquatic habitats,
it is found in swamps and on riverbanks that have a ready supply of
frogs, although it may also eat small mammals, lizards, and other snakes.
• **OCCURRENCE** E. and S.E. Australia. In swamps, streams,
and lagoons.
• **REPRODUCTION** Live-bearing, 8–40 neonates.
• **SIMILAR SPECIES** Spotted Blacksnake (*Pseudechis guttatus*).
• **REMARK** Numbers of Red-
bellied Blacksnakes (and of other
frog-eating snakes) have fallen
sharply since the arrival in
Australia of the Marine Toad
(*Bufo marinus*, p.224), a South
American species introduced to
control pests of sugar cane. This
toad is not only fatally poisonous
to the Australian snakes, it has
also killed many native frogs,
depriving the snakes of food.

AUSTRALIA

glossy or iridescent black upper surface

bright red underside

rounded head with large eyes

| Length 6½–9ft (2–2.7m) | Diet | Activity |

Family ELAPIDAE	Species *Pseudohaje goldii*	Status Rare

GOLD'S TREE COBRA ☠

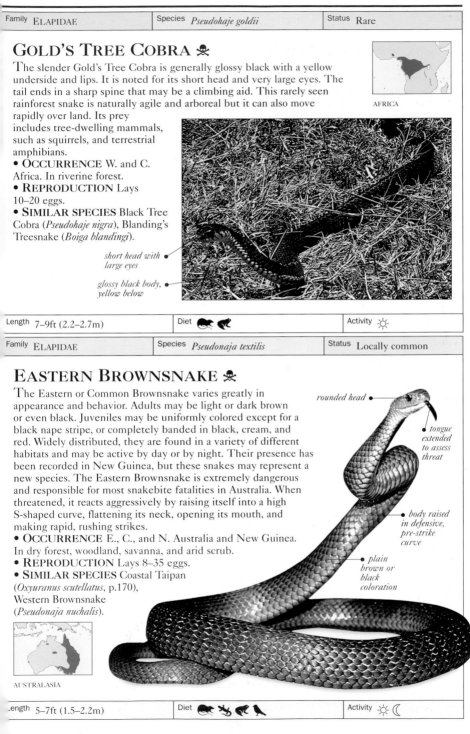

The slender Gold's Tree Cobra is generally glossy black with a yellow underside and lips. It is noted for its short head and very large eyes. The tail ends in a sharp spine that may be a climbing aid. This rarely seen rainforest snake is naturally agile and arboreal but it can also move rapidly over land. Its prey includes tree-dwelling mammals, such as squirrels, and terrestrial amphibians.

AFRICA

• **OCCURRENCE** W. and C. Africa. In riverine forest.
• **REPRODUCTION** Lays 10–20 eggs.
• **SIMILAR SPECIES** Black Tree Cobra (*Pseudohaje nigra*), Blanding's Treesnake (*Boiga blandingi*).

short head with large eyes

glossy black body, yellow below

Length 7–9ft (2.2–2.7m)	Diet 🐀🐸	Activity ☼

Family ELAPIDAE	Species *Pseudonaja textilis*	Status Locally common

EASTERN BROWNSNAKE ☠

The Eastern or Common Brownsnake varies greatly in appearance and behavior. Adults may be light or dark brown or even black. Juveniles may be uniformly colored except for a black nape stripe, or completely banded in black, cream, and red. Widely distributed, they are found in a variety of different habitats and may be active by day or by night. Their presence has been recorded in New Guinea, but these snakes may represent a new species. The Eastern Brownsnake is extremely dangerous and responsible for most snakebite fatalities in Australia. When threatened, it reacts aggressively by raising itself into a high S-shaped curve, flattening its neck, opening its mouth, and making rapid, rushing strikes.

rounded head

tongue extended to assess threat

body raised in defensive, pre-strike curve

plain brown or black coloration

• **OCCURRENCE** E., C., and N. Australia and New Guinea. In dry forest, woodland, savanna, and arid scrub.
• **REPRODUCTION** Lays 8–35 eggs.
• **SIMILAR SPECIES** Coastal Taipan (*Oxyuranus scutellatus*, p.170), Western Brownsnake (*Pseudonaja nuchalis*).

AUSTRALASIA

Length 5–7ft (1.5–2.2m)	Diet 🐀🦎🐸🐦	Activity ☼ ☾

Family ELAPIDAE	Species *Tropidechis carinatus*	Status Locally common

ROUGH-SCALED SNAKE ☠

With its strongly keeled scales, rounded head, and brown, mottled coloration, the highly venomous Rough-scaled Snake closely resembles the well-known, nonvenomous Common Keelback (*Tropidonophis mairii*) from the same area. However, the Common Keelback has a loreal scale on the side of the head, which is absent in the Rough-scaled Snake. Rough-scaled Snakes climb well and shelter in trees by day. They defend themselves by rearing with an S-bend in their necks, hissing and striking rapidly.

- **OCCURRENCE** E. Australia. In freshwater habitats, scrub, and wet woodland.
- **REPRODUCTION** Live-bearing, 5–8 neonates.
- **SIMILAR SPECIES** Common Keelback (*Tropidonophis mairii*).

strongly keeled scales unusual for an elapid

head and body flatten as a warning when snake approached

AUSTRALIA

Length 2–3ft (0.7–1m)	Diet 🐀 🐸 🐦 🦎	Activity ☾

Family ELAPIDAE	Species *Walterinnesia aegyptia*	Status Locally common

DESERT BLACK SNAKE ☠

Also known as the Desert Cobra, the Desert Black Snake is a glossy, smooth-scaled, black or dark gray snake, with a slightly paler underside. A nocturnal and primarily desert-dwelling species, it seems to move into areas that have been cultivated and irrigated. Prey includes mastigures (*Uromastyx* species), and this snake is especially common where these lizards occur. The Desert Black Snake hunts at night and spends hot days down mammal burrows. When threatened, it raises its body, hisses, and strikes. Bites can be fatal to humans.

- **OCCURRENCE** Egypt to Iran. In desert, rocky scrub, and irrigated areas.
- **REPRODUCTION** Lays eggs (clutch size unknown).
- **SIMILAR SPECIES** Small-scaled Burrowing Asp (*Atractaspis microlepidota*).

smooth body scales and dark coloration

head raised in threat posture

AFRICA, MIDDLE EAST

Length 3–4ft (1–1.3m)	Diet 🦎 🦎 🐀	Activity ☾

Family VIPERIDAE	Species *Agkistrodon bilineatus*	Status Rare

CANTIL ☠

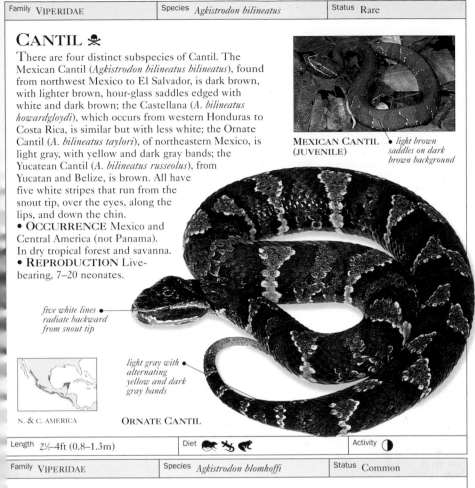

There are four distinct subspecies of Cantil. The
Mexican Cantil (*Agkistrodon bilineatus bilineatus*), found
from northwest Mexico to El Salvador, is dark brown,
with lighter brown, hour-glass saddles edged with
white and dark brown; the Castellana (*A. bilineatus
howardgloydi*), which occurs from western Honduras to
Costa Rica, is similar but with less white; the Ornate
Cantil (*A. bilineatus taylori*), of northeastern Mexico, is
light gray, with yellow and dark gray bands; the
Yucatean Cantil (*A. bilineatus russeolus*), from
Yucatan and Belize, is brown. All have
five white stripes that run from the
snout tip, over the eyes, along the
lips, and down the chin.
• **OCCURRENCE** Mexico and
Central America (not Panama).
In dry tropical forest and savanna.
• **REPRODUCTION** Live-
bearing, 7–20 neonates.

MEXICAN CANTIL
(JUVENILE)

• *light brown
saddles on dark
brown background*

• *five white lines
radiate backward
from snout tip*

• *light gray with
alternating
yellow and dark
gray bands*

N. & C. AMERICA

ORNATE CANTIL

Length 2½–4ft (0.8–1.3m)	Diet	Activity ◑

Family VIPERIDAE	Species *Agkistrodon blomhoffi*	Status Common

MAMUSHI ☠

This pitviper is pale gray to sandy colored, with dark, inverted-U-
shaped markings or large, dark-edged spots on the sides. A pair of
tiny indentations on each scale distinguish Mamushis from other
Asian *Agkistrodon* species. This snake is collected for food, for
making saki, and for traditional medicines.
• **OCCURRENCE** Japan and also on
mainland E. Asia. In grassland and cultivated
areas and on rocky hillsides.
• **REPRODUCTION** Live-
bearing, 2–13 neonates.
• **SIMILAR SPECIES**
Asian Pitviper (*Agkistrodon
intermedius*), Siberian
Pitviper (*A. halys*).

*arrow-
shaped head* •

*dark brown stripes
run through eyes from
snout to angle of jaw*

ASIA

Length 16–24in (40–60cm)	Diet	Activity ◑

Family VIPERIDAE	Species *Agkistrodon contortrix*	Status Locally common

COPPERHEAD ☠

The Copperhead is patterned with a series of red-brown
bands, or hour-glass-shaped markings, on a pale brown to
pink-brown background. The tan-colored head has a pair
of small, darker spots at the rear. A
fine, dark brown stripe separates the dark
crown from the pale lips.

distinctive brown
bands or hour-glass
markings on body •

• dark spots
on rear of
head crown

• OCCURRENCE S.E.
US and N.E. Mexico. On rocky,
wooded hillsides.
• REPRODUCTION Live-
bearing, 4–16 neonates.

N. AMERICA

• pale brown to
pink-brown
background color

Length 2–4ft (0.7–1.3m)	Diet	Activity ◐

Family VIPERIDAE	Species *Agkistrodon piscivorus*	Status Common

COTTONMOUTH ☠

Also known as the Water Moccasin, the Cottonmouth is
named for the pure white interior of its mouth.
Adults are very dark and uniform in color,
while juveniles (shown here) are lighter
with distinctive patterning.
• OCCURRENCE S.E. US. In swamps,
bayous, and slow rivers.

• fang sheaths and white
mouth interior visible
when snake threatened

• REPRODUCTION
Live-bearing,
1–16 neonates.
• SIMILAR SPECIES
American watersnakes
(*Nerodia* species, p.148).

N. AMERICA

Length 5–6ft (1.5–1.8m)	Diet	Activity ◐ ☾

Family VIPERIDAE	Species *Azemiops feae*	Status Rare

FEA'S VIPER ☠

Believed to be the most primitive of the
vipers, this little-known species is black-
brown, with a series of narrow pink or yellow
bands that sometimes meet over the center of
the back. Its most distinctive features are its
yellow head and neck, marked with a pair of
slightly darker longitudinal dorsal stripes. The
eyes are small, with vertical pupils.

head covered
in large scutes,
unusual for
vipers •

yellow head with
contrasting,
darker dorsal
• stripes

dark body
with narrow
pink or yellow
• bands

• OCCURRENCE
S. Himalayan foothills. In
montane rainforest.
• REPRODUCTION
Unknown, but probably
lays eggs.

ASIA

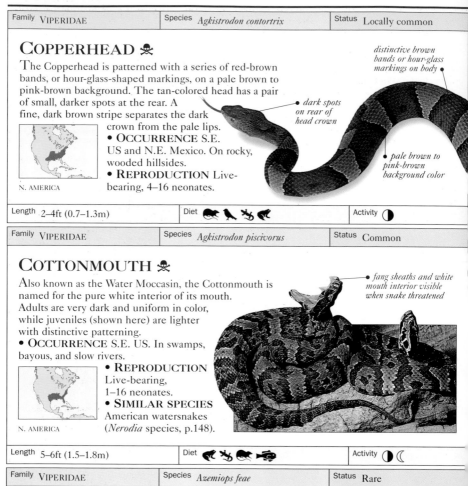

Length 20–35in (50–90cm)	Diet	Activity Unknown

Family VIPERIDAE	Species *Bitis arietans*	Status Common

PUFF ADDER ☠

The Puff Adder has a stout gray, yellow, or brown body, with light-edged dark chevrons that pass over the center of the back. The large, broad brown head has a pale line behind the eyes that extends to the back of the jaw. Large Puff Adders are so heavy they are forced to move in a straight-line, rectilinear motion, or a caterpillar crawl, like large boas.
• OCCURRENCE Africa and Yemen. In all habitats except desert and mountains.
• REPRODUCTION Live-bearing, 40–150 neonates.

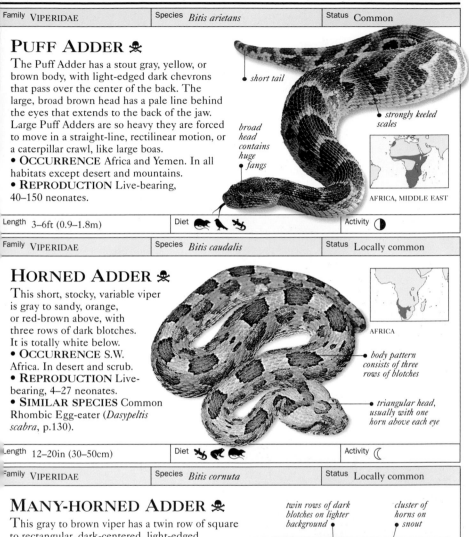

short tail

broad head contains huge fangs

strongly keeled scales

AFRICA, MIDDLE EAST

Length 3–6ft (0.9–1.8m)	Diet 🐀 🦎	Activity ◑

Family VIPERIDAE	Species *Bitis caudalis*	Status Locally common

HORNED ADDER ☠

This short, stocky, variable viper is gray to sandy, orange, or red-brown above, with three rows of dark blotches. It is totally white below.
• OCCURRENCE S.W. Africa. In desert and scrub.
• REPRODUCTION Live-bearing, 4–27 neonates.
• SIMILAR SPECIES Common Rhombic Egg-eater (*Dasypeltis scabra*, p.130).

AFRICA

body pattern consists of three rows of blotches

triangular head, usually with one horn above each eye

Length 12–20in (30–50cm)	Diet 🦎 🐸 🐀	Activity ☾

Family VIPERIDAE	Species *Bitis cornuta*	Status Locally common

MANY-HORNED ADDER ☠

This gray to brown viper has a twin row of square to rectangular, dark-centered, light-edged markings on its back. Smaller dark blotches are present on the sides, and the underside is dark-speckled. Most individuals have two to seven horns over each eye; some are hornless.
• OCCURRENCE E. South Africa and Namibia. On mountains and rocky plains.

AFRICA

twin rows of dark blotches on lighter background

cluster of horns on snout

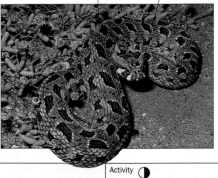

• REPRODUCTION Live-bearing, 6–8 neonates.
• SIMILAR SPECIES Plain Mountain Adder (*Bitis inornata*).

Length 10–13in (25–34cm)	Diet 🐀 🦎	Activity ◑

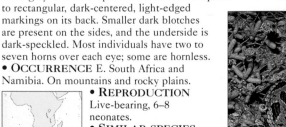

Family VIPERIDAE	Species *Bitis gabonica*	Status Locally common

GABOON VIPER ☠

The geometric patterning of browns, grays, and
purples, and the large, leaflike head, make the Gaboon
Viper one of the most cryptically patterned of African
forest-floor snakes. It is the longest and heaviest
African viper; slow moving and often sedentary, it lies
in wait for its unwary prey – rats, squirrels, even small
antelopes and porcupines. There are two subspecies:
Bitis gabonica gabonica (eastern and central Africa) and
B. gabonica rhinoceros (west Africa).
• OCCURRENCE Tropical Africa. In rainforest
and woodland.
• REPRODUCTION Live-bearing, 16–60 neonates.
• SIMILAR SPECIES
Rhinoceros Viper
(*B. nasicornis*,
opposite).

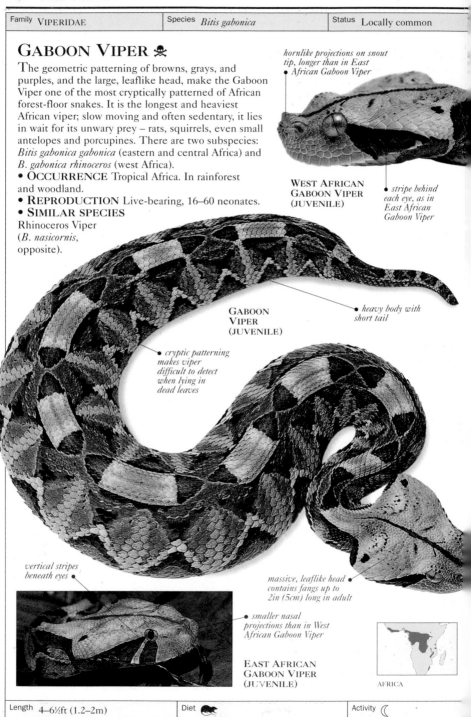

*hornlike projections on snout
tip, longer than in East
• African Gaboon Viper*

**WEST AFRICAN
GABOON VIPER
(JUVENILE)**

*• stripe behind
each eye, as in
East African
Gaboon Viper*

**GABOON
VIPER
(JUVENILE)**

*• heavy body with
short tail*

*• cryptic patterning
makes viper
difficult to detect
when lying in
dead leaves*

*vertical stripes
beneath eyes •*

*massive, leaflike head •
contains fangs up to
2in (5cm) long in adult*

*• smaller nasal
projections than in West
African Gaboon Viper*

**EAST AFRICAN
GABOON VIPER
(JUVENILE)**

AFRICA

Length 4–6½ft (1.2–2m)	Diet 🐀	Activity ☾

Family VIPERIDAE	Species *Bitis nasicornis*	Status Locally common

RHINOCEROS VIPER ☠

Also known as the River Jack, this large viper
is an ambusher of mammals and big frogs.
The patterning is as cryptic as that of its
relative, the Gaboon Viper (*Bitis gabonica*,
opposite), comprising a geometric carpet of
gray, blue, purple, orange, and velvet-black,
with a large black, arrow-shaped marking on
top of the long head. The hornlike
protuberances on the snout are
longer even than those of the
West African Gaboon Viper
(*B. gabonica rhinoceros*).
Although it is terrestrial,
the Rhinoceros Viper can
climb into low bushes and
swims well. The juvenile
is shown here.
• **OCCURRENCE** W. and
C. Africa. In rainforest and
riverine forest.
• **REPRODUCTION**
Live-bearing,
6–40 neonates.
• **SIMILAR
SPECIES** Gaboon
Viper (*B. gabonica*,
opposite).

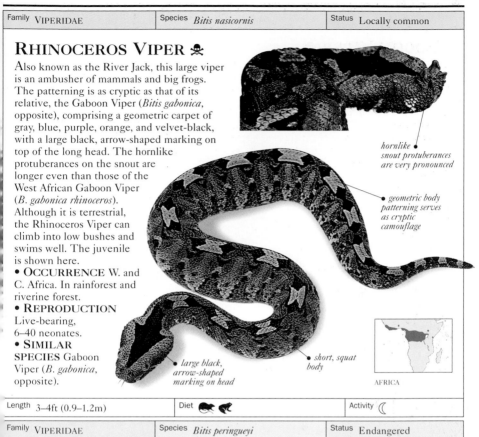

*hornlike
snout protuberances
are very pronounced*

*geometric body
patterning serves
as cryptic
camouflage*

*short, squat
body*

*large black,
arrow-shaped
marking on head*

AFRICA

Length 3–4ft (0.9–1.2m)	Diet 🐀 🐸	Activity ☾

Family VIPERIDAE	Species *Bitis peringueyi*	Status Endangered

PERINGUEY'S ADDER ☠

Also known as the Namib Desert Sidewinding
Viper, this adder moves rapidly over the loose
dune sands, using a diagonal, sidewinding
motion that leaves J-shaped markings in the
sand. Avoiding the heat of the day, it shuffles
into the shadow of vegetation, with only its
flatfishlike, dorsally positioned eyes visible
above the surface. It ambushes any diurnal
lizard that ventures close, and actively hunts
geckos at night.
• **OCCURRENCE** S.W. Africa. In desert
sand dunes.
• **REPRODUCTION** Live-bearing, 4–10
neonates.
• **SIMILAR SPECIES** Namaqua Dwarf
Adder (*Bitis schneideri*).
• **REMARK** Peringuey's Adder is the only
snake with dorsally positioned eyes.

AFRICA

*dorsally
positioned
eyes*

*pastel-
colored body
with black
tail tip that
lures lizards*

Length 10–12in (25–30cm)	Diet 🦎	Activity ☾

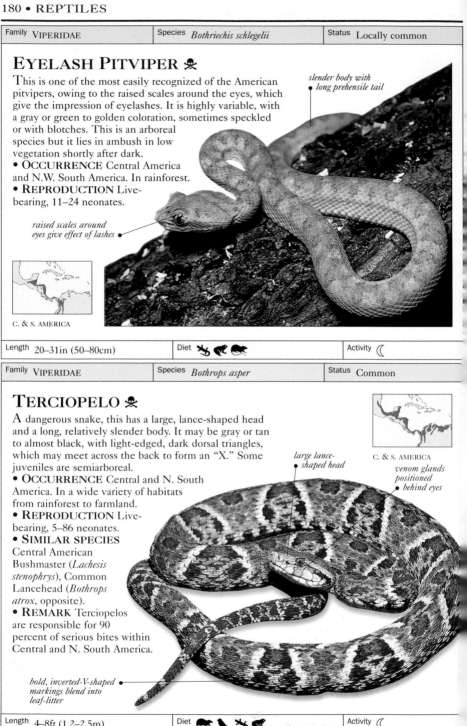

| Family VIPERIDAE | Species *Bothriechis schlegelii* | Status Locally common |

EYELASH PITVIPER ☠

This is one of the most easily recognized of the American pitvipers, owing to the raised scales around the eyes, which give the impression of eyelashes. It is highly variable, with a gray or green to golden coloration, sometimes speckled or with blotches. This is an arboreal species but it lies in ambush in low vegetation shortly after dark.
• **OCCURRENCE** Central America and N.W. South America. In rainforest.
• **REPRODUCTION** Live-bearing, 11–24 neonates.

slender body with long prehensile tail

raised scales around eyes give effect of lashes

C. & S. AMERICA

| Length 20–31in (50–80cm) | Diet | Activity ☾ |

| Family VIPERIDAE | Species *Bothrops asper* | Status Common |

TERCIOPELO ☠

A dangerous snake, this has a large, lance-shaped head and a long, relatively slender body. It may be gray or tan to almost black, with light-edged, dark dorsal triangles, which may meet across the back to form an "X." Some juveniles are semiarboreal.
• **OCCURRENCE** Central and N. South America. In a wide variety of habitats from rainforest to farmland.
• **REPRODUCTION** Live-bearing, 5–86 neonates.
• **SIMILAR SPECIES** Central American Bushmaster (*Lachesis stenophrys*), Common Lancehead (*Bothrops atrox*, opposite).
• **REMARK** Terciopelos are responsible for 90 percent of serious bites within Central and N. South America.

large lance-shaped head

C. & S. AMERICA

venom glands positioned behind eyes

bold, inverted-V-shaped markings blend into leaf-litter

| Length 4–8ft (1.2–2.5m) | Diet | Activity ☾ |

Family VIPERIDAE	Species *Bothrops atrox*	Status Common

COMMON LANCEHEAD ☠

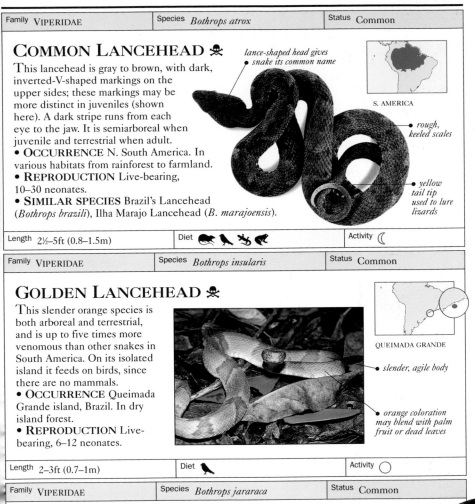

This lancehead is gray to brown, with dark, inverted-V-shaped markings on the upper sides; these markings may be more distinct in juveniles (shown here). A dark stripe runs from each eye to the jaw. It is semiarboreal when juvenile and terrestrial when adult.

- **OCCURRENCE** N. South America. In various habitats from rainforest to farmland.
- **REPRODUCTION** Live-bearing, 10–30 neonates.
- **SIMILAR SPECIES** Brazil's Lancehead (*Bothrops brazili*), Ilha Marajo Lancehead (*B. marajoensis*).

lance-shaped head gives snake its common name

S. AMERICA

rough, keeled scales

yellow tail tip used to lure lizards

Length 2½–5ft (0.8–1.5m)	Diet	Activity ☾

Family VIPERIDAE	Species *Bothrops insularis*	Status Common

GOLDEN LANCEHEAD ☠

This slender orange species is both arboreal and terrestrial, and is up to five times more venomous than other snakes in South America. On its isolated island it feeds on birds, since there are no mammals.

- **OCCURRENCE** Queimada Grande island, Brazil. In dry island forest.
- **REPRODUCTION** Live-bearing, 6–12 neonates.

QUEIMADA GRANDE

slender, agile body

orange coloration may blend with palm fruit or dead leaves

Length 2–3ft (0.7–1m)	Diet	Activity ○

Family VIPERIDAE	Species *Bothrops jararaca*	Status Common

JARARACA ☠

The Jararaca is brown in color, with variable and cryptic patterning. In some individuals, the dark, inverted-V shapes on a lighter background are well marked; in others they are barely visible. Although it is a terrestrial species, juveniles may be found in trees. Its preference for open areas brings it into frequent contact with humans, sometimes resulting in serious bites.

S. AMERICA

- **OCCURRENCE** S. Brazil and S.E. Paraguay. In dry forest, savanna, and cultivated areas.
- **REPRODUCTION** Live-bearing, 12–18 neonates.

strongly keeled body scales

large head accommodates long, hinged fangs

Length 3–5ft (1–1.6m)	Diet	Activity ○

Family VIPERIDAE	Species *Calloselasma rhodostoma*	Status Common

MALAYAN PITVIPER ☠

The Malayan Pitviper is brown with small, dark, inverted-V-shaped markings along its back. The lance-shaped head is brown above, bordered by a pair of yellow-brown stripes. A broad, dark brown stripe runs from each eye to the back of the jaw. The lips, chin, and throat are white. Unlike most vipers, this species lays eggs.
• **OCCURRENCE** Mainland S.E. Asia and Java. In dry woodland and on plantations.
• **REPRODUCTION**
Lays 20–40 eggs.
• **SIMILAR SPECIES**
Chinese Copperhead
(*Deinagkistrodon acutus*).

ASIA

inverted-V-shaped markings on paler background

vertical pupils

stripe runs from each eye to rear of jaw

dark, mid-dorsal line

body patterning blends in well with dead leaves

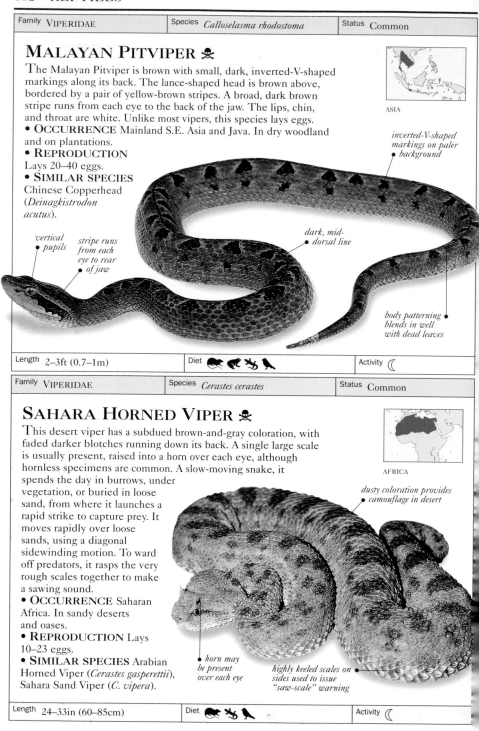

Length 2–3ft (0.7–1m)	Diet	Activity ☾

Family VIPERIDAE	Species *Cerastes cerastes*	Status Common

SAHARA HORNED VIPER ☠

This desert viper has a subdued brown-and-gray coloration, with faded darker blotches running down its back. A single large scale is usually present, raised into a horn over each eye, although hornless specimens are common. A slow-moving snake, it spends the day in burrows, under vegetation, or buried in loose sand, from where it launches a rapid strike to capture prey. It moves rapidly over loose sands, using a diagonal sidewinding motion. To ward off predators, it rasps the very rough scales together to make a sawing sound.
• **OCCURRENCE** Saharan Africa. In sandy deserts and oases.
• **REPRODUCTION** Lays 10–23 eggs.
• **SIMILAR SPECIES** Arabian Horned Viper (*Cerastes gasperettii*), Sahara Sand Viper (*C. vipera*).

AFRICA

dusty coloration provides camouflage in desert

horn may be present over each eye

highly keeled scales on sides used to issue "saw-scale" warning

Length 24–33in (60–85cm)	Diet	Activity ☾

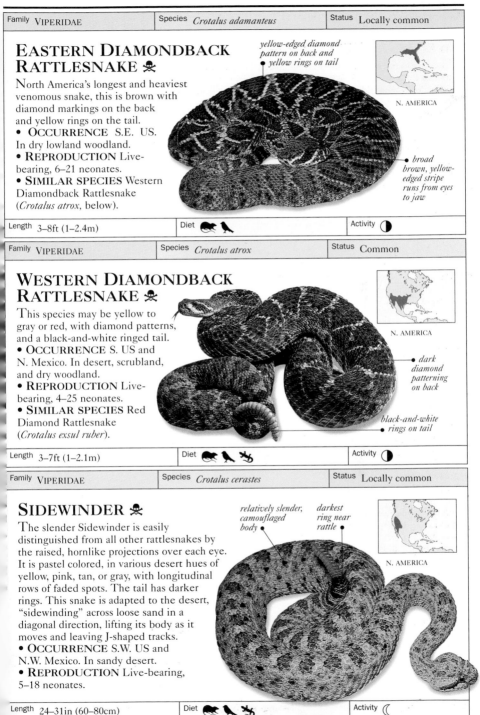

Family VIPERIDAE	Species *Crotalus adamanteus*	Status Locally common

EASTERN DIAMONDBACK RATTLESNAKE ☠

yellow-edged diamond pattern on back and yellow rings on tail

North America's longest and heaviest venomous snake, this is brown with diamond markings on the back and yellow rings on the tail.
- OCCURRENCE S.E. US. In dry lowland woodland.
- REPRODUCTION Live-bearing, 6–21 neonates.
- SIMILAR SPECIES Western Diamondback Rattlesnake (*Crotalus atrox*, below).

N. AMERICA

broad brown, yellow-edged stripe runs from eyes to jaw

Length 3–8ft (1–2.4m)	Diet	Activity

Family VIPERIDAE	Species *Crotalus atrox*	Status Common

WESTERN DIAMONDBACK RATTLESNAKE ☠

This species may be yellow to gray or red, with diamond patterns, and a black-and-white ringed tail.
- OCCURRENCE S. US and N. Mexico. In desert, scrubland, and dry woodland.
- REPRODUCTION Live-bearing, 4–25 neonates.
- SIMILAR SPECIES Red Diamond Rattlesnake (*Crotalus exsul ruber*).

N. AMERICA

dark diamond patterning on back

black-and-white rings on tail

Length 3–7ft (1–2.1m)	Diet	Activity

Family VIPERIDAE	Species *Crotalus cerastes*	Status Locally common

SIDEWINDER ☠

relatively slender, camouflaged body

darkest ring near rattle

The slender Sidewinder is easily distinguished from all other rattlesnakes by the raised, hornlike projections over each eye. It is pastel colored, in various desert hues of yellow, pink, tan, or gray, with longitudinal rows of faded spots. The tail has darker rings. This snake is adapted to the desert, "sidewinding" across loose sand in a diagonal direction, lifting its body as it moves and leaving J-shaped tracks.
- OCCURRENCE S.W. US and N.W. Mexico. In sandy desert.
- REPRODUCTION Live-bearing, 5–18 neonates.

N. AMERICA

Length 24–31in (60–80cm)	Diet	Activity

Family VIPERIDAE	Species *Crotalus durissus*	Status Common

NEOTROPICAL RATTLESNAKE ☠

The only rattlesnake south of Mexico, this species has twin dark stripes that run from the back of the head along the neck, and a raised vertebral ridge. There are 13 to 14 subspecies, including the endangered dwarf Aruba Island Rattlesnake (*Crotalus durissus unicolor*) and the Uracoan Rattlesnake (*C. durissus vegrandis*) from Venezuela. They may not rattle a warning.
• OCCURRENCE N.E. Mexico to N. Argentina (excluding Ecuador and Chile). In savanna and savanna woodland.
• REPRODUCTION Live-bearing, 2–47 neonates.
• SIMILAR SPECIES Mexican West Coast Rattlesnake (*Crotalus basiliscus*).

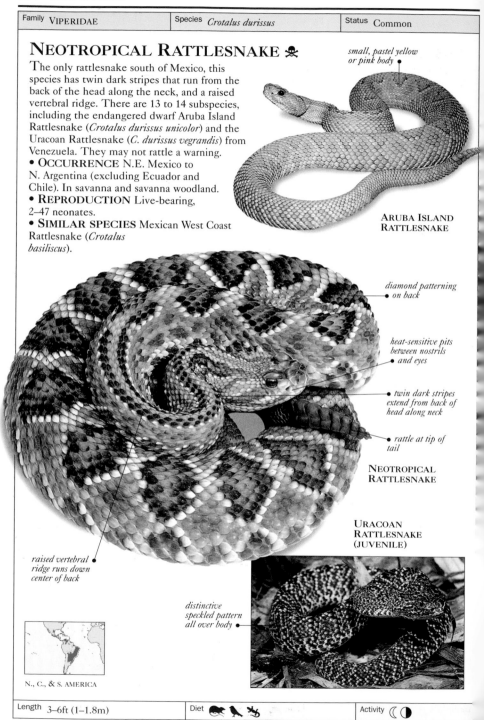

small, pastel yellow or pink body •

ARUBA ISLAND RATTLESNAKE

diamond patterning on back •

heat-sensitive pits between nostrils and eyes •

• twin dark stripes extend from back of head along neck

• rattle at tip of tail

NEOTROPICAL RATTLESNAKE

URACOAN RATTLESNAKE (JUVENILE)

raised vertebral • ridge runs down center of back

distinctive speckled pattern all over body •

N., C., & S. AMERICA

Length 3–6ft (1–1.8m)	Diet	Activity

Family VIPERIDAE	Species *Crotalus horridus*	Status Endangered

TIMBER RATTLESNAKE ☠

The first rattlesnake encountered by
European colonists, the Timber Rattlesnake
is also one of the most persecuted snakes in
the United States. It is highly variable in
coloration, ranging from black to dark brown,
light brown, yellow, or light gray, with an
overlying pattern of variable dark bands and
an almost entirely black tail. Light-colored
specimens may have orange vertebral stripes.
The scientific name, *Crotalus horridus*, refers
to the prickly, keeled scales.
• **OCCURRENCE** E. US. In montane
woodland and lowland swamps.
• **REPRODUCTION** Live-bearing,
3–19 neonates.
• **SIMILAR SPECIES** Blacktail Rattlesnake
(*Crotalus molossus*).
• **REMARK** The sole Canadian population
went extinct in 1941.

irregular
transverse
dark bands •

entirely
black tail •

N. AMERICA

Length 3–6ft (0.9–1.8m)	Diet	Activity

Family VIPERIDAE	Species *Crotalus viridis*	Status Common

WESTERN RATTLESNAKE ☠

The Western Rattlesnake has the widest range of any
rattlesnake in western North America. The basic
pattern is one of dark-edged blotches on a lighter
background, but there is much variation
between the nine subspecies. The Arizona
Black Rattlesnake (*Crotalus viridis
cerberus*) is very dark; the Prairie
Rattlesnake (*C. viridis viridis*, shown
here) is greenish or reddish brown;
the small Hopi Rattlesnake
(*C. viridis nuntius*) is reddish
brown; and the Midget Faded
Rattlesnake (*C. viridis concolor*)
may be almost cream-colored.
• **OCCURRENCE** E. North
America, from southern
Canada to Baja California,
Mexico. In many habitats,
from sea level and desert
edges to 10,850ft (3,300m).
• **REPRODUCTION** Live-
bearing, 3–25 neonates.
• **SIMILAR SPECIES** Mojave
Rattlesnake (*C. scutellatus*), Western
Diamondback Rattlesnake
(*C. atrox*, p.183).

short, dark-edged
blotches on paler
background •

N. AMERICA

• body coloration
continues on to
rattle

light stripes run
from camouflaged eyes
• to mouth corners

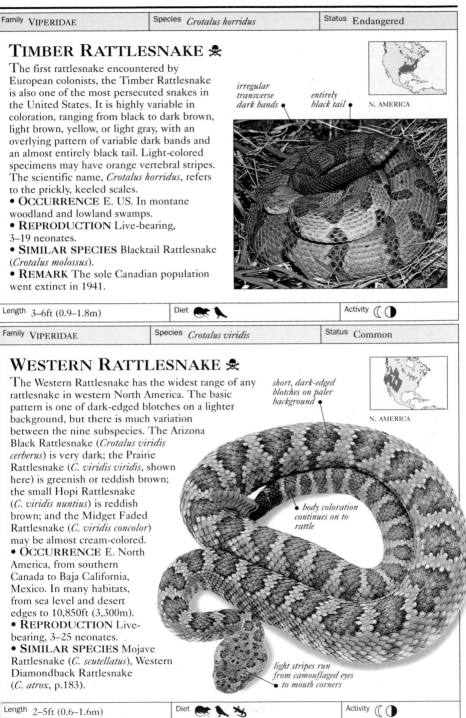

Length 2–5ft (0.6–1.6m)	Diet	Activity

| Family VIPERIDAE | Species *Daboia russelii* | Status Locally common |

RUSSELL'S VIPER ☠

This viper is unmistakable in both its appearance and behavior. The background color is orange, pink, or gray, broken by three longitudinal rows of large, dark-edged spots, often interspersed by two rows of smaller but similar markings. Curved markings of the same color are present on the head. If alarmed, Russell's Viper will issue a prolonged, very loud hiss.

- **OCCURRENCE** Pakistan to Thailand and Taiwan, and Indonesia (Java and the Lesser Sunda Islands). In dry woodland and grassy hills.
- **REPRODUCTION** Live-bearing, 30–60 neonates.
- **REMARK** This highly venomous snake causes more serious snakebites in Sri Lanka (where it is known as Tic Polonga) than cobras, kraits, or carpet vipers.

three rows of large, dark-edged spots

stout body shape

ASIA

| Length 3–5ft (1–1.5m) | Diet | Activity ☽ |

| Family VIPERIDAE | Species *Echis pyramidum* | Status Locally common |

EAST AFRICAN CARPET VIPER ☠

This is a short brown viper with a rounded head. The keels of the scales along the sides, which are arranged obliquely, are serrated. When alarmed, the carpet viper forms its body into a series of concentric curves and rasps the serrated scales together to produce a loud "saw-scaling" sound; it may strike simultaneously with a rapid jabbing motion.

- **OCCURRENCE** N. and N.E. Africa. In oases and on rocky and grassy terrain.
- **REPRODUCTION** Lays 4–20 eggs.
- **SIMILAR SPECIES** Burton's Painted Carpet Viper (*Echis coloratus*).

short, rounded head

eyes large in relation to head

keeled, serrated scales on sides adapted for "saw-scaling"

rounded head

AFRICA

| Length 20–33in (50–85cm) | Diet | Activity ☽ |

Family VIPERIDAE	Species *Lachesis muta*	Status Locally common

SOUTH AMERICAN BUSHMASTER ☠

This viper is brown, yellow, or pink, with contrasting dark brown or black rhomboid markings that pass over the back. A black stripe runs from the eyes to the jaw. The tail terminates in a short spine. There are two subspecies: the Amazonian Bushmaster (*Lachesis muta muta*) and the Atlantic Coastal Bushmaster (*L. muta rhombeata*), which is highly endangered.
• **OCCURRENCE** Amazon Basin and E. Brazil, along the Atlantic coast. In rainforest.
• **REPRODUCTION** Lays 5–18 eggs.
• **SIMILAR SPECIES** Black-headed Bushmaster (*Lachesis melanocephala*), Central American Bushmaster (*L. stenophrys*).
• **REMARK** Bushmasters (*Lachesis* species) are the largest and only egg-laying vipers in the Americas.

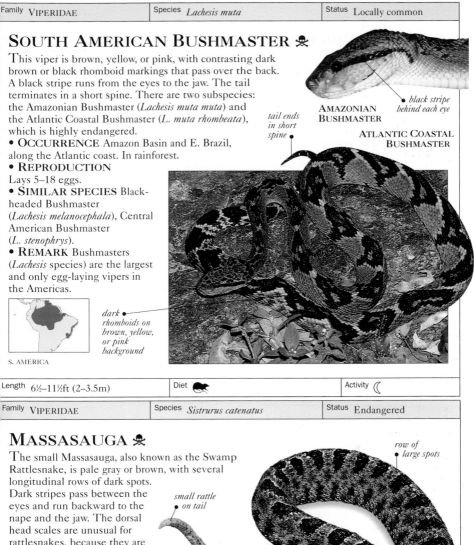

black stripe behind each eye

AMAZONIAN BUSHMASTER

tail ends in short spine

ATLANTIC COASTAL BUSHMASTER

dark rhomboids on brown, yellow, or pink background

S. AMERICA

Length 6½–11½ft (2–3.5m)	Diet 🐀	Activity ☾

Family VIPERIDAE	Species *Sistrurus catenatus*	Status Endangered

MASSASAUGA ☠

The small Massasauga, also known as the Swamp Rattlesnake, is pale gray or brown, with several longitudinal rows of dark spots. Dark stripes pass between the eyes and run backward to the nape and the jaw. The dorsal head scales are unusual for rattlesnakes, because they are large scutes rather than granular scales. Massasaugas swim well and some populations hibernate in crayfish burrows.
• **OCCURRENCE** S.E. Canada to N.E. Mexico. In swamps, meadows, and river beds.
• **REPRODUCTION** Live-bearing, 2–19 neonates.
• **SIMILAR SPECIES** Pygmy Rattlesnake (*Sistrurus miliarius*), Western Hognose Snake (*Heterodon nasicus*, p.138).

row of large spots

small rattle on tail

N. AMERICA

Length 2½–3ft (0.8–1m)	Diet 🦗 🐁 🦎 🐸 🐛	Activity ☼ ◑

Family VIPERIDAE	Species *Trimeresurus albolabris*	Status Common

WHITE-LIPPED PITVIPER ☠

One of several arboreal green pitvipers
in southern Asia, the White-lipped Pitviper
is vivid green with a broad red dorsal line on its
tail. Males have a white stripe along the lower
sides but this stripe is absent or indistinct in females.
Despite its name, the lips of this snake are actually
green, but the throat and underside are white.
The eyes are orange with vertical pupils.
Large, heat-sensitive loreal pits make
this an efficient predator of small
mammals and birds.
• **OCCURRENCE**
S. and S.E. Asia. In open
lowland and hilly woodland.
• **REPRODUCTION** Live-
bearing, 15–25 neonates.
• **SIMILAR SPECIES** Pope's Pitviper
(*Trimeresurus popeiorum*).

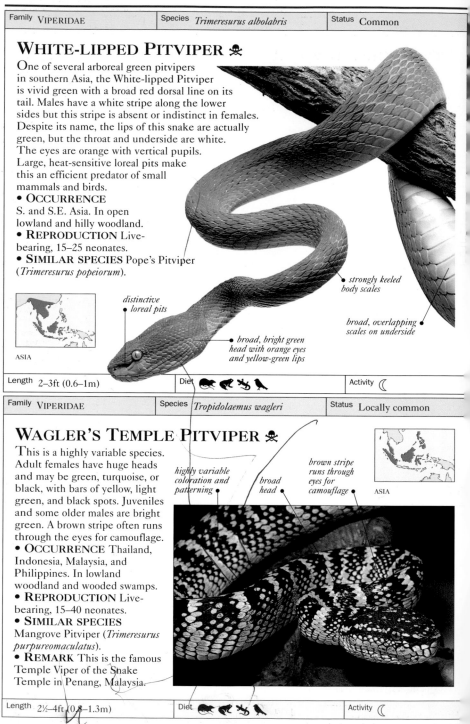

ASIA

distinctive
• loreal pits

strongly keeled
body scales

broad, overlapping
scales on underside

• broad, bright green
head with orange eyes
and yellow-green lips

Length 2–3ft (0.6–1m)	Diet 🐀 🐁 🦎 🐍 🐦	Activity ☾

Family VIPERIDAE	Species *Tropidolaemus wagleri*	Status Locally common

WAGLER'S TEMPLE PITVIPER ☠

This is a highly variable species.
Adult females have huge heads
and may be green, turquoise, or
black, with bars of yellow, light
green, and black spots. Juveniles
and some older males are bright
green. A brown stripe often runs
through the eyes for camouflage.
• **OCCURRENCE** Thailand,
Indonesia, Malaysia, and
Philippines. In lowland
woodland and wooded swamps.
• **REPRODUCTION** Live-
bearing, 15–40 neonates.
• **SIMILAR SPECIES**
Mangrove Pitviper (*Trimeresurus
purpureomaculatus*).
• **REMARK** This is the famous
Temple Viper of the Snake
Temple in Penang, Malaysia.

highly variable
coloration and
patterning •

broad
head •

brown stripe
runs through
eyes for
camouflage •

ASIA

Length 2½–4ft (0.8–1.3m)	Diet 🐀 🐸 🦎 🐍 🐦	Activity ☾

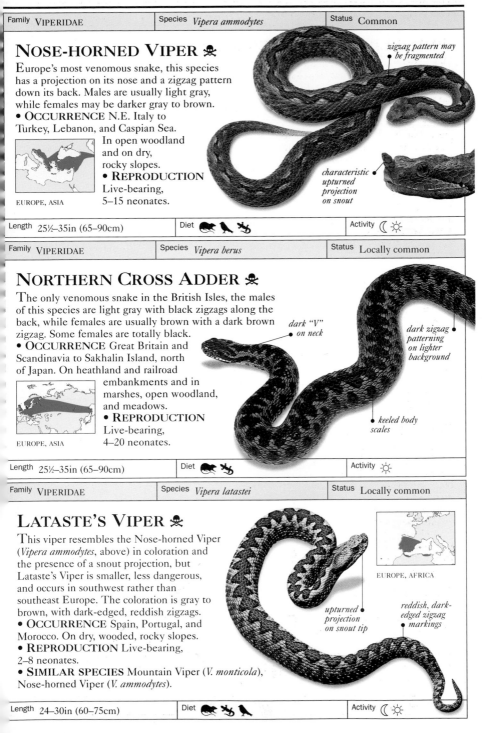

Family VIPERIDAE	Species *Vipera ammodytes*	Status Common

NOSE-HORNED VIPER ☠

Europe's most venomous snake, this species
has a projection on its nose and a zigzag pattern
down its back. Males are usually light gray,
while females may be darker gray to brown.
• OCCURRENCE N.E. Italy to
Turkey, Lebanon, and Caspian Sea.
In open woodland
and on dry,
rocky slopes.
• REPRODUCTION
Live-bearing,
5–15 neonates.

EUROPE, ASIA

zigzag pattern may be fragmented

characteristic upturned projection on snout

Length 25½–35in (65–90cm)	Diet	Activity ☾ ☼

Family VIPERIDAE	Species *Vipera berus*	Status Locally common

NORTHERN CROSS ADDER ☠

The only venomous snake in the British Isles, the males
of this species are light gray with black zigzags along the
back, while females are usually brown with a dark brown
zigzag. Some females are totally black.
• OCCURRENCE Great Britain and
Scandinavia to Sakhalin Island, north
of Japan. On heathland and railroad
embankments and in
marshes, open woodland,
and meadows.
• REPRODUCTION
Live-bearing,
4–20 neonates.

EUROPE, ASIA

dark "V" on neck

dark zigzag patterning on lighter background

keeled body scales

Length 25½–35in (65–90cm)	Diet	Activity ☼

Family VIPERIDAE	Species *Vipera latastei*	Status Locally common

LATASTE'S VIPER ☠

This viper resembles the Nose-horned Viper
(*Vipera ammodytes*, above) in coloration and
the presence of a snout projection, but
Lataste's Viper is smaller, less dangerous,
and occurs in southwest rather than
southeast Europe. The coloration is gray to
brown, with dark-edged, reddish zigzags.
• OCCURRENCE Spain, Portugal, and
Morocco. On dry, wooded, rocky slopes.
• REPRODUCTION Live-bearing,
2–8 neonates.
• SIMILAR SPECIES Mountain Viper (*V. monticola*),
Nose-horned Viper (*V. ammodytes*).

EUROPE, AFRICA

upturned projection on snout tip

reddish, dark-edged zigzag markings

Length 24–30in (60–75cm)	Diet	Activity ☾ ☼

CROCODILIANS

C ROCODILES, alligators, and gharials together form a group known as the Crocodilians. The bodies of animals in this group are covered in a tough, leathery skin, which may be strengthened with plates (known as osteoderms, or bone-skin). Unable to sweat through their tough skins, crocodilians loose heat by "gaping" (resting with their mouths open), permitting moisture to evaporate from the mucous membranes to cool them down. Despite their almost primeval appearance, modern crocodilians are actually quite advanced, possessing an elaborate, four-chambered heart similar to that of a mammal. In fact, it is generally accepted by biologists that birds, rather than other reptiles, are the nearest living relatives of modern crocodilians. Except for the American Alligator (*Alligator mississippiensis*), all crocodilian species are endangered in at least part of their ranges, and some are threatened with extinction as a result of habitat destruction, hunting, or pollution.

The 23 living crocodilian species are often divided into three separate families (Alligatoridae, Crocodylidae, and Gavialidae), as in this book; however, they are sometimes placed in three subfamilies of a single family.

Family ALLIGATORIDAE	Species *Alligator mississippiensis*	Status Common

AMERICAN ALLIGATOR

Juvenile American Alligators are black with irregular yellow cross-bands but, as they mature, the yellow markings become completely obscured by black pigment and algae. The American Alligator's broad, rounded snout and coloration distinguishes it from the American Crocodile (*Crocodylus acutus*), which also inhabits southern Florida but is brown with a tapered snout. Male alligators are much larger than females. In the breeding season, the huge males bellow to attract a mate, curving the body concavely and thrusting the head and tail out of the water. As they bellow, small jets of water vibrate upward from the scales of the alligator's back. Mating takes place in the water, and female alligators lay their eggs in mounds of vegetational debris, guarding them throughout the 65-day gestation period. Juvenile alligators feed on invertebrates, frogs, and fish, but adults prey on turtles, waterbirds, and mammals.

eyes have inner membraneous eyes for underwater vision

• OCCURRENCE
S.E. US. In freshwater
swamps, lakes,
and rivers.
• REPRODUCTION
Lays 20–50 eggs.
• SIMILAR SPECIES
Chinese Alligator (*Alligator sinensis*, opposite).
• REMARK There are few cases of humans being attacked and killed by alligators compared to crocodiles, but there are occasional accidents. Since American Alligators became protected from wholesale hunting in the 1960s, their populations have recovered; indeed, "nuisance" alligators are now being removed from some areas.

Length 9–16½ft (2.8–5m)	Diet 🦐🦅🐾	Activity ☼

Family ALLIGATORIDAE	Species *Alligator sinensis*	Status Endangered

CHINESE ALLIGATOR

The closest relative of the American Alligator (*Alligator mississippiensis*, opposite), the Chinese Alligator is greenish black, with yellow speckles and bars on its sides. Juveniles are more vivid, with yellow and black bands.
• OCCURRENCE China. In and around the Lower Yangtze River and in associated grass swamps and lakes.
• REPRODUCTION Lays 10–40 eggs.
• SIMILAR SPECIES American Alligator (*A. mississippiensis*, opposite).

short, broad, upturned snout

stout, olive-green body

ASIA

Length 5–6½ft (1.5–2m)	Diet	Activity ☾

reticulated yellow markings on black background

N. AMERICA

JUVENILE

powerful tail for swimming

ADULT

scales of back raised into hardened ridges

webbed hindfeet (only three out of five toes have toenails)

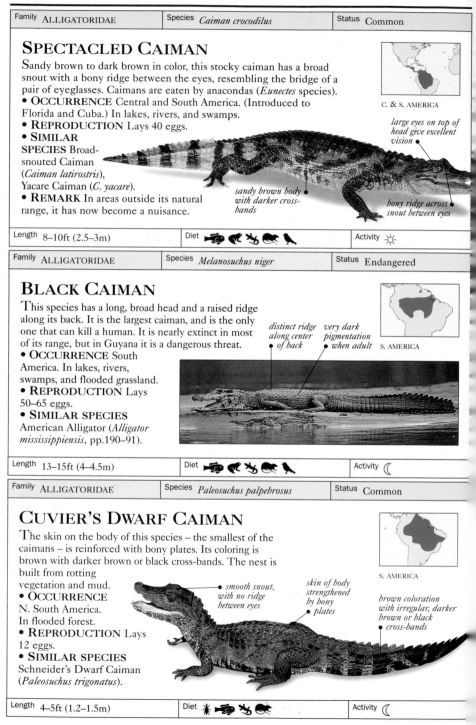

Family ALLIGATORIDAE	Species *Caiman crocodilus*	Status Common

SPECTACLED CAIMAN

Sandy brown to dark brown in color, this stocky caiman has a broad
snout with a bony ridge between the eyes, resembling the bridge of a
pair of eyeglasses. Caimans are eaten by anacondas (*Eunectes* species).
• **OCCURRENCE** Central and South America. (Introduced to
Florida and Cuba.) In lakes, rivers, and swamps.
• **REPRODUCTION** Lays 40 eggs.
• **SIMILAR**
SPECIES Broad-
snouted Caiman
(*Caiman latirostris*),
Yacare Caiman (*C. yacare*).
• **REMARK** In areas outside its natural
range, it has now become a nuisance.

C. & S. AMERICA

large eyes on top of
head give excellent
vision

sandy brown body
with darker cross-
bands

bony ridge across
snout between eyes

Length 8–10ft (2.5–3m)	Diet	Activity ☼

Family ALLIGATORIDAE	Species *Melanosuchus niger*	Status Endangered

BLACK CAIMAN

This species has a long, broad head and a raised ridge
along its back. It is the largest caiman, and is the only
one that can kill a human. It is nearly extinct in most
of its range, but in Guyana it is a dangerous threat.
• **OCCURRENCE** South
America. In lakes, rivers,
swamps, and flooded grassland.
• **REPRODUCTION** Lays
50–65 eggs.
• **SIMILAR SPECIES**
American Alligator (*Alligator
mississippiensis*, pp.190–91).

distinct ridge
along center
of back

very dark
pigmentation
when adult

S. AMERICA

Length 13–15ft (4–4.5m)	Diet	Activity ☾

Family ALLIGATORIDAE	Species *Paleosuchus palpebrosus*	Status Common

CUVIER'S DWARF CAIMAN

The skin on the body of this species – the smallest of the
caimans – is reinforced with bony plates. Its coloring is
brown with darker brown or black cross-bands. The nest is
built from rotting
vegetation and mud.
• **OCCURRENCE**
N. South America.
In flooded forest.
• **REPRODUCTION** Lays
12 eggs.
• **SIMILAR SPECIES**
Schneider's Dwarf Caiman
(*Paleosuchus trigonatus*).

S. AMERICA

smooth snout,
with no ridge
between eyes

skin of body
strengthened
by bony
plates

brown coloration
with irregular, darker
brown or black
cross-bands

Length 4–5ft (1.2–1.5m)	Diet	Activity ☾

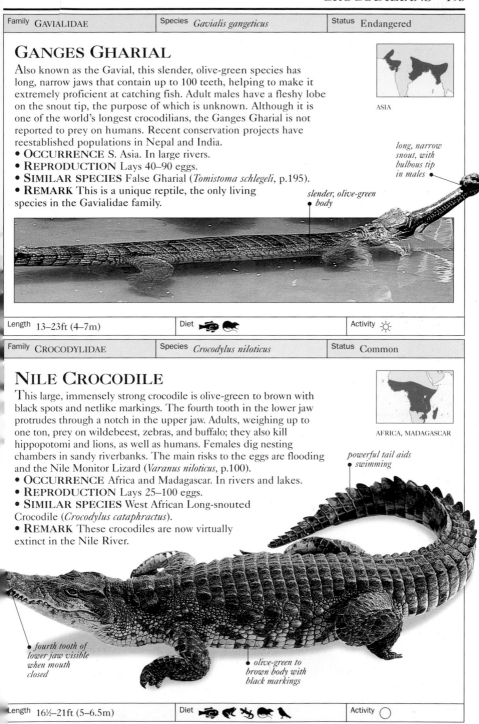

| Family GAVIALIDAE | Species *Gavialis gangeticus* | Status Endangered |

GANGES GHARIAL

Also known as the Gavial, this slender, olive-green species has long, narrow jaws that contain up to 100 teeth, helping to make it extremely proficient at catching fish. Adult males have a fleshy lobe on the snout tip, the purpose of which is unknown. Although it is one of the world's longest crocodilians, the Ganges Gharial is not reported to prey on humans. Recent conservation projects have reestablished populations in Nepal and India.
• **OCCURRENCE** S. Asia. In large rivers.
• **REPRODUCTION** Lays 40–90 eggs.
• **SIMILAR SPECIES** False Gharial (*Tomistoma schlegeli*, p.195).
• **REMARK** This is a unique reptile, the only living species in the Gavialidae family.

ASIA

long, narrow snout, with bulbous tip in males

slender, olive-green body

| Length 13–23ft (4–7m) | Diet | Activity |

| Family CROCODYLIDAE | Species *Crocodylus niloticus* | Status Common |

NILE CROCODILE

This large, immensely strong crocodile is olive-green to brown with black spots and netlike markings. The fourth tooth in the lower jaw protrudes through a notch in the upper jaw. Adults, weighing up to one ton, prey on wildebeest, zebras, and buffalo; they also kill hippopotomi and lions, as well as humans. Females dig nesting chambers in sandy riverbanks. The main risks to the eggs are flooding and the Nile Monitor Lizard (*Varanus niloticus*, p.100).
• **OCCURRENCE** Africa and Madagascar. In rivers and lakes.
• **REPRODUCTION** Lays 25–100 eggs.
• **SIMILAR SPECIES** West African Long-snouted Crocodile (*Crocodylus cataphractus*).
• **REMARK** These crocodiles are now virtually extinct in the Nile River.

AFRICA, MADAGASCAR

powerful tail aids swimming

fourth tooth of lower jaw visible when mouth closed

olive-green to brown body with black markings

| Length 16½–21ft (5–6.5m) | Diet | Activity |

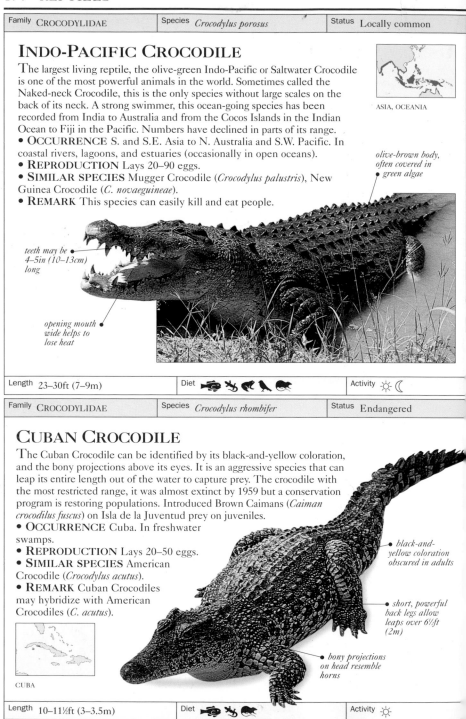

| Family | CROCODYLIDAE | Species | *Crocodylus porosus* | Status | Locally common |

INDO-PACIFIC CROCODILE

The largest living reptile, the olive-green Indo-Pacific or Saltwater Crocodile is one of the most powerful animals in the world. Sometimes called the Naked-neck Crocodile, this is the only species without large scales on the back of its neck. A strong swimmer, this ocean-going species has been recorded from India to Australia and from the Cocos Islands in the Indian Ocean to Fiji in the Pacific. Numbers have declined in parts of its range.
• **OCCURRENCE** S. and S.E. Asia to N. Australia and S.W. Pacific. In coastal rivers, lagoons, and estuaries (occasionally in open oceans).
• **REPRODUCTION** Lays 20–90 eggs.
• **SIMILAR SPECIES** Mugger Crocodile (*Crocodylus palustris*), New Guinea Crocodile (*C. novaeguineae*).
• **REMARK** This species can easily kill and eat people.

ASIA, OCEANIA

olive-brown body, often covered in green algae

teeth may be 4–5in (10–13cm) long

opening mouth wide helps to lose heat

| Length | 23–30ft (7–9m) | Diet | | Activity |

| Family | CROCODYLIDAE | Species | *Crocodylus rhombifer* | Status | Endangered |

CUBAN CROCODILE

The Cuban Crocodile can be identified by its black-and-yellow coloration, and the bony projections above its eyes. It is an aggressive species that can leap its entire length out of the water to capture prey. The crocodile with the most restricted range, it was almost extinct by 1959 but a conservation program is restoring populations. Introduced Brown Caimans (*Caiman crocodilus fuscus*) on Isla de la Juventud prey on juveniles.
• **OCCURRENCE** Cuba. In freshwater swamps.
• **REPRODUCTION** Lays 20–50 eggs.
• **SIMILAR SPECIES** American Crocodile (*Crocodylus acutus*).
• **REMARK** Cuban Crocodiles may hybridize with American Crocodiles (*C. acutus*).

black-and-yellow coloration obscured in adults

short, powerful back legs allow leaps over 6½ft (2m)

bony projections on head resemble horns

CUBA

| Length | 10–11½ft (3–3.5m) | Diet | | Activity |

Family CROCODYLIDAE	Species *Osteolaemus tetraspis*	Status Endangered

DWARF CROCODILE

The smallest crocodile, this is a secretive, short-headed species with two distinctly separate populations. Adults are black-brown but juveniles are light brown with black spots and bars. When threatened, the Dwarf Crocodile will dive into the water and hide in holes under the bank.
• **OCCURRENCE** W. and C. Africa. In rainforest swamps, ponds, and slow-moving rivers.
• **REPRODUCTION** Lays 10–17 eggs.
• **SIMILAR SPECIES** Dwarf caimans (*Paleosuchus* species, p.192).

AFRICA

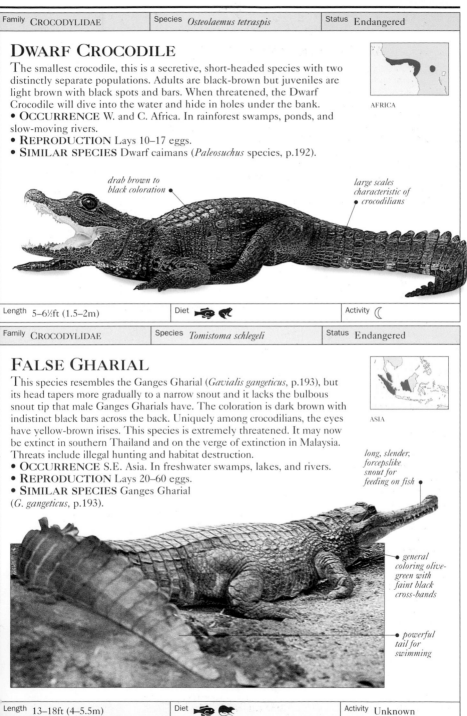

drab brown to black coloration

large scales characteristic of crocodilians

Length 5–6½ft (1.5–2m)	Diet	Activity ☾

Family CROCODYLIDAE	Species *Tomistoma schlegeli*	Status Endangered

FALSE GHARIAL

This species resembles the Ganges Gharial (*Gavialis gangeticus*, p.193), but its head tapers more gradually to a narrow snout and it lacks the bulbous snout tip that male Ganges Gharials have. The coloration is dark brown with indistinct black bars across the back. Uniquely among crocodilians, the eyes have yellow-brown irises. This species is extremely threatened. It may now be extinct in southern Thailand and on the verge of extinction in Malaysia. Threats include illegal hunting and habitat destruction.
• **OCCURRENCE** S.E. Asia. In freshwater swamps, lakes, and rivers.
• **REPRODUCTION** Lays 20–60 eggs.
• **SIMILAR SPECIES** Ganges Gharial (*G. gangeticus*, p.193).

ASIA

long, slender, forcepslike snout for feeding on fish

general coloring olive-green with faint black cross-bands

powerful tail for swimming

Length 13–18ft (4–5.5m)	Diet	Activity Unknown

AMPHIBIANS

NEWTS AND SALAMANDERS

T HERE ARE FIVE families in the order Urodela, consisting of 450 species of newts and salamanders (over half of the total number of species are lungless salamanders, belonging to the family Plethodontidae). Salamanders and newts are characterized by a long tail and a long, slender body. They have relatively short limbs, which are all of similar length. Coloration is very variable. Some species secrete poison from glands in their skin; they are often brightly colored to warn potential predators.

Newts and salamanders are usually active at night. They mostly crawl on the ground, hiding by day under logs and rocks or in the burrows of other animals. A few species can climb trees and many are good swimmers. Some permanently aquatic salamanders resemble eels.

Salamanders and newts typically lay their eggs in water. The eggs hatch into carnivorous larvae, which – unlike the tadpoles of frogs and toads – have long, slender bodies. A large number of salamanders, however, lay their eggs on land. The larval phase of such species is completed in the egg with the young emerging as miniature adults. The term "newt" generally refers to those species that return to water for a period of weeks or months each year to breed.

Family SIRENIDAE	Species *Siren lacertina*	Status Locally common

GREATER SIREN

The Greater Siren is a large, eellike animal with small forelimbs and no hindlimbs. The upper body is gray with dark spots, and the sides are lighter with irregular yellow-brown markings. Its finlike tail is laterally compressed, with a spine running through the center. This species uses its shovel-shaped head to search for food in the mud. It feeds on a variety of prey, especially snails and clams.
• OCCURRENCE S.E. US. In shallow, muddy, well-vegetated rivers, canals, lakes, ponds, and ditches.
• REPRODUCTION Lays eggs in water in spring.
• REMARK In drought conditions, sirens are able to survive for up to two years, encased in a cocoon in the mud, feeding on their very large fat reserves.

prominent external gills on sides of head

N. AMERICA

pale yellow-brown markings on sides

flattened head

Length 20–35in (50–90cm)	Habit Entirely aquatic	Activity ☾

Family PROTEIDAE	Species *Necturus maculosus*	Status Locally common

MUDPUPPY

Also known as the Waterdog, this large, aggressive salamander is usually gray or brown with paler markings. It has prominent, bushy, reddish brown external gills on either side of its head. Its long, flattened body shape enables it to hide under logs and rocks by day. The Mudpuppy is a voracious predator, feeding on a variety of invertebrates, fish, and other amphibians. The female digs a nest chamber and defends her clutch of eggs, which are attached to the underside of a log or rock.
• OCCURRENCE E. and C. North America. In streams, rivers, canals, and lakes.
• REPRODUCTION Lays eggs in water in autumn and winter.

large, feathery, reddish brown external gills

long, flattened body

N. AMERICA

Length 8–20in (20–50cm)	Habit Entirely aquatic	Activity ☾

Family CRYPTOBRANCHIDAE	Species *Cryptobranchus alleganiensis*	Status Rare

HELLBENDER

This large salamander has distinctive folds of skin along its brown, mottled body. The flattened head and body enable it to force its way beneath rocks, and its noxious, slimy skin secretion protects it from predators. In the breeding season, the male excavates a space beneath a rock into which it lures or drives a female. The female is prevented from leaving until she has laid a long string of eggs, onto which the male releases his sperm. The male then drives the female away and guards the eggs until they hatch.
• OCCURRENCE E. US. In large, rocky, fast-flowing streams.
• REPRODUCTION Lays eggs in water in autumn.
• REMARK Due to pollution, this once common species is now increasingly rare.

N. AMERICA

serrated crest of skin along back and tail

large, flattened head

folds of skin on lower body

Length 12–30in (30–75cm)	Habit Entirely aquatic	Activity ○

Family PROTEIDAE	Species *Proteus anguinus*	Status Rare

OLM

The Olm is an exclusively cave-dwelling salamander that never leaves the water. It is usually white in color, although some are gray, pink, or yellow. Olms do not metamorphose into adults, but become sexually mature while in the larval state. They retain their external gills throughout life. Their tails are large, enabling them to swim well, and their eyes are rudimentary, suited to the permanent darkness in which they live. During courtship, the male wafts odors by fanning his tail in front of the female's snout. Fertilization is internal, and the female lays up to 70 eggs, attached to the underside of a rock.
• **OCCURRENCE** Slovenia to Montenegro. In underground streams and pools in limestone caves.
• **REPRODUCTION** Lays eggs in water in spring.

EUROPE

very small eyes

bill-like snout

large external gills

white, gray, pink, or yellow body coloration

Length 8–12in (20–30cm)	Habit Entirely aquatic	Activity ○

Family DICAMPTODONTIDAE	Species *Dicamptodon tenebrosus*	Status Locally common

PACIFIC SALAMANDER

This stocky salamander is dark brown to black, with light brown mottling or spots. It progresses through an aquatic larval stage that lasts for several years. While some individuals become terrestrial at maturity, returning to water to breed, others never leave the water and retain their gills into adulthood. Those that leave the water are the largest terrestrial salamanders in the world.
• **OCCURRENCE** N.W. US. In and around streams in coastal forest.
• **REPRODUCTION** Lays eggs in water in spring and autumn.

N. AMERICA

dark brown to black coloration

light brown spots or mottling

tail laterally compressed toward rear

12 or 13 costal grooves on body

Length 6¾–13in (17–34cm)	Habit Terrestrial or aquatic	Activity ☾

Family AMPHIUMIDAE	Species *Amphiuma tridactylum*	Status Locally common

THREE-TOED AMPHIUMA

This large salamander, with slimy skin, a long tail, and tiny limbs (each with three toes), is similar to an eel in appearance. It has a black, gray, or brown upper side, and a pale gray underside. Males usually breed every year, females every other year; the female guards the eggs until they hatch. The Three-toed Amphiuma can deliver a painful bite.

N. AMERICA

• OCCURRENCE S. and C. US. On coastal plains, in ditches, swamps, streams, and ponds.
• REPRODUCTION Lays eggs in water in winter and spring.

slimy skin

black, gray, or brown coloration above, pale gray below

very small limbs, with three toes on each limb

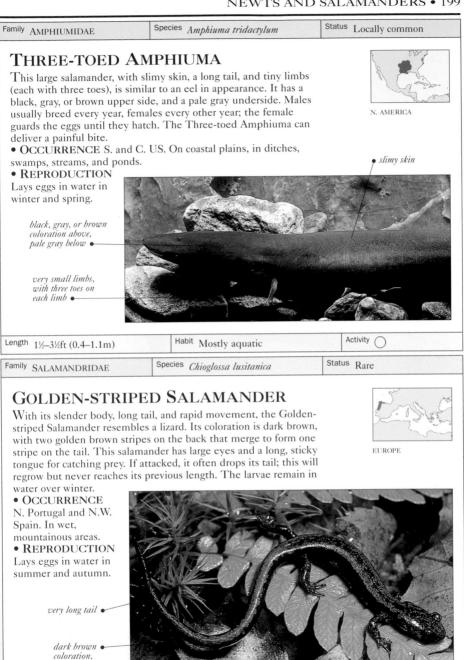

Length 1½–3½ft (0.4–1.1m)	Habit Mostly aquatic	Activity ○

Family SALAMANDRIDAE	Species *Chioglossa lusitanica*	Status Rare

GOLDEN-STRIPED SALAMANDER

With its slender body, long tail, and rapid movement, the Golden-striped Salamander resembles a lizard. Its coloration is dark brown, with two golden brown stripes on the back that merge to form one stripe on the tail. This salamander has large eyes and a long, sticky tongue for catching prey. If attacked, it often drops its tail; this will regrow but never reaches its previous length. The larvae remain in water over winter.

EUROPE

• OCCURRENCE N. Portugal and N.W. Spain. In wet, mountainous areas.
• REPRODUCTION Lays eggs in water in summer and autumn.

very long tail

dark brown coloration, with golden brown stripes

Length 4¾–5½in (12–14cm)	Habit Mostly terrestrial	Activity ☾

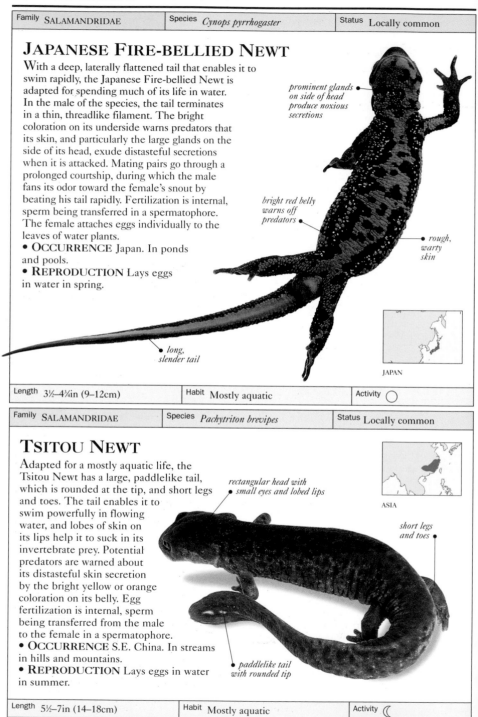

| Family SALAMANDRIDAE | Species *Cynops pyrrhogaster* | Status Locally common |

JAPANESE FIRE-BELLIED NEWT

With a deep, laterally flattened tail that enables it to swim rapidly, the Japanese Fire-bellied Newt is adapted for spending much of its life in water. In the male of the species, the tail terminates in a thin, threadlike filament. The bright coloration on its underside warns predators that its skin, and particularly the large glands on the side of its head, exude distasteful secretions when it is attacked. Mating pairs go through a prolonged courtship, during which the male fans its odor toward the female's snout by beating his tail rapidly. Fertilization is internal, sperm being transferred in a spermatophore. The female attaches eggs individually to the leaves of water plants.
• OCCURRENCE Japan. In ponds and pools.
• REPRODUCTION Lays eggs in water in spring.

prominent glands on side of head produce noxious secretions

bright red belly warns off predators

rough, warty skin

long, slender tail

JAPAN

| Length 3½–4¾in (9–12cm) | Habit Mostly aquatic | Activity ◯ |

| Family SALAMANDRIDAE | Species *Pachytriton brevipes* | Status Locally common |

TSITOU NEWT

Adapted for a mostly aquatic life, the Tsitou Newt has a large, paddlelike tail, which is rounded at the tip, and short legs and toes. The tail enables it to swim powerfully in flowing water, and lobes of skin on its lips help it to suck in its invertebrate prey. Potential predators are warned about its distasteful skin secretion by the bright yellow or orange coloration on its belly. Egg fertilization is internal, sperm being transferred from the male to the female in a spermatophore.
• OCCURRENCE S.E. China. In streams in hills and mountains.
• REPRODUCTION Lays eggs in water in summer.

rectangular head with small eyes and lobed lips

ASIA

short legs and toes

paddlelike tail with rounded tip

| Length 5½–7in (14–18cm) | Habit Mostly aquatic | Activity ☾ |

Family SALAMANDRIDAE	Species *Paramesotriton hongkongensis*	Status Locally common

HONG KONG WARTY NEWT

A species that spends most of its life in water, the Hong Kong Warty Newt swims by beating its long, laterally flattened tail. It has relatively short, thick legs, typical of an animal that spends very little time crawling on land. The numerous warts on its skin and the large parotid glands on its head produce a toxic secretion when it is attacked; it may also feign death, rolling over onto its back and exposing its brightly colored belly. In the breeding season, the male displays by beating its tail; this develops a white or bluish stripe along its length, which makes it more visible in dim light. Sperm is transferred to the female in a spermatophore. Eggs are laid singly, wrapped in leaves.
• OCCURRENCE Hong Kong. In streams.
• REPRODUCTION Lays eggs in water in winter.

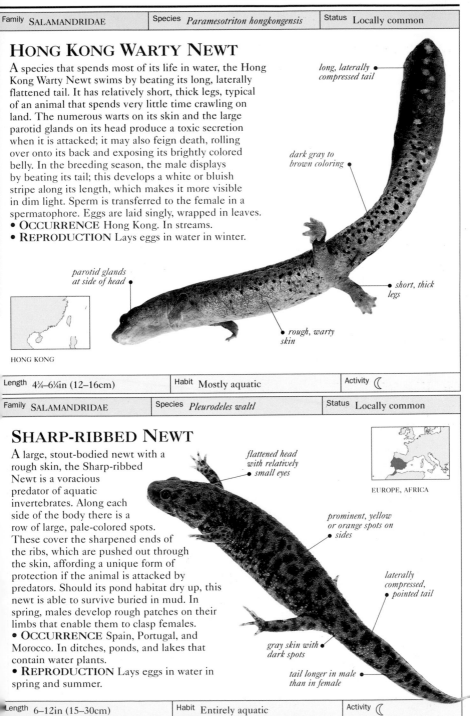

long, laterally compressed tail

dark gray to brown coloring

parotid glands at side of head

short, thick legs

rough, warty skin

HONG KONG

Length 4¾–6¼in (12–16cm)	Habit Mostly aquatic	Activity ☾

Family SALAMANDRIDAE	Species *Pleurodeles waltl*	Status Locally common

SHARP-RIBBED NEWT

A large, stout-bodied newt with a rough skin, the Sharp-ribbed Newt is a voracious predator of aquatic invertebrates. Along each side of the body there is a row of large, pale-colored spots. These cover the sharpened ends of the ribs, which are pushed out through the skin, affording a unique form of protection if the animal is attacked by predators. Should its pond habitat dry up, this newt is able to survive buried in mud. In spring, males develop rough patches on their limbs that enable them to clasp females.
• OCCURRENCE Spain, Portugal, and Morocco. In ditches, ponds, and lakes that contain water plants.
• REPRODUCTION Lays eggs in water in spring and summer.

flattened head with relatively small eyes

EUROPE, AFRICA

prominent, yellow or orange spots on sides

laterally compressed, pointed tail

gray skin with dark spots

tail longer in male than in female

Length 6–12in (15–30cm)	Habit Entirely aquatic	Activity ☾

Family SALAMANDRIDAE	Species *Salamandra salamandra*	Status Locally common

FIRE SALAMANDER

A robust animal with a short tail, the Fire
Salamander is almost entirely terrestrial once
it has completed its larval stage. Throughout
its range, there is considerable variation in
coloration and patterning: individuals may
be black with yellow markings, yellow with
black markings, or occasionally red or orange.
The limbs are short and stout, with broad toes,
and the tail is cylindrical in shape and shorter
than the body. There are two rows of poison
glands running along each side and, when
attacked, the Fire Salamander squirts toxins
from the large parotid glands on its head. Females
are slightly larger than males. Fire Salamanders
emerge at night, especially after rain, from
beneath logs and stones, to feed on worms, insects,
insect larvae, and slugs. During mating, the male
grasps the female from below. The eggs develop
inside the female and are released as larvae (in
clutches of between 12 and 50) into a pond or stream.
During their development in the oviduct, larvae may
be cannibalistic, eating their smaller siblings as eggs or
larvae. In some high-altitude populations, the larvae
remain in the oviduct until they have metamorphosed
into the adult form.
• **OCCURRENCE** Europe, N.W. Africa, and
S.W. Asia. In woodland on hills and mountains.
• **REPRODUCTION** Lays larvae in water in
spring and summer.
• **SIMILAR SPECIES** Alpine Salamander
(*Salamandra atra*).

*large parotid glands
with conspicuous
pores*

*black body
coloration with
yellow stripes
(variable)*

**STRIPED
SPECIMEN**

*tail shorter
than body*

*black background
color with yellow
spots (variable)*

cylindrical tail

*stout, short limbs
with broad toes*

**SPOTTED
SPECIMEN**

*large,
prominent
eyes*

EUROPE, AFRICA, ASIA

Length 7–11in (18–28cm)	Habit Mostly terrestrial	Activity ☾

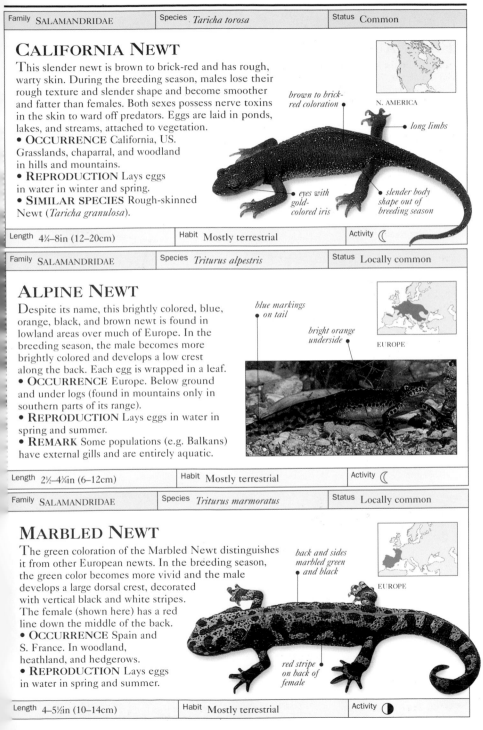

Family SALAMANDRIDAE	Species *Taricha torosa*	Status Common

CALIFORNIA NEWT

This slender newt is brown to brick-red and has rough, warty skin. During the breeding season, males lose their rough texture and slender shape and become smoother and fatter than females. Both sexes possess nerve toxins in the skin to ward off predators. Eggs are laid in ponds, lakes, and streams, attached to vegetation.
• OCCURRENCE California, US. Grasslands, chaparral, and woodland in hills and mountains.
• REPRODUCTION Lays eggs in water in winter and spring.
• SIMILAR SPECIES Rough-skinned Newt (*Taricha granulosa*).

brown to brick-red coloration

N. AMERICA

long limbs

eyes with gold-colored iris

slender body shape out of breeding season

Length 4¾–8in (12–20cm)	Habit Mostly terrestrial	Activity ☾

Family SALAMANDRIDAE	Species *Triturus alpestris*	Status Locally common

ALPINE NEWT

Despite its name, this brightly colored, blue, orange, black, and brown newt is found in lowland areas over much of Europe. In the breeding season, the male becomes more brightly colored and develops a low crest along the back. Each egg is wrapped in a leaf.
• OCCURRENCE Europe. Below ground and under logs (found in mountains only in southern parts of its range).
• REPRODUCTION Lays eggs in water in spring and summer.
• REMARK Some populations (e.g. Balkans) have external gills and are entirely aquatic.

blue markings on tail

bright orange underside

EUROPE

Length 2½–4¾in (6–12cm)	Habit Mostly terrestrial	Activity ☾

Family SALAMANDRIDAE	Species *Triturus marmoratus*	Status Locally common

MARBLED NEWT

The green coloration of the Marbled Newt distinguishes it from other European newts. In the breeding season, the green color becomes more vivid and the male develops a large dorsal crest, decorated with vertical black and white stripes. The female (shown here) has a red line down the middle of the back.
• OCCURRENCE Spain and S. France. In woodland, heathland, and hedgerows.
• REPRODUCTION Lays eggs in water in spring and summer.

back and sides marbled green and black

EUROPE

red stripe on back of female

Length 4–5½in (10–14cm)	Habit Mostly terrestrial	Activity ◑

Family SALAMANDRIDAE	Species *Triturus vulgaris*	Status Locally common

SMOOTH NEWT

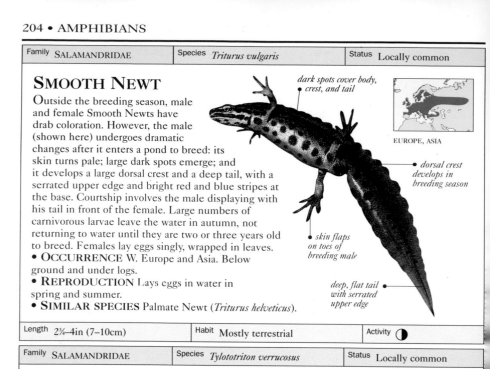

Outside the breeding season, male and female Smooth Newts have drab coloration. However, the male (shown here) undergoes dramatic changes after it enters a pond to breed: its skin turns pale; large dark spots emerge; and it develops a large dorsal crest and a deep tail, with a serrated upper edge and bright red and blue stripes at the base. Courtship involves the male displaying with his tail in front of the female. Large numbers of carnivorous larvae leave the water in autumn, not returning to water until they are two or three years old to breed. Females lay eggs singly, wrapped in leaves.
• OCCURRENCE W. Europe and Asia. Below ground and under logs.
• REPRODUCTION Lays eggs in water in spring and summer.
• SIMILAR SPECIES Palmate Newt (*Triturus helveticus*).

dark spots cover body, crest, and tail

EUROPE, ASIA

dorsal crest develops in breeding season

skin flaps on toes of breeding male

deep, flat tail with serrated upper edge

Length 2¾–4in (7–10cm)	Habit Mostly terrestrial	Activity ◑

Family SALAMANDRIDAE	Species *Tylototriton verrucosus*	Status Locally common

MANDARIN SALAMANDER

Also known as the Crocodile Newt, this robust animal, with rough, warty skin, lives most of its life on land but migrates to ponds to breed during the monsoon. It has a dark brown body and a bright orange head and tail. The orange dorsal ridge and large orange warts signal that the Mandarin Salamander will exude distasteful secretions if attacked. These are produced in the large parotid glands on either side of the head and in the skin. During mating, the male grasps the female and holds her for some time before transferring sperm in a spermatophore. The female lays about 50 eggs, which are attached to plants.
• OCCURRENCE China, N. India, N. Thailand, and N. Vietnam. In damp montane forest.
• REPRODUCTION Lays eggs in water in the rainy season.

ASIA

robust body with prominent, bright orange dorsal ridge

broad head with rounded jaw

laterally compressed tail

prominent, bright orange warts mark ends of ribs

large parotid glands produce distasteful secretions

Length 4¾–7in (12–18cm)	Habit Mostly terrestrial	Activity ☾

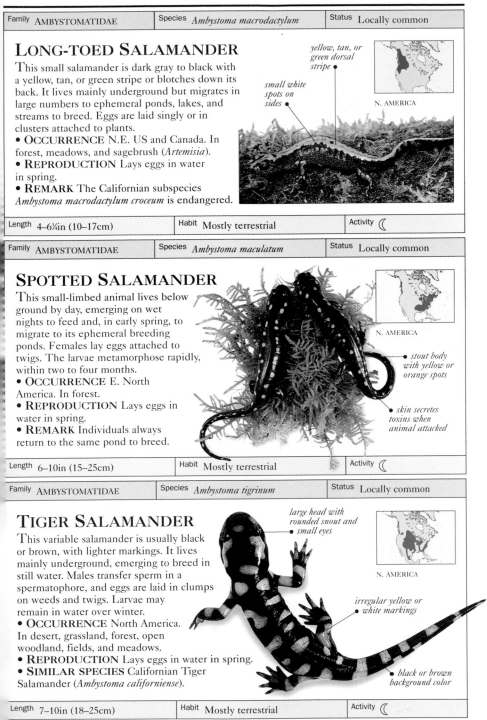

Family AMBYSTOMATIDAE	Species *Ambystoma macrodactylum*	Status Locally common

LONG-TOED SALAMANDER

This small salamander is dark gray to black with
a yellow, tan, or green stripe or blotches down its
back. It lives mainly underground but migrates in
large numbers to ephemeral ponds, lakes, and
streams to breed. Eggs are laid singly or in
clusters attached to plants.
• OCCURRENCE N.E. US and Canada. In
forest, meadows, and sagebrush (*Artemisia*).
• REPRODUCTION Lays eggs in water
in spring.
• REMARK The Californian subspecies
Ambystoma macrodactylum croceum is endangered.

yellow, tan, or
green dorsal
stripe

small white
spots on
sides

N. AMERICA

Length 4–6¾in (10–17cm)	Habit Mostly terrestrial	Activity ☾

Family AMBYSTOMATIDAE	Species *Ambystoma maculatum*	Status Locally common

SPOTTED SALAMANDER

This small-limbed animal lives below
ground by day, emerging on wet
nights to feed and, in early spring, to
migrate to its ephemeral breeding
ponds. Females lay eggs attached to
twigs. The larvae metamorphose rapidly,
within two to four months.
• OCCURRENCE E. North
America. In forest.
• REPRODUCTION Lays eggs in
water in spring.
• REMARK Individuals always
return to the same pond to breed.

N. AMERICA

stout body
with yellow or
orange spots

skin secretes
toxins when
animal attacked

Length 6–10in (15–25cm)	Habit Mostly terrestrial	Activity ☾

Family AMBYSTOMATIDAE	Species *Ambystoma tigrinum*	Status Locally common

TIGER SALAMANDER

This variable salamander is usually black
or brown, with lighter markings. It lives
mainly underground, emerging to breed in
still water. Males transfer sperm in a
spermatophore, and eggs are laid in clumps
on weeds and twigs. Larvae may
remain in water over winter.
• OCCURRENCE North America.
In desert, grassland, forest, open
woodland, fields, and meadows.
• REPRODUCTION Lays eggs in water in spring.
• SIMILAR SPECIES Californian Tiger
Salamander (*Ambystoma californiense*).

large head with
rounded snout and
small eyes

N. AMERICA

irregular yellow or
white markings

black or brown
background color

Length 7–10in (18–25cm)	Habit Mostly terrestrial	Activity ☾

Family AMBYSTOMATIDAE	Species *Ambystoma mexicanum*	Status Endangered

AXOLOTL

The Axolotl provides the classic example of an amphibian that reaches sexual maturity while still in the larval state. In the wild, individuals do not metamorphose into a terrestrial form but, in captivity, they are sometimes induced to do so. Naturally dark gray or black in color, captive-bred variants include animals that are albino or yellow, or white with large blotches of gray or black. Males transfer sperm in a spermatophore. Eggs are laid on the bottom of the lake.
• OCCURRENCE Lake Xochimilco, Mexico.
• REPRODUCTION Lays eggs in water in autumn and spring.
• REMARK Once eaten as a delicacy in Mexico City, the Axolotl is now a protected species.

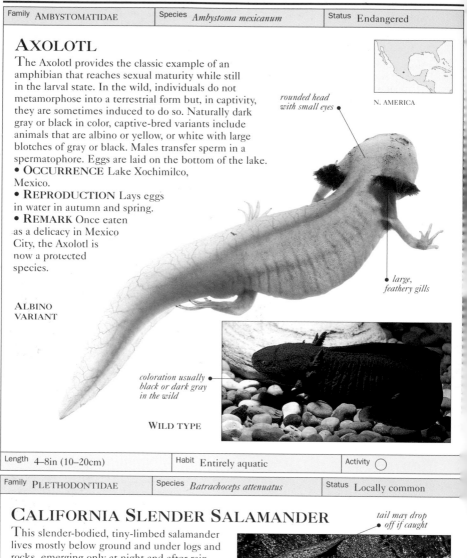

rounded head with small eyes

N. AMERICA

large, feathery gills

ALBINO VARIANT

coloration usually black or dark gray in the wild

WILD TYPE

Length 4–8in (10–20cm)	Habit Entirely aquatic	Activity ◯

Family PLETHODONTIDAE	Species *Batrachoceps attenuatus*	Status Locally common

CALIFORNIA SLENDER SALAMANDER

tail may drop off if caught

This slender-bodied, tiny-limbed salamander lives mostly below ground and under logs and rocks, emerging only at night and after rain. Several females may lay their eggs in the same cavity. The eggs hatch directly into small adults, without an aquatic larval stage.
• OCCURRENCE California and Oregon, US. In grassland, chaparral, pine forest, and woodland.
• REPRODUCTION Lays eggs underground in autumn.

N. AMERICA

Length 3–5½in (7.5–14cm)	Habit Entirely terrestrial	Activity ☾

Family PLETHODONTIDAE	Species *Desmognathus ochrophaeus*	Status Common

MOUNTAIN DUSKY SALAMANDER

The Mountain Dusky Salamander is very abundant in some
localities, but is rarely seen. It has highly variable coloration and
patterning. Most individuals are dark gray, with a stripe or row of
large patches down the back, which may be yellow, orange, olive-
green, gray, tan, brown, or reddish brown. The sides are generally
pale gray or ocher. Adults live mostly underground, emerging only at
night, and the larvae live in streams. Breeding males have two small
teeth, with which they abrade the skin of
females, and a gland under the chin that
produces an aphrodisiac secretion, which
they rub into the
skin. Mating occurs
on land, then the
eggs are deposited
underground, in clusters,
attached to rocks or logs.
Individuals may breed more
than once in a season.
• OCCURRENCE
E. US. In forest.
• REPRODUCTION
Lays eggs underground from
spring to autumn.

N. AMERICA

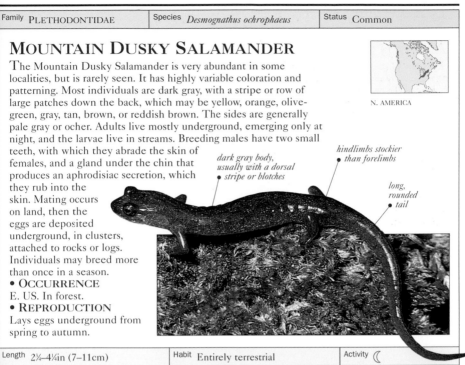

dark gray body,
usually with a dorsal
• stripe or blotches

hindlimbs stockier
• than forelimbs

long,
rounded
• tail

Length 2¾–4¼in (7–11cm)	Habit Entirely terrestrial	Activity ☾

Family PLETHODONTIDAE	Species *Plethodon cinereus*	Status Locally common

RED-BACKED SALAMANDER

This slender salamander has a narrow body, short,
slender limbs, and a round tail forming half of its total
body length. The common name derives from the broad
red, black-edged stripe that runs along the length of its
body and much of its tail. In many
individuals, however, the stripe may
be orange, yellow, or gray. An
inhabitant of leaf-litter, the Red-
backed Salamander eats ants and
termites. Males leave droppings
around their territories, and females
examine these intently, usually mating
with those males that have eaten a lot
of termites. During courtship, the
male scrapes the female's skin with
two protruding teeth. Females lay only
6 to 13 large eggs, attached to the roof
of an underground chamber.
• OCCURRENCE E. and C. US
and S.E. Canada. In forest.
• REPRODUCTION Lays eggs
underground from autumn to spring.

broad red, orange,
yellow, or gray
stripe on back •

N. AMERICA

Length 2¾–4¾in (7–12cm)	Habit Entirely terrestrial	Activity ☾

| Family PLETHODONTIDAE | Species *Plethodon jordani* | Status Locally common |

JORDAN'S SALAMANDER

This is a relatively large salamander, with a long, slender, gray to black body and a long, narrow head with very prominent eyes. Some populations are uniform in color, while others have bright red cheeks or legs. When attacked, Jordan's Salamander produces a distasteful slimy secretion from its tail. The tail itself may become detached to distract the predator while the salamander escapes. This species hides under logs by day and is active only at night, especially after rain. During courtship, the male uses large glands under its chin to tap the female's snout. Males breed every year, whereas females breed in alternate years.
• **OCCURRENCE**
S. Appalachian mountains, E. US. In montane forest.
• **REPRODUCTION** Lays eggs in summer and autumn.

N. AMERICA

tail round in cross section •   *16 costal grooves* •   *red marking on cheeks* •

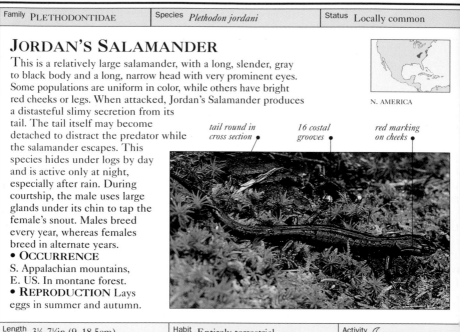

| Length 3½–7¼in (9–18.5cm) | Habit Entirely terrestrial | Activity ☾ |

| Family PLETHODONTIDAE | Species *Pseudotriton ruber* | Status Locally common |

RED SALAMANDER

With its stout body and its short tail and legs, this species is less agile than other salamanders but nonetheless sometimes preys on them. Its head is relatively small with distinctive yellow eyes. Its bright red coloration, with irregular black spots, tends to get darker in older individuals. The coloration is believed to mimic that of the highly poisonous juvenile stage of the Red-spotted Newt (*Notophthalmus viridescens*). When attacked, the Red Salamander raises and waves its tail.
• **OCCURRENCE** E. US. Under logs and stones near springs and clear streams.
• **REPRODUCTION** Lays eggs in autumn on land or in water.
• **REMARK** This species may not lay its eggs until several months after mating.

N. AMERICA

costal grooves on body •   *short tail and legs* •

bright yellow iris •

| Length 4–6¾in (10–17cm) | Habit Mostly terrestrial | Activity ☾ |

CAECILIANS

F REQUENTLY mistaken for large earthworms, caecilians have long bodies, no limbs, and virtually no tail. Many have distinct grooves that form rings around the body. Some species have long, thin bodies, while others are shorter and stockier. Caecilians have pointed, heavily boned heads, which help them to burrow into the soil. Their primary sense is smell, and their eyes are very rudimentary.

There are five families of caecilians in the order Gymnophiona (also known as the Apoda), comprising approximately 165 species. Most caecilians are found in loose soil or deep leaf-litter in tropical forest, but some live in rivers and streams. All are carnivorous, feeding on a variety of prey including earthworms, termites, and other invertebrates. They are "sit and wait" predators rather than hunters, lunging at prey when it comes close and holding onto it with a double row of teeth in the upper jaw, and a single or double row in the lower jaw.

In all caecilian species, fertilization is internal, the male extruding part of his cloaca to insert sperm into the female's body. Some species lay eggs in water, which hatch into swimming, gilled larvae; others lay their eggs in soil, where they hatch into miniature adults. Several species retain the eggs in their body and give birth to live young.

Family ICHTHYOPHIDAE	Species *Ichthyophis glutinosus*	Status Locally common

CEYLON CAECILIAN

The numerous rings (approximately 400) around the dark brown, cylindrical body make the Ceylon Caecilian look like a very large earthworm. The underside is a paler brown, and a distinctive yellow stripe extends along each side from the head to the tail. The head is oval and relatively small. A small, retractable tentacle between the eye and the nostril picks up chemical cues in the environment, enhancing the animal's sense of smell. The eyes, which are covered by a layer of skin, are minute and barely visible. The tail is extremely short. The Ceylon Caecilian lives mostly below ground, emerging to the surface only very occasionally. It feeds mainly on earthworms and other invertebrates. The female lays up to 54 eggs in a burrow close to water and guards them until they hatch. The aquatic larvae immediately swim to a nearby pond or stream.
- OCCURRENCE Sri Lanka. In muddy soil and swamps.
- REPRODUCTION Lays eggs on land in the rainy season.

SRI LANKA

rings around body similar to those of earthworms

female coils body around eggs to protect them

brown coloration with blue sheen

Length 12–16in (30–40cm)	Habit Entirely terrestrial	Activity ○

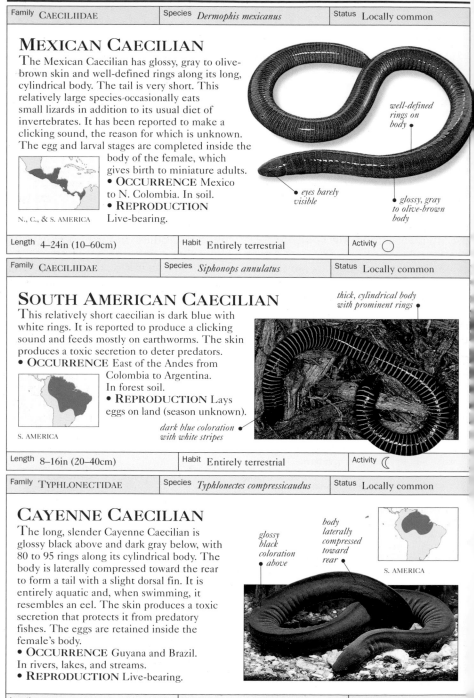

| Family CAECILIIDAE | Species *Dermophis mexicanus* | Status Locally common |

MEXICAN CAECILIAN

The Mexican Caecilian has glossy, gray to olive-brown skin and well-defined rings along its long, cylindrical body. The tail is very short. This relatively large species occasionally eats small lizards in addition to its usual diet of invertebrates. It has been reported to make a clicking sound, the reason for which is unknown. The egg and larval stages are completed inside the body of the female, which gives birth to miniature adults.

• OCCURRENCE Mexico to N. Colombia. In soil.

• REPRODUCTION Live-bearing.

N., C., & S. AMERICA

well-defined rings on body

eyes barely visible

glossy, gray to olive-brown body

| Length 4–24in (10–60cm) | Habit Entirely terrestrial | Activity ○ |

| Family CAECILIIDAE | Species *Siphonops annulatus* | Status Locally common |

SOUTH AMERICAN CAECILIAN

This relatively short caecilian is dark blue with white rings. It is reported to produce a clicking sound and feeds mostly on earthworms. The skin produces a toxic secretion to deter predators.

• OCCURRENCE East of the Andes from Colombia to Argentina. In forest soil.

• REPRODUCTION Lays eggs on land (season unknown).

S. AMERICA

thick, cylindrical body with prominent rings

dark blue coloration with white stripes

| Length 8–16in (20–40cm) | Habit Entirely terrestrial | Activity ☾ |

| Family TYPHLONECTIDAE | Species *Typhlonectes compressicaudus* | Status Locally common |

CAYENNE CAECILIAN

The long, slender Cayenne Caecilian is glossy black above and dark gray below, with 80 to 95 rings along its cylindrical body. The body is laterally compressed toward the rear to form a tail with a slight dorsal fin. It is entirely aquatic and, when swimming, it resembles an eel. The skin produces a toxic secretion that protects it from predatory fishes. The eggs are retained inside the female's body.

• OCCURRENCE Guyana and Brazil. In rivers, lakes, and streams.

• REPRODUCTION Live-bearing.

glossy black coloration above

body laterally compressed toward rear

S. AMERICA

| Length 12–24in (30–60cm) | Habit Entirely aquatic | Activity ☾ |

FROGS AND TOADS

T HERE ARE more than 4,100 species of frogs and toads, making the order Anura much the largest group of amphibians. The majority live in the tropics, mostly in or close to freshwater. Frogs and toads are characterized by the absence of a tail in the adult. Most have hindlimbs that are much larger than the forelimbs, enabling them to jump, sometimes very long distances. Many species are beautifully colored. This coloration may serve either as camouflage or as a warning to potential predators that their skin produces toxic secretions. Not all of the attractively colored species are poisonous, but certain species produce some of the most deadly poisons in nature. There is much diversity among frogs and toads. In terms of movement alone, there are species that (in addition to

jumping and crawling) use their legs to swim, burrow into the soil, climb trees, and glide through the air. The primary senses of frogs and toads are vision (for which they have very large eyes) and hearing. Many frogs and toads use loud calls to communicate with one another, especially during breeding. In the mating season, species may congregate in large numbers in or around freshwater. Frogs and toads typically lay their eggs in water. The eggs hatch into larvae (known as "tadpoles"), which have spherical bodies and are herbivorous. Adult frogs and toads, however, are carnivorous, feeding mostly on insects. They are generally active only at night. The term "toad" strictly refers to the approximately 250 species in the genus *Bufo*, but it is widely used for any slow-moving anuran with rough, warty skin.

Family ASCAPHIDAE	Species *Ascaphus truei*	Status Locally common

TAILED FROG

A unique tail-like appendage gives this species its name. Present only in males, it is not actually a tail but is an extension of the cloaca. The body of the Tailed Frog is slightly flattened, and the rough skin is olive-green, brown, gray, or reddish brown. There is a dark stripe through the eye and usually a yellow or pale green triangular patch on the head. The male develops dark, rough pads on the forearms and chest in the breeding season. Fertilization is internal, the male inserting sperm into the female using his tail-like cloaca. The female lays eggs in strings under rocks in fast-moving streams. The tadpoles, which have large, suckerlike mouths that enable them to attach to rocks in fast-flowing water, take two years to complete their development.
• OCCURRENCE N.W. US. In humid forest. Also in grassland and scrub, to an altitude of 6,500ft (2,000m).
• REPRODUCTION Lays eggs in water in summer.

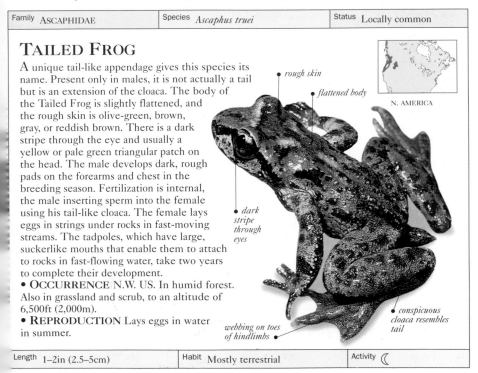

rough skin

flattened body

N. AMERICA

dark stripe through eyes

webbing on toes of hindlimbs

conspicuous cloaca resembles tail

Length 1–2in (2.5–5cm)	Habit Mostly terrestrial	Activity ☾

Family DISCOGLOSSIDAE	Species *Alytes muletensis*	Status Endangered

MAJORCAN MIDWIFE TOAD

Smaller than its mainland relatives, this tiny toad is able
to live in very narrow and deep crevices. It is usually
yellow to brown, with distinctive dark mottling. Both
males and females call to locate each other. Females
produce several small clutches of eggs in a year. During
mating, the female passes a batch of eggs to the male,
which carries them wrapped around the hindlegs.
When the eggs are ready to hatch, they
are deposited in a pool. The tadpoles
grow very large, and little growth
occurs after metamorphosis into
the adult form.
• OCCURRENCE Majorca,
Spain. In high-altitude ravines.
• REPRODUCTION Male
releases eggs into water from
spring to autumn.
• REMARK One of the world's
rarest frogs, it has been the subject of
a successful conservation program, in
which captive-bred animals are released
into new localities on Majorca.

dark, blotchy patterning

MAJORCA

vertical pupils

dry, warty skin

Length 1¼–1¾in (3–4.5cm)	Habit Mostly terrestrial	Activity ☾

Family DISCOGLOSSIDAE	Species *Alytes obstetricans*	Status Locally common

MIDWIFE TOAD

A small, plump species, the Midwife Toad has powerful forelimbs
adapted for digging. It may be pale green, gray, or brown, often
with darker markings. The name derives from the fact that the
male cares for the eggs, carrying them in strings
wrapped around the hindlegs. Males call to
females from a crevice or burrow,
producing a distinctive high-
pitched "poo...poo" sound.
The eggs are transferred from
female to male during mating.
The male carries them until
they are ready to hatch and then
releases them into shallow water.
• OCCURRENCE W. Europe.
In woodland, gardens, drystone
walls, quarries, sand dunes, and
rock slides.
• REPRODUCTION Male
releases eggs into water in
spring and summer.
• SIMILAR SPECIES
Spanish Midwife Toad (*Alytes
cisternasii*).

prominent eyes with vertical pupils

EUROPE

strings of pale eggs

Length 1¼–2in (3–5cm)	Habit Entirely terrestrial	Activity ☾

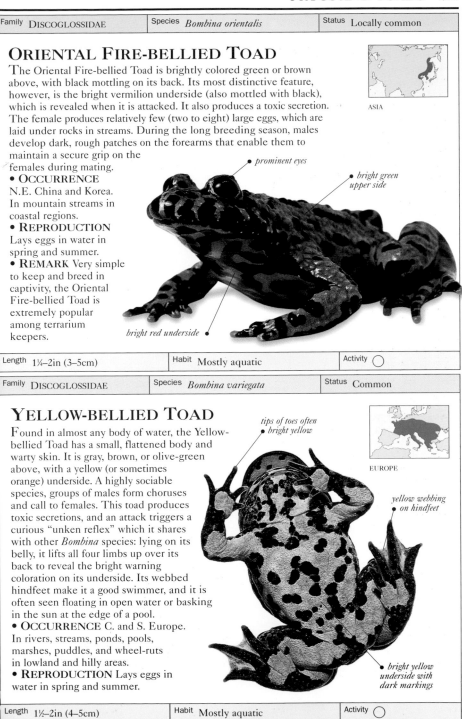

| Family DISCOGLOSSIDAE | Species *Bombina orientalis* | Status Locally common |

ORIENTAL FIRE-BELLIED TOAD

The Oriental Fire-bellied Toad is brightly colored green or brown above, with black mottling on its back. Its most distinctive feature, however, is the bright vermilion underside (also mottled with black), which is revealed when it is attacked. It also produces a toxic secretion. The female produces relatively few (two to eight) large eggs, which are laid under rocks in streams. During the long breeding season, males develop dark, rough patches on the forearms that enable them to maintain a secure grip on the females during mating.

ASIA

• OCCURRENCE
N.E. China and Korea.
In mountain streams in coastal regions.

• REPRODUCTION
Lays eggs in water in spring and summer.

• REMARK Very simple to keep and breed in captivity, the Oriental Fire-bellied Toad is extremely popular among terrarium keepers.

prominent eyes

bright green upper side

bright red underside

| Length 1¼–2in (3–5cm) | Habit Mostly aquatic | Activity ◯ |

| Family DISCOGLOSSIDAE | Species *Bombina variegata* | Status Common |

YELLOW-BELLIED TOAD

Found in almost any body of water, the Yellow-bellied Toad has a small, flattened body and warty skin. It is gray, brown, or olive-green above, with a yellow (or sometimes orange) underside. A highly sociable species, groups of males form choruses and call to females. This toad produces toxic secretions, and an attack triggers a curious "unken reflex" which it shares with other *Bombina* species: lying on its belly, it lifts all four limbs up over its back to reveal the bright warning coloration on its underside. Its webbed hindfeet make it a good swimmer, and it is often seen floating in open water or basking in the sun at the edge of a pool.

tips of toes often bright yellow

EUROPE

yellow webbing on hindfeet

• OCCURRENCE C. and S. Europe.
In rivers, streams, ponds, pools, marshes, puddles, and wheel-ruts in lowland and hilly areas.

• REPRODUCTION Lays eggs in water in spring and summer.

bright yellow underside with dark markings

| Length 1½–2in (4–5cm) | Habit Mostly aquatic | Activity ◯ |

Family PIPIDAE	Species *Xenopus laevis*	Status Common

AFRICAN CLAWED TOAD

Also known as the Platanna, this species is highly
adapted for aquatic life. It has a flattened, streamlined
body and strong, muscular hindlimbs with long,
webbed toes that make it a powerful swimmer.
There are characteristic white stitchlike markings
running along each side of the body.
The forelimbs are small, with three
clawed toes, which are used to
shovel food into the mouth
of this voracious feeder.
The small eyes point
upward, enabling it to
see predators such as herons.
• OCCURRENCE Angola,
S.E. Africa. In ponds and lakes.
• REPRODUCTION Lays eggs in
water in the rainy season.
• REMARK The white "stitch" marks,
which run along either side of the body,
contain special sense organs that detect
vibrations in the water, enabling the
African Clawed Toad to locate predators
and food in murky water.

*distinctive
clawed toes*

AFRICA

*white "stitch"
marks along sides*

*color changes
from gray to
black to match
background*

*very
muscular
hindlegs*

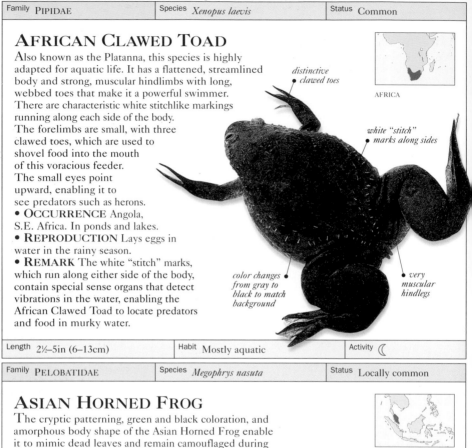

Length 2½–5in (6–13cm)	Habit Mostly aquatic	Activity ☾

Family PELOBATIDAE	Species *Megophrys nasuta*	Status Locally common

ASIAN HORNED FROG

The cryptic patterning, green and black coloration, and
amorphous body shape of the Asian Horned Frog enable
it to mimic dead leaves and remain camouflaged during
the day. Its name is derived from the conspicuous,
hornlike projections on the eyelids. The head is large,
with a prominent snout, and there is a bony shield
embedded in the skin on its back.
The Asian Horned Frog is a "sit
and wait" predator that feeds on
smaller frogs and invertebrates.
The tadpoles, which hang
vertically in the water to feed,
have large, umbrella-shaped
mouths that act as a funnel to
suck in tiny organisms.
• OCCURRENCE S.E. Asia.
In tropical forest.
• REPRODUCTION Lays eggs
in water in the rainy season.

*hornlike
projections
on eyelids*

ASIA

*green background color
with black markings*

pointed snout

Length 2¾–5½in (7–14cm)	Habit Mostly terrestrial	Activity ☾

Family PELOBATIDAE	Species *Pelobates fuscus*	Status Locally common

COMMON SPADEFOOT TOAD

A pale, horny lump on the hindfeet of the Common Spadefoot Toad enables it to burrow backward into the soil (hence its name). Other features of this species include a plump body, relatively smooth skin, and a distinctive lump on top of its head. Coloration and patterning are highly variable, ranging from creamy white to gray or brown. This toad is most active in wet weather and often gives off an odor resembling garlic. When attacked, it squeals, inflates its body, and raises itself on all fours. When breeding, the male calls to the female from below water.
• **OCCURRENCE** Europe and E. Asia. In sand dunes, heathland, and cultivated areas.
• **REPRODUCTION** Lays eggs in water in spring.

EUROPE, ASIA

large eyes with vertical pupils

characteristic lump on top of head

plump, smooth-skinned body

Length 1½–3¼in (4–8cm)	Habit Mostly terrestrial	Activity ☾

Family PELOBATIDAE	Species *Scaphiopus couchii*	Status Locally common

COUCH'S SPADEFOOT

This toad's name is derived from the spadelike black ridge on its hindfeet, which it uses to scrape away the soil as it digs into the ground. It has a plump body, which is covered in small, pale tubercles. Coloration is green, yellow-green, or brown, with black, brown, or dark green markings, and a uniformly off-white underside. This species spends most of its life in a cocoon underground, having burrowed into soft soil. It breeds in ephemeral pools in semiarid habitats. The eggs hatch extremely quickly, about three or four days after they are laid, and the larvae grow rapidly so that they become adults before the temporary pools dry up.
• **OCCURRENCE** S. US and Mexico. In grassy plains, bush desert, and thorn forest.
• **REPRODUCTION** Lays eggs in water in summer.

N. AMERICA

vertical pupils

smooth white underside

plump body

Length 2¼–3½in (5.5–9cm)	Habit Mostly terrestrial	Activity ☾

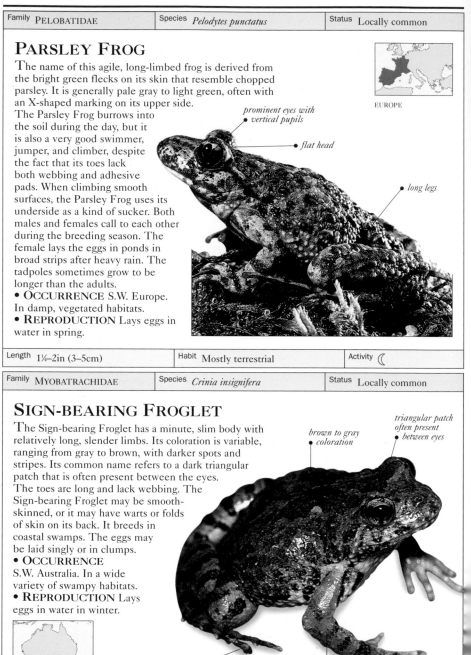

Family PELOBATIDAE	Species *Pelodytes punctatus*	Status Locally common

PARSLEY FROG

The name of this agile, long-limbed frog is derived from the bright green flecks on its skin that resemble chopped parsley. It is generally pale gray to light green, often with an X-shaped marking on its upper side. The Parsley Frog burrows into the soil during the day, but it is also a very good swimmer, jumper, and climber, despite the fact that its toes lack both webbing and adhesive pads. When climbing smooth surfaces, the Parsley Frog uses its underside as a kind of sucker. Both males and females call to each other during the breeding season. The female lays the eggs in ponds in broad strips after heavy rain. The tadpoles sometimes grow to be longer than the adults.
• OCCURRENCE S.W. Europe. In damp, vegetated habitats.
• REPRODUCTION Lays eggs in water in spring.

EUROPE

prominent eyes with vertical pupils

flat head

long legs

Length 1¼–2in (3–5cm)	Habit Mostly terrestrial	Activity ☾

Family MYOBATRACHIDAE	Species *Crinia insignifera*	Status Locally common

SIGN-BEARING FROGLET

The Sign-bearing Froglet has a minute, slim body with relatively long, slender limbs. Its coloration is variable, ranging from gray to brown, with darker spots and stripes. Its common name refers to a dark triangular patch that is often present between the eyes. The toes are long and lack webbing. The Sign-bearing Froglet may be smooth-skinned, or it may have warts or folds of skin on its back. It breeds in coastal swamps. The eggs may be laid singly or in clumps.
• OCCURRENCE S.W. Australia. In a wide variety of swampy habitats.
• REPRODUCTION Lays eggs in water in winter.

triangular patch often present between eyes

brown to gray coloration

long, unwebbed toes

long, slender limbs

AUSTRALIA

Length ⅗–1¼in (1.5–3cm)	Habit Mostly terrestrial	Activity ☾

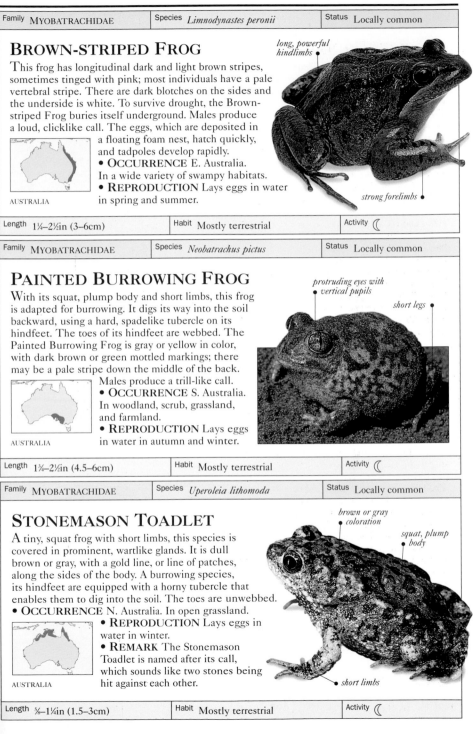

| Family MYOBATRACHIDAE | Species *Limnodynastes peronii* | Status Locally common |

BROWN-STRIPED FROG

long, powerful hindlimbs •

This frog has longitudinal dark and light brown stripes, sometimes tinged with pink; most individuals have a pale vertebral stripe. There are dark blotches on the sides and the underside is white. To survive drought, the Brown-striped Frog buries itself underground. Males produce a loud, clicklike call. The eggs, which are deposited in a floating foam nest, hatch quickly, and tadpoles develop rapidly.
• OCCURRENCE E. Australia. In a wide variety of swampy habitats.
• REPRODUCTION Lays eggs in water in spring and summer.

AUSTRALIA

strong forelimbs •

| Length 1¼–2⅓in (3–6cm) | Habit Mostly terrestrial | Activity ☾ |

| Family MYOBATRACHIDAE | Species *Neobatrachus pictus* | Status Locally common |

PAINTED BURROWING FROG

protruding eyes with • vertical pupils

short legs •

With its squat, plump body and short limbs, this frog is adapted for burrowing. It digs its way into the soil backward, using a hard, spadelike tubercle on its hindfeet. The toes of its hindfeet are webbed. The Painted Burrowing Frog is gray or yellow in color, with dark brown or green mottled markings; there may be a pale stripe down the middle of the back. Males produce a trill-like call.
• OCCURRENCE S. Australia. In woodland, scrub, grassland, and farmland.
• REPRODUCTION Lays eggs in water in autumn and winter.

AUSTRALIA

| Length 1¾–2½in (4.5–6cm) | Habit Mostly terrestrial | Activity ☾ |

| Family MYOBATRACHIDAE | Species *Uperoleia lithomoda* | Status Locally common |

STONEMASON TOADLET

brown or gray • coloration

squat, plump • body

A tiny, squat frog with short limbs, this species is covered in prominent, wartlike glands. It is dull brown or gray, with a gold line, or line of patches, along the sides of the body. A burrowing species, its hindfeet are equipped with a horny tubercle that enables them to dig into the soil. The toes are unwebbed.
• OCCURRENCE N. Australia. In open grassland.
• REPRODUCTION Lays eggs in water in winter.
• REMARK The Stonemason Toadlet is named after its call, which sounds like two stones being hit against each other.

AUSTRALIA

short limbs •

| Length ⅝–1¼in (1.5–3cm) | Habit Mostly terrestrial | Activity ☾ |

Family SOOGLOSSIDAE	Species *Sooglossus gardineri*	Status Endangered

SEYCHELLES FROG

A very small terrestrial species, the Seychelles Frog varies in color from creamy white or yellowish green to brown. It has relatively big, protruding eyes with horizontal pupils, and its toes lack adhesive disks or webbing. The large, yolky eggs do not hatch into tadpoles but into tiny froglets that have only rudimentary eyes. The male sits in the egg mass and the froglets crawl onto his back, where they become glued on by mucus. They remain attached to the male until they have used up their yolk and their legs are fully developed.
• OCCURRENCE Seychelles, Indian Ocean. In woodland and forest.
• REPRODUCTION Lays eggs on land in the rainy season.
• SIMILAR SPECIES Seychelles Frog (*Sooglossus seychellensis*).
• REMARK Populations have declined owing to habitat destruction.

protruding eyes with horizontal pupils

tiny brown, creamy white, or yellowish green body

SEYCHELLES

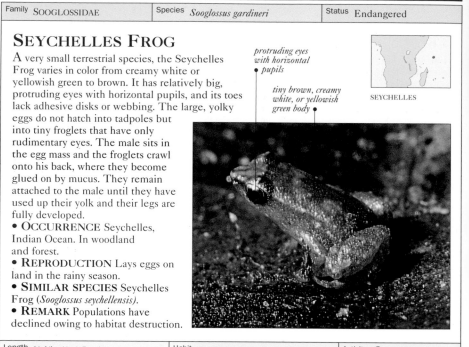

Length ⅜–⅝in (1–1.5cm)	Habit Entirely terrestrial	Activity ☾

Family HELEOPHRYNIDAE	Species *Heleophryne purcelli*	Status Locally common

CAPE GHOST FROG

An inhabitant of fast-flowing streams, the Cape Ghost Frog is perfectly adapted for aquatic life. Long, powerful hindlimbs with webbed toes make it a good swimmer; a flattened body enables it to hide by squeezing between boulders; and flattened tips to its toes give it a secure grip on slippery surfaces. Its smooth skin is yellow, brown, or green, mottled with dark red or brown. In the breeding season, the male develops numerous tiny spines all over its body, which enable it to grip its mate. Males call to females, and mating is preceded by a unique form of behavior in which partners rub each other with their forelimbs. Tadpoles have suckerlike mouths to attach themselves to rocks.
• OCCURRENCE S. and W. Cape, S. Africa. In fast-flowing streams running through boulder-strewn gorges.
• REPRODUCTION Lays eggs in or just out of water (season unknown).

AFRICA

flattened body

large, prominent eyes

webbing on toes of hindlimbs only

Length 1¼–2½in (3–6cm)	Habit Mostly aquatic	Activity ☾

Family LEPTODACTYLIDAE	Species *Physalaemus pustulosus*	Status Common

TÚNGARA FROG

This small, toadlike frog is dark brown with warty skin. It is rarely seen outside the breeding season. Following the first rains of the year, male Túngara Frogs appear in any pool of water, from large ponds to wheel-ruts, from where they call to females. The call is very loud, as the male repeatedly inflates its huge vocal sacs. The call is variable, consisting of a basic "whine," which is followed by one or several "chucks." However, the call may also attract the attention of predatory bats that swoop over Túngara Frog choruses, eating frogs whole. During mating, the female produces a secretion that the male whips into a floating foam nest with its hindlimbs. After heavy rain, the eggs are laid in the nest. The eggs hatch quickly and tadpole development is very rapid.
• **OCCURRENCE** Central America. In a wide variety of habitats, from scrub to forest; also found in gardens and other urban habitats.
• **REPRODUCTION** Lays eggs in water in the rainy season.

C. AMERICA

body floating at surface (photographed from above) •

CALLING TO FEMALES

• *inflated vocal sacs*

protruding eyes with horizontal pupils •

MALE

dark brown body with paler mottling •

rough, warty skin •

• *dark brown coloration provides camouflage in mud puddles*

• *eggs laid in frothy, floating foam nest*

PAIR SPAWNING IN A FOAM NEST

Length 1¼–1½in (3–4cm)	Habit Mostly terrestrial	Activity ☾

Family LEPTODACTYLIDAE	Species *Ceratophrys cornuta*	Status Locally common

AMAZONIAN HORNED FROG

The massive, plump body of the Amazonian Horned Frog is as wide as it is long. The head and mouth are also huge. Coloration of this species is red or brown, with a dark brown pattern of spots, stripes, and blotches. Incapable of rapid movement, this frog hides among the leaf-litter until its prey comes along. Its huge mouth enables it to catch animals nearly as large as itself. Its "horns" are actually projections of the eyelids and enhance its camouflage among leaves. Males produce loud mating calls that resemble the bellowing of cattle.
• OCCURRENCE N.E. Brazil, Guyana, and W. Ecuador. In tropical forest.
• REPRODUCTION Lays eggs in water in the rainy season.

S. AMERICA

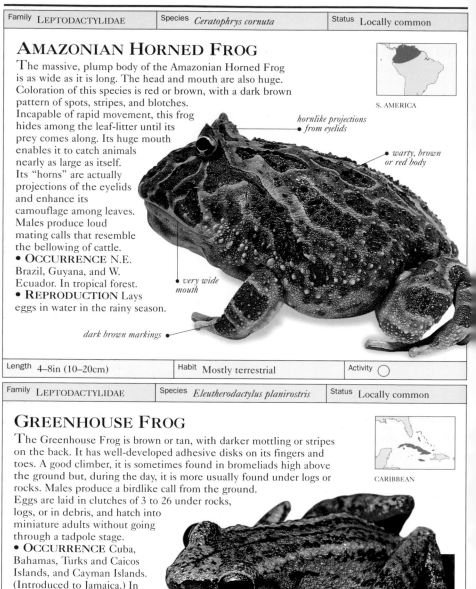

hornlike projections from eyelids

warty, brown or red body

very wide mouth

dark brown markings

Length 4–8in (10–20cm)	Habit Mostly terrestrial	Activity ○

Family LEPTODACTYLIDAE	Species *Eleutherodactylus planirostris*	Status Locally common

GREENHOUSE FROG

The Greenhouse Frog is brown or tan, with darker mottling or stripes on the back. It has well-developed adhesive disks on its fingers and toes. A good climber, it is sometimes found in bromeliads high above the ground but, during the day, it is more usually found under logs or rocks. Males produce a birdlike call from the ground. Eggs are laid in clutches of 3 to 26 under rocks, logs, or in debris, and hatch into miniature adults without going through a tadpole stage.
• OCCURRENCE Cuba, Bahamas, Turks and Caicos Islands, and Cayman Islands. (Introduced to Jamaica.) In wooded habitats and gardens.
• REPRODUCTION Lays eggs on land in summer.

CARIBBEAN

large pupils

adhesive disks on fingers and toes

Length 1–1½in (2.5–4cm)	Habit Entirely terrestrial	Activity ☽

Family LEPTODACTYLIDAE	Species *Leptodactylus pentadactylus*	Status Locally common

SOUTH AMERICAN BULLFROG

This bullfrog is yellow or pale brown, with red, dark brown, and black markings. Large and powerfully built, it can be highly aggressive. Males defend territories at the edges of ponds and, when fighting with rivals, use a sharp, black spur on their thumbs as a weapon. Mating occurs in cavities next to the edges of flooded pools after heavy rain. Large numbers of eggs are deposited in a foam nest, which the male whips up with his hindlegs. The muscular hindlegs are eaten by humans.
• OCCURRENCE Central and South America. In forest in and around swamps, pools, lakes, and streams.
• REPRODUCTION Lays eggs in water in the rainy season.
• REMARK When caught, this frog emits a loud scream that often causes its captor to release it in surprise.

C. & S. AMERICA

muscular • forearms

prominent • eardrum

pale brown or • yellow background color

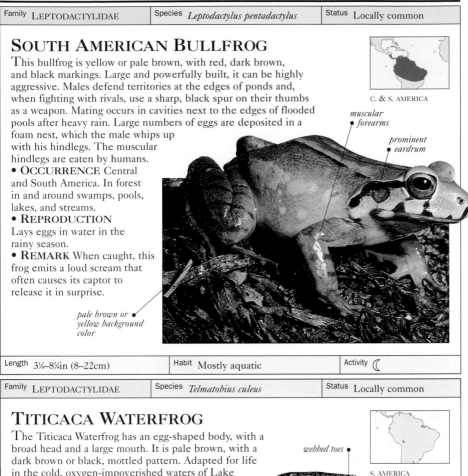

Length 3¼–8¾in (8–22cm)	Habit Mostly aquatic	Activity ☾

Family LEPTODACTYLIDAE	Species *Telmatobius culeus*	Status Locally common

TITICACA WATERFROG

The Titicaca Waterfrog has an egg-shaped body, with a broad head and a large mouth. It is pale brown, with a dark brown or black, mottled pattern. Adapted for life in the cold, oxygen-impoverished waters of Lake Titicaca in the high Andes, the Titicaca Waterfrog has very small lungs and relies primarily on oxygen taken in through the skin. Extensive folds in the skin increase the animal's surface area. This frog further enhances oxygen uptake by gently swaying from side to side in the water. It has fully webbed hindfeet, which enable it to swim strongly in the mud in search of prey. Little is known about the breeding habits of this frog. The male has a weak call, and clasps the female around her waist.
• OCCURRENCE Lake Titicaca, South America.
• REPRODUCTION Lays eggs in water in summer.

webbed toes •

S. AMERICA

pale brown with darker • mottling

small eyes

Length 3¼–4¾in (8–12cm)	Habit Entirely aquatic	Activity ○

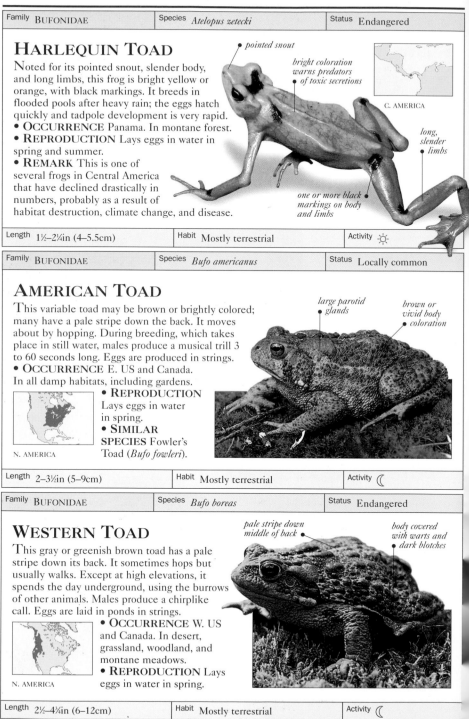

Family BUFONIDAE	Species *Atelopus zetecki*	Status Endangered

HARLEQUIN TOAD

pointed snout

bright coloration warns predators of toxic secretions

C. AMERICA

Noted for its pointed snout, slender body, and long limbs, this frog is bright yellow or orange, with black markings. It breeds in flooded pools after heavy rain; the eggs hatch quickly and tadpole development is very rapid.
• OCCURRENCE Panama. In montane forest.
• REPRODUCTION Lays eggs in water in spring and summer.
• REMARK This is one of several frogs in Central America that have declined drastically in numbers, probably as a result of habitat destruction, climate change, and disease.

long, slender limbs

one or more black markings on body and limbs

Length 1½–2¼in (4–5.5cm)	Habit Mostly terrestrial	Activity ☼

Family BUFONIDAE	Species *Bufo americanus*	Status Locally common

AMERICAN TOAD

large parotid glands

brown or vivid body coloration

This variable toad may be brown or brightly colored; many have a pale stripe down the back. It moves about by hopping. During breeding, which takes place in still water, males produce a musical trill 3 to 60 seconds long. Eggs are produced in strings.
• OCCURRENCE E. US and Canada. In all damp habitats, including gardens.
• REPRODUCTION Lays eggs in water in spring.
• SIMILAR SPECIES Fowler's Toad (*Bufo fowleri*).

N. AMERICA

Length 2–3½in (5–9cm)	Habit Mostly terrestrial	Activity ☾

Family BUFONIDAE	Species *Bufo boreas*	Status Endangered

WESTERN TOAD

pale stripe down middle of back

body covered with warts and dark blotches

This gray or greenish brown toad has a pale stripe down its back. It sometimes hops but usually walks. Except at high elevations, it spends the day underground, using the burrows of other animals. Males produce a chirplike call. Eggs are laid in ponds in strings.
• OCCURRENCE W. US and Canada. In desert, grassland, woodland, and montane meadows.
• REPRODUCTION Lays eggs in water in spring.

N. AMERICA

Length 2½–4¾in (6–12cm)	Habit Mostly terrestrial	Activity ☾

Family BUFONIDAE	Species *Bufo bufo*	Status Common

EUROPEAN COMMON TOAD

The European Common Toad is a robust species and grows to a very large size in the southern parts of its range, where the warts on its skin become horny spines (a northern specimen is shown here). Males arrive at breeding ponds and lakes up to 20 days before females and outnumber them by about three to one. Females are substantially larger than males and start to breed one year later. Males have no vocal sac and only rarely produce a mating call. Eggs are laid in long strings of jelly wrapped around vegetation.

EUROPE, AFRICA, ASIA

large, half-moon-shaped parotid glands

green, brown, or gray warty skin

• OCCURRENCE Europe, N.W. Africa, and Asia. In woodland, gardens, and fields.
• REPRODUCTION Lays eggs in water in spring.
• REMARK This species is known as the "gardener's friend" because it eats slugs and snails.

male has thicker forearms than female

Length 3¼–8in (8–20cm)	Habit Mostly terrestrial	Activity ☾

Family BUFONIDAE	Species *Bufo calamita*	Status Locally common

NATTERJACK TOAD

With shorter legs than other toads, the Natterjack Toad moves in a scuttling motion, like a mouse. It is brown, gray, or green with darker markings, usually with a bright yellow stripe down its back. By day, it hides in holes made by other animals or in a burrow that it digs itself. Breeding males have large vocal sacs and repeatedly produce a loud call lasting one or two seconds. The breeding season is longer than that of most toads, and some individuals mate more than once a year. Breeding takes place in ponds and lakes, and eggs are laid in strings among weeds.

yellow stripe down middle of back

EUROPE

numerous small, flat warts on back

• OCCURRENCE W. and C. Europe and Russia. In various habitats, including sand dunes, heath, and mountains.
• REPRODUCTION Lays eggs in water in spring and summer.
• REMARK The Natterjack Toad is an endangered species in the UK.

short limbs enable Natterjack to run rather than hop

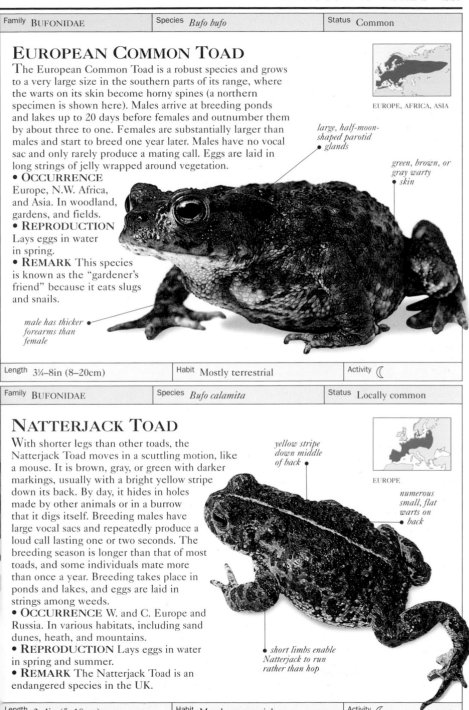

Length 2–4in (5–10cm)	Habit Mostly terrestrial	Activity ☾

Family BUFONIDAE	Species *Bufo marinus*	Status Locally common

MARINE TOAD

Also known as the Cane Toad, this formidable creature is the world's largest toad. It is extremely robust, with a massive head. The warty skin is brown or tan, with darker patches, and its underside is creamy white. The diet of this species includes other frogs and toads.

WORLDWIDE

• OCCURRENCE Central and South America. (Introduced to other parts of the world.) In most habitats, including towns.
• REPRODUCTION Lays eggs in water at any time of year.
• REMARK Since 1920, the Marine Toad has been introduced to many countries to control insect pests of sugarcane. In Australia, it has become a serious pest that has had a harmful effect on native frogs and toads.

parotid glands secrete toxin

tough, leathery, warty skin

brown or tan body

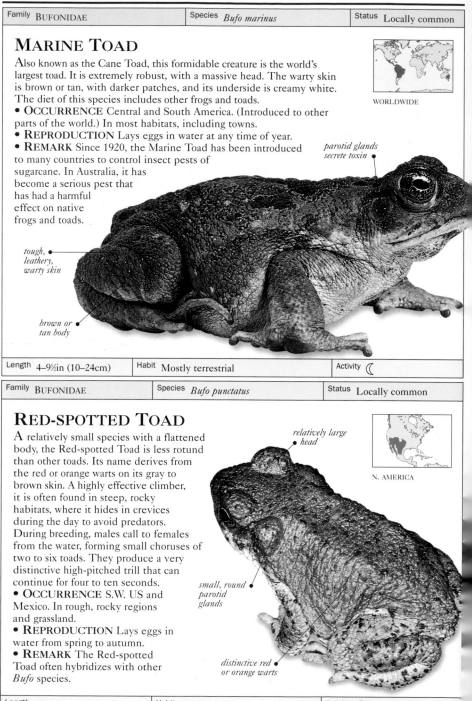

Length 4–9½in (10–24cm)	Habit Mostly terrestrial	Activity ☾

Family BUFONIDAE	Species *Bufo punctatus*	Status Locally common

RED-SPOTTED TOAD

A relatively small species with a flattened body, the Red-spotted Toad is less rotund than other toads. Its name derives from the red or orange warts on its gray to brown skin. A highly effective climber, it is often found in steep, rocky habitats, where it hides in crevices during the day to avoid predators. During breeding, males call to females from the water, forming small choruses of two to six toads. They produce a very distinctive high-pitched trill that can continue for four to ten seconds.

relatively large head

N. AMERICA

• OCCURRENCE S.W. US and Mexico. In rough, rocky regions and grassland.
• REPRODUCTION Lays eggs in water from spring to autumn.
• REMARK The Red-spotted Toad often hybridizes with other *Bufo* species.

small, round parotid glands

distinctive red or orange warts

Length 1¼–2¾in (3–7cm)	Habit Mostly terrestrial	Activity ☾

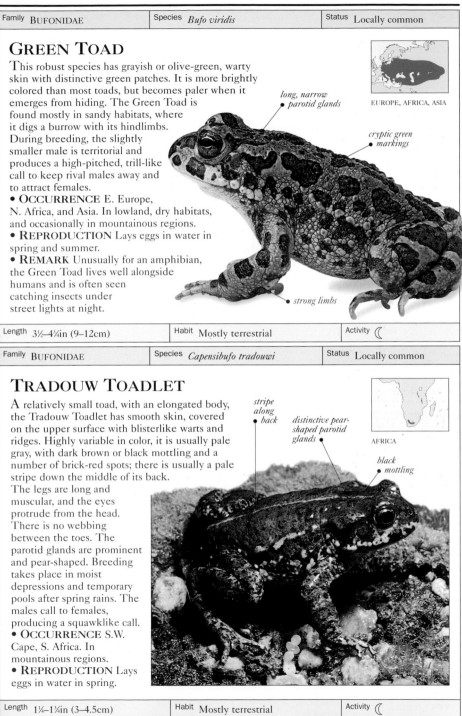

Family BUFONIDAE	Species *Bufo viridis*	Status Locally common

GREEN TOAD

This robust species has grayish or olive-green, warty skin with distinctive green patches. It is more brightly colored than most toads, but becomes paler when it emerges from hiding. The Green Toad is found mostly in sandy habitats, where it digs a burrow with its hindlimbs. During breeding, the slightly smaller male is territorial and produces a high-pitched, trill-like call to keep rival males away and to attract females.
• OCCURRENCE E. Europe, N. Africa, and Asia. In lowland, dry habitats, and occasionally in mountainous regions.
• REPRODUCTION Lays eggs in water in spring and summer.
• REMARK Unusually for an amphibian, the Green Toad lives well alongside humans and is often seen catching insects under street lights at night.

long, narrow parotid glands

EUROPE, AFRICA, ASIA

cryptic green markings

strong limbs

Length 3½–4¾in (9–12cm)	Habit Mostly terrestrial	Activity ☾

Family BUFONIDAE	Species *Capensibufo tradouwi*	Status Locally common

TRADOUW TOADLET

A relatively small toad, with an elongated body, the Tradouw Toadlet has smooth skin, covered on the upper surface with blisterlike warts and ridges. Highly variable in color, it is usually pale gray, with dark brown or black mottling and a number of brick-red spots; there is usually a pale stripe down the middle of its back. The legs are long and muscular, and the eyes protrude from the head. There is no webbing between the toes. The parotid glands are prominent and pear-shaped. Breeding takes place in moist depressions and temporary pools after spring rains. The males call to females, producing a squawklike call.
• OCCURRENCE S.W. Cape, S. Africa. In mountainous regions.
• REPRODUCTION Lays eggs in water in spring.

stripe along back

distinctive pear-shaped parotid glands

AFRICA

black mottling

Length 1¼–1¾in (3–4.5cm)	Habit Mostly terrestrial	Activity ☾

Family BUFONIDAE	Species *Pedostibes hosii*	Status Locally common

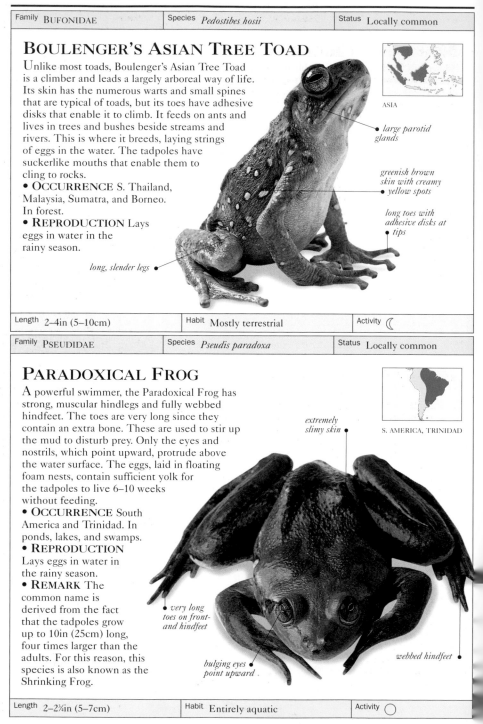

BOULENGER'S ASIAN TREE TOAD

Unlike most toads, Boulenger's Asian Tree Toad
is a climber and leads a largely arboreal way of life.
Its skin has the numerous warts and small spines
that are typical of toads, but its toes have adhesive
disks that enable it to climb. It feeds on ants and
lives in trees and bushes beside streams and
rivers. This is where it breeds, laying strings
of eggs in the water. The tadpoles have
suckerlike mouths that enable them to
cling to rocks.
• OCCURRENCE S. Thailand,
Malaysia, Sumatra, and Borneo.
In forest.
• REPRODUCTION Lays
eggs in water in the
rainy season.

ASIA

*large parotid
glands*

*greenish brown
skin with creamy
yellow spots*

*long toes with
adhesive disks at
tips*

long, slender legs

Length 2–4in (5–10cm)	Habit Mostly terrestrial	Activity ☾

Family PSEUDIDAE	Species *Pseudis paradoxa*	Status Locally common

PARADOXICAL FROG

A powerful swimmer, the Paradoxical Frog has
strong, muscular hindlegs and fully webbed
hindfeet. The toes are very long since they
contain an extra bone. These are used to stir up
the mud to disturb prey. Only the eyes and
nostrils, which point upward, protrude above
the water surface. The eggs, laid in floating
foam nests, contain sufficient yolk for
the tadpoles to live 6–10 weeks
without feeding.
• OCCURRENCE South
America and Trinidad. In
ponds, lakes, and swamps.
• REPRODUCTION
Lays eggs in water in
the rainy season.
• REMARK The
common name is
derived from the fact
that the tadpoles grow
up to 10in (25cm) long,
four times larger than the
adults. For this reason, this
species is also known as the
Shrinking Frog.

*extremely
slimy skin*

S. AMERICA, TRINIDAD

*very long
toes on front-
and hindfeet*

*bulging eyes
point upward*

webbed hindfeet

Length 2–2¾in (5–7cm)	Habit Entirely aquatic	Activity ○

Family HYLIDAE	Species *Acris crepitans*	Status Common

NORTHERN CRICKET FROG

This small frog has rough skin, a blunt snout, and relatively short legs, with webbing between the toes of the hindlimbs. Found in or around water, the Northern Cricket Frog does not climb, but it is able to hop large distances. It is often seen raising its body temperature by basking in the sun. In the breeding season, large numbers converge at ponds. The males call loudly, producing a series of metallic clicks reminiscent of the sound of crickets. In some areas, the tadpoles have black tips to their tails. These distract predatory dragonfly larvae, thus protecting more vulnerable parts of the body from attack.
• OCCURRENCE S.E. and E. US. In vegetation near water.
• REPRODUCTION Lays eggs in water in spring.
• SIMILAR SPECIES Southern Cricket Frog (*Acris gryllus*).

dark triangular marking between eyes *short legs* *rough skin*

N. AMERICA

Length ⅝–1½in (1.5–4cm)	Habit Mostly terrestrial	Activity ☾ ☼

Family HYLIDAE	Species *Agalychnis callidryas*	Status Locally common

RED-EYED TREEFROG

This bright green treefrog has yellow and blue stripes on its sides and blue inner thighs, but this distinctive coloring can be seen only when the frog moves. An excellent climber, it has very long legs and adhesive pads on its toes. Mating takes place in trees overhanging water, with many frogs gathering in the same tree. Males attract females by making a soft, clicking sound. The smaller male climbs onto the back of a female, and she then takes up water from the pond before climbing up into the tree. She lays a batch of eggs on foliage and then, still carrying the male, returns to the water before laying another batch. After about five days the eggs hatch into tadpoles, which drop into the water.
• OCCURRENCE Central America. In forest.
• REPRODUCTION Lays eggs on land in summer.

C. AMERICA

bright green coloring gives camouflage among foliage

large red eyes with vertical pupils

extremely long, delicate legs

well-developed toe pads

Length 1½–2¾in (4–7cm)	Habit Entirely terrestrial	Activity ☾

Family HYLIDAE	Species *Gastrotheca monticola*	Status Locally common

MOUNTAIN MARSUPIAL FROG

A compact, plump frog with a wide head and a rounded
snout, this upland species is usually brown with green
areas on its back, although some frogs are entirely
green. It has webbed toes on its hindlimbs, but not
on its forelimbs. Its common name is derived from
the enclosed brood pouch on the back of the
female. As the fertilized eggs are laid, the
male packs them into the pouch and this is
where they develop. They are eventually
released into pools of water as well-
grown tadpoles, the female helping
them to escape by opening the
pouch with her toes.
• OCCURRENCE
S. Ecuador and N. Peru.
In montane forest.
• REPRODUCTION
Tadpoles released from
brood pouch into water
in spring and summer.

*position of
brood pouch
on back of
female*

S. AMERICA

broad head

*large,
prominent
eyes*

Length 1½–2⅜in (4–6cm)	Habit Entirely terrestrial	Activity ☾

Family HYLIDAE	Species *Hyla arborea*	Status Locally common

EUROPEAN TREEFROG

An expert climber and jumper, the European Treefrog has slender
limbs and adhesive disks on its toes. It is typically bright green in
color, with a dark stripe running through the eyes and almost the
length of its body, but it may also be yellow or
brown. Individuals are able to change color
quite rapidly. In the breeding season,
males gather in trees and bushes beside
ponds, calling in loud choruses to attract
females. Mating pairs descend to the water
to lay their eggs.
• OCCURRENCE Most of Europe.
In well-vegetated habitats.
• REPRODUCTION Lays
eggs in water in spring
and summer.
• SIMILAR
SPECIES
Stripeless
Treefrog (*Hyla
meridionalis*).

EUROPE

*conspicuous dark
stripe along head
and body*

*adhesive disks
on toes*

Length 1¼–2in (3–5cm)	Habit Mostly terrestrial	Activity ☾

Family HYLIDAE	Species *Hyla cinerea*	Status Common

GREEN TREEFROG

Usually bright green, this treefrog changes color fairly rapidly, turning yellow when calling in the breeding season, and becoming gray when inactive in cold weather. It is an accomplished climber, with adhesive disks on its toes, and it is able to leap large distances. It often appears at night at windows, where it feeds on insects drawn to the light. Breeding takes place near water. Males call very loudly in choruses, although some, known as satellite males, stay silent and attempt to intercept females attracted to those who do call.
• OCCURRENCE S.E. US. In woods.
• REPRODUCTION Lays eggs in water in spring.
• REMARK It is colloquially known as the "rain frog" because it calls just before and during wet weather.

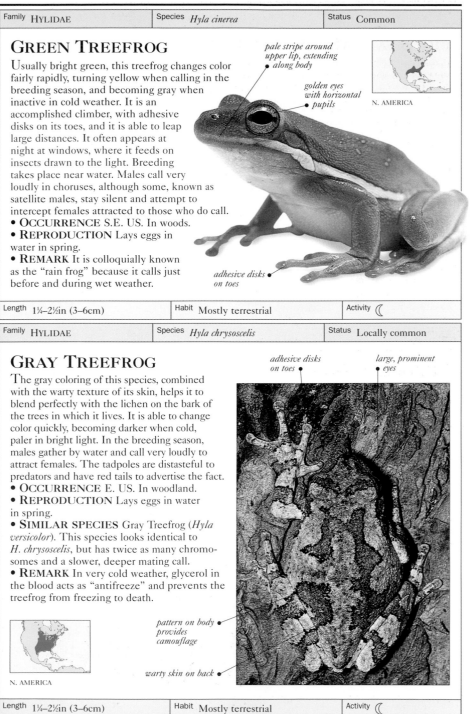

pale stripe around upper lip, extending along body

golden eyes with horizontal pupils

N. AMERICA

adhesive disks on toes

Length 1¼–2⅓in (3–6cm)	Habit Mostly terrestrial	Activity ☾

Family HYLIDAE	Species *Hyla chrysoscelis*	Status Locally common

GRAY TREEFROG

The gray coloring of this species, combined with the warty texture of its skin, helps it to blend perfectly with the lichen on the bark of the trees in which it lives. It is able to change color quickly, becoming darker when cold, paler in bright light. In the breeding season, males gather by water and call very loudly to attract females. The tadpoles are distasteful to predators and have red tails to advertise the fact.
• OCCURRENCE E. US. In woodland.
• REPRODUCTION Lays eggs in water in spring.
• SIMILAR SPECIES Gray Treefrog (*Hyla versicolor*). This species looks identical to *H. chrysoscelis*, but has twice as many chromosomes and a slower, deeper mating call.
• REMARK In very cold weather, glycerol in the blood acts as "antifreeze" and prevents the treefrog from freezing to death.

adhesive disks on toes

large, prominent eyes

pattern on body provides camouflage

warty skin on back

N. AMERICA

Length 1¼–2⅓in (3–6cm)	Habit Mostly terrestrial	Activity ☾

Family HYLIDAE	Species *Litoria caerulea*	Status Locally common

WHITE'S TREEFROG

Despite its obese appearance, this treefrog is an agile climber and leaper. It is usually pale green, sometimes with small, cream-colored spots. White's Treefrog has a voracious appetite and, while it feeds mostly on insects, it has been known to eat small rats. It is often found living in or close to human habitations. During mating, the male calls loudly from perches close to the pond edge, then the pair enters the water. The female ejects her eggs forcibly, dispersing them into the pond, where they sink to the bottom.

AUSTRALASIA

• **OCCURRENCE** N.E. Australia and S. New Guinea. In woodland.

• **REPRODUCTION** Lays eggs in water in summer.

• **REMARK** The skin of White's Treefrog contains various compounds that are antiviral and antibacterial. One of these compounds (caerulein) is known to reduce blood pressure in humans.

horizontal pupils

pale green or bluish coloration, sometimes with small, cream-colored spots

large, well-developed adhesive pads on toes

Length 2–4in (5–10cm)	Habit Mostly terrestrial	Activity ☾

Family HYLIDAE	Species *Litoria infrafrenata*	Status Locally common

GIANT TREEFROG

One of the largest treefrogs, this species is uniform green or bronze above, and white or off-white below. The limbs are long and slender, with stripes (white in females, pink in males) on the lower legs. The Giant Treefrog is extremely agile when moving in vegetation but moves clumsily on the ground. During the breeding season, males gather around ponds, calling from perches 10–13ft (3–4m) above the ground.

very large eyes with horizontal pupils

white stripe on upper lip

AUSTRALASIA

• **OCCURRENCE** New Guinea and extreme N.E. Australia. In forest and gardens.

• **REPRODUCTION** Lays eggs in water in summer.

well-developed adhesive pads

Length 4–5½in (10–14cm)	Habit Mostly terrestrial	Activity ☾

| Family HYLIDAE | Species *Ololygon rubra* | Status Locally common |

RED-SNOUTED TREEFROG

A slender silver, gray, or yellow frog with long limbs, the Red-snouted Treefrog (sometimes known as *Scinax rubra*) gathers to breed in ephemeral ponds, following rain. Males gather in large groups, calling loudly to attract females. Females select males on the basis of their body size, preferring males that are about 20 percent smaller than they are; this ratio provides the closest contact with the male's cloaca and so maximizes the proportion of eggs that are fertilized. During mating, the female scatters her eggs widely in the pond to reduce the impact of predation.
• **OCCURRENCE** Panama, N. South America, Trinidad, Tobago, and St. Lucia. In savanna and near human settlements.
• **REPRODUCTION** Lays eggs in water in autumn and again in spring and summer.

flat yellow, silver, or gray body with darker markings

C. & S. AMERICA

slightly pointed head

adhesive disks on toes

| Length 1–1½in (2.5–4cm) | Habit Mostly terrestrial | Activity ☾ |

| Family HYLIDAE | Species *Phyllomedusa hypochondrialis* | Status Locally common |

ORANGE-SIDED LEAF FROG

Native to dry habitats, this small green-and-orange frog reduces water loss by wiping a waxy secretion of the skin glands over its body. When attacked, it feigns death, rolling onto its back with its legs tucked up. It produces an unpleasant odor when handled and may be toxic or distasteful to predators. Eggs are wrapped in leaves hanging over water; the female surrounds the eggs with empty egg capsules to provide moisture in dry weather.
• **OCCURRENCE** Panama and Colombia. In arid habitats.
• **REPRODUCTION** Lays eggs on land in spring and summer.

very large eyes

C. & S. AMERICA

opposable toes enable frog to grasp very small branches

long, delicate limbs help agility

| Length 1½–2in (4–5cm) | Habit Entirely terrestrial | Activity ☾ |

| Family CENTROLENIDAE | Species *Centrolenella valerioi* | Status Locally common |

LA PALMA GLASS FROG

A small and delicate creature, the La Palma Glass Frog is so called because the skin on its underside is transparent, and its internal organs are visible. It is an expert climber with long, slender limbs and very well-developed adhesive disks on the toes, enabling it to climb stems and cling to smooth leaves. The eyes are very large and prominent. Eggs are attached to leaves hanging over streams, and the male guards them against insect predators such as wasps. Tadpoles drop into the water as they hatch and burrow into the mud on the bottom of the stream.
• **OCCURRENCE** Central America. In tropical forest.
• **REPRODUCTION** Lays eggs over water in the rainy season.

prominent eyes with horizontal pupils

C. AMERICA

long hindlimbs

adhesive disks on toes

| Length ¾–1¼in (2–3cm) | Habit Mostly terrestrial | Activity ☾ |

| Family DENDROBATIDAE | Species *Dendrobates auratus* | Status Locally common |

BLACK-AND-GREEN POISON-DART FROG

This brilliantly colored species has glossy black-and-green skin, which provides ideal camouflage in lush tropical forest, and a rounded snout. As its name suggests, its deadly poison was used by tribesmen to coat darts that were fired from blowpipes. Females play the more active role in initiating mating and lay several clutches of 5 to 13 eggs in leaf-litter. Males care for the young, often protecting more than one clutch at once. When the eggs hatch, the male carries the tadpoles, one or two at a time, to small pools in the leaves of bromeliads or in tree holes.
• **OCCURRENCE** Panama and N.W. Colombia. In tropical forest.
• **REPRODUCTION** Lays eggs on land in the rainy season.
• **REMARK** This species is common in cocoa plantations, where it eats insects feeding on rotting fruit.

C. & S. AMERICA

smooth, bright green skin with black markings

adhesive pads on toes

long hindlimbs

| Length 1–2½in (2.5–6cm) | Habit Entirely terrestrial | Activity ☼ |

| Family DENDROBATIDAE | Species *Dendrobates azureus* | Status Endangered |

BLUE POISON-DART FROG

A brilliant electric-blue coloration, flecked with black, warns predators that this species is highly poisonous. Females produce several clutches of 5 to 13 eggs in leaf-litter on the forest floor. Males care for the eggs, often protecting more than one clutch at once. When the eggs hatch, the tadpoles wriggle onto the male's back. The male carries them, one or two at a time, to small pools in the leaves of bromeliads or in tree holes.
• **OCCURRENCE** N.E. South America. On vegetation in tropical forest.
• **REPRODUCTION** Lays eggs on land in the rainy season.

bright blue skin with black mottling •

S. AMERICA

extremely long forelimbs with adhesive pads on toes •

| Length 1¼–2in (3–5cm) | Habit Entirely terrestrial | Activity ☼ |

| Family DENDROBATIDAE | Species *Dendrobates pumilio* | Status Locally common |

STRAWBERRY POISON-DART FROG

The coloration in this species is highly variable from one locality to another. Individuals in some areas are brilliant blue or red; in other areas, they may be brown, blue, or green. Males call loudly to attract females. Females produce clutches of only four to six eggs, which are laid in leaf-litter. When the eggs hatch, the tadpoles wriggle onto the back of the female, which carries them to water-filled tree holes and bromeliads, placing a single tadpole in each pool. The females then return to the tadpoles at frequent intervals, feeding them on unfertilized eggs. The tadpoles complete their development in approximately six weeks.
• **OCCURRENCE** Nicaragua, Costa Rica, and Panama. On vegetation in tropical forest.
• **REPRODUCTION** Lays eggs on land in the rainy season.
• **REMARK** For centuries, tribesmen have heated this frog over fires to extract the deadly poison.

• *rounded snout*

C. AMERICA

• *large eyes*

long, slender forelimbs with adhesive pads •

| Length ¾–1in (2–2.5cm) | Habit Entirely terrestrial | Activity ☼ |

Family DENDROBATIDAE	Species *Dendrobates tinctorius*	Status Locally common

DYEING POISON-DART FROG

The largest species of the dendrobatid frogs, the Dyeing Poison-dart Frog has a black-and-yellow-striped body and blue legs, spotted with black. A good jumper and climber, it has muscular hindlegs and adhesive disks on its toes. The female lays up to 20 eggs on a leaf; the male guards them and, when they hatch, carries the tadpoles individually to pools of water, where he leaves them.
• OCCURRENCE French Guiana and N.E. Brazil. In tropical rainforest.
• REPRODUCTION Lays eggs on land in the rainy season.

S. AMERICA

adhesive disks on toes

Length 1¼–2½in (3–6cm)	Habit Entirely terrestrial	Activity ☼

Family RANIDAE	Species *Ceratobatracus guentheri*	Status Rare

SOLOMON ISLAND HORNED FROG

This frog's common name derives from the projections, or "horns," on its head. These help to break up the outline of the frog's head, improving its camouflage against a background of leaves. Other features include a flat, triangular head and large, adhesive disks on its outer toes. Coloration is highly variable. Unusually for a frog, this species has tusks in its lower jaw; these are bony projections rather than true teeth, and are larger in males than in females. The female lays clumps of large eggs, which hatch directly into froglets, in streams. The froglets have folds in their skin, which enhance absorption of yolk from eggs.
• OCCURRENCE Solomon Islands. In wooded habitats.
• REPRODUCTION Lays eggs in water in the rainy season.

hornlike projections on head

flat, triangular head

SOLOMON ISLANDS

adhesive disks on toes

Length 2–3¼in (5–8cm)	Habit Mostly terrestrial	Activity ☾

Family RANIDAE	Species *Conraua goliath*	Status Rare

GOLIATH FROG

The largest frog in the world, the Goliath Frog is well adapted
for its aquatic lifestyle. A good swimmer and diver, it has smooth,
slippery skin, very powerful hindlegs, and long, webbed toes. It is
blue-gray to green, with brown markings. This species rarely comes
far out of water and, if disturbed on land, it immediately jumps
toward the nearest stream. It feeds mostly on other vertebrates.
Unusually for frogs and toads, the male is larger than the
female and also has larger eardrums.
• OCCURRENCE
Cameroon and Equatorial
Guinea. Along streams
in jungle.
• REPRODUCTION
Lays eggs in the rainy
season (location unknown).

AFRICA

*powerful hindlegs
for swimming*

*long, webbed
toes*

Length 4–16in (10–40cm)	Habit Mostly aquatic	Activity ☾

Family RANIDAE	Species *Hylarana albolabris*	Status Locally common

WHITE-LIPPED RIVER FROG

A good climber, the green-and-black White-lipped River
Frog has large adhesive pads on its toes. It has a pointed
head, a white upper lip, and prominent folds of skin down
each side of its back. The very visible eardrum is larger in
the male than it is in the female, which is unusual for
frogs. In the breeding season, males
have large glands on the upper
arm, which probably help them
maintain a good grip on females
in running water. Eggs are laid
in clumps in streams.
• OCCURRENCE
W. and C. Africa. In
rainforest and woodland.
• REPRODUCTION
Lays eggs in water
in summer.

*prominent
folds in skin
on back*

AFRICA

*large eyes with
round pupils*

Length 2½–4in (6–10cm)	Habit Mostly terrestrial	Activity ☾

Family RANIDAE	Species *Mantella auriantiaca*	Status Endangered

GOLDEN MANTELLA

The Golden Mantella varies in color from yellow, through orange, to red. Juveniles are green and black. It is a poisonous frog from the rainforests of Madagascar, and is active by day. It is believed that, unusually for frogs, fertilization is internal. Males call to the females from the ground, rather than from vegetation or from the water. The eggs are laid in moist leaf-litter, and the tadpoles are washed into small pools by rain.

• **OCCURRENCE** W. central Madagascar. In sunny patches in rainforest.

• **REPRODUCTION** Lays eggs on land in the rainy season.

• **REMARK** These frogs are endangered because of destruction of their forest habitat. There is also serious concern about trade to developed countries, but this is being controlled.

MADAGASCAR

black eyes with horizontal pupils

yellow, orange, to red coloration

pointed snout

slender body with long, delicate limbs

Length ¾–1¼in (2–3cm)	Habit Entirely terrestrial	Activity ☼

Family RANIDAE	Species *Mantella viridis*	Status Rare

GREEN MANTELLA

The Green Mantella is yellow or pale green on the back and sides, with a patch of black on the side of its head and the front part of its body. It has a white stripe along the upper lip and has adhesive disks on the toes of both fore- and hindlimbs. The male's call consists of a series of clicks. Mating takes place on land and the eggs are laid close to streams, in which its tadpoles develop.

• **OCCURRENCE** N. and E. Madagascar. In tropical forest.

• **REPRODUCTION** Lays eggs on land in the rainy season.

• **REMARK** This species is threatened by habitat destruction and collection for the pet trade.

pale green or yellow on back and upper sides

white stripe on upper lip

adhesive disks on toes of hind- and forelimbs

MADAGASCAR

Length ¾–1¼in (2–3cm)	Habit Entirely terrestrial	Activity ☼

| Family RANIDAE | Species *Pyxicephalus adspersus* | Status Locally common |

AFRICAN BULLFROG

A large and aggressive species, the African Bullfrog has a massive body, wide head, large mouth, and muscular hindlegs. The coloration is olive-green, with dark green, brown, or black markings along ridges in its skin. Males are larger than females. Bullfrogs spend up to ten months a year underground, encased in a cocoon that prevents them from drying out. They have a hard tubercle on the hindfeet, which helps them dig into the soil. Males call to attract females. After mating in flooded pools, males guard the eggs and dig channels to allow the tadpoles to swim away.
• OCCURRENCE Sub-Saharan Africa. In wet and dry savanna.
• REPRODUCTION Lays eggs in water in the rainy season.
• REMARK In dry localities with only occasional rain, these bullfrogs may remain underground for several years.

AFRICA

olive-green body with darker markings

large head and very wide mouth

hindfeet possess tubercles for digging

| Length 3¼–9in (8–23cm) | Habit Mostly terrestrial | Activity ○ |

| Family RANIDAE | Species *Rana catesbeiana* | Status Locally common |

NORTH AMERICAN BULLFROG

The largest frog in North America, this species is olive-green above, with darker markings. It is often pale green on the head, and the legs are banded and blotched with brown or black. A voracious predator, it feeds on a variety of prey, including small mammals, reptiles, and other frogs. In the breeding season, males defend spawn sites and females lay thousands of eggs. Tadpoles may take up to four years to develop.
• OCCURRENCE C. and E. US. (Introduced to W. US and elsewhere.) In large ponds and lakes.
• REPRODUCTION Lays eggs in water in spring and summer.
• REMARK This bullfrog has been introduced to many parts of the world, where it has had a very destructive effect on native frog species.

prominent eardrums, larger in males

N. AMERICA

brown or olive-green coloration

| Length 3½–8in (9–20cm) | Habit Mostly aquatic | Activity ☾ ☀ |

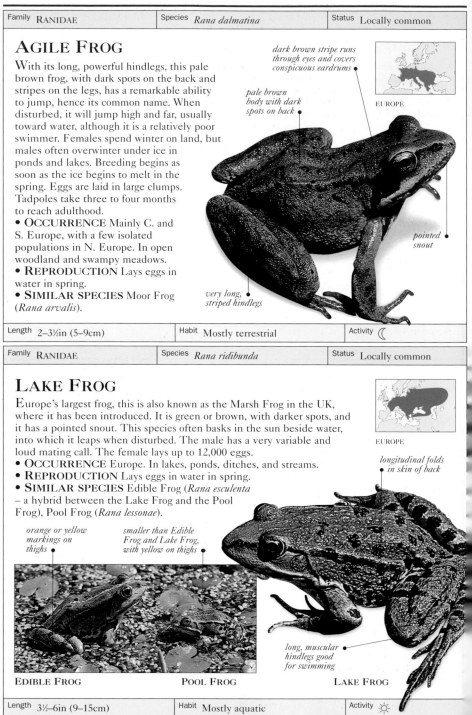

Family RANIDAE	Species *Rana dalmatina*	Status Locally common

AGILE FROG

With its long, powerful hindlegs, this pale brown frog, with dark spots on the back and stripes on the legs, has a remarkable ability to jump, hence its common name. When disturbed, it will jump high and far, usually toward water, although it is a relatively poor swimmer. Females spend winter on land, but males often overwinter under ice in ponds and lakes. Breeding begins as soon as the ice begins to melt in the spring. Eggs are laid in large clumps. Tadpoles take three to four months to reach adulthood.
• **OCCURRENCE** Mainly C. and S. Europe, with a few isolated populations in N. Europe. In open woodland and swampy meadows.
• **REPRODUCTION** Lays eggs in water in spring.
• **SIMILAR SPECIES** Moor Frog (*Rana arvalis*).

dark brown stripe runs through eyes and covers conspicuous eardrums

pale brown body with dark spots on back

EUROPE

pointed snout

very long, striped hindlegs

Length 2–3½in (5–9cm)	Habit Mostly terrestrial	Activity ☾

Family RANIDAE	Species *Rana ridibunda*	Status Locally common

LAKE FROG

Europe's largest frog, this is also known as the Marsh Frog in the UK, where it has been introduced. It is green or brown, with darker spots, and it has a pointed snout. This species often basks in the sun beside water, into which it leaps when disturbed. The male has a very variable and loud mating call. The female lays up to 12,000 eggs.
• **OCCURRENCE** Europe. In lakes, ponds, ditches, and streams.
• **REPRODUCTION** Lays eggs in water in spring.
• **SIMILAR SPECIES** Edible Frog (*Rana esculenta* – a hybrid between the Lake Frog and the Pool Frog), Pool Frog (*Rana lessonae*).

EUROPE

longitudinal folds in skin of back

orange or yellow markings on thighs

smaller than Edible Frog and Lake Frog, with yellow on thighs

long, muscular hindlegs good for swimming

EDIBLE FROG   POOL FROG   LAKE FROG

Length 3½–6in (9–15cm)	Habit Mostly aquatic	Activity ☼

Family RANIDAE	Species *Rana temporaria*	Status Locally common

EUROPEAN COMMON FROG

Highly variable in color, the European Common Frog
is usually green or brown, but occasionally red or yellow
individuals are seen. Some specimens have black spots.
Also known as the Grass Frog, it lives most of its life
on land, but migrates to ponds in early spring to breed.
Breeding is usually completed within two or three
days. Some males spend the winter in ponds and may
die if their pond freezes over. Breeding males have
much thicker forelimbs than
females and also prominent
dark nuptial pads on their
thumbs, which ensure a
firm grasp on the female
during mating. Females
deposit eggs in clumps in
communal spawn sites in
ponds, ditches, and canals.
• OCCURRENCE Europe.
In a wide variety of damp
habitats.
• REPRODUCTION Lays eggs
in water in spring.
• SIMILAR SPECIES Moor
Frog (*Rana arvalis*).

thick forelimbs of male, with dark • pads on thumbs

EUROPE

green or brown coloration, sometimes • with black spots

distinct • eardrum

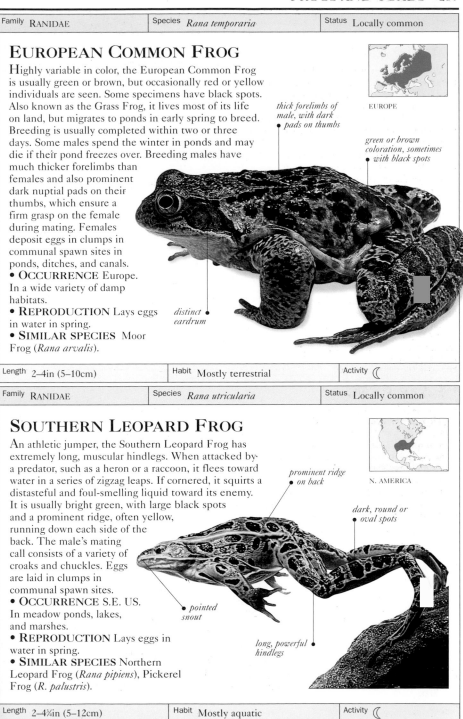

Length 2–4in (5–10cm)	Habit Mostly terrestrial	Activity ☾

Family RANIDAE	Species *Rana utricularia*	Status Locally common

SOUTHERN LEOPARD FROG

An athletic jumper, the Southern Leopard Frog has
extremely long, muscular hindlegs. When attacked by·
a predator, such as a heron or a raccoon, it flees toward
water in a series of zigzag leaps. If cornered, it squirts a
distasteful and foul-smelling liquid toward its enemy.
It is usually bright green, with large black spots
and a prominent ridge, often yellow,
running down each side of the
back. The male's mating
call consists of a variety of
croaks and chuckles. Eggs
are laid in clumps in
communal spawn sites.
• OCCURRENCE S.E. US.
In meadow ponds, lakes,
and marshes.
• REPRODUCTION Lays eggs in
water in spring.
• SIMILAR SPECIES Northern
Leopard Frog (*Rana pipiens*), Pickerel
Frog (*R. palustris*).

prominent ridge • on back

N. AMERICA

dark, round or • oval spots

pointed snout

long, powerful • hindlegs

Length 2–4¾in (5–12cm)	Habit Mostly aquatic	Activity ☾

Family RANIDAE	Species *Hemisus marmoratus*	Status Locally common

MOTTLED SHOVEL-NOSED FROG

This burrowing species, which spends most of its life underground, has a squat, slightly bloated body, powerful limbs, and a tiny, pointed head with small eyes and a sharp, toughened snout. The coloration is yellow or gray, with brown or black mottled patterning. Males call to females from the banks of pools, making a buzzing sound. The eggs are laid in an underground chamber close to the pool. When they hatch, the female digs a tunnel to release the tadpoles into the pond.
• OCCURRENCE S.E. Africa. In savanna and dry scrub.
• REPRODUCTION Lays eggs on land in the rainy season.
• REMARK Unusually for a burrowing frog, this species digs into the soil head-first (most use their hindfeet to dig backward).

AFRICA

stout
• *limbs*

pointed snout •

Length 1¼–1½in (3–4cm)	Habit Mostly terrestrial	Activity ☾

Family HYPEROLIIDAE	Species *Afrixalus fornasinii*	Status Locally common

GREATER LEAF-FOLDING FROG

With its long, slender limbs and adhesive disks on its toes, the Greater Leaf-folding Frog is well equipped for its life in vegetation. Its coloration is highly variable, from yellowish brown to yellowish green, but this species is distinguished by its dark vertebral stripe, bordered by a paler stripe on either side. Males call from elevated positions in vegetation, producing a series of rapid clicks. Smaller males often do not call but sit in a flat posture close to calling males to try to intercept a female. Eggs are laid in small clutches on a leaf, which is then folded and glued with a secretion produced by the female. When the eggs hatch, the tadpoles fall into the water.
• OCCURRENCE S.E. Africa. In low vegetation.
• REPRODUCTION Lays eggs over water in the rainy season.

dark stripe along center of back, bordered by paler • *stripes*

AFRICA

vertical pupils •

long toes with • *adhesive pads*

Length 1¼–1½in (3–4cm)	Habit Entirely terrestrial	Activity ☾

| Family HYPEROLIIDAE | Species *Hyperolius tuberilinguis* | Status Locally common |

TINKER REED FROG

A very agile climber and jumper, the Tinker Reed Frog
has a slim body, long, slender hindlimbs, and adhesive
disks on its toes. The coloration is bright green,
yellow, or brown, with no patterning
on the skin, and the inner surfaces
of the legs are bright orange or
yellow (this flash coloration is
visible only when the frog leaps).
The large eyes are yellow or orange,
with horizontal pupils. Despite their small
size, reed frogs have among the loudest
of frog calls. Choruses of calling males
frequently number several thousand.
Eggs are laid in a mass of jelly on
vegetation overhanging a swamp,
pond, or lake.
• OCCURRENCE Africa. In
lowland habitats in vegetation.
• REPRODUCTION Lays
eggs above water in spring.

large eyes with horizontal pupils

AFRICA

slender body

long toes with adhesive disks

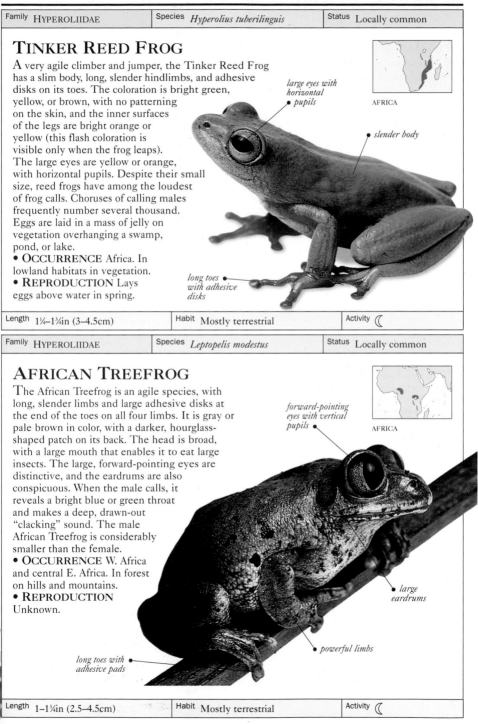

| Length 1¼–1¾in (3–4.5cm) | Habit Mostly terrestrial | Activity ☾ |

| Family HYPEROLIIDAE | Species *Leptopelis modestus* | Status Locally common |

AFRICAN TREEFROG

The African Treefrog is an agile species, with
long, slender limbs and large adhesive disks at
the end of the toes on all four limbs. It is gray or
pale brown in color, with a darker, hourglass-
shaped patch on its back. The head is broad,
with a large mouth that enables it to eat large
insects. The large, forward-pointing eyes are
distinctive, and the eardrums are also
conspicuous. When the male calls, it
reveals a bright blue or green throat
and makes a deep, drawn-out
"clacking" sound. The male
African Treefrog is considerably
smaller than the female.
• OCCURRENCE W. Africa
and central E. Africa. In forest
on hills and mountains.
• REPRODUCTION
Unknown.

forward-pointing eyes with vertical pupils

AFRICA

large eardrums

powerful limbs

long toes with adhesive pads

| Length 1–1¾in (2.5–4.5cm) | Habit Mostly terrestrial | Activity ☾ |

| Family ARTHROLEPTIDAE | Species *Trichobatrachus robustus* | Status Locally common |

HAIRY FROG

The "hairs" that give this species its name are a unique adaptation that enables the male Hairy Frog to remain submerged without surfacing to breathe while it is caring for its eggs. These hairlike skin projections along its sides and legs increase the area of skin through which oxygen can be absorbed from the water. The Hairy Frog is a relatively large species with a huge head. The tadpoles have a suckerlike disk on the abdomen that enables them to adhere to stones.
• OCCURRENCE E. Nigeria, Guinea, Cameroon, and Zaire. In rainforest.
• REPRODUCTION Lays eggs in water in the rainy season.

numerous hairlike projections on back

dark stripe along center of back

AFRICA

pointed snout

| Length 2¾–5in (7–13cm) | Habit Mostly terrestrial | Activity ☾ |

| Family RHACOPHORIDAE | Species *Chiromantis xerampelina* | Status Locally common |

FOAM-NEST FROG

An excellent climber, the Foam-nest Frog has long, slender limbs and adhesive disks on its toes. It is able to change color, allowing it to be camouflaged while resting during the day. Breeding occurs in trees overhanging pools. The female produces a secretion that is whipped into a foam by her legs, with help from one or several males. The foam dries on the outside and the tadpoles develop within the nest. They then burrow out of the nest to fall into the water below.
• OCCURRENCE S. Africa. In wooded savanna.
• REPRODUCTION Lays eggs over water in the rainy season.

AFRICA

large, protruding eyes

body changes color for camouflage

long, slender limbs

adhesive disks on toes

| Length 2–3½in (5–9cm) | Habit Entirely terrestrial | Activity ☾ |

Family RHACOPHORIDAE	Species *Rhacophorus reinwardti*	Status Locally common

JAVAN FLYING FROG

The Javan Flying Frog gets its name from its ability
to glide considerable distances when it jumps from a
tree (it does not fly in the true sense). This gliding
motion is achieved by the frog spreading its large,
webbed toes, which act as a parachute. The limbs
are long and slender, making this species an agile
climber. The coloration is green, with black marks
on the webbing between the toes. The female lays
eggs in a foam nest over water.
• OCCURRENCE Malaysia, Sumatra, and Java.
In woodland and forest.
• REPRODUCTION Lays eggs above water
in the rainy season.

flattened head

ASIA

long, slender limbs with webbed feet

large, protruding eyes with horizontal pupils

Length 2–3¼in (5–8cm)	Habit Mostly terrestrial	Activity ☾

Family RHINOPHRYNIDAE	Species *Rhinophrynus dorsalis*	Status Locally common

MEXICAN BURROWING FROG

Unlike any other frog in appearance, the unique shape
of this large species is adapted for life underground.
The cone-shaped head and pointed, calloused snout
enable it to burrow through the soil, propelled by its
short but powerful legs. It emerges onto the surface
only after rain, moving clumsily to ephemeral ponds
to breed. Its prey consists of
termites and ants.
• OCCURRENCE Central America.
In lowland forest and open habitats.
• REPRODUCTION Lays eggs in
water in the rainy season.

red dorsal stripe

C. AMERICA

cone-shaped head with tiny eyes

short limbs

Length 2½–3¼in (6–8cm)	Habit Mostly terrestrial	Activity ☾

Family MICROHYLIDAE	Species *Breviceps adspersus*	Status Locally common

BUSHVELD RAIN FROG

A burrowing species, the Bushveld Rain Frog has a stout,
globular body, short limbs, and a flattened face. The
coloration is pale or dark brown, with bands of black,
yellow, and orange spots. This frog moves backward
when digging, using horny tubercles on its hindfeet
to move the soil. When disturbed, it can
inflate its body with air, lodging itself firmly in
its burrow. It emerges only on rainy nights to
feed on termites and ants.
• OCCURRENCE South Africa and
Zimbabwe. In wooded areas with sandy soils.
• REPRODUCTION Lays eggs on land in
the rainy season.

flattened face

bands of spots on body

AFRICA

plump, rounded body

powerful limbs

Length 1¼–2⅜in (3–6cm)	Habit Mostly terrestrial	Activity ☾

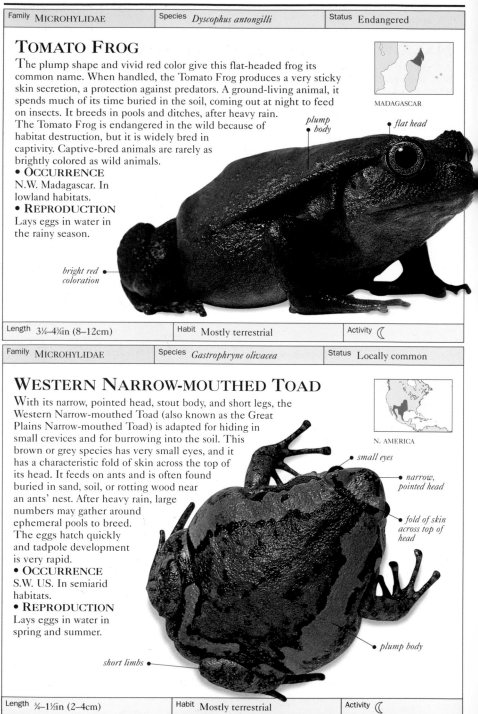

Family MICROHYLIDAE	Species *Dyscophus antongilli*	Status Endangered

TOMATO FROG

The plump shape and vivid red color give this flat-headed frog its common name. When handled, the Tomato Frog produces a very sticky skin secretion, a protection against predators. A ground-living animal, it spends much of its time buried in the soil, coming out at night to feed on insects. It breeds in pools and ditches, after heavy rain. The Tomato Frog is endangered in the wild because of habitat destruction, but it is widely bred in captivity. Captive-bred animals are rarely as brightly colored as wild animals.
• OCCURRENCE
N.W. Madagascar. In lowland habitats.
• REPRODUCTION
Lays eggs in water in the rainy season.

MADAGASCAR

plump body

flat head

bright red coloration

Length 3¼–4¾in (8–12cm)	Habit Mostly terrestrial	Activity ☾

Family MICROHYLIDAE	Species *Gastrophryne olivacea*	Status Locally common

WESTERN NARROW-MOUTHED TOAD

With its narrow, pointed head, stout body, and short legs, the Western Narrow-mouthed Toad (also known as the Great Plains Narrow-mouthed Toad) is adapted for hiding in small crevices and for burrowing into the soil. This brown or grey species has very small eyes, and it has a characteristic fold of skin across the top of its head. It feeds on ants and is often found buried in sand, soil, or rotting wood near an ants' nest. After heavy rain, large numbers may gather around ephemeral pools to breed. The eggs hatch quickly and tadpole development is very rapid.
• OCCURRENCE
S.W. US. In semiarid habitats.
• REPRODUCTION
Lays eggs in water in spring and summer.

N. AMERICA

small eyes

narrow, pointed head

fold of skin across top of head

plump body

short limbs

Length ¾–1½in (2–4cm)	Habit Mostly terrestrial	Activity ☾

Family MICROHYLIDAE	Species *Kaloula pulchra*	Status Locally common

MALAYSIAN NARROW-MOUTHED TOAD

A burrowing species, the Malaysian Narrow-mouthed Toad has a rotund
body and short limbs. It is brown to dark brown, with broad, beige or pink
stripes along its body. When mating, the male glues himself to the female's
back with secretions from glands on his abdomen.
• OCCURRENCE India and S.W. Asia. In a wide variety of habitats with
loose soil, including farmland and urban areas.
• REPRODUCTION Lays eggs in
water in the rainy season.

ASIA

*body inflated with
air for defense*

DEFENSE
POSTURE

*relaxed body
posture*

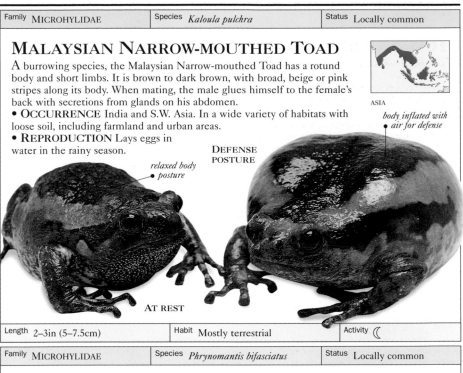

AT REST

Length 2–3in (5–7.5cm)	Habit Mostly terrestrial	Activity ☾

Family MICROHYLIDAE	Species *Phrynomantis bifasciatus*	Status Locally common

BANDED RUBBER FROG

A creature that runs or walks, the Banded Rubber Frog has
small limbs and a long, relatively flat body. The striking red
or pink stripes, blotches, or spots on its smooth black skin are
a warning to potential enemies. In defense, it raises itself up
on its legs and inflates its body
while producing a toxic skin
secretion. Individuals may
change color as they mature
(the black may turn to gray,
the red to pink or almost
white). Breeding occurs in
ponds after rain. Males
produce a trill-like call from
the pond edge. Eggs are laid
in a clump attached to plants.
• OCCURRENCE
S. and E. Africa. In savanna.
• REPRODUCTION Lays
eggs in water in spring.

*red stripes act
as warning to
predators*

AFRICA

long body

small limbs

Length 1½–2⅜in (4–6cm)	Habit Mostly terrestrial	Activity ☾

GLOSSARY

Some of the definitions below have been simplified and apply only to the use of the terms in the study of reptiles and amphibians. Words printed in **bold** type are defined elsewhere in the glossary.

- **ALLIGATOR**
Subtropical **crocodilian**, differing from a **crocodile** in having a broader snout.
- **AMPHIBIAN**
Cold-blooded vertebrate, typically living on land but breeding in water.
- **AMPHISBAENIAN**
Wormlike, **burrowing reptile** with a long, slender body, short tail, and **scales** arranged in rings (also known as a worm-lizard).
- **ARBOREAL**
Adapted for living in trees.
- **AUTOTOMIZATION**
See Caudal autotomy.
- **BARBEL**
Long, fleshy projection or **tubercle**, usually under the chin of a **turtle** or **tortoise**.
- **BONY PLATE**
Plate that strengthens the tough, leathery skin of a **crocodilian**.
- **BRILLES**
Immovable, transparent coverings of the eye, characteristic of all **snakes** and some **lizards** (also known as "spectacles").
- **CAECILIAN**
Earthwormlike **amphibian** with a long body, often with rings around it, no limbs, and virtually no tail.
- **CAIMAN**
South American relative of the **alligator**.
- **CARAPACE**
Upper side of a **turtle** or **tortoise** shell.
- **CASQUE**
Raised adornment on the head of a **lizard**, usually on the rear.
- **CAUDAL AUTOTOMY**
Process in which a **lizard** or other animal sheds its tail, to enable it to escape when attacked (also known as autotomization).
- **CHELONIAN**
Member of a group of **reptiles** that includes **turtles** and **tortoises**, distinguished by a protective **shell**.
- **CLOACA**
Genital and excretory opening.

- **CLOACAL SPUR**
Remnant of the pelvic girdle or hindlimb that remains as a **spur** or claw in boas and pythons, and is used by the male for stroking the female in courtship.
- **CLUTCH**
Group of eggs from one female.
- **COLLAR**
Narrow band of pigment that extends across the nape of the neck.
- **CONSTRICTION**
Method of killing used by many nonvenomous **snakes** involving coiling around the prey and tightening the coils until the prey suffocates.
- **COSTAL GROOVES**
Parallel, vertical grooves on the sides of some **salamanders**, **newts**, and their **larvae**.
- **CREST**
Raised ridge of skin that is present on the back and tail of some **lizards** and that develops in some male **newts** in the breeding season.
- **CROCODILE**
Tropical **crocodilian**, differing from an **alligator** in having a narrower snout.
- **CROCODILIAN**
Generic term for all **alligators**, **caimans**, **crocodiles**, and **gharials**, characterized by a streamlined body; long tail; thick, leathery skin, strengthened by **bony plates**; and a usually narrow snout.
- **CROSS-BAND OR -BAR**
Narrow marking that passes over the back of the body but does not meet on the underside.
- **CRYPTIC PATTERNING**
Patterning or coloration that breaks up the outline of an animal or helps it blend into its surroundings.
- **DEWLAP**
Large flap under a **lizard's** throat, sometimes used for **display**.
- **DISPLAY**
Pattern of behavior in which a **reptile** or **amphibian** attracts attention while it is courting or defending its territory.
- **DIURNAL**
Active mainly during the day.
- **DORSAL**
Pertaining to the back.
- **EPHEMERAL POOL OR POND**
Pool or pond that usually dries up in the course of a year.

- **FANG**
Long, hollow or grooved tooth of a venomous **snake** through which venom is injected.
- **FROG**
Amphibian characterized by the absence of a tail in the adult and, typically, hindlimbs that are much larger than the frontlimbs.
- **FRONT-FANGED SNAKE**
Venomous **snake** that has **fangs** in the front of the upper jaw.
- **GHARIAL**
Asian, fish-eating **crocodilian** with a very narrow snout.
- **HATCHLING**
Animal that has just emerged from an egg.
- **HEAT-SENSITIVE PIT**
Organ that helps certain **snakes** locate their warm-blooded prey. In boas and pythons, these border the mouth (labial pits); in pitvipers, they are between the nostril, the eye, and the mouth (loreal pits).
- **IMMACULATE**
Of skin, unmarked and usually white.
- **INTERSTITIAL SKIN**
Skin between a **snake's scales**.
- **JUVENILE**
Reptile that is not yet fully mature. *See also* **Hatchling**, **Subadult**.
- **KEELED SCALE**
Scale that has one or more ridges down the center, giving a rough, matt appearance and texture.
- **LABIAL**
Pertaining to the lips. *See also* **Heat-sensitive pit**.
- **LARVA (pl. LARVAE)**
Young form of all **amphibians**, before undergoing **metamorphosis** into the adult form (the larvae of **frogs** and **toads** are more commonly called **tadpoles**).
- **LATERALLY COMPRESSED**
High and narrow in cross section, rather than rounded or flattened.
- **LIVE-BEARING**
Of an animal that gives birth to **neonates**, rather than lays eggs.
- **LIZARD**
Reptile, typically with four legs, a relatively long tail, movable eyelids, and external ear openings.
- **LOCALLY COMMON**
Uncommon or absent over most of its range but relatively common in one or more specific localities.

• **LOREAL**
Pertaining to the area between the eye, the nostril, and the mouth. *See also* **Heat-sensitive pit**.

• **METAMORPHOSIS**
Transformation of a **larva** or **tadpole** into an adult, a process that occurs in most **amphibians**.

• **MIDVEIN**
Fine line down the head or back of a **snake** or **lizard**, usually enhancing the **cryptic patterning**.

• **NEONATE**
Newborn **snake** or **lizard** when it is the product of a live birth.

• **NEWT**
Small, semiaquatic **amphibian** with a long, slender body, long tail, short limbs, and in some species a **crest** on the male in the breeding season. Returns to water to breed.

• **NOCTURNAL**
Active mainly at night.

• **NUPTIAL PAD**
Swelling, usually dark in color and rough in texture, that develops in some male **frogs** and **toads** in the breeding season.

• **OCCIPITAL FLAP**
Movable fold of skin on the rear of a chameleon's head.

• **OCELLUS (pl. OCELLI)**
Eyelike spot with a light center that contrasts with its border.

• **OPPOSABLE THUMB**
Thumb that can be pushed tightly against any of the other digits.

• **OVERSHOT JAW**
Top jaw overhanging the lower one.

• **PAROTID GLAND**
Gland behind the back of the eye in many **amphibians**, particularly conspicuous in true **toads**. It may produce a noxious secretion.

• **PARTHENOGENETIC**
Of an all-female population or species that reproduces without sexual contact with a male.

• **PINEAL EYE**
Third eye in the forehead of **tuataras** and many **lizards** that can register light intensity and may help to regulate body temperature.

• **PLASTRON**
Flat underside of a **tortoise** or **turtle shell**.

• **POST-OCCIPITAL SCALE**
One of a pair of round **scales** on the rear of the head of a King Cobra, distinguishing it from other cobras.

• **PREHENSILE TAIL**
Tail that can grip, characteristic of **arboreal** animals.

• **PROBOSCIS**
Long snout or mouthparts.

• **RATTLE**
Loosely interlocking remnants of shed skin, present on a rattlesnake's tail, that are vibrated to make a rattling sound to deter predators.

• **REAR-FANGED SNAKE**
Venomous **snake** that has **fangs** at the rear of the upper jaw.

• **REPTILE**
Cold-blooded vertebrate characterized by the presence of lungs, and **scales**, **scutes**, or **bony plates**.

• **RETICULATED**
Arranged in a network pattern.

• **RING**
Narrow marking that completely encircles the body.

• **ROSTRAL SCALE**
Scale at the very tip of the snout on the upper jaw.

• **SADDLE**
Broad marking that passes over an animal's back and extends a short distance down the sides.

• **SALAMANDER**
Typically terrestrial **amphibian** with a long body and tail and short limbs. Some species return to water to breed; others lay eggs on land.

• **SAW-SCALING**
Action of a **snake** curving its body in concentric curves and rasping its **keeled scales** together to make a sawing sound as a warning.

• **SCALE**
Soft, usually overlapping body covering in **snakes**, **lizards**, and **amphisbaenians** (may be smooth, **keeled**, granular, or **tuberculate**).

• **SCUTE**
Large, well-defined **scale**, e.g. on a **tortoise** or **turtle carapace**.

• **SEMIBURROWING**
Pertaining to an animal that lives some of the time below ground or lives in leaf-litter.

• **SHELL**
Protective outer covering of a **turtle** or **tortoise**, comprising a **carapace** and a **plastron**.

• **SNAKE**
Reptile with a long, slender body covered in smooth or keeled **scales**, flexible jaws, forked tongue, no limbs, fixed "spectacles" (**brilles**) rather than movable eyelids, and no external ear. Some are highly venomous, but many are harmless.

• **SPECTACLES**
See **Brilles**.

• **SPERMATOPHORE**
Gelatinous mass of sperm deposited by the male and picked up by the cloacal lips of the female.

• **SPUR**
Pointed, projecting structure on the limbs. *See also* **Cloacal spur**.

• **STRIPE**
Marking that usually runs longitudinally down the body.

• **SUBADULT**
Animal that is older than a **juvenile** but is not yet fully mature.

• **SUBOCULAR SCALE**
Scale that separates the eye from the **labial scales** in some **snake** species.

• **TADPOLE**
The **larva** of a **frog** or **toad**, before undergoing **metamorphosis** into the adult form.

• **TERRAPIN**
Colloquial term often used to describe a freshwater **turtle**.

• **TOAD**
Member of the family Bufonidae. The term is also used more generally to describe any slow-moving **frog** or toad with rough, warty skin.

• **TORTOISE**
Terrestrial **chelonian**.

• **TRUNCATED**
Short and blunt, often of a tail.

• **TUATARA**
Primitive, lizardlike **reptile** found only on islands off New Zealand.

• **TUBERCLE**
Fleshy protuberance.

• **TUBERCULATE**
Covered in raised, fleshy protuberances.

• **TURTLE**
Freshwater or marine **chelonian**.

• **VENTRAL SCALE**
Scale on the underside of a **snake's** body (usually broader than other scales).

• **VERTEBRAL**
Along the center of the back.

• **VESTIGIAL**
Pertaining to part of an animal that is in the process of being lost in the course of evolution and is small, imperfectly formed, and serves little or no function.

• **VOCAL SAC**
Soft, baglike structure that inflates and acts as a resonator, amplifying the mating calls of some male **frogs** and **toads**.

• **WORM-LIZARD**
See **Amphisbaenian**.

INDEX

ACKNOWLEDGMENTS

THE AUTHORS would like to thank Chris Mattison, who contributed a great number of photographs and helped with the Introduction, and Roger Avery and David Dickey, who read and commented on all the text. They would also like to thank all the photographers and agencies who submitted photographs for inclusion, and especially the following people who were instrumental in obtaining the final few difficult images: Jim Bridges, Indraneil Das, Carl Gans, Bill Love, Louis Porras, John Tashjian, Wayne van Devender, and Harold Voris. Thanks are also due to: West Midland Safari Park, for their leniency in time-keeping as the book neared completion; Wolverhampton University, for the long-term loan of several relevant books; John Wilkinson, who helped with the amphibians section; and finally to Barbara O'Shea, who proofread most of the reptiles section in search of typographical and grammatical errors.

DORLING KINDERSLEY would like to thank Monica Byles, Elaine Hewson, Peter Cross, and Sean O'Connor for their help in planning the contents of this book.

STUDIO CACTUS would like to thank Jane Baldock, Alison Copland, and Fiona Wild for editorial assistance; Sharon Moore, Laura Watson, Claire Moore, and Melanie Brown for design assistance; Peter Bull for illustrations; Chris Bernstein for the index; John Sturgess for proofreading; and Neale Chamberlain for picture research. Special thanks to Chris Mattison and Roger Avery for their expert advice throughout the project. Thanks also to David Roberts from DK cartography.

PHOTOGRAPHY: Special photography for this book by Chris Mattison.

PICTURE CREDITS: The publisher would like to thank the following for their kind permission to reproduce the photographs: a = above, b = below/bottom, c = center, l = left, r = right, t = top

JACKET: DK Picture Library: Jerry Young: front cover tl, b; Chris Mattison: front cover c, clb, cla, back cover cra, br; Charlie Wooding: inside back flap tr; Yorkshire/Associated Producers: inside back flap tl.

INSIDE: A.N.T. Photo Library: Ken Griffiths 173b; G.E. Schmida 170b; J. Weigel 170t; Ardea London Ltd: Hans & Judy Beste 82t, 216b, 217b; Liz & Tony Bomford 18br; Hans D. Dossenbach 11cr, 203c; Kenneth W. Fink 95c; Francois Gohier 69b; Nick Gordon 191t; M. Watson 48b; Alan Weaving 240t; Wardene Weisser 206b; BBC Natural History Unit: Michael Fogden 7b; Dietmar Hill 219t; Steven David Miller 100b; Pete Oxford 98t, 192c; Tony Phelps 161b; Michael Pitts 99c; Premaphotos 75c; Rico & Ruiz 146t, 199b; Jeff Rotman 21; Peter Scoones 7cl; Yuri Shibnev 175b; Tom Vezo 54t; Doug Wechsler 45t, 208t; Mike Wilkes 74t; Dr. W.R. Branch: 31br, 108b, 171b, 218b, 225b, 243b; Studio Cactus: 32cl, 32cr; Bruce Coleman Ltd.: Fred Bruemmer 174b; John Cancalosi 143c, 168c; Jack Dermid 10tc, 207t; M.P.L. Fogden 9c, 232t; Dr. M.P. Kahl 215b; P. Kaya 22t, 238bl; George McCarthy 89c; Joe McDonald 23tr, 110c, 139t, 176c; Dr. Scott Nielsen 222c; John Shaw 227t; Gunter Ziesler 20crb, 23b; David M. Dennis: 47t, 94c, 102b, 196, 197t, 199c, 221b; DK Picture Library: Natural History Museum 31t, 74b; Royal Museum of Scotland 6c; Jerry Young 1, 2tr, 2cl, 2cr, 8bl, 8br, 9bc, 15tr, 17ca, 19br, 26cl, 45c, 50bl, 53c, 53b, 54b, 55t, 60t, 62c,

80t, 86c, 87b, 97b, 97t, 100t, 177t, 195t, 223t, 225t, 226b, 227b, 235b, 244b, 244t; Michael & Patricia Fogden: 5tr, 10bc, 10br, 11cl, 210t, 219b, 222t; Carl Gans: 107b; Daniel Heuclin: 88t, 169b, 216t; Dr. Indraneil Das: 87t, 161t, 242t; FLPA - Images of nature: Frank W. Lane 100c; Mandal Ranjit 159b; G. Saltini/Panda 198t; Silvestris 118t; Chris Mattison: 5cl, 5b, 6b, 11tr, 12tl, 12cl, 12c, 12cr, 12bl, 14tr, 15c, 16c, 16cb, 17tl, 18tr, 19cr, 19cbl, 23cr, 26cr, 26bl, 28cl, 28bl, 28br, 29tr, 29cl, 29bc, 30cl, 30t, 32tr, 32bc, 33tl, 33tr, 33cl, 44, 45b, 46c, 46b, 51c, 51b, 51t, 52t, 59c, 59t, 60c, 60b, 61b, 62t, 63c, 65t, 66b, 66t, 69t, 71c, 71t, 72c, 77b, 77t, 83t, 84b, 91c, 95t, 99t, 105t, 106b, 106t, 108t, 112br, 112t, 114c, 114b, 116t, 117t, 120b, 121bl, 122t, 125b, 129b, 130b, 130t, 131tr, 131cr, 132-133, 132b, 133cr, 133b, 134t, 135cr, 135b, 135t, 136b, 137b, 138b, 138t, 139b, 140b, 141c, 144c, 144t, 145t, 149t, 150cr, 150b, 152b, 152t, 153b, 156t, 164b, 165, 178tr, 178c, 179c, 179br, 181b, 184c, 186bl, 186br, 187b, 188t, 189tl, 189tr, 189b, 203t, 204t, 206c, 208b, 210c, 212t, 214b, 217t, 219c, 220b, 224b, 228t, 229b, 231b, 232b, 233b, 233t, 238t, 241b, 241t, 242b, 243t, 245b; Nature Photographers: S.C. Bisserot 218t; Colin Carver 238br; Don Smith 205t; Paul Sterry 65b; Natural Science Photos: C. Dani & I. Jeske 14bl, 76c; Ken Hoppen 156b; David Lawson 75b; Chris Mattison 90t; Jim Merli 207b; O.C. Roura 63t; Kennan Ward 222b; N.H.P.A.: A.N.T. 47b, 76t; Anthony Bannister 124t, 150t, 160b; James Carmichael Jr 67b; Nigel J. Dennis 167t; Robert Erwin 197b; Pavel German 64b, 136t, 158t, 209; Ken Griffiths 172b; Brian Hawkes 88b; Daniel Heuclin 62b, 107c, 107t, 129t, 144b, 235t; Ralph and Daphne Keller 174t; T. Kitchin & V. Hurst 237b; Gerald Lacz 142b; Haroldo Palo 105b; Jany Sauvanet 70t, 91b, 210b, 221t; Karl Switak 92t; Dave Watts 75t; Martin Wendler 23cl; Mark T. O'Shea: 15br, 19cl, 25tr, 25b, 27br, 29crb, 31c, 46t, 49b, 55b, 56t, 58, 61c, 61t, 63b, 64t, 68b, 68t, 71b, 72b, 72t, 73c, 73b, 73t, 79bl, 80b, 81b, 82c, 82b, 83c, 83b, 84c, 84t, 85c, 86c, 90c, 90t, 91t, 92b, 93b, 93t, 96c, 96b, 101, 102c, 103c, 103b, 103t, 104c, 104b, 109bl, 109br, 110b, 111b, 112bl, 113tl, 113tr, 113br, 114t, 117b, 118c, 119c, 119t, 120t, 121t, 122bc, 122br, 124b, 125t, 126bl, 128b, 128t, 134b, 137t, 140t, 141bt, 145t, 145b, 147t, 148t, 149c, 151b, 151t, 152c, 153tr, 153cl, 154t, 155b, 155t, 157b, 159t, 160t, 162c, 162b, 163b, 164t, 166b, 169cr, 171t, 172t, 175t, 177c, 177b, 178bl, 179tr, 180t, 181c, 182b, 183b, 183t, 184tr, 184br, 185t, 186t, 187tl, 187tr, 188b, 191cl, 192b, 193t, 194b, 194t, 195b; Oxford Scientific Films: Kathie Atkinson 217c; J.A.L. Cooke 163t; David M. Dennis 143b, 143t; Michael Fogden 22c, 157t, 176b; Zig Leszczynski 87c, 146b; John Mitchell 119b; G. Synatzschke Okapia 215t; Babs & Bert Wells 64c, 168b; Louis W. Porras: 95b, 240b; Stephen Spawls: 173t; John Tashjian (specimen courtesy of Latoxan): 158b; R.W. Van Devender: 86b, 211b; Harold Voris: 162t; W. Wuster: 168t.